Dedicated to the 400th Anniversary
of the House of Romanov

Russia & Europe

Dynastic Ties

By

Galina Korneva & Tatiana Cheboksarova

Expanded and Edited by

Arturo E. Beéche

ISBN: 978-0-9854603-2-7

EUROHISTORY.COM

ЛИКИ РОССИИ

TRAIN TRANSSIBERIEN
DE LA Cⁱᵉ INTERNATIONALE DES WAGONS-LITS
VOYAGE DE
MOSCOU à PEKIN

Introduction

During the reign of Peter the Great, the Czar-Reformer, Russia first turned to the West and started to actively communicate with the scientific and cultural wealth that had been amassed in European countries. The first dynastic ties between the House of Romanov and representatives of Royal Houses of Europe stem from this era. Tsarevich Alexei, the son of Peter I and his first wife Evdokiia Lopukhina, at the command of his father, in 1711 married Princess Sophie Charlotte Brünswick-Wolfenbüttel, and Peter's daughter Anna Petrovna married Duke Karl Friedrich Schleswig-Holstein-Gottorp. This last marriage would later have great implications for the Romanov Dynasty.

Two centuries later numerous representatives of the Russian Imperial Family had come to be close relatives of the ruling Houses of Europe. Extremely close dynastic ties were established by this time with the German Empire and the many small Principalities, Duchies, Grand Duchies and Kingdoms that fell within its borders. It was from Germany that two Hesse and by Rhine Princesses came to Russia, Marie – Empress Maria Alexandrovna – and Alix – Empress Alexandra Feodorovna.

In 1866, Princess Dagmar, daughter of King Christian IX of Denmark, married the son of Emperor Alexander II, the Tsarevich Alexander Alexandrovich. This marriage was responsible, for over half a century, for establishing the close dynastic ties of Russia, not only with Denmark, but also with several other European nations, England and Greece being the most prominent examples among these dynasties. The Tsarevna Maria Feodorovna's (i.e. the former Princess Dagmar) own brother ascended the throne of Greece in 1863. Four years later, King George I chose as his bride the Russian Grand Duchess Olga Konstantinovna. For the next half a century years, the Greek monarchs involved themselves in transforming the land of the Hellenes, while also establishing dynastic alliances of great importance for their children.

As a result of ambitious dynastic marriages, two more Russian Grand Duchesses became consorts of two ruling German sovereigns. In July 1846, Olga Nikolaevna, a daughter of Nicholas I, married the Heir to the Throne of Württemberg. Three decades later, the only daughter of Grand Duke Michael Nikolaevich, Anastasia Mikhailovna, became the Grand Duchess of Mecklenburg-Schwerin. Her own three children would reiinforce this web of alliances by marrying into the dynasties of Denmark, Hannover and Prussia.

We set as a goal for ourselves to replicate, through the prism of dynastic ties, the kind of life that was led by these people. They were determining factors in the development of the countries in which they reigned. They were also able to characterize their influence on the enhancement of cultural ties between Russia and the countries of Europe.

We have selected a series of photographs that allow one to see the faces of Russian monarchs and their closest relatives living in Europe; we have also allowed them to speak for themselves, by providing excerpts from their memoirs, written by German, Greek, Danish princes and princesses, as well as political leaders and representatives from the world of art at the time.

We also provide descriptions and show pictures of the various residences where princesses who became Russian Empresses spent their childhood and early youth. Many of these palaces are grand architectural monuments. They were the depositories of the best works of a wide range of art, including also gifts given by brothers and sisters, parents and children, during family holidays or important events in the history of these countries. Today, most of the palaces of these former rulers, at least those buildings that have survive, are museums, open to the public, or they serve as residences for presidents or offices for government officials.

When the young princesses arrived in Russia from Europe, they became true helpers to their husbands and assisted them in the difficult task of service to their new country. They raised their children in accordance to traditions of their newly acquired families, doing everything possible to prepare them to faithfully fulfill their duty to their homeland in whatever post or responsibility destiny and fate had chosen for them to serve.

During the last several years a lot has been said about the role of the Romanov dynasty in all areas of development in Russia. Books have been published about the influence of members of the family in one or another sphere, particularly those in which Grand Dukes and Grand Duchesses held high-level positions. But little has been said about the families from which the future Empresses and Grand Duchesses of Russia came. The contemporary reader has only the names of residences, no visual image with which to associate their childhood and youth.

Russian Emperors often accompanied their wives to visit their nearest relatives – parents, brothers, sisters. Detailed descriptions of these visits were provided on the pages of periodicals and were accompanied by photographs of residences, including views of rooms and halls in which official and family gatherings took place. Fredensborg and Tatoi, Jugenheim and Schwerin – practically every contemporary knew these names at the time; however, today, few Russians are familiar with them.

A Russian saying proclaims – "better to see once, than to hear a hundred times" (i.e. "a picture is worth a thousand words"). That is why we decided to reveal our theme mainly through photographs.

In selecting our illustrations we asked for the assistance of the leading photo archives, museums and libraries of our country, Denmark, Germany and England. Priceless assistance was received from owners of private collections.

The earliest type of photographic images used is daguerreotypes – those with the images of Empress Maria Alexandrovna and Mikhail Glinka. They date from the 1860s. The latest type used, archival photos, are the images documenting the death of the Dowager Empress Maria Feodorovna in Denmark in 1928.

The pioneers of photography in Russia were A. Denier, S. Levitsky, K. Bergamasco and others, who made a wonderful contribution to the development of the art of photography at its earliest stages of development. Our book (photo album) contains many photographs by these famous masters.

Photography at that time was an extremely expensive pleasure, and that is why we were able to find photo images of most members of Imperial families and representatives of the upper classes on portrait photographs. However, images in photographs on file in Russian archives are often not fully identified. To completely identify personages included in group photographs is a very difficult task, and we turned to specialists from many countries in order to master this problem. The list of people to whom we would like to express our gratitude is very large. At the end of this photo album we have provided the names of those who supported us in this project. To them we are deeply indebted.

The authors were able to visit most of the residences described in this book. Some contemporary photographs will help the reader see the present day conditions of these monuments of history and culture.

We are, presently, trying to restore a torn thread of history and to re-establish Russia's path of cooperation with the countries of Europe. A view through a camera's lens on the events of the past, when the progressive actions of our nation corresponded to those of European nations in the most varied aspects of life, will maybe cause the reader to ponder and to reflect.

Table of Contents

Russia and Germany

Introduction   8
Emperor Alexander II, Empress Maria Alexandrovna and Kaiser Wilhelm I   12
The Kingdom of Württemberg – Queen Olga   40
Princess Charlotte of Württemberg – Grand Duchess Helen Pavlovna and her heirs in Russia   50
Grand Duchess Vera Konstantinovna, Duchess Eugen of Württemberg   56
The dawn of the automotive industry in Stuttgart and in Russia   60
Contacts with Germany during the reign of Emperor Alexander III   65
The St. Vladimir Brotherhood in Berlin   72
Baden-Baden – the "Summer Capital of Europe"   77
The Duchy of Saxe-Coburg and Gotha. Grand Duchess Maria and her daughter Victoria Melita   81
Victoria Melita's second marriage. The familial home of Grand Duke Kirill Vladimirovich   96
The Engagement of Tsarevich Nicholas Alexandrovich and Princess Alix of Hesse and by Rhine   111
The Grand Duchy of Hesse. Princess Alix, her brother Grand Duke Ernst Ludwig and her sister Ella   117
The Coronation of Emperor Nicholas II and Empress Alexandra Feodorovna   125
Grand Duchess Elisabeth Feodorovna   130
The Grand Duchy of Hesse and Russia   134
Russia and Germany during the years of the reign of Emperor Nicholas II and Kaiser Wilhelm II   144
The Grand Duchy of Mecklenburg-Schwerin   151
The Mikhailovich – The Family of Grand Duchess Anastasia Mikhailovna   154
The Mecklenburg-Schwerin Relatives of Grand Duchess Anastasia Mikhailovna   161

Russia and Denmark

Introduction   174
The Family of King Christian IX – The Amalienborg Palace   177
Princess Dagmar and Tsarevich Nicholas Alexandrovich   182
The Engagement of Princess Dagmar and Tsarevich Alexander Alexandrovich   187
Tsarevich Alexander Alexandrovich and Tsarevna Maria Feodorovna   192
Gatchina – the residence of Emperor Alexander III's family   200
The Visits of Emperor Alexander III and His Family to Denmark   205
Empress Maria Feodorovna and Her Siblings   215

Important Events for in the Life of Emperor Nicholas II   224
The Dowager Empress Maria Feodorovna   239

Russia and Greece

Introduction   255
The Konstantinovich – The Family of Grand Duchess Olga Konstantinovna   256
Queen Olga of Greece   261
Crown Prince Constantine   272
Prince George   274
Queen Olga's Charities   277
Prince Nicholas and Grand Duchess Helen Vladimirovna   280
PrincessAlexandra and Grand Duke Paul Alexandrovich   286
Princess Marie and Grand Duke George Mikhailovich   292
The Tragic End – The Final Years   297

Addendum

       Family Tree: The Russian Imperial House   306
       Family Tree: The German Descendants of Tsar Paul I   308

Bibliography   310

Index of Names   312

Last Word...   318

Russia and Germany

Unter den Linden – Berlin's main thoroughfare (1913)

*F*or three centuries of dynastic rule, members of the Romanov Imperial Family entered into marriages with princes and princesses from various kingdoms and princicipalities, grand duchies and duchies, located within the geographic territory of present-day Germany. The marriage of Grand Duke Nicholas Pavlovich, which took place in July of 1817, established familial ties between the Russian Imperial House and the Prussian Royal Family, the Hohenzollerns. Nicholas Pavlovich and Charlotte of Prussia, who adopted the name Alexandra Feodorovna, had a large family. All seven children of this Imperial couple established marital ties with representatives of German ruling houses. German princesses, upon their arrival in St. Petersburg, took up residence in the best palaces of the Russian capital and brought with them the best traditions of their homeland, which were then ingrained into Russian culture. Consequently, by the end of the XIX century the House of Romanov had extremely close familial ties with many of the realms within what in 1871 became the powerful German Empire, ruled by the Hohenzollerns.

Starting with Peter the Great, when the Russian Tsar traveled to Europe as head of the Great Diplomatic Mission, Russia has shown an interest in the achievements of Germany in the areas of science, industry and culture. A simple listing of members of the first Russian Academy of Science, founded in 1725, will show that Russian scientific development was greatly influenced by the influx of German scientists. By the end of the XIX century representatives of German families were successfully employed in the government and the military, in industry and finances; they also built palaces, man sions, and cathedrals throughout all of Russia.

In 1838–1839, when Tsarevich Alexander Nikolaevich traveled around Europe, he met his fated bride, Princess Marie of Hesse and by Rhine, who was to become Empress Maria Alexandrovna.

In 1894 in Coburg the grandson of Alexander II, Tsarevich Nicholas Alexandrovich was engaged to Princess Alix of Hesse and by Rhine, who at the end of that same year together with her husband ascended the throne of Russia. Alix's father, Grand Duke Ludwig IV was a nephew of Empress Maria Alexandrovna, his father being the Empress' older brother. Nicholas' father, Alexander III, was therefore a first cousin of Alix's own father.

Russian Grand Duchesses, as a rule, entered into marriages with representatives of German ruling houses. When they settled in the residences of their husbands, very often they would not change their religion. As a result, many Russian Orthodox cathedrals and chapels were constructed in various German capitals, smaller cities and resort towns. These were widely visited by the Russian elite, from the middle of the XIX century. Funds for their construction were, for the most part, sent as donations from Russia, and some of the leading Russian architects and masters of iconography participated in their architectural and interior designs. The Emperor, the Empress, and other members of the Imperial Family provided a considerable amount of the funding.

Indeed, there are very many Russian Orthodox church buildings throughout Germany. This is tied to the initiatives of the St. Vladimir Brotherhood, founded in Berlin in 1890. It was affiliated to the Russian embassy and was under the patronage of Grand Duke Vladimir Alexandrovich.

In this image we see four generations of Prussian royalty. Seated at center is German Kaiser Wilhelm I holding his great-grandson Prince Wilhelm. To the Emperor's right is his only son, the future Kaiser Friedrich III, while to his left is his grandsonthe future Kaiser Wilhelm II. Tsar Alexander II of Russia was a nephew of Kaiser Wilhelm I. (1882) Photograph by H. Selle. [RGAKFD]

Emperor Alexander II and his wife Empress Maria Alexandrovna. An image dating from the 1860s.
Photograph by Levitsky. [TsGAKFFD Spb]

Tsarevich Nicholas Alexandrovich and Princess Alix of Hesse and by Rhine (the future Empress Alexandra Feodorovna) after their engagement – Coburg, April 20, 1894. Photograph by Uhlenhuth. [RGAKFD]

Emperor Alexander II, Empress Maria Alexandrovna and Kaiser Wilhelm I

Having come to Russia from a small German principality, both Hessian princesses found themselves on the throne of one of the most powerful nations on earth. For Maria and Alix, Russia became the country where they would create their own identities; here they converted to a new religion, that aided both empresses to overcome the trials and tribulations that they were to face in later years. In Russia they would find familial bliss, and here they would raise their children. Their official place of residence was the Winter Palace in St. Petersburg.

The Winter Palace was constructed in 1754–1762 according to the project of Francesco Bartolomeo Rastrelli (1700–1771). In December of 1837 there was a fire that ravaged the palace. It took more than thirty hours to put under control; it destroyed the luxurious interiors of the second and third floors. In order to start the renovation process a special commission was established, under the leadership of His Serene Highness Prince P. Volkonsky. Every day from one to ten thousand people worked at the palace. The imperial residence was restored in a very short period of time, fifteen months. According to the plans of leading St. Petersburg architects Alexander Pavlovich Brullov and Vasily Stasov several halls were totally renovated. Some others were returned to their former glory, as expressed by Rastrelli's designs – the imposing Jordanian staircase and the Main Church, and also the interiors decorated by Giacomo Quarenghi and Auguste de Montferrand.

Up until the October Revolution, the interiors of the palace complex were being constantly redecorated by the leading architects of the time, including A. Stakenschneider and G. Bosse. The rooms of the Winter Palace were to house a priceless collection of art, sculpture, furniture, china and other articles of applied art. Today, the

The Imperial flower garden in front of the West façade of the Winter Palace.
In the center is the personal entrance of their Highnesses. Before the 1880s the rooms of Empress Maria Alexandrovna were located on the second floor and in the right resolute; to the left of the entrance was the study of Emperor Alexander II. In 1896-1898 the rooms to the left of the entrance were the private apartments of Emperor Nicholas II and Empress Alexandra Feodorovna, *c. 1910s.* [TsGAKFFD Spb]

Alexander II, Maria Alexandrovna & Kaiser Wilhelm I

Winter Palace and adjoining buildings, the pavilion created according to the plans of J.B. Vallin de la Mothe, the Main Hermitage and the New Hermitage, and also the side facing Palace Square with the grandiose building of the General Staff, have become known to the world as the State Hermitage Museum.

Empress Maria Alexandrovna, according to official versions, was the daughter of the Grand Duke Ludwig II and his wife Wilhelmine of Baden, who was the sister of the Russian Empress Elisabeth Alexeievna. However, rumor had it that the real father of Maria was considered to be Baron Auguste Senarclens de Grancy, the Grand Master of Stables of the Grand Duke of Hesse and by Rhine. In order to avoid unnecessary rumors, the Grand Duke declared

During his 26-year reign Emperor Alexander II passed many important reforms in Russia, and, having abolished serfdom, is remembered as the "Tsar-Liberator." "His most important gift to humanity was his heart, his kind, warm, human-loving heart, which naturally, led him to perform all that was great, for which his reign is remembered."

Anna Tiutcheva

The study of Emperor Alexander II in the Winter Palace.
The following portraits hung on the walls: in the top row Empress Maria Feodorovna, the wife of Emperor Paul I (Alexander's grandmother), in the bottom row (from left to right): Empress Alexandra Feodorovna and Emperor Nicholas I (his parents) and Empress Maria Alexandrovna (his wife). It was in this study on March 1, 1881, that Emperor Alexander II died, after a terroritt attack on his life on the Ekaterininky Canal.

Maria and her brother Alexander to be his own children. Since Grand Duchess Wilhelmine died early, Maria and her brother were raised away from the grand ducal court. Their childhood home was a mountainside castle, Heiligenberg, nestled on a hill overlooking the village of Jugenheim, located some 20 kilometers from Darmstadt.

Tsarevich Alexander Nikolaevich first met Maria in 1839, when she was 15 years old. At that time the Russian heir wrote to his mother, Empress Alexandra Feodorovna: "My dear Maman, I absolutely do not care about the secrets of Maria. I love her, and I would sooner abdicate the throne, than give her up. I will marry only her, that is my decision!"

During the spring of the following year, just before Easter, their engagement was announced, and later that September, the festive arrival of the Tsarevich's bride took place in St. Petersburg.

In later times Empress Maria Alexandrovna's Lady in Waiting, Anna Tiutcheva, was to write about the feelings experienced by the young German princess: "Having been raised in seclusion and even, one might say, in austerity, in the little castle of Jugenheim (sic. Heiligenberg), where she saw her father only rarely, she was more

View to the Palace Embankment and the Winter Palace – St. Petersburg, c. 1900. Photograph by K. Bulla. [TsGAKFFD Spb]

frightened than bedazzled, when she was suddenly brought to Court, to the most opulent, most splendid, most brilliant Court of all European nations. She told me that many times, after constant battles of overcoming her timidity and awkwardness, later on, under cover of darkness and in the stillness of her own room, she would give freedom to her tears and muffled cries..."

After their wedding, which took place on April 16, 1841, the young couple settled in the Winter Palace, and during the next two decades they were blessed with six sons and two daughters. The eldest daughter, Alexandra (1842–1849) died at the age of seven, and the young parents were quite distraught at the loss of their beloved child. The entire family spent the winter months at the official Imperial residence. Here, in the Winter Palace, the children had their own rooms, places to play and places to study. On Sunday evenings they would invite guests of their own age – the Adlerbergs, Meindorfs, Baryatinskys and children from other notable

Notwithstanding her height and built, she was in fact so thin and slender, that at first glance she gave no impression of a "belle dame;" however, she was extremely graceful, that special kind of grace, which can only be found in old German pictures, or Madonnas by Albrecht Dürer ... her facial features were correct. Her hair beautiful, her facial coloring delicate, her large blue, slightly bulging, eyes, looked at you with timidity and perception."

Anna Tiutcheva

Portrait of Empress Maria Alexandrovna, née Princess of Hesse and by Rhine. Second half of the 1860s. S.L. Levitsky. [RNB]

families. Their best friend and cohort in childhood mischief, the young Count Sergei Sheremetiev would remember, that he would wait with great anticipation for the time, when the carriage would drive him to the palace. He was allowed to dress in the same hussar uniform that was worn by the sons of Alexander II. There were many children, and they would have rather noisy games. Count Sheremetiev wrote: "After all, we were children, and everyone would have as much fun as he could, not paying much attention to court etiquette."

The family liked to spend the summer months in Tsarskoe Selo. The apartments of the Tsarevich and his wife were located in the Zubovsky wing of the Catherine Palace; it was so called because this was the last name of one of Catherine II's aides, Count Platon Zubov. On the first floor, where Catherine's aides had lived, one after the other, Alexander Nikolaevich arranged his private rooms, and on the second floor, previously gloriously decorated for Catherine II herself, were the apartments of Maria Alexandrovna. During the 1850s the architect

The fireplace in the White Hall of the Winter Palace.
[TsGAKFFD Spb]

Ippolit Monighetti redecorated these rooms, and, in particular, he chose a Western decor for the "Asian Room," which was designated as a showcase for a collection of arms; hence a very bright and functional interior was created.

Not surprisingly, for the children of the Imperial couple Tsarskoe Selo became a very dear haven, where they would live, sometimes for several months of the year.

When the Imperial family was in residence, the Catherine Palace would become the location for many festive events. The most opulent hall, where official receptions, dinners and balls were held, was richly decorated in gold-covered stucco. The large Rastrelli Hall covers an area of over 1000 square meters. But the "pearl" of the summer residence from the XVIII century on, was the one of its kind in the whole world Amber Room, encrusted entirely with this "stone of the sun."

During the reign of Alexander II, Tsarskoe Selo became the main summer residence, where the Imperial family would pass not only part of their summers, but also the autumn months. After the accession to the throne of Alexander Nikolaevich, work was expanded on the remodeling of the rooms in the Catherine Palace, and

Tsarevich Nicholas Alexandrovich.
Early 1860s. Photograph by I. Geffert.
[TsGAKFFD Spb]

Grand Duke Alexander Alexandrovich.
Early 1860s. [TsGAKFFD Spb]

Grand Duke Alexei Alexandrovich.
[RGAKDF]

Grand Duke Paul Alexandrovich.
Photograph by K. Bergamasco. [RGAKDF]

Grand Duchess Maria Alexandrovna.
[RGAKDF]

Grand Dukes Paul and Sergei Alexandrovich.
[RGAKDF]

Grand Dukes Alexander and Vladimir
Alexandrovich.
[RGAKDF]

Monighetti received the first assignment: to reconstruct the Grand Staircase. This project so pleased the Emperor that its creator was designated the official architect of the Imperial Court, and he was also given the honor of constructing a residence for the Imperial family in the newly acquired estate of Livadia in the Crimea.

Livadia (which when translated from the Greek means a "a small meadow"), the Imperial family's new Crimean residence, was named so in memory of an ancient settlement on that site. The estate was purchased by Emperor Alexander II in 1860 from the daughters of Count L. Pototsky and was soon transferred as a gift to his "beloved wife." Maria Alexandrovna saw her new estate for the first time in 1861, and she was thoroughly beguiled by the southern flora, the mild climate and the beautiful house and park. Ippolit Monighetti, as Chief Architect of palaces to the Imperial Court, was put in charge of the remodeling. Here, on the shores of the Crimea, the Empress, who was already showing the first signs of consumption, was hoping to improve her health. Maria Alexandrovna took an active role in the creation of a new image for her southern home. The plans of the Large Palace, the Smaller Palace (that had been set aside for the Grand Dukes), staff quarters and other buildings met with complete approval by the august client. Materials for the construction and the decoration, marble for the Krestovozdvizhensky ("Raising of the Holy Cross") church, pieces of furniture, all were often ordered in European countries. In 1866, after several years of stressful labor, working simultaneously on building construction, interior decoration, furniture designs, china and silverware pieces, as well as landscaping the parks, Ippolit Monighetti was able to create one of the most beautiful summer residences imaginable, and with a glorious surrounding park. Climentii Gekkel, who had arrived in Russia in 1832 from Dresden, where he had been the Royal Gardener to the Court of Saxony, worked with the architect on the winter gardens, the formal and the rose garden.

New buildings had appeared in Livadia, and old ones had been remodeled, to satisfy the wishes of the new masters; they totaled around 70. The Imperial Couple was extremely satisfied with the work of Monighetti, and in appreciation awarded him with the Order of St. Anne, Second Rank, with a diamond decoration in the form of an Imperial crown.

Emperor Alexander II and his family.
Seated in the first row, left to right, are: Emperor Alexander II, Tsarevna Maria Feodorovna with her son Nicholas Alexandrovich, and Empress Maria Alexandrovna. In the second row, same order: Grand Duke Paul Alexandrovich, Grand Duke Sergei Alexandrovich, Grand Duchess Maria Alexandrovna, Grand Duke Alexei Alexandrovich, Tsarevich Alexander Alexandrovich, and Grand Duke Vladimir Alexandrovich, c. 1870. [Eurohistory Archive]

Alexander II, Maria Alexandrovna & Kaiser Wilhelm I

View of the Catherine Palace from the side of the large plaza, c. 1910.
[TsGAKFFD SPb]

The room of Empress Maria Alexandrovna in the Zubovsky wing of the Catherine Palace in Tsarskoe Selo.
On the desk is a large oval photograph of her deceased son Tsarevich Nicholas Alexandrovich, c. 1870.
[TsGAKFFD SPb]

Many joyful days were spent on this estate of Alexander II. His family would come to the Crimea almost every year. The last time Empress Maria Alexandrovna saw her beloved Livadia was in 1879, by then she understood that she would not be able to win the battle with her dreadful disease.

Wishing to have a convenient rest stop during his travels from St. Petersburg to Livadia, Emperor Alexander II turned his attention to the Tsar's palace in Kiev, which had been constructed at the request of Empress Elisabeth Petrovna. It was built using the plans of the famed Court Architect F.B. Rastrelli. The decision to erect this palace was made by the Empress in the summer of 1744, during a pilgrimage she was taking to the Kievan Cave Monastery. The expansive baroque palace was built during a long period of fifteen years, and when it was finally completed, Empress Elisabeth Petrovna was ill, and could not visit the banks of the Dniepr River once again. In fact, the first Imperial guest of the Kievan residence was Catherine II. During later years the Governor-General of Kiev used the palace; however in the beginning of the XIX century a fire destroyed the wooden section of the second floor. It remained in this condition until 1867, when Emperor Alexander II directed architect Karl Maievsky to restore the building. Work

Emperor Alexander II's study in the Large Palace, Livadia.
[IIMK RAN]

The Smaller Palace, Livadia.
It was built by renowned Architect
I. Monighetti.

View of the Mariinsky Palace in Kiev.
[IIMK RAN]

The Imperial Mariinsky Theater.
To the left of the theater one can see the monument of M. Glinka; it was later moved from Glinka Street to the public garden next to the
Conservatory, c. 1908. Photograph by K. Bulla. [TsGAKFFD SPb]

Mikhail Ivanovich Glinka.
Daguerreotype by S.L. Levitsky.

was performed from 1868 to 1870, and the Kievan Palace became known as the Mariinsky Palace, in honor of Empress Maria Alexandrovna. Up until the October revolution members of the Imperial Family would stop there frequently. In fact, during the First World War, right before the time of her forced exile to the Crimea, the Dowager Empress Maria Feodorovna resided at the palace.

The Mariinsky Theater in St. Petersburg is also named in honor of Empress Maria Alexandrovna. This building was built in 1859–1860, according to the plans of Albert Cavos, son of the Italian composer Katarino Cavos, who had taken up residence in St. Petersburg. The famous art historian Alexander Benois wrote the following about the creation of this building in a letter to his grandfather: "The decorative designs of the main hall of the Mariinsky Theater are in their own way perfection ... the total decorative effect is unusually delicate, and has absolutely nothing obtrusive, the combination of light blue draperies in the loges and the decoration of the paneling and the armchairs in gold, create a harmony of rare festivity with an atmosphere of coziness." Notwithstanding the replacement of wooden construction sections with metal ones, and the introduction of other modern developments into the

View of the Berlin City Palace (Stadtschloß) and the Kaiser Wilhelm I Monument from the Schloßbrücke.

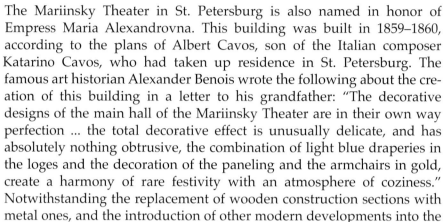

entire theater complex (completed in the 1890s by German born architect Victor Schreter,) the decor of the viewing hall had remained intact.

The first performance in the new building took place on October 2, 1860; it was Michael Glinka's opera "Life for the Tsar."

Emperor Alexander II and his wife very often traveled to Berlin, the capital of Imperial Germany. These journeys were sometimes for official meetings, but oftentimes to visit their nearest relatives. Kaiser Wilhelm I, the reader will remember, was an uncle of the Russian Emperor.

The main winter residence of the Markgraf and Kürfürsts of Brandenburg, and later the main residence of the German Kaisers, was the city palace on the river Spree in central Berlin. Its construction was started in the XVI century, and in later years the palace complex was expanded several times. In 1694 Andreas Schlüter came to Berlin, where he was commissioned to oversee the construction of the Berlin palace and to decorate its interiors. It was under this Court architect that the palace became a glorious example of northern German baroque architecture. The expansion of the Berlin residence of the Hohenzollerns continued in the XIX century. The building with the grand cupola, which became a part of its architectural complex, was constructed in 1845–1853 by Friedrich Schlüter and Albert Schadov, based on the plans of another famous architect of the Prussian Court, Karl Schinkel. To this very day, Schinkel's architectural monuments continue to beautify the squares of Berlin and Potsdam.

An interior view of the Knight's Hall, Berlin City Palace, c. early 1900s. The hall was the work of A. Schlüter.

Schinkel, as well as Schlüter, also worked on architectural projects in St. Petersburg. Schinkel was responsible for the plans of the pseudo-gothic Chapel in Peterhof, which served as a private church for the parents of Alexander II, Emperor Nicholas I and Empress Alexandra Feodorovna, sister of Kaiser Wilhelm I.

The Berlin City Palace from the side of the Lustgarden. The steeds designed by Klodt feature prominently in the image.

The Berlin city palace is not merely an architectural monument, but a building that in itself is of historical importance. It was from the palace balcony that Kaiser Wilhelm II called for the German people to unite behind at the beginning of the First World War. It was also here on November 9, 1918, that Karl Liebknecht announced the overthrow of the monarchy and declared Germany to be a socialist republic. After the revolution in 1918 the palace was turned into a museum. During the Second World War, as a result of an air raid, there was a fire in the Berlin city palace, and the ensuing fire consumed most of the massive structure. By order of the government of Walter Ulbricht, the building was blown up because it was deemed a symbol of Prussian absolutism. In 1950 the ruins were cleared and the empty space used as a parade ground.

During 1821–1823, according to the plans of Karl Schinkel, in the environs of the Berlin city palace of the Prussian kings, a bridge was constructed, which was named Schlossbrücke ("Castle Bridge"). This bridge is one of the major tourist attractions in Berlin. Eight marble groupings adorn it, each representing Hero at various moments of his life, from early youth to the meeting with death upon a battlefield, and to his transport to Mount Olympus. These sculptures were made according to the sketches of Schinkel. They were erected on the bridge during the reign of Friedrich Wilhelm IV.

In the capitals of both Russia and Germany there are sculptural and architectural monuments that remind one of the close ties shared by the two countries during the reign of Emperor Nicholas I, who had married the daughter of King Friedrich Wilhelm III of Prussia.

During a leisurely stroll in Berlin one can see in Kleistpark the sculptures familiar to every citizen of St. Petersburg – the famous horses of Peter Klodt. At the base of the figures there are plaques, and although the words are in Latin, one can clearly understand that these sculptures are a gift from Emperor Nicholas I to his brother-in-law King Friedrich Wilhelm IV. So popular were these figures of "man conquering the horse," that Klodt had to make several copies, first to adorn the Anitchkov Bridge over the Fontanka River in St. Petersburg, then as a gift to the King of Naples and to the Prussian King. In return, the King of Prussia sent a gift of his own – today this gift adorns the entrance of Konnogvardeisky Boulevard ("the Boulevard of the Mounted Guards") on the side of St. Isaac's Cathedral Square in St. Petersburg. Modeled by Christian Rauch, it is a bronze monument of the goddess Nike, atop a ten-meter column, erected during the middle of the XIX century.

When King Friedrich Wilhelm IV died in 1861, childless, his brother Wilhelm I ascended the throne of Prussia. The new Prussian king was Empress Alexandra Feodorovna's older brother. Wilhelm was born in 1797, and at age 16 had already participated in the famous Battle of Leipzig (also known as Battle of the Nations), a grand victory of the united forces against Napoleon Bonaparte. For his valor Wilhelm received the Iron Cross. In 1814 Emperor Alexander I awarded the young man the Russian Order of St. George. Three years later Wilhelm traveled with his sister, Princess Charlotte, to St. Petersburg and was present at the wedding of Grand Duke Nicholas Pavlovich, who later would become Emperor Nicholas I.

Nike's column at the entrance of Konnogvardeisky Boulevard, St. Petersburg. (C. Rauch, Sculptor; C. Rossi, Architect)

A view of the Anitchkov Bridge and the Palace of the Princes Beloselsky-Belozersky on St. Petersburg's Nevsky Prospekt. This lithograph dates from the 1850s from a drawing by I. Charlemagne. The palace was built by the famed architect A. Stakenschneider. It was later the home of Grand Duke Sergei Alexandrovich and his wife Elisabeth Feodorovna. [RNB]

The Palace of Wilhelm I at Berlin's Unter den Linden No. 37, c. 1879.
Photograph by Hermann Rueckwardt.

Kaiser Wilhelm I in his study, February 1877. [TsGAKFFD SPb]

Alexander II, Maria Alexandrovna & Kaiser Wilhelm I

The main goal in the life of King Wilhelm I was the unification and growth of Germany. He was very successful in accomplishing his goal. When Prussia, with the support of armies from other German principalities, won the war against France in January 1871, it was decided to form one united nation. In Versailles Wilhelm was declared German Kaiser, while also holding the title of King of Prussia. His right hand man in the unification process was Chancellor Otto von Bismarck. In his memoirs he described Wilhelm as an old-fashioned, gracious and personable gentleman, a true Prussian officer, with a good sense of propriety, but easily beguiled by "a women's charms."

In 1829, Wilhelm I married Princess Augusta Saxe-Weimar-Eisenach. The wedding took place in Berlin, where the couple eventually settled in the palace built at No. 37 Unter den Linden. Augusta was a niece of Wilhelm's Russian brother-in-law since she was the daughter of Grand Duchess Maria Pavlovna, an older sister of Emperor Nicholas I. The couple had two children, a son and a daughter: Kaiser Friedrich III and Grand Duchess Luise of Baden. The name Unter den Linden ("under-the-linden trees") comes from the fact that the central section of this wide boulevard consists of two rows of majestic linden trees. Unter den Linden is one of the is one of the oldest thoroughfares in the capital city, as well as home to the most luxurious palaces and estates of Berlin.

The future Kaiser Wilhelm I's palace was constructed in 1834–1837, under the direction of Karl Ferdinand Langhans. It was here, from the window on the first floor, farthest to the left, that the Kaiser would greet the citizens of Berlin on festive occasions. It was also here that Wilhelm I died on March 9, 1888.

During the reign of Emperor Alexander II, there were very many Germans at the Imperial Court and in government service in Russia. One illustrious representative of the German nation was the Adjutant-General of the Imperial Suite, Count Peter Andreevich Kleinmikhel (1793–1869). He was also famous as the chief Director of Transport and Public Buildings, and it was under his supervision that the first railroad, the Nikolaevskaia, connecting Moscow and St. Petersburg, was constructed. The railroad line was named in honor of Emperor

A view of the interior of Kaiser Wiilhelm I's Palace at Unter den Linden No. 37, c. 1879.

Nicholas I, due to the fact that the Emperor was personally involved in the completion of this grandiose project. Trains started to run in both directions on November 1, 1851, exactly on the date assigned by the Emperor at the beginning of the project. The construction of the railroad cost the nation an enormous amount of money – 6.4 million rubles, but it was hard to underestimate the importance of this new method of transportation for Russia.

Under the supervision of Count Kleinmikhel the construction of the Blagoveschensky Bridge, the first permanent bridge over the Neva River, was also completed. After the death of Emperor Nicholas I the Blagoveschensky Bridge was renamed the Nikolaevsky Bridge, in his honor. There was also a chapel on the bridge, to St. Nicholas the Wonderworker, constructed under the plans of architect A. Stakenschneider.

During the middle of the XIX century the building for the first Imperial art museum in Russia was constructed. This was the New Hermitage and it was built by decree of Emperor Nicholas I and under the plans of the leading German architect Leo von Klenze (1784–1864). As the Court architect of the Kingdom of Bavaria, Klenze was famous throughout Europe, and had worked for many European rulers. The New Hermitage is unique in its overall unified conception – everything, even the interiors, the furniture, the demonstration tables and Von Klenze conceived stands.

The glorious opening of the Imperial museum took place on

Count Peter Kleinmichel (1793-1869), c. 1851. Painting by Franz Krüger.

St. Petersburg's Nikolaevsky Railroad Station, c. 1910. [TsGAKFFD SPb]

February 5, 1852. The new building was attached to the Winter Palace, and many pieces that had been collected privately by the Imperial family became part of the exhibition in this new temple to the arts. In decorating the museum halls the German architect always remembered that his creation was an integral part of "the palace, the residence of the Russian monarchs."

In those days, in order to see the exhibition in the museum, visitors needed to obtain special permission from the Ministry of the Imperial Court, and during the day, for around one hour and a half in the middle of the day, the museum would be closed to the public, because Emperor Nicholas I had the habit of "visiting the Hermitage personally, every day." But already by the reign of Emperor Alexander II the museum became open to all, and admission was free.

On "Namesdays," days of birth, weddings and important church holidays, it was a tradition with members of the House of Romanov to give each other beautiful works of art. With time, many of these pieces also became part of the Hermitage collection.

On March 1, 1881 a violent and tragic explosion took place on the Ekaterininsky Canal Embankment – a plot conjured by the terrorist group "Narodnaya Volya" ("Peoples' Will") mortally wounded Emperor Alexander II. In memory of this tragedy, which ended the life of the Tsar-Reformer, on September 14, 1883 the corner stone of a new cathedral was laid at the very spot where the horrible event took place. This was to become the Cathedral of the Resurrection of Our Lord, known to all as the "Saviour on Spilled Blood." This monument is now considered one of the dominant historical structures in the center of St. Petersburg. It was built in "a purely Russian style," in the traditions of Moscow and Yaroslavl church architecture of the XVII century. Plans were

The Nikolaevsky Brideg with the Chapel of St. Nicholas the Wonderworker, c. 1913.
Photograph by K. Bulla. [TsGAKFFD SPb]

The Hall of History and Sculpture at the New Hermitage Museum.
"Vsemirnaya Illyustratsiya" [International Illustrations]

provided by Archimandrite Ignatiy (Malyshev) and architect Alfred Parland, who was born in St. Petersburg in 1842, in a family of merchants. His grandfather Alfred John Parland was formerly the English tutor to the children of Emperor Paul I. Parland worked on the construction of one of the churches on the monastery grounds of the Trinity Sergius Monastery near Strelna with Archimandrite Ignatiy. When work was completed in 1881 Parland received the title of Academic of Architecture with the right to teach courses at the Academy of Art. During the construction of the Cathedral "Saviour on the Spilled Blood" and then later, during work on its interior, the architect taught first at the Academy of Art, and then at the School of Technical Drawing of Baron A. Stiglitz, in the "Aquarelle" (Watercolor) department.

Emperor Alexander III expressed the wish that the embankment railing, on which his mortally wounded father had leant, and the fragment of cobblestones, on which his blood was spilled, should become part of the new cathedral, and that these relics should be on the inside of the new building. Because of this, it was necessary to move a section of the foundation by eight meters, thus having the

The New Hermitage. [TsGAKFFD SPb]

building enter into the waters of the canal. The completion of this difficult architectural task took several years; in total the cathedral itself was constructed in 24 years.

This cathedral monument is very often called a "museum of mosaics." The mosaic decoration of the façades and of the interior covers a total area of over seven thousand square meters. Designs were provided by famous Russian artists, including V. Vasnetsov, N. Kharlamov, A. Riabushkin, M. Nesterov, A. Parland and also from the studios of the Frolov Brothers. The etched marble icon screen, made according to the designs of A. Parland, was cut in Genoa, by the firm of Giuseppe Novi. The central altar doors (the "Tsar's Gate") were made by the master jewelers of Moscow, the brothers Grachev, in 1900. Donations for the construction of this cathedral were collected from all corners of Russia, while funds for the construction of the belfry were donated by Slavic nations of the Balkans, as a sign of gratitude for being liberated from the Turkish yoke. The bells were forged in a foundry in Finland in 1896. Total expenses for the construction were over 4.6 million rubles, of which over a million were donated by members of the House of Romanov. Because of this the etched golden cross above the belfry is

Architect A. Parland.
[From the author's collection]

adorned with the Imperial crown; this is the only such occurrence in the city of St. Petersburg. The consecration of the "Saviour on Spilled Blood" occurred on August 19, 1907, in the presence of Nicholas II and members of the Imperial family. The upkeep of such an expensive cathedral required massive funding; together with St. Isaacs' Cathedral in St. Petersburg, the main cathedral of the capital, and also the Cathedral of Christ the Saviour in Moscow, this was provided for by the national budget.

Parland was also responsible for the design of the artfully decorated metal ironwork fencing of the Mikhailovsky Park on the side of the Griboiedov (formerly the Ekaterininsky) Canal. The fencing, covered with a rich botanical ornamentation, was forged at the St. Petersburg factory of Karl Winkler (1845-1900). He was an engineer and entrepreneur, was originally from the German town of Nürnberg; there are many examples of ironwork masterpieces in the architecture of this city. Winkler opened his shop in St. Petersburg in 1876, and had just four workers; eventually he was to

The Cathedral of the resurrection of Our Lord, St. Petersburg, c. 1907.

Karl Winkler, Purveyor of the Imperial Court.
[From the collection of J. Heusler]

turn this shop into one of the leading construction and decorative works enterprises in Russia. Its specialty was the creation of cast iron pieces; the technology necessary for this production was developed in Nürnberg, and was equal to the best pieces produced at the San Galli factory. Under the direction of his widow and the active participation of his three sons, until 1914, the factory continued to work after the death of Karl Winkler. Cast iron fencing, decorating famous buildings in St. Petersburg, for example the Singer Company building and the Eliseev Store on Nevsky Prospect, the palace of Grand Duke Alexei Alexandrovich on the River Moika, the Nabokov House on the Bol'shaya Morskaia Street – all were produced at the Karl Winkler factory.

Both the Berlin cathedral in memory of Kaiser Wilhelm (Kaiser Wilhelm Gedaechtness Kirche), as well as the Cathedral of the "Saviour on Spilled Blood" in St. Petersburg, are memorial buildings. They were constructed between the end of the XIX and beginning of the XX centuries. But if the cathedral in St. Petersburg was considered to be a place of sorrow, in memory of the loss of Emperor Alexander II, then the gothic cathedral in Berlin was in memory of the triumph of Kaiser Wilhelm I, who had united Germany and transformed it into a leading European nation. The same idea served as inspiration for the national monument to Kaiser Wilhelm I, erected at the end of the 1890s across from the Berlin city palace.

The Berlin cathedral was constructed according to the plans of the German architect Franz Schwechten. It was built in 1891–1895, and then the interior decoration took another ten years. The construction of the building was financed by voluntary donations given by the German people and the total cost equaled 6.8 million German marks (3 million 128 thousand rubles). The central tower, out of a total of five, was 113 meters in height, and the cathedral became the highest building in Berlin. The walls, vaults and plafond of the memorial cathedral are covered in mosaics. Pictured on the mosaics are the rulers of Germany from the Hohenzollern Dynasty.

The cover of the firm's catalogue. Drawing by Karl Winkler (1896).
[From the collection of J. Heusler]

In November of 1943, during a British air raid, the walls of the cathedral were destroyed, there was a fire, and the memorial cathedral to Kaiser Wilhelm became a pile of debris. In 1950 the Berlin city administration decided to demolish the cathedral entirely, but the citizens of Berlin came to the rescue. The building was preserved, and within the restored halls a museum was opened.

The idea of erecting a monument to the Tsar-Liberator in Moscow came about in March 1881, almost immediately after the tragic assassination of Emperor Alexander II in St. Petersburg. However, realization of this idea took a long and exhausting path. First, one could not come to a consensus on the design. Three competitions, one after another, did not produce the desired results, and it was only after the direct intervention of Emperor Alexander III himself, that a decision was finally made.

In 1890, on a Kremlin hilltop, overlooking the Moscow River, work was commenced on the project designed by architect N. Sultanov, sculptor A. Opekushin and artist P. Zhukovsky. The three of them foresaw not simply a monument, but a whole architectural complex, with several sculptured figures. A foundation of 17 meters was required, and it alone was under construction for three years. The corner stone was laid in May 1893, with Emperor Alexander III and members of the Imperial family present.

Monument to Kaiser Wilhelm I in Berlin. G.F. Halmguber, sculptor P. Begas.
[From the collection of Yu. Saveliev]

The Cathedral in memory of Kaiser Wilhelm I, Breit Square, Berlin.

The five-meter high statue of the Emperor, in Imperial robes, over a General's parade uniform, was forged at the St. Petersburg factory of N. Stange. It was erected under a canopy, topped with an Imperial two-headed eagle, over 36 meters in height. The plaque at the base of the monument read: "To Emperor Alexander II, with the love of his nation." On three sides the monument was surrounded with a spacious gallery-arcade, 110 meters in length; the vaults of this arcade were decorated in 33 mosaics with portraits of Russian rulers, from Prince Vladimir to Nicholas I. The designs were by Paul Zhukovsky and the mosaics themselves were made in Venice. The unveiling of the monument was on August 16, 1898, with Emperor Nicholas II and members of his family present.

Donations for this main monument to the Emperor were collected throughout Russia, and the costs turned out to be enormous – 1.8 million rubles. But the fate of this monument was similar to that of many others, created for the "eternal memory" of the rulers of Russia. In 1918 the five meter colossus was thrown off of the pedestal, and later, in the 1930s, the entire architectural ensemble, at one time created with the "voluntary support of the Russian people," was totally demolished.

Before the October revolution, there were several thousand monuments to Emperor Alexander II throughout Russia. This was tied not merely to the tragedy of his death, but, more importantly, to the most memorable event of his reign, the liberation of the serfs. Today, out of all of the thousands, only rare examples remain. In Finland, in the capital city Helsinki, the memory of Alexander II was best preserved.

On April 17, 1894, on the day of his birth, a monument to Emperor Alexander II was erected on a central square of Helsinki, the main city of the Great Principality of Finland, which at that time was part of the Russian Empire.

Senate Square, as almost the entire city of Helsinki, was constructed under the plans of Karl Ludwig Engel (1778–1840), a German architect from Berlin, who studied together with Schinkel, and in later years lived and worked in Finland. The Cathedral of St. Nicholas, the Senate buildings, and the university all were constructed according to his designs in a pure classical style. The monument to Alexander II was designed

Mosaic from the Berlin Cathedral in memory of Kaiser Wilhelm I.
From left to right: Queen Louise and King Friedrich Wilhelm III of Prussia, King Friedrich Wilhelm IV and his brother Kaiser Wilhelm I, Kaiser Friedrich III, his son Kaiser Wilhelm II with his wife Augusta Viktoria, and their daughter-in-law Crown Princess Cecilie.

The unveiling of the monument to Emperor Alexander II in the Moscow Kremlin, August 16, 1898.
Photograoh K. Bula. [TsGAKFFD SPb]

The central portion of the Alexander II monument in the Kremlin. [TsGAKFFD SPb]

The monument to Emperor Alexander II on Senate Square, Helsinki.
On March 1 (13), 1899, the anniversary of Emperor Alexander II's death, citizens of Helsinki came to the monument dressed in mourning and laid flowers at the foot of the monument. Doing so they expressed their respect for the Tsar-Liberator, as well as their protest against Nicholas II's decree limiting Finnish autonomy.
Photograph by Daniel Nyblin. [National Library of Finland, Helsinki]

by the Finnish sculptors B. Runeberg and I. Takanen.

Back in Germany, the difficult task of uniting separate lands into a strong nation, which was the main goal of Wilhelm I, was successfully completed due in large part to the strong politics of the "Iron Chancellor" Otto von Bismarck. In the 1890s monuments to this political leader were erected in many large cities; in Berlin, a grand monument was created right in front of the Reichstag, in the very heart of the capital.

On an old photograph one can see a view of the Reichstag; to the right of the monument to Bismarck stands another famous monument – the Column to Victory (Siegessaeule). This monument was erected by order of Kaiser Wilhelm I in 1873 and was in memory of Prussia being victorious in wars against Denmark, Austria and France. At the top of the column, constructed from cannons taken in battle, there is an eight-meter figure of "Victoria," the Goddess of Victory. Berliners call this feminine figure "Golden Elsa" in memory of the heroine of a popular novel, printed in the magazine Die Gartenlaube in the 1870s; however, it would have been better to call her "Golden Margarita," since the sculptor's (Friedrich Drack's) daughter Margarita served as inspiration for the figure of the goddess.

Today, both monuments shown in the photograph are located on a new spot, on Big Star Square (Grosser Stern) in the center of the Tiergarten. At a height of fifty meters, there is a viewing platform on the Victory Column, from which one has a wonderful panorama of the city.

The monument to Chancellor Prince Otto von Bismarck and the Franco-Prussian War Victory Column, Tiergarten, Berlin.

THE KINGDOM OF WÜRTTEMBERG

Queen Olga
(Grand Duchess Olga Nikolaevna)
(1822-1892)

The House of Württemberg, one of the ruling Houses of Germany, was famous in Europe from the 13th century. In 2005 it celebrated its 510th anniversary, from the moment of the founding of the Duchy; this was also the 190th anniversary of the declaration of the Kingdom.

The capital city of the Kingdom of Württemberg was Stuttgart.

The first dynastic ties between Württemberg and the Russian Imperial House were established in September 1776, when Princess Sophia Dorothea of Württemberg (1759– 1828) became the second wife of the future Emperor Paul I. These dynastic ties between Russia and Württemberg would be strengthened in generations to come.

Forty years later, in January 1816, the daughter of this Imperial couple, Catherine Pavlovna (1788–1819), widowed from her first husband Duke George of Oldenburg (1784–1812), was wed secondly to her first cousin Crown Prince Wilhelm of Württemberg (1781–1864), who was a widower as well. He succeeded his father as King later that same year. The citizens of the kingdom greatly appreciated the humanitarian activities of Queen Catherine, although she was fated to live only three years in Stuttgart, where she died in 1819. Institutions of learning that she founded still carry the name of this beloved Russian Grand Duchess. Queen Catherine is buried in a church built especially for her, a cathedral-mausoleum, situated on a hill in Rotenberg, not far from Stuttgart.

Grand Duchess Olga Nikolaevna, from 1846 the Crown Princess, and from 1864 the Queen of Württemberg. Gravure by J. Lindner, 1875.
[Archives of the city of Stuttgart]

The most significant pages in the history of relations between Russia and the Kingdom of Württemberg were the years in the reign of King Karl I (1823–1891) and his wife Queen Olga (1822–1892). Olga was the second of three daughters of Emperor Nicholas I and his wife Alexandra Feodorovna (née Prussia). Olga lived in Württemberg for 46 years, and she was famous for her charitable works. Under her initiative several charitable institutions were opened, among them: a women's gymnasium, a pedagogical institute, a hospital named after Karl and Olga. Not having children of her own, Queen Olga adopted her niece, Grand Duchess Vera Konstantinovna (1854–1912), who, at the suggestion of her physicians, needed to change the damp and cold climate of St. Petersburg for a warmer, more southern locale. The ten-year old young child came to live in Stuttgart, where she found a new loving family that welcomed her with open arms. In 1874 Princess Vera further strengthened the ties between Russia and her aunt's kingdom when she married Duke Wilhelm Eugen of Württemberg (1846–1877).

In the capital of Württemberg the memory of these three wonderful Russian women survives in the names of streets and squares.

King Karl I (1823–1901) was the only son of King Wilhelm I of Württemberg from his third wife, the former Princess Pauline of Württemberg. Wilhelm I's second wife Grand Duchess Catherine Pavlovna was the sister of Russian Emperors Alexander I and Nicholas I. Fate had tied Prince Karl with Russia from childhood. By the age of fifteen, Karl was awarded with the highest Russian Order, and was to become the seventh Knight of the Order of St. Andrew the First-Called who came from the House of Württemberg. The engagement of Karl and Olga Nikolaevna was announced in January 1846 in Palermo, Sicily. The announcement took place in such an unlikely spot because Nicholas I, along with his family, had decided to spend the winter season in sunny Italy, so that Empress Alexandra Feodorovna could improve her health. While in Sicily, they stayed in a villa belonging to Varvara Petrovna, née Princess Shakhovskaia, the widow of the Neapolitan Ambassador, Prince Butera di Radali.

The wedding of Karl and Olga took place on July 1, 1846, in Peterhof, the favorite residence of the family of Emperor Nicholas I. For this gala event a rich dowry was being prepared for the beautiful bride. For example, her parents had ordered for Olga an exquisite silver table service. On each of the 500 pieces a two-headed eagle was engraved under the crown and insignia of Grand Duchess Olga Nikolaevna. But aside from traditional wedding presents, the daughter of the Emperor also received her very own little "kingdom" – an island with a three-story pavilion, with a vine covered pergola, a staircase leading down to a boat dock, and all of this

The New Royal Palce in Stuttgart built by Architects Leopold M. Retti, Philippe de la Guinuepe and Nikolaus F. von Tourett.
In 1841 a memorial column to honor the Silver Anniversary of the reign of King Wilhelm I was erected on the main palace square.
[Archives of the city of Stuttgart]

The White Hall in the New Royal Palace, Stuttgart. [Archive of the city of Stuttgart]

The combined coat-of-arms of Queen Olga of Württemberg.

surrounded by flower gardens. It took just several months to construct this pavilion in a Neapolitan style, in memory of the happy event that had taken place in Palermo. The pavilion, island and surrounding pond in Peterhof still carry the name of "Olga," in honor of Nicholas I daughter. The serene, demure building, with simple decoration on the outside, is topped with a viewing platform, from which one can see Tsaritsyn Island, the Kolonistky and Lugovoy (Meadow) parks. Next to the staircase, at the water's edge, a gondola would always be on the ready, to take guests to this secluded little corner of Italy in Russia.

During the second half of the 19th century grand firework displays and illumination shows would be organized on "Olga Island," in honor of birthdays of members of the Imperial family or visits of important foreign guests. For example, on July 27, 1876, in honor of the arrival in Peterhof of the King and Queen of Denmark and the King and Queen of Greece, a grand spectacle was held on Olga Island, a production of an act from the ballet "Two Stars," with music composed by C. Pugni and choreographed by M. Petipa.

Queen Olga of Württemberg

Grand Duchess Olga Nikolaevna moved to Württemberg in 1846 and took up residence with her husband Crown Prince Karl in the palace on Königstrasse. A house chapel was set up for the mistress of the palace; this temporary chapel was consecrated in honor of St. Nicholas. In 1864 after the death of King Wilhelm I, when Olga Nikolaevna's husband, Karl I, ascended the throne, the church of St. Nicholas was moved into the New Royal Palace, which had become the residence of the august couple.

The entrance of the New Palace is adorned with two pylons, on which are situated statues of a lion and a deer, the two symbols on the coat-of-arms of the lands of Baden-Württemberg.

This was the official residence of the Kings of Württemberg and it is situated on the central square of Stuttgart. It was erected during the reign of Duke Karl Eugen of Württemberg (1744–1793). During the 19th century the palace was expanded, and new rooms were added, and decorated in the "Empire" style. Queen Olga's apartments were in the palace extension next to the park.

The private church was located in a large room with a high ceiling and it was very richly decorated. There was a two-tiered carved wooden altar screen, made in St. Petersburg, and designed by Feodor Bruni. In total, there were about 80 holy icons. The overall design was under the direction of architect Konstantin Ton. The personal priest of Queen Olga for a period of over forty years, starting from 1851, was Protopriest Ivan Bazarov (1819–1895). Queen Olga's brother, Emperor Alexander II prayed in this private chapel numerous times,

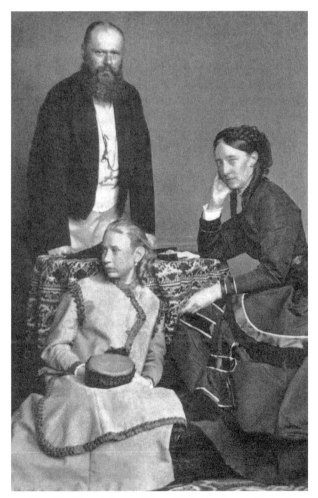

The celebration on Olga Island, July 14, 1876.
["Vsemirnaya Illyustratsiya" – 1876]

King Karl I and Queen Olga of Württemberg with their
adopted daughter Grand Duchess Vera Konstantinovna.
[Eurohistory Archive]

The gondola, on exhibition in the State Museum of
Peterhof, Olga Island.
[Photograph by Galina Korneva]

Queen Olga's apartment building, which Grand Duchess Vera inherited from her aunt in 1892.
[Archive of the city of Stuttgart]

The church of St. Nicholas in the New Royal palace, Stuttgart.

whenever he would come "for the cure" to Germany. It was here that Olga's niece, Grand Duchess Vera Konstantinovna, was married to Duke Wilhelm Eugen of Württemberg. This church was also the site for the wedding of Duke George Maximilianovich of Leuchtenberg (1852–1912), a nephew of Queen Olga, and Duchess Theresa of Oldenburg (1852–1883). After the death of Queen Olga, the church was moved to the villa Berg outside the city and placed in two small rooms on an upper floor.

Back in 1829, medicinal springs were discovered in the residential park of the Württemberg Kings at Rosenstein. King Wilhelm I ordered architect Karl Ludwig von Tsant to create a convalescent complex with a pavilion in a Mauritanian style. The King's House Master had brought him a present from his travels in Spain, an elaborate album with illustrations and descriptions of palaces in Granada's Alhambra. It was this architectural marvel that served as the model for the construction of several sites, the entrance and bathing pavilion, with an orangerie (winter garden), a hall for gala events, a gallery and gazebo. At the King's

Queen Olga of Württemberg

On the Silver Anniversary of King Karl I's reign, the Royal Family reunited.
Seated, from left to right: Princess Catharine, Princess Charlotte (née Schaumburg-Lippe), Princess Pauline, King Karl I, Queen Olga,
Princess Augusta of Saxe-Weimar-Eisenach. Standing, same order: Duke Albrecht, Prince Wilhelm, Grand Duchess Vera
Konstantinovna flanked by her daughters Elsa and Olga, and Prince Hermann of Saxe-Weimar-Eisenach. ["Vsemirnaya Illyustratsiya" – 1889]

desire the "marvels of the Alhambra were carried to the valley of the river Nekar." All of these exotic structures were scattered in a luxurious park, with ponds, fountains, flowerbeds, and sculptures. Rare species of birds and animals strolled on the paths of the park.

Two months after their wedding the newlyweds Crown Prince Karl and Grand Duchess Olga Nikolaevna finally moved to Stuttgart, and the gala celebration of their marriage took place in the "Wilhelma" park.

The official summer residence of the newlyweds became the Villa Berg. During his travels in Italy in 1845 the Crown Prince of Württemberg was totally enamored with the architectural style of that country. Having returned home, and knowing that his wedding was not far off, he assigned the young architect Christian Friedrich Leinz to develop the plans for a summer palace on the river Nekar. This was the architect's first assignment, and he fulfilled it brilliantly. The idea of erecting a palace in the Italian Renaissance style was met with approval by the Grand Duchess Olga Nikolaevna – thoughts of Sicily, where she made the acquaintance of her future husband, always brought back very fond and bright memories. The Olga Nikolaevna not only received a very rich dowry, but she also possessed not insignificant personal funds, part of

Queen Olga in middle-age. [RGAKFD]

45

which she set aside for the construction of the palace. On the first floor of the villa was the largest and most richly decorated Grand White Hall, with gold overlay. It was adorned with two rows of Corinthian marble columns, and inlaid parquet floor from rare types of wood, Carrara marble, a grandiose chandelier, unique landscape works of art, sculptures of the god Amour, created by I. Dannecker, and porcelain vases given as a gift to Grand Duchess Olga by the Chinese Empress. Located on this floor also were the Blue Living Room, the Dining Room, the Billiard Room, the Arsenal, Library and another Living Room with a terrace. The interior of the palace was also home to many pieces from Olga's dowry, including an English silver table service, very rare porcelain from the Imperial Porcelain Factory in St. Petersburg, furniture from the famous House of Heinrich Gambs. On the floor above the grand reception area there were twelve rooms set aside as private apartments for the family and their guests. Over a period of four decades many noted artists and musicians, scientists and architects, representatives of the most enlightened families of different countries of the world, had frequented these rooms; these included German Kaisers Wilhelm I and Wilhelm II, the French Emperor Napoleon III, and the Russian Emperor Alexander II, to name but a few. In June of 1867 Grand Duke Vladimir Alexandrovich visited Stuttgart with his father. The 20-year-old youth was greatly impressed with the beauty of the Villa Berg, and, when planning the decor of his own palace on the Neva embankment in St. Petersburg, construction of which took place in 1867–1872, the Grand Duke ordered architects Ieronim (Jerome) Kitner and Andrei Goon to visit Stuttgart and to use some of the motifs of the interiors in the summer residence of the King of Württemberg for his own magnificent palace.

A park, in which one can find, intermingled, natural and landscaped sections, fruit trees, flowerbeds, and

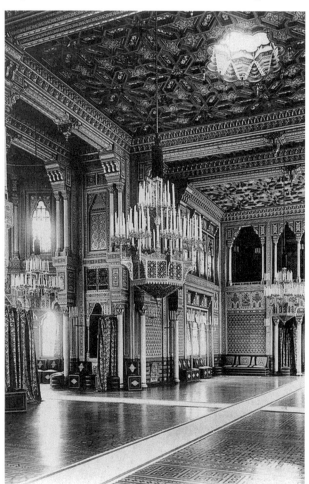

The Hall for grand receptions inside the Royal palace in Stuttgart was decoartedin Mauritanian style. This image dates from around 1900.
[Archives of the city of Stuttgart]

The Bathing Pavillion by Architect K.L. Tsant.
[Archives of the city of Stuttgart]

Queen Olga's Clinic in Stuttgart.
[Archives of the city of Stuttgart]

magnificent marble statuary surround the Villa Berg. The statue of the goddess Venus, for example, was delivered to the Villa Berg from St. Petersburg. The park was famous for its winter gardens (orangeries). On the eastern side, right next to the villa, there was a glorious rose garden.

Queen Olga easily earned the love of the citizens of Württemberg. She had received a very good education at home, she played the piano skillfully, and she could also paint and carve. When she came to Stuttgart she brought with her, as a memento, an album of pictures of Russia's northern capital; many of the graphic illustrations were in her own hand. Her tutor, the famous Russian poet Vasily Zhukovsky, instilled in Olga a love for literature, and helped her develop her artistic talents. In 1881 Queen Olga wrote her memoirs, about her childhood and teenage years, called the "Dream of Youth" (*Traum der Jugend goldener Stern*), and dedicated them to her nieces Olga and Vera, the daughters of Grand Duke Konstantin Nikolaevich.

Her contemporaries often recalled the beauty and high moral qualities of Queen Olga. For her active role in helping the poor and the downtrodden, she was known in Württemberg as the "virtuoso of charity."

In Europe, at the initiative of Swiss-born Henri Dunant, the International Committee for the provision of aid to those wounded in war was organized, and on October 29, 1863, the Geneva Convention officially founded the International Red Cross. In less than two months, as a direct result of the charitable activities of Queen Olga, chapters of this volunteer medical association appeared in Württemberg.

The Villa Berg.
[IIMK RAN]

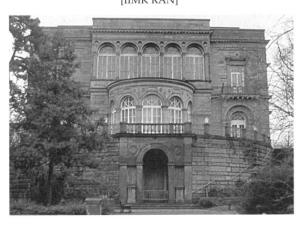

The Villa Berg in 2008.
[Photograph by Galina Korneva]

The inner courtyard in the Old Royal palace in Stuttgart.
[Archives of the city of Stuttgart]

Queen Olga of Württemberg toward the end of her life.
[Eurohistory Archive]

Queen Olga of Württemberg

Queen Olga also founded many charitable medical and educational facilities in Stuttgart. These include a children's hospital called the "Olgale," one of the first children's clinics in Germany. Of the 468 thousand marks that were necessary for its founding, Queen Olga donated 379 thousand out of her own personal funds.

During the Franco-Prussian War of 1870–1871, she was in charge of helping the wounded. Special workshops were set up in the royal palaces, where the citizens of Stuttgart would sew, knit and prepare bandages for the wounded. In 1871 King Karl I of Württemberg, officially installed an Order in honor of his wife, the Order of Olga. It was granted for acts of valor in charitable work.

Olga was also deeply interested in natural sciences and had her own collection of minerals, which she bequeathed to the State Museum of Natural Sciences in Stuttgart.

Queen Olga died on October 18 (30), 1892, in the royal palace at Friedrichshafen, on the northern shores of Lake Constance. She was buried next to her husband in a crypt in the palace church of the Old Castle in Stuttgart.

King Karl I and Queen Olga of Württemberg's final resting place, Old Royal Palace in Stuttgart. [TsGAKDDFD SPb]

Princess Charlotte of Württemberg –

Grand Duchess Helen Pavlovna and her Heirs in Russia

Grand Duchess Helen Pavlovna.
[Archives of the city of Stuttgart]

"... the existence of the Red Cross today is greatly indebted to the noble example of tencding to the wounded during the Crimean War, as set by Helen Pavlovna; she was an inspiration to the cause."

J. H. Dunant, first Nobel Peace Laureate.
[From a letter to the Russian Red Cross Society]

Fate willed that Grand Duchess Olga Nikolaevna live many years outside of Russia, and her activities in charitable work brought great aid to the citizens of the Kingdom of Württemberg.

In St. Petersburg, meanwhile, a German-born princess, Frederika Charlotte Maria of Württemberg (1806–1873), provided, for more than half a century, help for the poor and needy of Russia. The seventeen-year-old niece of Wilhelm I came to Russia, where in February 1824 her marriage to Grand Duke Michael Pavlovich took place. When she converted to Orthodoxy, she received the name of Helen Pavlovna. Very soon her mother-in-law, the Dowager Empress Maria Feodorovna, passed on to her the patronage of the Mariinsky Birthing and Obstetric Institutes. In her will the Empress wrote: "Knowing full well the steadfastness and gentleness of the character of my daughter-in-law, I am certain that in this way both institutes will always thrive and be a benefit to our country." Eventually, Grand Duchess Helen Pavlovna also became the patron of the Pavlovsky Institute for Young Ladies and the Maximilian Hospital. In memory of two of her daughters, Elisabeth (1826–1845) and Maria (1825–1846), both of whom had died at an early age, she established charitable institutions in St. Petersburg and in Pavlovsk.

Having founded the Krestovozdvizhenskaya ("Raising of the Holy Cross") Community of Nurses, the Grand Duchess became totally inspired by the ideas of Jean Henri Dunant, the founder of the International Red Cross. During the Crimean War of 1854–1855, she was able to obtain permission for nurses to be present on the battlefield. For the first time in the history of warfare, a public organization, not the military, provided care for the wounded in battle on the Crimean Peninsula. However, the greatest achievement of Helen Pavlovna was the creation of the first in the world Institute for the Re-education (i.e. the professional development) of Doctors. Her daughter Grand Duchess Catherine Mikhailovna in 1885 further developed the work of this Institute.

Having a very wide spectrum of interests and a very independent character, Grand Duchess Helen Pavlovna, three years before the official reform was announced by Alexander II, freed all 15,000 serfs that inhabited her estate of Karlovka. Her experience in this area was highly appreciated and even used during the formulation of the "Status Statement of February 19, 1861" (i.e. the Emancipation Proclamation).

In gratitude for her support of scientific and geographic expeditions, the explorer Miklukho-Maklay named several mountains and a strait in her honor in New Guinea.

The influence of Helen Pavlovna on the most varied aspects of Russian life is hard to underestimate. She was a grand supporter of the arts, a brilliant conversationalist, and a bright personality – the Grand Duchess played a major role in the cultural life of the country. In St. Petersburg her salon was attended by some of the country's most renowned intellectuals.

The names of Grand Duchess Helen Pavlovna and Anton Rubinstein are greatly intertwined in the establishment of the Russian Music Society and the famous St. Petersburg Conservatory.

In the Mikhailovsky Palace, home of the Grand

The Mikhailovsky Palace in St. Petersburg – a gift from Emperor Alexander I to his brother Mikhail Pavlovich upon his marriage to Frederika of Württemberg, Grand Duchess Helen Pavlovna. Built by Architect K. Rossi. Photograph by K. Bulla.
[TsGAKFFD SPb]

The Crimson Room of Grand Duchess Catherine Mikhailovna in a side wing of the Mikhailovsky Palace, c. 1894. [IIMK RAN]

The main building of the Clinical Institute, c. 1890 (presently the St. Petersburg Academy of Medicine, Post-graduate School).

Grand Duchess Catherine Mikhailovna.
[Eurohistory Archive]

Duke George of Mecklenburg-Strelitz.
[Eurohistory Archive]

Duchess, the sound of music was heard everywhere. Helen Pavlovna had a great talent for discovering and liberally supporting gifted artists. Anton Rubinstein, who had conquered Europe, as a ten-year-old child during his two-year tour, in the 1850s became the chief accompanist and soloist at the Court of the Grand Duchess. The biographer of Helen Pavlovna, the famous attorney A.F. Koni, wrote that Helen Pavlovna became involved in the establishment of the Conservatory, "with the gusto and steadfastness inherent to her character, not stopping even in the face of personal financial problems, having sold her diamonds for the cause." The Grand Duchess' right hand was always Anton Grigorievich Rubinstein. For many years Helen Pavlovna was the august patron of the Russian Music Society, which sponsored the establishment of educational facilities and organization of concerts in many different cities of Russia; she was always donating personal funds for this cause. For the support of teachers, talented students and for other needs of the Conservatory in St. Petersburg she would annually transfer from 8 to 10 thousand rubles into the Conservatory's account.

The Grand Duchess would also spare no small amount of money in order to invite to St. Petersburg the most famous European musicians. Hector Berlioz stayed at the Mikhailovsky Palace six times to conduct concerts; Richard Wagner would come on tour. This famous German composer would discuss librettos for his operas with Helen Pavlovna, and he also gave her as a gift an exquisite edition of Der Ring des Nibelungen. After one visit to Russia, Wagner wrote to one of the Grand Duchess' ladies in waiting, Baroness E. Raden, "A week ago I wanted to leave for St. Petersburg and to stay there for good. I wanted to throw myself at the feet of the Grand Duchess and to ask her to receive me in any position, to allot for me a small room, a servant, a little money for personal expenses, just a few hundred rubles a year. The horrible climate no longer scared me."

In 1872 Helen Pavlovna announced a competition for the composition of an opera based on N.V. Gogol's novel "Noch pered Rozhdestvom" ("Night before Christmas"). A prize of 2,000 rubles was announced for the best production, but the unexpected death of the Grand Duchess placed in doubt the completion of this project. It was only due to the support of the idea by her daughter Catherine Mikhailovna that the competition took place. The winner's laurels were bestowed upon P.I. Tchaikovsky, who dedicated the opera composed by him, "Vakula Kuznets "("Vakula the Blacksmith") to the memory of Grand Duchess Helen Pavlovna.

Grand Duchess Helen Pavlovna and Her Heirs in Russia

After the death of Helen Pavlovna on January 9 (21), 1873, her daughter Grand Duchess Catherine Mikhailovna became the mistress of the Mikhailovsky Palace in St. Petersburg, and of Oranienbaum in the environs of the capital. According to the Grand Duchess' will Catherine Mikhailovna also became the owner of Kamenny Ostrov ("Stone Island") along with the former Imperial residence, the palace of Paul I. This palace used to belong to the younger son of the Emperor, Michael Pavlovich, and in 1843 he gave it as a gift to his wife, Helen Pavlovna.

In 1851 Catherine Mikhailovna married Duke George Mecklenburg-Strelitz (1824–1876). He had close ties to the Imperial Family, as George was a first cousin of Empress Alexandra Feodorovna. His father, Grand Duke George (1779–1860), was the brother of Queen Louise of Prussia, the mother of Alexandra Feodorovna. In Russia, the head of the "Russian" branch of the Duchy of Mecklenburg-Strelitz became known as George Georgievich.

Just like the other Grand Duchesses from the House of Romanov, Catherine Mikhailovna was actively involved in many charitable causes. For many years she was a member of the Council of the Imperial Ladies Patriotic Society, and in 1870 became its Chairwoman. Catherine Mikhailovna continued to patronize the institutions founded by her mother, which were eventually combined into the Office of the Grand Duchess Helen Pavlovna.

In her spiritual will Catherine Mikhailovna asked her children to always remember that, "the Almighty God gave us certain advantages as far as position and wealth, but He also demands of us, that we use these gifts with dignity." Duke George Georgievich and the Grand Duchess had three children: Helen (1857–1936), George Alexander (1859–1909) and Michael (1863–1934). Not ignoring the fact that they, like their parents, were citizens of the Grand Duchy of Mecklenburg-Strelitz, Russia became a second home for the entire family. In his memoirs, Grand Duke Alexander Mikhailovich wrote about the Mecklenburg-Strelitz family saying, "they were half-German by birth, but totally Russian in spirit."

The children of Catherine Mikhailovna and Duke George of Mecklenburg-Strelitz were raised in the Mikhailovsky Palace, where they were literally surrounded by music. They were all gifted with perfect pitch; they were taught by the best teachers of the capital and during the day one constantly heard the sounds of musical scales and other melodies coming from the

The Northern façade of the Chinese Palace. From a postcard from the beginning of the XX century.

The Grand Palace, Oranienbaum. Photograph taken at the beginning of the XX century. [Archives of the Princes Golitsyn Famiy]

The St. Petersburg residence of Countess von Carlow, located at No. 46 Fontanka Embankmen, c. 2003. [Photograph by E. Zakharov]

music classrooms. In the evenings, in the grand halls, the stars of Europe would perform. For George Alexander, the oldest son (who was also known as George Georgievich, just to confuse matters), music even became a calling. At one time he considered having a professional career as a cellist. From the time George Alexander was 12-years-old, his teacher was the composer, and professor of the St. Petersburg Conservatory, Karl Davydov, whom Tchaikovsky called "the king of cellists of our time." It was no surprise that George Alexander would become the head of the committee for the anniversary festivities of the 50-year career of Anton Rubinstein, celebrated in 1889. It was then that the famous musician was given a very unusual gift – a unique instrument (with the number 10000) created especially for him by the firm of Jacob Bekker, the official purveyor to the Courts of Russia, Austria, Sweden, Denmark and Norway, created a piano. This anniversary instrument, made out of the best types of wood by the masters of the firm, was given to the most outstanding pianist of the time, and on the cover a wreath of laurel leaves was engraved with the name "Anton Rubinstein." After the death of this master, Rubinstein's relatives gave his conducting baton to Duke George Alexander.

Duke George Georgievich Jr. and his family, the Carlows. George Georgievich and Natalia surrounded by their children: Ekaterina, Maria, Natalia and George, who later became Duke of Mecklenburg. [GARF]

In the 1890s George Georgievich Jr. fulfilled his dream – he organized a string quartet. Members of this ensemble played on instruments made by Guarneri, which the Duke had purchased for them in Europe. The quartet's first performance took place in Oranienbaum, the suburban residence of the Mecklenburg-Strelitzes, on October 31, 1896. The group of musicians consisted of the greatest masters, and they were to see European fame – they were the first Russian string quartet to go on a European tour, and they took Europe by storm. The London newspaper, the "Morning Post" in 1907 wrote: "It is doubtful that London will ever hear more illustrious chamber music, than that which was performed by the St. Petersburg string quartet."

Concert performed at his residence on the Fontanka Embankment by Duke George Georgievich of Mecklenburg-Strelitz's string quartet. Photograph attributed to G.A. Popova and estimated to have been taken c. mid-1900s. [RGAKFD]

Music also helped George Georgievich Jr. to find marital bliss. In 1890 he wed his mother's lady-in-waiting, Natalia Vanliarsky. The love of music had brought together the Duke and the young lady, renowned for possessing a beautiful voice. Natalia not being of royal background, the marriage was considered morganatic and she was granted the title of Countess von Carlow. A great mutual love allowed them to overcome court demands, and, with the passing of time, Countess Natalia Feodorovna Carlow, who had a kind heart and a very honorable disposition, became loved by all of her Imperial relatives. The

newlyweds first settled in the western extension of the Mikhailovsky Palace, where fifteen rooms were reserved as their apartment. With the death of Catherine Mikhailovna, the Romanov line leading back to Grand Duke Mikhail Pavlovich ended; so, the palace erected for him, was purchased by Emperor Nicholas II from the Mecklenburg-Strelitz's during the winter of 1895, and in its luxurious halls it was decided to house the collection of the Russian Museum, named in honor of Emperor Alexander III.

George Georgievich Jr. and his wife settled in their residence at No. 46 Fontanka Embankment. Children born to them – daughters Catherine, Maria and Natalia, and their younger brother George, were very close and always ready to do something kind for their relatives. Their aunt, Helen Georgievna, was also very kind to the children. She had married at the age of 34 to the widowed Prince Albert of Saxe-Altenburg, a first cousin of Grand Duchess Alexandra Iosifovna, the wife of Grand Duke Konstantin Nikolaevich, Emperor Alexander II's brother. Not having children of her own, Helen Georgievna took to raising the children of her husband from his previous marriage to Princess Marie of Prussia, Olga and Maria. Princess Helen was very musically gifted. Alexander Benois remembered her, "her voice is beautiful, full-sounding, precise ... She could easily have become one of the premier performers of Bach, but her position and a natural self-consciousness, did not allow her ... Whenever concerts were given at the grand palace on Kamenny Island, she herself was one of the best performers."

Princess Albert of Saxe-Altenburg.
[Eurohistory Archive]

Her gift of music helped Helen Georgievna overcome many difficulties, which were thrown upon her, like on so many other exiled Russians. After the revolution of 1917 she was exiled to Copenhagen, where she supported herself through voice lessons. During these years she would very often visit the Dowager Empress Maria Feodorovna, and support her, spiritually.

After the fall of Emperor Nicholas II, the only son of George Georgievich Jr., Count George Alexander of Carlow, escaped Russia and settled in Germany. Grand Duke Adolf Friedrich VI of Mecklenburg-Strelitz having committed suicide early in 1918, Duke Michael, George Georgievich Jr.'s only brother, inherited the throne. Michael was still in Russia at the time, but eventually reached Strelitz, where he settled in exile. By then, however, the German Empire had also fallen and the grand ducal throne had ceased to exist. Since Duke Michael did not have any children, he adopted his nephew Georg Alexander as heir. Today, the grandson of Georg Alexander, Duke Borwin, is the Head of the House of Mecklenburg.

Grand Duchess Vera Konstantinovna
Duchess Wilhelm Eugen of Württemberg

Grand Duke Konstantin Konstantinovich wrote, "Vera, notwithstanding all of her good qualities, is prone to a lack of tactfulness. She has become distant to Russia, to our customs and mannerisms, she criticizes far too much, with no sense or reason."

Grand Duke Konstantin Konstantinovich of Russia. (1858-1915)

Duke Wilhelm Eugen of Württemberg and Grand Duchess Vera Konstantinovna. [Eurohistory Archive]

Grand Duchess Vera Konstantinovna came to Stuttgart in December 1863 as a nine-year-old girl, and all of her young and adult life was tied to Württemberg. Vera was sent to live in Stuttgart because her many physical ailments made living in Russia's inclement weather impossible. In order to help the little girl get used to her new surroundings in a strange country, Crown Princess Olga assigned to her a Russian governess from St. Petersburg, and would invite the children of Admiral Efim Putiatin to come and play with her. Half a year after Vera's arrival, in June 1864, King Wilhelm I of Württemberg died. At this very time Vera and Crown Princess Olga were in Kissingen, where they were visiting with many of their Russian relations. Having heard the news of the death Wilhelm I, they all rushed off to Stuttgart to attend the funeral ceremonies. Wilhelm I was buried next to his second wife, the Russian Grand Duchess Catherine Pavlovna, who had passed away in 1819. Their resting place is found in the Orthodox Church of St. Catherine on Rotenberg hill.

Grand Duchess Vera Konstantinovna

Notwithstanding the fact that Olga's life changed entirely, and she was now responsible for carrying out the duties of Queen of Württemberg, she still found the time to raise her niece.

Slowly, but surely, Vera became accustomed to her new surroundings and started to feel herself at home. In 1871 Queen Olga and her husband, who were childless, decided to adopt their niece. In 1874, Vera Konstantinovna married to Duke Wilhelm Eugen of Württemberg (1846–1877), a cousin of King Wilhelm. The fact that she was constantly abroad left an imprint of Grand Duchess Vera. Her own brother, Grand Duke Konstantin Konstantinovich wrote: "Vera, notwithstanding all of her good qualities, is prone to a lack of tactfulness. She has become distant to Russia, to our customs and mannerisms, she criticizes far too much, with no sense or reason." Vera, not surprisingly, had become a German through and through. Being surrounded by Protestants, during the reign of Alexander III she thought of adopting the Protestant faith, but, under the influence of her Russian relatives, this undertaking was delayed until 1909.

Grand Duchess Vera's bedroom, assumed to be in the Villa Berg, Stuttgart.
[TsGAKFFD SPb]

Sadly, married life was a short experiment for Vera and her husband. The couple lived together for only three years, and Duke Wilhelm Eugen suddenly died in 1877. At the age of 23 Duchess Vera, whose firstborn son had died, found herself alone with two twin baby girls, Olga and Elsa. Vera raised her daughters in Württemberg, where she continued enjoyed a privileged position.

Queen Olga's will, left her adopted daughter the Villa Berg. It was here that Vera had passed her childhood years, and it was here, since it was her main residence, that Duchess Vera had spent many years after the death of her husband.

Like her aunt, Vera Konstantinovna invested a lot of time and spent considerable sums of money helping various charitable institutions. In 1908, having sold many of her precious family jewels for the incredible sum of 166.000 gold German marks, she donated the money for the establishment of a home for the "poorest sisters in Christ." A new building, with a surrounding garden, was built in Stuttgart especially for this institution. During the first two years of its existence the home cared for 373 women and 112 children. Today, the institution continues to help the needy and it carries the name of Weraheim, or "The Haven of Duchess Vera."

At the initiative of Duchess Vera a new Orthodox cathedral was

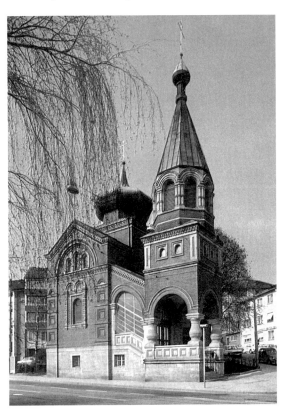

The Cathedral of St. Nicholas, Stuttgart.

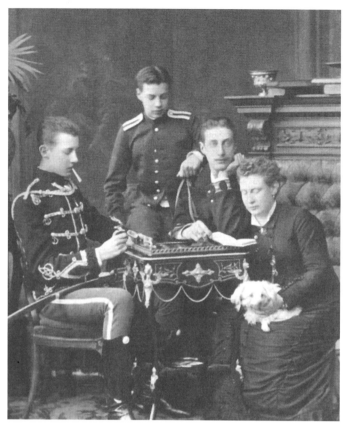

From left: Grand Duke Dimitry Konstantinovich, Grand Duke Vyacheslav Konstantinovich, Grand Duke Konstantin Konstantinovich, and their sister Grand Duchess Vera Konstantinovna. [Eurohistory Archive]

built in Stuttgart. Previously Orthodox believers had to attend services in a private chapel on the grounds of the Villa Berg; but it was situated rather far from the center of town and not equipped to house the large number of holy items and icons that had been collected by Queen Olga. The parcel of land for the new cathedral was bought in April 1894. Emperor Alexander III donated 75 thousand rubles for its purchase. But laying the foundation stone occurred after the death of the Russian Emperor. On May 6 (18) 1895, on the birthday of Nicholas II, the cathedral was festively consecrated, and on December 6 (18) of the same year, it was blessed and named in honor of St. Nicholas the Wonder Worker. The altar screen and many church utensils and icons were moved to the cathedral from the Villa Berg. Vera Konstinovna donated the main bell for the belfry, as well as three golden panikadilo (church chandeliers). She would arrive for church services in a Russian coach, driven by coachman Vasily Vasilievich Shatin, whom nature had blessed with a huge Russian beard; he had previously served Queen Olga of Württemberg. This new cathedral was also attended by Vera Konstantinovna's sister, Queen Olga, during her many regular visits to Stuttgart.

The cathedral of St. Nicholas was intended for the occupancy of 250 people. Its basement rooms house the library of Württemberg's Queen Olga.

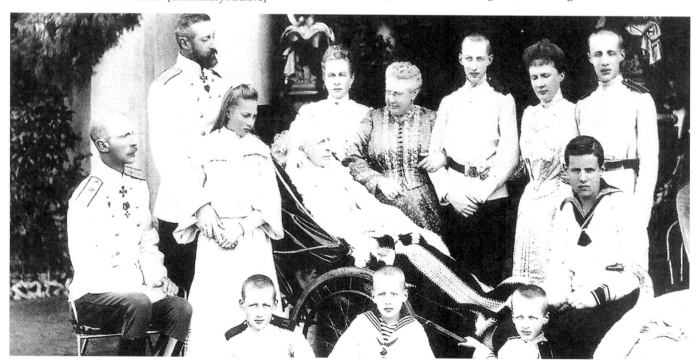

The Konstantinovich, c. 1904.
From left to right: Grand Duke Dimitry Konstantinovich, Grand Duke Konstantin Konstantinovich with daughter Tatiana, Grand Duchess Alexandra Iosifovna, Queen Olga of Greece, Grand Duchess Vera Konstantinovna, Prince Ioann Konstantinovich, Grand Duchess Elisabeth Mavrikievna, Prince Gabriel Konstantinovich and Prince Christopher of Greece. On the floor: Princes Konstanin, Igor and Oleg Konstantinovich, Strelna, 1903.
Photograph by D.S. Zdobnov. From the collection of I. Filimonov.

Grand Duchess Vera Konstantinovna

Grand Duchess Vera Konstantinovna with her daughters, Olga and Elsa, and her grandchildren.
[Eurohistory Archive]

Grand Duchess Vera Konstantinovna in later years. Although her eyesight was challenged by hereditary ailments, Vera remained an avid reader. [Eurohistory Archive]

Grand Duchess Vera Konstantinovna surrounded by her family.
From left to right: Prince Eugen of Schaumburg-Lippe, Princess Elsa of Schaumburg-Lippe, Princess Olga of Schaumburg-Lippe, Grand Duchess Vera Konstantinovna, Princess Bathildis of Schaumburg-Lippe, Prince Maximilian of Schaumburg-Lippe, Prince Albrecht of Schaumburg-Lippe, Prince Alexander of Schaumburg-Lippe, Prince Albrecht Jr. of Schaumburg-Lippe. [Eurohistory Archive]

The Dawn of the Automotive Industry
in Stuttgart and Russia

Very close familial ties between Russia and Germany also led to important cooperation between these two nations in other areas, such as economics and industry.

One of these areas was the automotive industry. The automobile, which saw its beginning at the end of the 19th century, was destined to drastically change the lives of common citizens. Stuttgart, the capital of the Kingdom of Württemberg became the "home of the self-moving transport system" – one of the status symbols of life in the 20th century. Some of the first buyers of these costly "motors" were members of the various royal families who stood at the helm of European nations. The Romanovs, without a doubt, were early enthusiasts of this new form of transportation.

Gotlieb Daimler (1834–1900) and Karl Benz (1844–1929) are names synonymous with the development of the motor industry. A graduate of the Stuttgart Polytechnic Institute, Daimler received in 1883 a patent for the internal combustion engine he was developing. Having attached it to a bicycle with wooden ironbound wheels and a wooden frame, two years later he started out on his first journey. The patented "motorcycle," with a gas or benzene engine, could climb to a speed of 12 km/hour. But there was one hindrance to its further development: one needed to find a cheaper way of obtaining benzene. In 1881 Daimler set off for Russia and visited Moscow, St. Petersburg, Nizhny Novgorod, Odessa and other cities. He spent an entire year in Russia, studying methods of refining oil into fuel. A few more years were required, before this new method of transportation would become a comfortable "motor coach" on four wheels, with an engine capable of providing speeds greater than horsepower. In 1890 Daimler established the world's first automotive plant – Daimler Motoren Gesellschaft.

Karl Benz was a student at the Karlsruhe Polytechnic School – one of the best technical universities of Germany. Like Daimler, Benz also worked on inventing and developing an internal combustion engine. At the beginning of 1886 he received a "birth certificate" for his newest invention, the automobile – a three-wheeled motor wagon. However, no one was willing to purchase the display model.

Gotlieb Daimler
(1834-1900)
[Daimler AG Archives and
Collection]

Karl Benz at the wheel of his
"motor wagon." [Daimler AG
Archives and Collection]

The Automotive Industry

Although the two famous German inventors never worked together (it is possible that they never met either), the firms that they had established were united in 1926 into the world-famous company known as "Daimler-Benz." The logo for the new firm was the emblem created by Daimler and it is used to this very day. The three-pointed star symbolizes that a vehicle produced at Daimler factories is subject to the will of three aspects of nature – air, water and earth. Automobiles sold by the company have the trademark of "Mercedes-Benz."

The name "Mercedes" came about because of another motoring enthusiast who believed in the future of the automobile invented by Daimler. Of Czech origin, Emil Jellinek, who was a successful businessman, arrived in Nice in 1899 as Consul of the Austro-Hungarian Empire. He was thrilled with the possibilities of the new means of transportation and started to work together with Gotlieb Daimler. As a result, Jellinek sold German cars in different countries. In 1900 in a car race organized in Nice, the first and second place winners were cars produced by Daimler's company. Seeing opportunity, Jellinek, the enterprising diplomat, agreed to purchase 36 cars from Daimler for a total amount of 550,000 gold marks. From 1900 through 1909 Jellinek was a member of the board of Daimler Motoren Gesellschaft. Having invested large sums in the company, he finally won the right to name a new model, which he did, in honor of his daughter – Mercedes. On February 23, 1902, this name was officially registered as a trademark.

Back in 1881, during his travels through Russia, Gotlieb Daimler was thoroughly impressed with the industrial advancements he witnessed, of which, according to him, "the West was completely unaware, or, in any case, had great misconceptions." It was at this time, that due to the activities of the "Union of Oil Industrialists of the Brothers Nobel," great advances were being made in oil refining.

When he returned to Germany, Daimler gave an accounting of his trip, and he was offered to open a representative office of his automobile concern in St. Petersburg; however, he was so busy with other projects that he refused. In a few years, however, another person appeared on the scene, and this entrepreneur was who would develop future ties between the Daimler Company and Russia.

His name was Boris Lutzky (1865–1926). This talented young man, after finishing high school in Sevastopol in 1882, was sent to continue his education abroad, and entered the Münich Technological Institute. In 1888, at the Münich exposition a gas engine developed by him was made public, and the patent for it immediately purchased. Just two years hence, the 23-year-old inventor was invited to Nürnberg to become the chief engineer at one of the largest machine building enterprises of Germany, the Maschinenbau AG, Nürnberg. In six years' time he was able to organize the serial production of internal combustion engines and to develop several new

"Mercedes," the daughter of Emil Jellinek. In Spanish her name means "mercy."
[Daimler AG Archives and Collection]

"Mercedes" automobiles at the first International Auto Show in St. Petersburg. The show was held at the Mikhailovsky Manege in 1907.

Opening of the IV International Auto Show in the Mickhailovsky Manege.
In the front row (left to right) are Grand Duchesses Maria Pavlovna and Victoria Feodorovna, and Grand Duke Dmitri Pavlovich. St. Petersburg 1913. Photograph by K. Bulla. [TsGAKFFD SPb]

St. Petersburg. Trials of the engine developed by Lutzky and produced at the German factory. [TsGAKFFD SPb]

experimental models. From 1897 Boris Lutzky set as his goal solving the problems of automotive production. Together with Gotlieb Daimler, Rudolf Diesel and other inventors, Lutzky become one of the founders of the "European Automotive Union." Auto cars with the name of "Lutzky" first appeared at the Berlin Exposition of 1899. From then on, the life of this talented inventor was tied with several firms, including the Daimler Company, where he was involved in the creation of the first freight automobiles (trucks).

"I wish to be useful to my fatherland," wrote Boris Grigorievich to the Russian Military Attaché in Berlin in 1900, Prince P.N. Engalychev. He proposed for Russia his concept of a new automobile, equipped with armament. Lutzky wrote: "Lately, I have concentrated my work on how to make the automobile useful for the military. I have attained major results, and, as a loyal Russian citizen, I feel morally obligated to make my results known to Your Excellency…"

Unfortunately, the Directory of Artillery could not find the 4 thousand rubles necessary for the realization of this project, but the Directory of the Navy was very interested in Lutzky's proposal and ordered three military vehicles (trucks) from Germany. They were delivered to St. Petersburg in March 1901. One year later a contract was signed with the St. Petersburg firm of "G.A. Lessner" for the right to produce automobiles with the "Daimler-Lutzky" engine in Russia. According to the contract, all engines produced by the firm carried the label "Lutzky-Daimler," and during the summer of 1904 the first automobiles came off the assembly line.

In 1894, the first "Benz" automobile was delivered to Russia. This newfangled piece of technology was of great interest to Russians, and in 1900 the very first Automobile Club was organized in Moscow. A similar club was organized in St. Petersburg in 1902, and very soon the Russian Automobile Society appeared, which, from 1910 obtained the right to be called the "Imperial" Russian Auto Society ("IRAO"). The first Chairman of IRAO was Member of the Imperial Suite, Commander of the Life-Guard Chevalier Corps, Major-General V.M. Bezobrazov. Another high-ranking Court official would replace him in this post, and in 1910-1916 the head of IRAO was Minister of the Imperial Court, Adjutant-General Baron V.B. Fredericks. IRAO organized the 1907 auto show in St. Petersburg's Mikhailovsky Manege. The event was the first Russian international auto show and it displayed the latest developments of the automotive industry. It proved to be a huge success.

The most notable event in advertising the new industry was the IV International Auto Show, which was tied to the celebrations of the 300th Anniversary of the Reign of the House of Romanov, as well as the 10th Anniversary of the establishment of IRAO. The show had the patronage of Emperor Nicholas II himself, and many members of the Romanov Family participated.

Emperor Nicholas II was one of the first to appreciate the advantages of this new form of transportation. But, the first attempts of Minister of the Court Baron Fredericks at showing the Emperor the "speed" of new automobiles proved to be a failure. The Baron was forced to push the car himself, to the amusement of other members of the Court. When the Emperor traveled to Germany with his family, Empress Alexandra Feodorovna's brother, the Grand Duke Ernst Ludwig, drove the Imperial family around the outskirts of Darmstadt on one of his new automobiles. At this time Nicholas II became seriously interested in this new invention, which had become so popular in Europe.

In 1905 Prince Vladimir Orlov purchased the first cars for Nicholas II. These were elegant limousines, produced by the

Prince V.N. Orlov (second from the left) and Grand Duchesses Olga, Maria and Tatiana during a parade in 1913.
[TsGAKFFD SPb]

firm "Delaunnay-Belleville" for short excursions, and two Mercedes – for longer journeys. In the beginning Prince Orlov himself fulfilled the duty of chauffeur to the Imperial family, but very soon the trips of Nicholas II became regular events, and using the services of his Fliegel-Adjutant became awkward for the Emperor. A 26-year-old French engineer, Adolphe Kegresse was appointed the Head of the Imperial Garage. He was not only an excellent driver, but he was also a master of invention. Knowing, through personal experience, the quality of Russian roads, Kegresse set about inventing a snowmobile, and also a "caterpillar" car, capable of maneuvering in gullies, fields and marshes. A 45-horsepowered Mercedes was equipped with skies on the front wheels and a caterpillar belt, attached to special drums.

With time, Kegresse vehicles proved to be very useful and greatly in demand during the First World War. In 1916 when the very first field testing of semi-caterpillar automobiles took place in Russia, the testing commission expressed its approval in the following words: "One should make every effort to produce as quickly as possible Kegresse attachments in the necessary quantities for all types of automobiles: armored, freight and light." It was also intended to equip the entire Russian military auto fleet with Kegresse engines.

The emblem of the IRAO. Brass plates with enamel fittings adorned the cars of the society's members.

Emperor Nicholas II's Imperial "Benz" driven by Adolphe Kegresse, his private chauffeur. The image was taken outside the Catherine Palace, Tsarskoe Selo. September 9, 1911 – Photograph by K. Bulla. [TsGAKFFD SPb]

An image of Emperor Nicholas II, who has just stepped off the Imperial "Benz," arriving at an official event in the later part of his reign.
[Eurohistory Archive]

Contacts with Germany During the Reign
of Emperor Alexander III

Having ascended the throne on the day of the assassination of Emperor Alexander II, March 1 (13), 1881, Alexander III's foreign policy, at least initially, continued his father's alliance with Imperial Germany. This was true, at least, during the first years of the new Tsar's reign. However, his official visits to this country were rather rare, as Alexander III's attention drifted towards Denmark and away from Germany. His brother, Grand Duke Vladimir Alexandrovich, who, in reality, was the "second person in charge in the Empire, after Alexander III," as a rule, represented the House of Romanov at gatherings of the Russian Imperial Family's large web of relations with various German ruling families, the Hohenzollerns among them. In 1887 the Imperial State Secretary Alexander Alexandrovich Polovtsov wrote to the Grand Duke: "You are now the only family tie between Germany and our nation's government; it is desirable that you keep this position and influence, for the good of Russia."

The organization of any official visit by any representative of Russia to Berlin always fell on the shoulders of the Russian Embassy staff. The embassy was located on Unter den Linden, the capital's elegant main thoroughfare. The assignment to the post of Ambassador to Germany was one of the most prestigious in the Russian Ministry of Foreign Affairs. During the second half of the XIX Century this post was held by representatives of Russia's elite: Privy Counselor Baron Andrei Feodorovich Budberg (in 1851–1856 and again in 1858–1862), Privy Counselor Count Paul Petrovich Ubri (1862–1879), Peter Alexandrovich Saburov (1880–1884), Lieutenant-General Count Paul Andreevich Shuvalov (1885–1894), Count Nikolai Dmitrievich von Osten-Sacken (1895–1912), Privy Counselor Sergei Nikolaevich Sverbeev (1912–1914).

Emperor Alexander III.
(1845-1894)
[TsGAKFFD SPb]

Diplomats working in the embassy in Berlin, and in other missions in Germany, were not only the organizers, but also the participants in the meetings with royal guests. The arrival of a member of the Imperial family, or a Grand Duke and his family, from Russia always became a notable political affair in Germany.

In a letter to his wife on September 29, 1889, Emperor Alexander III wrote the following about his stay in Berlin: "Our arrival was most impressive, we were greeted by all of the troops of the Berlin garrison, who later paraded in a ceremonial march past our Embassy, while the Emperor and I, and others, stood in the street. Then there was a grand breakfast, with music, in our embassy, which was hosted by Count Shuvalov and his wife, with around fifty people at the table. After that George [his son] and I made official visits to Guillome [Prince of Schleswig-Holstein, the brother of Danish King Christian IX], the Empress [Augusta Victoria], "Vicky"

Count Paul Andreievich Shuvalov (1830-1908). From a photograph by Bergamasco. "Vsermirnaya Illyustratsiya" [International Illustrations 1895]

Both brothers – Counts Peter and Paul Shuvalov, the first the Ambasador in London, and the second in Berlin, were for the longest time true friends of Germany, and always strove to maintain the very best relations between the two Courts, and neighboring countries. Count Peter Andreevich, and his brother Paul Andreevich a bit later, were very close friends with Prince Otto von Bismarck. In 1885 Count Paul Shuvalov was appointed the Imperial Russian Ambassador to the Court of the King of Prussia. His almost ten year term at this post was the most brilliant in the existecne of the Russian Embassy at Unter-den-Linden, No. 7. Paul Andreevich Shuvalov, and his adorable wife Maria Alexandrovna soon were the hearts of Berlin society, and never before, and never after, was there such a lively and unpretentious rapport between Germans and Russians, as during the stay of the "friend of arms" of Emperor Wilhelm. This title our Ambassador soon received also in official German circles."

L. Knorring, member of the Russian Ambassadorial staff in Berlin

The Russian Embassy in Berlin, Unter den Linden No. 7.

German Emperor Wilhelm II.
(1859-1941)
[Eurohistory Archive]

[Victoria, the Dowager German Empress], and I saw all of her daughters. She cried a lot, telling me about her poor husband and his last days ... At four thirty we received Prince Bismarck, who came here especially to meet with me, he was even at the station; this is something he does not do, not even for the Emperor of Austria, nor the King of Italy, and, of course, all of the Prussians were quick to point this out to me."

In January 1837 Emperor Nicholas I bought a house on Unter den Linden, No. 7, not far from Alexanderplatz, a square named in honor of his late Imperial brother. During 1840–1841, by order of the Russian Emperor, the building was expanded inwards on the lot by Frankfurt architect Eduard Knoblauch, a follower of Karl Schinkel. The design of the front, the formal enfilade, was left intact. The White Hall, built with strict adherence to the Schinkel style, was situated in the new left extension.

The Russian Embassy moved into the building at Unter den Linden, No. 7, and a private chapel, consecrated in honor of St. Vladimir, was also built in this palace. The church was located on the bottom floor and was rather small in size, since at most 150 people could attend service. In time the church was adorned with beautiful icons, some of which were donated from the main spiritual center of Russia, the St. Sergius – Trinity Monastery. Some of the icons were painted on a gold leaf background by archimandrite Ignatiy Malyshev.

The White Hall in the Russian Embassy, Berlin.

The reign of Emperor Alexander III is characterized by a great rise in the development of both Russian industry and the banking sector. It is this time that is connected to the success of the "young electrical technology." In the 1880s the first electric substation appeared in St. Petersburg. According to the plans of Vasiliy Pashkov, a graduate of the Technological Institute named in honor of Emperor Nicholas I, the first "factory of electricity" was created; it completely transformed the imperial residence. On Christmas day in 1887 the Winter Palace was ablaze with electrical light. At the time, St. Petersburg had the largest electrical station in Europe. However, the installation of electrical lighting had a high cost, and only a few of St. Petersburg's elite could allow themselves this luxury. In 1889, the brother of Alexander III, Grand Duke Vladimir Alexandrovich, ordered that an electric station be built on a lot belonging to him. The cost of electrical lighting in the Vladimir Palace for the year 1891 alone ran up to 31,779 rubles.

At this time, several renowned German companies started investing capital into Russian industry. The most notable investments into the Russian electrical industry were made by the Siemens family, which worked both in Russia and in Germany.

In 1847 Werner von Siemens, together with mechanical engineer J. Halske, founded in Germany the telegraph construction company Telegraphenbauanstalt Siemens & Halske. Starting from 1853 the firm "Siemens &

Siemens & Halske stock with a value of 1000 marks. [From the collection of J. Heusler]

Engineer Johann Halske.
[Siemens Forum, Munich]

Karl von Siemens (1829-1906).
[Siemens Forum, Munich]

Werner von Siemens (1816-1892).
[Siemens Forum, Munich]

The factory of "Siemens & Halske" on Vasilievsky Island, St. Petersburg. [Siemens Forum, Munich]

The first electrical railroad, built by Siemens in 1879.
[Siemens Forum, Munich]

Halske" installed telegraph lines in Russia. They connected St. Petersburg with Kronstadt, Helsingfors and other cities.

Six years later, Karl von Siemens opened a representative office of his older brother Werner's company in St. Petersburg, "Siemens & Halske." He lived and worked in Russia from 1853 to 1867 and again from 1880 to 1892; he even became a Russian citizen. After the death of Werner, Karl von Siemens was the General Director of "Siemens & Halske" from 1892 to 1904. For his faithful service Emperor Nicholas II bestowed on him the title of Russian nobility.

The Siemens brothers established joint stock companies – "The Russian Society of Electrical Companies Siemens & Halske," and the Russian stock company "Siemens – Shukert." Their factories did almost everything that was demanded on the Russian market, from telephones and electrical apparatus, to electrical equipment for trolleys and railroads, to the needs of enterprises and mining concerns.

Emperor Alexander III, and subsequently his son Michael, at the end of the XIX century were often called the "promoters of electricity in Russia." In order to prepare new qualified personnel a School for Postal and Telegraph Workers was founded in St. Petersburg in 1886, under the auspices of the Ministry of Internal Affairs. The Imperial Order for its founding was signed by Emperor Alexander III. In 1891 the School was transformed into the Electro-Technical Institute (ETI) – the first school of higher learning in Russia whose graduates were specialists in the areas of telegraphy and electricity. At the end of the 1890s ETI became known as the Emperor Alexander III Electro-Technical Institute, and Tsarevich Michael Alexandrovich became its August patron.

The stock company "Siemens & Halske" provided great help to ETI by donating laboratory equipment, and Karl von Siemens himself became an honorary electrical engineer.

Grand Duke Michael Alexandrovich (1878-1918), the august patron of ETI.

The ETI campus on Aptekarsky (Apothecary) Island, at the crossing of Aptekarsky Prospect and Pesochnaia (Sandy) Street (present-day Prof. Popov Street), c. 1903. Photograph K. Bulla. [TsGAKFFD SPb]

Thanks to the sponsorship of the Siemens Company, ETI graduate students were sent to study abroad in 1897 with the goal of obtaining production experience. The Director of ETI, Nicholas Kachalov approached Karl von Siemens with the request of giving his students the "chance to freely inspect all of the equipment in the factories of Siemens & Halske in Berlin." The text of his request was sent to the company by telegraph, and in a few days Karl von Siemens instructed that "400 rubles be allocated to cover living expenses of students" staying in Berlin. The students had the chance to get acquainted with the capital of Germany, with the latest improvements in telegraphy and electrical engineering. While there, they even saw the latest newfangled idea – the "Siemens tram run by electrical power."

Seventeen students, who had gone through study in Berlin, successfully graduated from ETI, became leading specialists in the electrification of railroads, and eventually would become heads of scientific and study centers in various cities of Russia: St. Petersburg, Moscow, Riga, Samara, Irkutsk, Rostov-on-Don, Grozny.

"Hallesches Tor" subway station, Berlin. [Siemens Forum, Munich]

In Berlin the first group of electro-technician students from St. Petersburg were warmly greeted not only in German factories and postal institutions, but also in the leading study center of Germany, where electrical engineers were prepared – the Polytechnic Institute. Professor Adolf Slabi himself read a special lecture to the Russian students, and the students gave a ball in honor of their St. Petersburg guests. The Russian Embassy in Berlin provided a lot of support for the realization of this project, the study abroad program for Russian students in Germany.

The St. Vladimir Brotherhood
in Berlin

In 1886, at the celebration of the Russian Ambassador Paul Shuvalov's birthday, the priest assigned to the Embassy, Rev. Alexei Petrovich Maltsev, expressed the idea of founding in Germany the first ever Russian educational and charitable society located outside of Russia, an Orthodox Brotherhood. This idea found support in the Russian Ministry of Foreign Affairs and in the Holy Synod. In 1890 the official opening of the St. Vladimir Orthodox Brotherhood took place. It was meant to provide spiritual support to Russian citizens, who, for some reason or another, found themselves outside of Russia, and also to help in the building of new Orthodox churches across Europe. Grand Duke Vladimir Alexandrovich was chosen as the Imperial patron of this new society, and this helped to attract to it not only the help and support of other members of the Romanov family, but also that of leading St. Petersburg socialites and elites. Emperor Alexander III donated 5,000 rubles, while Grand Dukes Alexei, Sergei and Paul Alexandrovich also donated large sums; Grand

Protopriest Alexei Maltsev.
(1854-1915)

The august patrons of the St. Vladimir Brotherhood, Grand Duke Vladimir Alexandrovich and his wife, Grand Duchess Maria Pavlovna.
[GARF]

A letter from V. Rev. Alexei Maltsev having to do with the study program for Russian students in Berlin.
The postal paper has scenes of the following – the Church of Sts. Konstantin and Helen, the "love of work" house (community hall) in memory of Emperor Alexander III in Tegel, the St. Alexander Nevsky Cathedral in Potsdam, and the interior of the St. Vladimir Church at the Russian Embassy in Berlin.

St. Vladimir Brotherhood in Berlin

The Church of Sts. Konstantin and Helen at the Russian Cememetery in tegel, Berlin.

The Cathedral of St. Sergei of Radonezh in Bad Kissingen.

Architect Victor Schröter. (1839-1891)

The house of V.A. Schröter in St. Petersburg, located at Moika River Embank-ment No. 114.

Duchesses Elisabeth Feodorovna and Catherine Mikhailovna, Queen Olga of Württemberg and Grand Duchess Anastasia of Mecklenburg-Schwerin became honorary members of the society. Representatives of the diplomatic community – Count N.N. Adlerberg and Baron L.K. Knorring became members, as did other leading members of the Russian aristocracy, among them: Prince Nikolai Borisovich Yousoupov, Count P.A. Shuvalov, bankers and famous patrons – V.A. Rat'kov-Rozhnov, A.G., P.S. and L.D. Eliseev. The famous pianist, A.G. Rubinstein donated 2,000 marks to the society from monies collected from a concert given by him in Berlin. The Brotherhood helped many in need, and successfully fulfilled its mission right up to the beginning of the First World War. For over a quarter of a century it was a spiritual center – responsible for intertwining the cultures of Russia and Germany.

From the very founding of the Brotherhood its Secretary, Treasurer and overall inspiration for all activities was the Protopriest Alexei Maltsev. He was a graduate of the St. Petersburg Divinity Academy, had a penchant for scientific studies, and was well versed in European languages – English, French, Greek and German. Kind, with a responsive nature, always ready to come to anyone's aid, Maltsev was able to attract to the Brotherhood many similarly minded individuals. He also served as head priest at the Russian Orthodox Embassy Church in Berlin for nearly thirty years. His scientific works and translations of holy literature into German comprise over 14,000 pages. Without a doubt, Protopriest Maltsev played a major role in establishing the position of the Russian Orthodox Church in Western Europe.

When Grand Duke Vladimir Alexandrovich died very suddenly in February 1909, his widow Grand Duchess

The titlte page of the magazine "Ogonyok."

Maria Pavlovna inherited her late husband's position within the Brotherhood. At that time the overall financial worth of the Brotherhood was quite large – around 370,000 marks, including real estate and investments. A quarter of a million German marks were collected by members of the society for the building fund for the construction of an Orthodox cathedral in Berlin. Protopriest Alexei Maltsev remained at his post up until 1914, the beginning of the First World War. On July 21, having left everything in Tegel, he, together with one of his daughters and his son Vladimir, returned to Russia on the Russian Embassy train.

One of the important activities of the Brotherhood was the establishment of the first cemetery for Orthodox Christians in Berlin. At the beginning of the 1890s, members of the society were able to purchase two plots of land in the northern suburbs of Berlin, close to Tegel. With the permission of Emperor Alexander III in 1893, Maltsev organized the delivery, in railroad cars, of forty tons of Russian soil, which was thrown over the newly purchased land, so that Orthodox Russians, who passed away abroad, could find their last resting place in "native" soil.

The cemetery, with its Orthodox cathedral, the Brotherhood House, with its studios, gardens and winter gardens, which were set up on the second parcel of land, became known to the local Germans as "ein Stück Russlands," a "little corner of Russia" in Berlin.

Tegel cemetery has the grave sites of many famous Russians, among whom are the Minister of the Armed Forces, General Vladimir Alexandrovich Sukhomlinov; attorney Vladimir Dmitrievich Nabokov, father of the famous novelist by the same name; Russian Minister of Agriculture, active in the formation of the White Army, Alexander Vasilievich Krivoshein; the Russian Ambassador to Germany Sergei Nikolaevich Sverbeev; the artist Nikolai Petrovich Bogdanov-Belsky.

The grand opening of the cemetery church took place on May 21 (June 2), 1893, with members of the Embassy

St. Vladimir Brotherhood in Berlin

The Church of St. Martyr Alexandra in Bad Ems was built on land donated by Emperor Wilhelm I.
The cost of building this church totaled 19.6 thalers: 14,000 were donated by Emperor Alexander II and members of his family. It was consecrated on May 2, 1876, in memory of the deceased Empress Alexandra Fedorovna. The carved wooden altar screen was produced in the atelier of E. Schröder in St. Petersburg, the four large icons with a gold background were written by court artist Timothy Neff. In the altar the image of the Resurrection of Christ was painted by Vasiliy Vereshchagin, who donated his work to the church after having come for a cure at the spa. Church holy items were donated by Moscow tradesmen, headed by famous philanthropist Sergei Tretiakov. The august patron of the church building fund was Queen Olga of Württemberg.

staff and residents of the little village of Alexandrovka present. Shuvalov, the Russian Ambassador, participated in the ceremonies and donated to the church two silver trikiri, candle holders used specifically during services officiated by higher clergy. The stone building was erected using the plans of the German Court architect Albert Bohm. In 1894 the church was consecrated to Sts. Konstantin and Helen. Several days later V. Rev. Alexei Maltsev sent a letter and photographs of the building to the august patron of the St. Vladimir Brotherhood, Grand Duke Vladimir Alexandrovich, in which he expressed the following idea:

"The auspicious coincidence that the consecration of the church fell upon the Names Day of Your Imperial Highness' august daughter, Helen Vladimirovna, our Brotherhood sees as a fortuitous sign, tying the Brotherhood even closer to the patronage of Your Imperial Highness."

V. Rev. Alexei Maltsev asked that the large donations made by statesman and businessman A.G. Eliseev receive specially recognized. A.G. Eliseev and his wife donated funds for the altar screen and icon holders, and also had five bells forged for the belfry over the entrance to the cemetery. The largest bell had images of four saints engraved on it, and another one – verses from the Imperial Russian poet, Grand Duke Konstantin Konstantinovich (he wrote under the pseudonym of "K.R."): "... and from a distance, very gently, toll the bells of the motherland."

Another important direction of the activities of the Brotherhood was the construction of Russian Orthodox churches in different locations of Germany. According to Maltsev, it was most important to erect churches in places of relaxation and caring, i.e. spas, where many Russians would "come for the cure." In these churches travelers could find solace and comfort far from home, hear familiar sounds, participate in church services.

The first such "spa" cathedral was built in the city of Bad Homburg, not far from Frankfurt-on-Main. Later, churches were also built in Bad Kissingen, Herbersdorf, Bad Nauheim and Brückennau. Famous Russian architects, artists and other masters participated in their construction.

The planning and construction of the cathedral in Bad Kissingen, named for St. Sergei of Radonezh and dedicated to the memory of the Holy Coronation of Emperor Nicholas II, was carried out by Professor of the Academy of Art, Victor Schröter, who also studied in Berlin's Construction Academy. The architect, free of charge, completed the project. The consecration of the cathedral took place on July 5 (18), 1901. V. Rev. Alexei Maltsev addressed the congregation in German: "We now experience great comfort and feel a true sense of joy – to see this glorious edifice, which is a site of beauty for the city, and for us – a center of spiritual life. From this day forward, under the plafonds of this holy building, people shall gather, to find, together with physical healing, spiritual health as well..." The cathedral was built in a Russo-Byzantine style, with a light, three-colored sandy exterior. Artists from St. Petersburg painted the interior in a "Vasnetsov" (a Russian painter of the 19th century) style. V.A. Schröter produced the two-tiered altar screen using sketches. The belfry had seven bells, forged at the Okhtinskaia Foundry owned by V. Orlov, and brought here from St. Petersburg.

Bad Homburg was famous for its cardio-vascular medicinal springs, and was yearly visited by many Russians, sometimes as many as 13,000 a year. The foundation of the All-Saints Cathedral, in memory of the Holy Coronation of Their Imperial Highnesses, occurred on October 4 (16), 1896. Emperor Nicholas II himself was present, as well as the Empress Friedrich (Kaiser Wilhelm II's English mother), Empress Alexandra Feodorovna, her sister Grand Duchess Elisabeth Feodorovna, their brother the Grand Duke of Hesse and by Rhine, and several others. Funding for the cathedral came from five major sources, notable St. Petersburg businessmen and bankers: the Chairman of the First Russian Insurance Society, Actual Privy Counselor Alexander Provorov; the owner of the steamship company Samolet ["Flies on its own"], millionaire lumber-entrepreneur, Actual Privy Counselor Vladimir Rat'kov-Rozhnov; St. Petersburg tradesman of the First Guild, Actual Counselor Alexander Eliseev; Actual Counselor Nicholas Brusnitsyn; and owner of the tobacco factory, Alexander Bogdanov. The stone cathedral was erected according to the plans of Professor of the Imperial Academy of Arts Leon Benois. It was located on land donated for this purpose by the town's magistrate. This architect was already well known in Russia. He was responsible for the building of the cathedral of St. Alexander Nevsky in Warsaw in the 1890s, the building for the Chapel Royal in St. Petersburg, the St. George Cathedral in Gus-Khrustalny, at the request of the owner of the glass works Yurij S. Nechaev-Maltsev, and the St. Petersburg mansion of V.A. Rat'kov-Rozhnov.

The consecration of the Bad Homburg church was celebrated on September 10 (22), 1899. All of the benefactors, who had donated large sums of money, were present. Not that large in size, the stone church, topped by a spire with a gold cross, was built in the Moscow-Yaroslavl' architectural style of the 16–17th centuries. By the decision of the Metropolitan of St. Petersburg, Anthony, the new church was considered to be under the jurisdiction of the Embassy church in Berlin. A.I. Provorov was elected honorary citizen of Bad Homburg and a street in the little town was named in his honor.

The first Russian Insurance Society – the oldest insurance company in Russia, was founded in 1827. Among its founders were Count N.S. Mordvinov and Baron L.I. Stiglitz. The business turned out to be a success; within the first twenty years over half a million buildings were insured. The company by-laws, very scrupulously written, became a model for other insurance companies. From 1880 and for over twenty years, Alexander Ivanovich Provorov led the First Russian Insurance Society. During his leadership the company purchased and refurbished, according to the plans of Leon Benois, its headquarters on Bolshaia Morskaia (Greater Marine) Street, No. 40, in St. Petersburg, where the company's main offices were located.

Today, Bad Homburg is a sister city with Peterhof, the famous "City of Fountains," or "the Versailles of St. Petersburg."

Baden-Baden – "The Summer Capital of Europe"

During the 19th century Baden-Baden, a small town in the South of Germany became famous as the "Summer Capital" of Europe, attracting many visitors with its medicinal mineral springs. Royalty and aristocratic families from around the world would gather here. Russia has a special tie to the former capital of the Grand Duchy of Baden: it was from here that in 1792 the fourteen-year-old Princess Louisa came to Russia, soon to become the wife of the Heir to the Throne, Tsarevich Alexander Pavlovich, and who, upon converting to Orthodoxy, received the name of Elisabeth Alexeevna. The second dynastic tie of the Russian Imperial Family with the Grand Dukes of Baden occurred in 1857, when Princess Cecilia of Baden (in Russia she became known as Grand Duchess Olga Feodorovna) was engaged to Grand Duke Mikhail Nikolaevich in Peterhof. Her own brother, Wilhelm (1829–1897) was also to tie his fate to Russia – in 1863 he married the granddaughter of Emperor Nicholas I, Princess Maria Maximilianovna Romanovskaya, Duchess of Leuchtenberg (1841–1914). Friedrich I, an older brother of Olga Feodorovna, ruled Baden for more than half a decade, between 1852-1907. His residence was in Baden-Baden's New Castle, located on the side of a mountain. When Empress Elisabeth Alexeievna lived in this castle in 1813, she called it "one of the most beautiful places in the world." Other Russian rulers also stayed here – Nicholas I, Alexander II, Nicholas II, as well as

"During the summers, Russians play a very important role in Baden. Among European aristocracy there are many representatives of the "Duchy of Moscovy," and they should be given their due: many of them are exquisite in their manners and in the gntility of their character. Not a single nation can compare to their politeness, their fine taste, their elegant mannerisms, and their liberal thinking. Having seen and heard them, one instantly disregards old prejudices. This nation is represented to us as barbarious, due to being under the yoke of tyrants. But in Baden, Russians are rehabilitated in the eyes of the world, and as a result, one can only sing praises to the Tsar of Russia."

Eugene Guinot, "L'eté a Bade."
Paris, 1861.

The Friedrichsbad at Baden-Baden.
[Galina Korneva]

Monument to Ivan Turgenev.
[Galina Korneva]

Monument to Louise of Baden.
[Galina Korneva]

The Crown Prince's Palace, Unter den Linden No. 29, c. 1910.

The Crown Prince's Palace in Berlin, Unter den Linden No. 29, c. 1910.

their children, Grand Dukes and Grand Duchesses with their families. Ties with the Grand Duchy of Baden became even stronger due to the marriage of Grand Duke Friedrich I with Princess Louise of Prussia, a first cousin of Emperor Alexander II. Later, Prince Max of Baden was briefly engaged to Grand Duchess Helen Vladimirovna. Although the marriage was called off, Max later married Princess Marie Louise of Hannover, a first cousin of Emperor Nicholas II.

From the windows of the New Castle one could see the main attraction of Baden-Baden – the thermal baths of Friedrichsbad. The building where one took mineral baths was erected in the style of Renaissance palaces in 1875–1877. It was considered one of the most beautiful and comfortable in Europe. Over its central portal, in front of a gold azure background stood a large bust of Grand Duke Friedrich I, in honor of whom the thermal complex was named.

Prince Maximilian of Baden.
(1867-1929)
[Eurohistory Archive]

Towards the end of the 19th, the beginning of the 20th century over fifty-thousand visitors would come to Baden-Baden a year, a great part of them were Russian, and at that time there were two hotels that catered to them, with names tied to their native land – the "Petersburger Hof" and the hotel "De Russie." Well-off Russian families would rent not merely rooms in luxury hotels, but sometimes whole houses for the season, and sometimes they even purchased villas in Baden-Baden. Up until the present day some of the tourist attractions of this resort town are the Gagarin Palace, remodeled by Isabella Gagarina from an old mill, and the former grand villa of Prince Vladimir Menshikov. Another famous building tied to Russian culture is the Russian Orthodox Church of the Transfiguration, built according to the plans of David Grimm, with the interior design done by Prince Gregory Gagarin. The church was gloriously consecrated in 1882, with Wilhelm of Baden and his wife Maria Maximilianovna present, the latter being the patron of the project.

Baden-Baden is known not only for it thermal springs, but also for its internationally famous casino, the oldest and most beautiful in Germany. It was built using the plans of architect Friedrich Weinbrenner in 1821–1824 in the very center of the city, and was called the "Maison de Conversation." The Florentine Hall, the Red Living Room, the Marquisa de Pompadour Room – leave visitors breathless to this day.

Grand balls would be held in the Court Hall – over 1,000 guests could be present at one time. One such ball was held in September 1847 in honor of Tsarevich Alexander Nikolaevich and his sister, Olga, the Crown Princess of Württemberg.

Baden-Baden is tied to the names of famous Russian writers Vasily Zhukovsky, Leo Tolstoy, Nicholas Gogol, Feodor Dostoevsky, and Vladimir Sologub. A street in the town has the name of Ivan Turgenev (1831–1883), the author of the novel "Dym" ("Smoke"), the narrative of this important literary work taking place in this town. In the 1990s a Turgenev Society was organized in Baden-Baden, due, mostly, to the huge energy of Mrs. Renate Effern, and in the year 2000 a bust of this Russian author was placed on the famous Lichtentahl Lane, with funds allocated by the Ministry of Culture of the Russian Federation.

The Duchy of Saxe-Coburg & Gotha

Grand Duchess Maria Alexandrovna and Her Daughter Victoria Melita of Edinburgh – Grand Duchess of Hesse and by Rhine, Grand Duchess of Russia

*I*n the 19th century, the rather small Duchy of Saxe-Coburg and Gotha became the link binding the reigning houses of two great nations – England and Russia.

Both Duke Ernst II of Saxe-Coburg and Gotha (1818–1893), who ruled from 1844 and was the older brother of Albert, consort to Queen Victoria, and wife Alexandrine (1820–1904), had familial ties to Russia. She was born a Princess of Baden and was the sister to Grand Duchess Olga Feodorovna, wife of Grand Duke Michael Nikolaevich.

In January 1874 the ruling houses of Russia and England became tied by marriage for the first time in history. This dynastic link was provided by the marriage of Grand Duchess Maria Alexandrovna, the daughter of Alexander II, and the Duke of Edinburgh, Prince Alfred, who was Queen Victoria's second son. Their wedding, celebrated with the pomp due to the marriage of a daughter of the Tsar, took place in St. Petersburg.

Afterward, the royal couple initially lived in England, where some of their children were born. Within ten years four

The Veste Coburg. [ILN]

daughters and one son were born to them. Alfred and Maria also lived on the island of Malta and eventually she built a spacious home in Coburg. In 1893, when Duke Ernst II died childless, Prince Alfred inherited his uncle's throne. The Edinburghs moved to Coburg, a small and picturesque town in central Germany built on the river Itz, a tributary of the Main. From that time the ties between Coburg and Russia became ever stronger.

In April 1894 the marriage of the second daughter of the ducal couple, Victoria Melita, provided an opportunity for a large royal gathering in Coburg. The bride was marrying her first cousin Grand Duke Ernst Ludwig of Hesse and by Rhine, whose sisters Elisabeth and Alexandra were already destined to have a future in Russia. Besides Queen Victoria, countless other royals attended the wedding ceremonies, among them: Kaiser Wilhelm II and Tsarevich Nicholas Alexandrovich, both of these distinguished guests were first cousins of the bride. Wilhelm II was also a first cousin of the groom, while Nicholas Alexandrovich's father was a first cousin of the groom's late father.

"The Grand Duchess Maria Alexandrovna possessed a very clear view of things around her. She had remained thoroughly Russian, but, on the other hand, after living many years in England and in Germany, had obtained a more liberal point of view about the conditions of life in Russia."

S.M. Volkonsky,
"My Memoirs."

Grand Duchess Maria Alexandrovna (1853-1920), the Duchess of Edinburgh, and from 1893 the Duchess of Saxe-Coburg & Gotha, c. 1874. By C. Bergamasco.
[Eurohistory Archive]

Grand Duchess Maria Alexandrovna and Coburg

Grand Duchess Maria Alexandrovna and her husband,
Prince Alfred, Duke of Edinburgh.
[Eurohistory Archive]

At the wedding ceremonies, three brothers of Grand Duchess Maria Alexandrovna accompanied her: Grand Duke Vladimir Alexandrovich (with his wife Maria Pavlovna), Grand Duke Sergei Alexandrovich (with his wife Elisabeth Feodorovna), and Grand Duke Paul Alexandrovich. Emperor Alexander III being ill, could not attend the wedding festivities of his niece, thus his son Nicholas represented him.

German Kaiser Wilhelm II came to congratulate his cousins Ernst Ludwig and Victoria Melita, while also taking advantage of the gathering to ingratiate himself with the future Nicholas II. Also present among the royal mob were Ernst Ludwig's other sisters, Victoria of Battenberg, Irene of Prussia and young Alix of Hesse and by Rhine.

Queen Victoria, who had played an important role in matching the couple, decided to attend the wedding of her two grandchildren. She was also particularly attached to Coburg, a place very dear to her heart. It was here, at Schloß Rosenau, that her dearly beloved husband, alas, already departed, Prince Albert, was born in 1819. He passed away unexpectedly in 1861 and Queen Victoria wore mourning for him for the rest of her days.

Queen Victoria was rightfully called "the Grandmother of Europe." The wedding of "Ducky" and "Ernie," where countless cousins of Kaiser Wilhelm II were present, proved to be a demonstration of the might and power of the English dynasty.

One of the people accompanying Queen Victoria was the Court photographer James Russell, "the Younger," who was able to capture on photographic paper all of the most brilliant moments of this happy family event. A compilation of his photographs was published as a special addition to the most popular English magazine of the time, the "Illustrated London News" (the "ILN").

Also very busy was the Coburg Court photographer, E. Uhlenhuth, who took countless photos of the royals attending the wedding. So that the illustrious guests would remember this event, he prepared for them a special album with the best photographs, on gold edged paper, bound in natural leather.

From 1543 the Ehrenburg Palace served as a main residence for the Duke of Saxe-Coburg & Gotha. By the end of the 17th century, the simple building had been transformed into a baroque ensemble, with an internal courtyard and a "cour d'honneur," or a three-sided courtyard, created by flanking the main central block, or corps de logis, with symmetrical advancing secondary wings containing minor rooms.

During the reign of Duke Ernst I the palace was completely remodeled, according to the plans of the Court architect to the Prussian King, Karl Friedrich Schinkel. The architect modeled the façade in a neo-Gothic English style. In 1816–1840 the French architect André Marie Renie-Gretry refurbished many rooms. Luxurious

Grand Duchess Maria Alexandrovna.
[Eurohistory Archive]

Prince Alfred, The Duke of Edinburgh.
[Eurohistory Archive]

Royals attending the wedding festivities pose for a photograph outside the Edinburgh Palais' Winter Garden, Coburg, 1894.
1. Princess Beatrice of Saxe-Coburg & Gotha, 2. Princess Feodora of Saxe-Meiningen, 3. Kaiser Wilhelm II, 4. Queen Victoria, 5. the Empress Friedrich, 6. Hereditary Prince Alfred of Saxe-Coburg & Gotha, 7. Tsarevich Nicholas Alexandrovich, 8. Princess Alix of Hesse and by Rhine, 9. Princess Victoria of Battenberg, 10. Princess Irene of Prussia, 11. Grand Duchess Maria Pavlovna of Russia, 12. Grand Duchess Maria Alexandrovna, Duchess of Edinburgh and Saxe-Coburg & Gotha, 13. The Prince of Wales (Edward VII), 14. Princess Beatrice of Battenberg, 15. Princess Louise of Saxe-Coburg & Gotha, 16. Princess Alexandra of Saxe-Coburg & Gotha, 17. Hereditary Princess Charlotte of Saxe-Meiningen, 18. The Duchess of Connaught, 19. Prince Louis of Battenberg, 20. Grand Duke Paul Alexandrovich, 21. Prince Henry of Battenberg, 22. Prince Philipp of Saxe-Coburg & Gotha, 23. Count Albert von Mensdorff-Pouilly, 24. Grand Duke Paul Alexandrovich, 25-26. Crown Princess Marie and Crown Prince Ferdinand of Romania, 27. Grand Duchess Elisabeth Feodorovna, 28. Grand Duke Vladimir Alexandrovich, 29. The Duke of Connaught, 30. The Duke of Saxe-Coburg & Gotha.
[Eurohistory Archive]

furnishings, clocks and candelabra were brought from Paris. In designing the interior of the classical Throne Room, the architect used the Tuilleries Palace of Napoleon I as a model. In the square in front of the castle there is a monument to Duke Ernst I.

An interesting fact about the history of the castle is tied to Queen Victoria's visit to the hometown of her husband in 1860. For this occasion, a "water closet" with running water, was brought to the castle from England. This was the first time that Europeans saw this new-fangled apparatus. The "WC" had red wood paneling, and it was installed in the rooms of very special guests. During this same visit, at the request of the Queen, who had difficulty in climbing stairs, a special "lift machine" was constructed, but it was manually operated.

Queen Victoria and her daughter-in-law Grand Duchess Maria Alexandrovna both possessed very strong and independent characters. For the first few years after her wedding, Maria Alexandrovna did not have a spiritual connection with her meddling and domineering mother-in-law. She would never fully identify with the English, and instead remained particularly close to her many German cousins, with whom she shared a deeper sense of family.

Maria Alexandrovna had special sympathies towards her Coburg relatives. After the Russo-Turkish War of 1877–1878, for a long while she resided in Coburg, as her husband was, by then, expected to succeed his ageing uncle. It was for that reason that Alfred and Maria, with the aid of her large fortune, built a palace for their

Queen Victoria's sons while attending the wedding ceremonies in Coburg, 1894.
From the left: The Duke of Saxe-Coburg & Gotha and Edinburgh, The Prince of Wales, The Duke of Connaught.
[Eurohistory Archive]

family. The structure, known as the Edinburgh Palais, was built across the central square facing the Ehrenburg Palace and next to the town's respected Opera Hall. On the first floor there was a chapel, living room and din-

ing room. The royal couple's rooms were on the second floor, while on the third – the bedrooms of the four princesses, their daughters. Both Alfred and his wife were avid collectors. Inside the Edinburgh Palais there were many objects that reminded Maria Alexandrovna of her beloved homeland. The more exotic parts of their collections, objects purchased in Japan, China and India, and silver models of ships, the couple had donated to the Coburg Museum.

As a reminder of Russia, the Maria Alexandrovna would organize "Russian Evenings" with all sorts of good things to eat and lots of entertainment. During the winters young people would slide down hills of ice, which in Coburg were known as "Russian hills."

In 1893, when Prince Alfred ascended the throne of the Duchy of Saxe-Coburg and Gotha, the couple settled permanently in Coburg. Maria particularly liked their summer residence in Rosenau, with its beautiful castle on a hill, from which one had a wonderful view of the surrounding countryside, a little stream flowing through the valley, and exquisite hunting reserves.

Now, let us return to the newlyweds, Victoria Melita and Ernst Ludwig. As a wedding gift Queen Victoria gave her granddaughter a beautiful diamond broach, made, according to her own design, by the jeweler Phillips.

From her groom Victoria Melita

The palace square in front of the Ehrenburg, the traditional residence of the Dukes of Saxe-Coburg & Gotha. In the center is a monument to Duke Ernst I. Photograph by E. Uhlenhuth. [RNB]

The Hall of Giants in the Ehrenburg Palace
A memorial plaque in the room marks the spot where Queen Victoria met Emperor Franz Joseph of Austria in 1863. This was also the room where, on the eve of the wedding of his daughter to the Grand Duke of Hesse and by Rhine, Prince Alfred organized a musical and theatrical performance for the wedding guests. *Photograph by E. Uhlenhuth.* [RNB]

received an unusual diamond tiara (Master J.W. Bensen), which could also be turned into a broach. Emperor Alexander III sent the bride, his niece, a diamond and sapphire garniture.

Queen Victoria on a donkey carriage. With her is her daughter Princess Beatrice of Battenberg. They are in the inner courtyard of the Ehrenburg Palace, Coburg, 1894. Behind the Queen is her loyal Scottish ghillie, John Brown. Photograph by E. Uhlenhuth. [RNB]

From the very moment of birth and up until her very last days, the life of Princess Victoria Melita was tied to different nations. She was born on Malta, and in honor of that island nation received the name of "Melita." Her childhood years were spent in England, in the London residence of her father, Clarence House; she received the name of Victoria in honor of her grandmother, the Queen of Great Britain. During her youth the family moved to Coburg, where she married her cousin from her father's side, Ernst Ludwig, the brother of the future Empress Alexandra Feodorovna of Russia.

Victoria Melita had a brother, Alfred Jr. (1874–1899), who died in tragic circumstances, and three sisters: Marie (1875–1938), who was to become the Queen of Romania; Alexandra (1878–1942), who married the hereditary Prince Ernst of Hohenlohe-Langenburg; and Beatrice (1884–1966), who married Infante Alfonso of Spain. Marie and Victoria Melita, the two older sisters, were practically the same age, and from childhood were very close. They were to remain close for their entire lives.

Victoria Melita was a very talented young lady, she spoke five languages fluently, she was a good artist, and played the piano well. She inherited her talent for music from her father. He played the violin; the Duke of Cambridge had given to him a Stradivarius as a gift, and Thomas Gladstone a bow, as a wedding present.

The Edinburgh Palace seen from the Ehrenburg Palace Square. From 1889 onward, the Edinburgh palace served as the family home of the Duke and Duchess of Edinburgh. [ILN]

Grand Duchess Maria Alexandrovna and Coburg

The Edinburghs with German and English cousins, Coburg,c. 1891. Photograph by E. Uhlenhuth.
From the left: Prince Alfred Jr. of Edinburg, Grand Duchess Maria Alexandrovna (Duchess of Edinburgh), Princess Beatrice and
Princess Alexandra of Edinburgh, Hereditary Grand Duke Ernst Ludwig of Hesse and by Rhine, The Duke of Edinburgh,
Prince Max of Baden, Princess Marie and Princess Victoria Melita of Edinburgh and Prince George of Wales.
[Eurohistory Archive]

Her family called Young Victoria Melita "Ducky." She had a very independent character, and she never forgot that she was the granddaughter of Emperor Alexander II and Queen Victoria, the two most powerful rulers of the time.

On their wedding day, Victoria Melita and her husband Ernst Ludwig left for Darmstadt.

Queen Victoria had been concerned about her daughter Alice, when she married the Hessian Prince Ludwig (1837–1892), and she ordered that a palace be built for the young couple in Darmstadt. The New Palace (Neues Palais) was built in 1864–1865, according to the plans of German architect Conrad Kraus. It was in this very palace that the young Ernst Ludwig and Victoria Melita were destined to start their married life. It was their Darmstadt residence.

Usually, the young couple spent the summer in the hunting lodge at Wolfsgarten, where they areceived count-less visitors. The days were in games and marriement, and while there everyone acted like "schoolchildren on holiday." Having married at the young age of 17, Victoria Melita very soon came to realize that she had made a mistake in choosing her mate. With each day the young couple felt like strangers to each other. They led thor-oughly independent lives, each with their own unending stream of amusements. Everyone in the family knew, even eventually Queen Victoria, that the couple was ill suited.

Grand Duchess Maria Alexandrovna.
[Eurohistory Archive]

Duke Alfred of Saxe-Coburg & Gotha and Edinburgh.
[Eurohistory Archive]

Princess Victoria Melita of Edinburgh.
[Eurohistory Archive]

Grand Duke Ernst Ludwig of Hesse and by Rhine.
[Eurohistory Archive]

The wedding photo of Princess Victoria Melita of Edinburgh and Grand Duke Ernst Ludwig of Hesse and by Rhine, Coburg 1894.
[Eurohistory Archive]

Ernst Ludwig was totally engulfed in the theater and the world of art; he invited to Hesse young artists and architects, the future founders of the "jugendstil," the art nouveau movement.

Ernst Ludwig adored his little daughter Elisabeth, born in 1895. He even ordered that a special little house be built especially for her; it was surrounded by a private garden, and adults were not allowed to enter. Josef Maria Olbrich created this house, famous for the exhibition center called "Secession" in Vienna.

During the late 1890s the couple visited Russia many times, where his sisters always warmly greeted Ernst Ludwig. While in Russia, the Hessians also visited Sergei Alexandrovich's famed property at Illinskoe. A very nonchalant atmosphere was present there. The Grand Duke inherited the estate from his mother and created a well-manicured and peaceful hideout where

The brooch given by Queen Victoria to Victoria Melita as a wedding present. [ILN]

The Ehrenburg Palace church, Coburg, 1894. Photograph by E. Uhlenhuth. [RNB]

"The palace church was brightly decorated with garlands of evergreen and white flowers. At midday, while the bells were chiming on the belfry, the Hofmarshal, Prince von Ratibor, escorted by the other chief courtiers, appeared at the entry to the church. He hit the floor with his staff three times, and thus ordered the procession to commence. German Kaiser Wilhelm II, in the Hessian General's uniform was in the first pair, leading the Duchess of Coburg, Maria Alexandrovna, they were followed by his mother, the German Empress, after them came the eldest son of Queen Victoria, Edward Albert, in the uniform of the First Dragoon Queen Victoria Leib-Guards, together with the Russian Cesarevich Nicholas in the uniform of the Russian Hussars ... The Hofmarshal appeared once again and announced the arrival of Queen Victoria, who is led by her son, the Duke of Coburg, Alfred. In the second row were the Grand Dukes Vladimir and Sergei Alexandrovich, further Grand Duke Paul Alexandrovich and Grand Duchess Maria Pavlovna the Elder. The guests are seated and the groom entered, wearing the uniform of a Hessian General. After a short pause the bride arrived ... At the end of the wedding ceremony Mendelsohn's Wedding March as performed on the organ."

Illustrated London News, 1894.

Princess Victoria Melita of Edinburgh c. 1881.
[Eurohistory Archive]

Princesses Marie and Victoria Melita of Edinburgh c. 1887.
[Eurohistory Archive]

he found the tranquility that his position as Governor-General of Moscow denied him.

A not-too-large house made from old oak, on the very banks of the Moscow River, surrounded by forests, was the favorite place to rest for not only Sergei and his wife Elisabeth Feodorovna ("Ella"), but also for their numerous relatives. Illinskoe was the place of many happy, beautiful childhood memories for Maria Pavlovna "the Younger" and her brother Dmitri. The children were taken in as wards by Sergei and Ella when their father, Paul Alexandrovich, entered into a morganatic marriage. The Grand Duchess Maria Pavlovna "the Younger" recalled: "This estate did not provide any income. On the contrary, Uncle Sergei spent enormous sums of money to maintain it. Every year he would have a new hobby: once he bought pedigreed cows – a special, as I believe, Swiss breed, of a light beige color .... he loved beautiful horses and purchased an Ardent stallion, the only one of its kind in Russia. He was continuously busy with some kind of construction: one year he was building a new school, the next year – he was expanding the hot houses, and so forth."

Princesses Alexandra and Victoria Melita
of Edinburgh c. 1887.
[RGAKFD]

*A sample of the iron lattice work over the arch leading
to the courtyard of the Grand Ducal Palace, Darmstadt.
Photograph by G.Korneva, 2008.*

Schloß Wolfsgarten near Darmstadt.
[Eurohistory Archive]

Princess Victoria Melita's bedroom, Coburg c. 1894. Photograph by E. Uhlenhuth.
[ILN]

Grand Duchess Maria Alexandrovna and Coburg

The Hessian siblings. Standing in back, left to right: Tsarevich Nicholas Alexandrovich, Princess Alix of Hesse and by Rhine, Princess Victoria of Battenberg, Grand Duke Ernst Ludwig of Hesse and by Rhine. Seated, same order: Princess Heinrich of Prussia, Grand Duchess Elisabeth Feodorovna, Grand Duchess Victoria Melita of Hesse and by Rhine, Grand Duke Sergei Alexandrovich. Darmstadt, April 11 (23), 1894. Photograph by K. Bachofen. [RGAKFD]

Emperor Nicholas II visits Illinskoe after his coronation ceremonies, 1896.
From the left, standing: Crown Prince Ferdinand of Romania, Tsar Nicholas II, Grand Duke Sergei Alexandrovich, Grand Duchess Victoria Melita and Grand Duke Ernst Ludwig of Hesse and by Rhine. Seated, same order: Grand Duke Dmitri Pavlovich, Crown Princess Marie of Romania, Empress Alexandra Feodorovna with her daughter Olga Nikolaevna, Princess Elisabeth of Hesse and by Rhine with her grandmother Grand Duchess Maria Alexandrovna, Grand Duchess Elisabeth Feodorovna. On the floor: Princess Alice of Battenberg, Grand Duchess Maria Pavlovna the "Younger," Grand Duke Paul Alexandrovich, and Princess Victoria of Battenberg. [TsGAKFFD SPb]

Grand Duke Kirill and Princess Victoria Melita of Edinburgh
"Her Second Marriage"

In December 1901 Victoria Melita's marriage to Ernst Ludwig finally unraveled and ended in divorce. Both agreed that their marriage was at an end. Both parents shared custody of their only daughter, the adorable Elisabeth (1895–1903). Sadly, she died of typhus two years later while visiting her Russian cousins at an Imperial hunting lodge in Poland. Ernst Ludwig and Victoria Melita were devastated by the loss of their daughter, but it brought a final, and painful, end to their prior history together.

By that time, Victoria Melita had fallen in love with a young Russian officer whom she had known for many years. Luckily for her, this time the feeling was mutual. He was Grand Duke Kirill Vladimirovich, a first cousin (like her first husband), but this time from her mother's side. Much to the surprise of their extended family, on September 25 (October 8), 1905, in Tegernsee, not far from Münich, they became husband and wife. However, their marriage was not approved by Emperor Nicholas II, and, also, the Orthodox Church considered a marriage between such close relatives to be against Church laws. Such was the seriousness of the situation that in Russia a special committee was created to examine this question. Emperor Nicholas II ordered that "His Imperial Highness Grand Duke Kirill Vladimirovich be removed from his post, entry into Russia be forbidden, and he be denied all ranks, privileges and revenue."

"I cannot accept the marriage of Grand Duke Kirill Vladimirovich. The Grand Duke and any of his heirs are disallowed from any rights of succession. In showing my caring for the future of the Grand Duke Kirill's heirs, should any children be born to him and his wife, I give them the name Princes Kirillovsky, with the title of Serene Highness and allocate for each of them a pension for their upbringing and education of 12,500 rubles a year, until they attain civil majority."

Resolution of Emperor Nicholas II, part of the protocols of the Committee meeting, December 4 (17), 1906.

[Eurohistory Archive]

Kirill Vladimirovich and Victoria Melita

Grand Duke Boris Vladimirovich.
He was Fliegel-Adjutant (1897), a Major of the Suite (1914), veteran of the Russo-Japanese and First World Wars. In 1915-1917 he served as a patrol Cossack Ataman. In 1919 he left for exile in France, where he died in 1943. He is buried in Contrexéville. [RGAKFD]

The headstrong and steadfast decision made by Victoria Melita and Kirill closed for them any possibility of settling in Russia. For the next five years, and up until 1910 the family was forced to live abroad.

The strictness of Emperor Nicholas II's decision – he was, after all, a first cousin to both Grand Duke Kirill and Princess Victoria Melita – shocked not only the newlyweds, but it also deeply wounded Grand Duke Vladimir Alexandrovich. Kirill's father, as a sign of protest, left his post as head of the Guard regiment, and his position as head of the St. Petersburg military region. But even with the loss of position and titles, Kirill Vladimirovich was overjoyed at the possibility of being close to the person he loved. "Our three years in exile, corresponding to the first three years of our married life, are tied to the most intimate and blissful moments of my life," Kirill recalled in his memoirs. At the end of 1906 Victoria Melita converted to Orthodoxy and received the name of Victoria Feodorovna. In 1907, in Coburg's Edinburg Palais she gave birth to the first daughter of this union, who was named Maria, in honor of both grandmothers. In that same year, by degree of Emperor Nicholas II, the marriage of Kirill and Victoria Feodorovna was declared valid in Russia. Two years later, this time in Paris, in their own house

The structure to the right of the image is known as the Kirill Palais, and served as the first home of Grand Duke Kirill Vladimirovich and Grand Duchess Victoria Feodorovna. Today it houses a kindergarten.
Photograph by G. Korneva, 2008.

"It is with great joy that I remember Grand Duke Vladimir Alexandrovich ... I served under his command for 31 years – a rather long period of time, enough to develop a good sense of the person. He was a kindhearted, straightforward, fairminded individual, without any roughness of manner with his subordinates. Some considered him abrupt, but I knew Grand Duke Vladimir Alexandrovich well, and I totally disagree with this opinion. Some said that he could be rude in his behavior with others, but that can be explained by his bashfulness, and in his desire to overcome this fault and not to appear inadequate, he would sometimes raise his baritone voice. Sharp tongues would say that "the Grand Duke speaks in whispers."

N.A. Epanchin, "At the Service of Three Emperors."

[Eurohistory Archive]

on Avenue d'Henri Martin, their second daughter, Kira, came into the world. Soon after, word came from Russia that the couple was completely exonerated, and in 1910 the family moved to St. Petersburg.

Throughout those difficult years of exile, Kirill Vladimirovich and Victoria Feodorovna received strong support from their parents, both in Coburg, and in St. Petersburg; probably their strongest ally, who tried to help them by any possible means, was Kirill's brother, Grand Duke Boris Vladimirovich.

Grand Duke Kirill Vladimirovich from the moment of birth found himself in the company of very August relatives. His father was Grand Duke Vladimir Alexandrovich, the third son of Emperor Alexander II. After his brother, Alexander III ascended the throne Vladimir Alexandrovich played a key role in matters of politics and

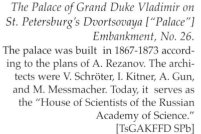

The Palace of Grand Duke Vladimir on St. Petersburg's Dvortsovaya ["Palace"] Embankment, No. 26.
The palace was built in 1867-1873 according to the plans of A. Rezanov. The architects were V. Schröter, I. Kitner, A. Gun, and M. Messmacher. Today, it serves as the "House of Scientists of the Russian Academy of Science."
[TsGAKFFD SPb]

Kirill Vladimirovich and Victoria Melita

Grand Duchess Maria Pavlovna with her children: Kiril and Helen (standing), and Boris and Andrei (seating).[TsGAKFFD SPb]

the military life of the capital. Vladimir was only two years younger than Alexander. From early childhood the brothers had the same teachers; they shared joys and sorrows. Having become Emperor, Alexander continued to take advice from Vladimir and trusted him when the time came to making difficult decisions. Thus, in 1885 Grand Duke Vladimir Alexandrovich was the head of the Commission on changing the Laws of Succession. The Grand Duke was member of the Government Council, a Senator, and for a quarter of century held the post of Commander-in-Chief of the St. Petersburg Military Region.

From childhood Vladimir Alexandrovich was interested in history and collected works of art. In 1869 the young Grand Duke was assigned as Fellow to the President of the Imperial Academy of Art, and later, for 33 years, he directed the activities of this institution as its President.

A vase of Meißen china, made from a model by Kendler. This superb piece was a wedding gift to Maria Pavlovna from her father, Grand Duke Friedrich Franz II of Mecklenburg-Schwerin. Photograph by G. Korneva, 1993.

It was not merely his close relation to Emperors, but the wide scope of his knowledge, his high human qualities that determined his special place in society. Vladimir Alexandrovich and his wife Maria Pavlovna entertained in their palaces in St. Petersburg and in Tsarskoe Selo famous politicians, diplomats, and government officials. The Court of the Grand Duke would set the tone for St. Petersburg high society.

Every year, the Grand Duke would spend a large amount of time in Europe, on official visits as a representative of the Imperial Family, as a military officer, or simply to visit his numerous relatives – the heads of state of European countries. Vladimir Alexandrovich was considered to be a gourmet, a lover and expert on the cuisine of many nations. In his palace he had a unique collection of menus, with notes on the sides made by him personally; at the present time they are stored in the State Archives of the Russian Federation.

Maria Alexandrina Elisabeth Eleonora, the daughter of the Grand Duke of Mecklenburg-Schwerin Friedrich Franz II (1823–1883) and his wife Augusta Mathilda Wilhelmina, née the Princess Reuß-Schleiz-Köstritz (1822–1862), was born on May 2 (14), 1854, at Lüdwigslust Palace, the official country residence of the Grand Dukes of Mecklenburg-Schwerin.

As a twenty-year-old Duchess of Mecklenburg-Schwerin she came to St. Petersburg in 1874, not long before her marriage with Grand Duke Vladimir Alexandrovich; she would reside in Russia for 46 years. For the first time in over 150 years the bride of one of the Grand Dukes of Russia did not convert to Orthodoxy, but remained a Lutheran. Their wedding took place first according to the Orthodox rite and was performed by the Isidor, Metropolitan of St. Petersburg in the Large, Church of the Winter Palace. Her brothers, Friedrich Franz and Paul Friedrich of Mecklenburg-Schwerin, held the crown over the head of Duchess Maria; his younger brothers, Grand Dukes Alexei and Sergei, held the crown over Vladimir's head. Later, in the Alexander Hall, the

Grand Duke Friedrich Franz III of Mecklenburg-Schwerin with his sister Grand Duchess Maria Pavlovna. [RGAKFD]

Grand Duchess Maria Pavlovna wearing some exquisite pieces from her legendary and fabulous jewel collection. [RGAKFD]

Kirill Vladimirovich and Victoria Melita

"As far as I can recall Father was an extremely kind person, respected by all for his righteous nature, his cultured mannerisms and his brilliant knowledge. And although he could be somewhat brusque in his attitude with others, and could even scare people away upon first acquaintance, beyond his outer rough exterior was hidden a heart of gold. Later in life he was to become my closest friend."

Grand Duke Kirill Vladimirovich, "My Life in Russia's Service."

From left: Grand Duke Boris, Grand Duke Vladimir, Grand Duchess Helen, Grand Duke Kirill and Grand Duke Boris. Standing behind is Grand Duchess Maria Pavlovna.
[Eurohistory Archive]

Bishop of the Evangelical Lutheran General Consistory Richter performed a marriage according to Lutheran rites.

With time, this marriage proved to be very successful. Five children were born to the couple: sons Alexander (1875–1877), Kirill (1876–1938), Boris (1877–1943), Andrei (1879–1956) and a daughter, Helen (1882–1957).

Grand Duchess Maria Pavlovna had exquisite taste, and together with her husband, they acquired a grand collection of works of art, china, and furniture. In particular, they had a unique collection of jewelry from the famous firm of Fabergé, which was considered one of the best such collections in the world.

The jewelry expert Bainbridge considered the Grand Duchess Maria Pavlovna "one of the most wonderful, one of the most illustrious of ladies in Europe," and General A.A. Mosolov once wrote the following about her exceptional diplomatic qualities; he had just complimented her on a successful event, and she responded: "One needs to know one's trade." And the author attested: "One should confess, the Grand Duchess certainly knew her "trade" to the utmost."

In 1909, after the untimely death of her husband, Grand Duchess Maria Pavlovna became President of the Imperial Academy of Art, the Chairman of the Russian Imperial Firemen's Society, the Honorary Chairman of the St. Petersburg Imperial Architects' Society. She also took over her husband's post as the Patron of the St. Vladimir's Orthodox Brotherhood in Berlin.

At the end of the 19th century there were over twenty luxurious palaces in St. Petersburg belonging to members of the Imperial family. The palace of Vladimir Alexandrovich, in comparison with other Grand Ducal residences, has been maintained remarkably well, strange as that may be. On the exterior it reminds one of the Palazzo Strozzi, chef d'ouvre of Florentine architecture of the XV century. The interiors were designed using the best St. Petersburg architects, who utilized various artistic styles, characteristic of the capital at the end of the XIX century. The ensemble of the Vladimir Palace was put together during the lifetime of just one generation of Grand Dukes, and thus, it greatly reflects the tastes of its owners.

Breakfast for members of the Life-Guard Dragoon Regiment in the Grand Ballroom of the Vladimir Palace. Grand Duchess Maria Pavlovna was the Honorary Chief of the the Regiment. Photograph by Bulla. [TsGAKFFD SPb]

Among its many grand palace halls and private apartments, created according to the traditions and new styles of interior design in European countries, two halls stand out, because they are decorated in a purely "Russian style." These are the Grand Dining Room and the private Orthodox Chapel. They are unique in their carvings, reminding one of ornaments in village huts. An important influence on their design, were paintings by Vasiliy Vereshchagin, a professor of the Academy of Art. At that time he was well known in Russia, and abroad. He had been brought up in a poor provincial family, whose parents and grandparents were iconographers. Without any money, even for paints and brushes, he arrived in St. Petersburg, and, after his studies at the Imperial Academy of Art, went on to receive every possible award. The important assignment for designing the palace of Grand Duke Vladimir Alexandrovich brought him fame, and, a few years later, he was one of the artists who worked on the icons of the main altar screen in the Christ the Savior Cathedral in Moscow. He also worked on the Uspensky ["Dormition"] Cathedral in the Kievan-Cave Monastery and the Cathedral of St. Mary Magdalene in Jerusalem.

The private chapel in the Vladimir palace, c. 1893. Photograph by K. Bulla. [TsGAKFFD SPb]

The paintings for the Grand Dining Room in the Vladimir Palace were done on a ribbed canvas, which resembled tapestries. One of them, the "Maiden

Dawn," won the grand prize at the International Fair in Paris in 1877. Other outstanding canvases of this artist are the "Baptism of St. Vladimir," the "Introduction of Orthodoxy to Kievan Rus'" and the "Laying of the Foundation of the Church," all painted for the private chapel of the Grand Duke in 1879.

In August 1874, the private chaplain to Vladimir Alexandrovich, Father Vasiliy Bazhanov, consecrated the Vladimir Palace chapel in the name of the Annunciation of the Virgin Mary. The church had a one-tiered altar screen made of walnut; 25 icons were placed on the screen, artists V.V. Vasiliev and N.A. Likhutin painted them on a gold background. The holy items were made of gold-plated silver and ordered specially from the firm of P.A. Ovchinnikov in Moscow. The carved heads of angels, eagles, lions and lambs, symbolizing the four Evangelists, were situated on the side beams.

The largest and the most elaborate hall in the Vladimir Palace was the Grand Ballroom. It was decorated in the style of Louis XV, and it left one in awe of its splendor and magnificence: the numerous stucco decorations, the mirrors, and the luxurious selection of lighting fixtures – six bronze and gold-plated chandeliers and nine seven-candled bras, all made to order at the atelier of I. Betz. The ceiling was decorated with an illustration of the "Triumph of Venus" and two round medallions with the images of instrument-playing cherubs, painted by V.P. Vereshchagin. The owners of the Vladimir Palace were very gracious hosts; the balls and gatherings hosted by the Grand Duke and Duchess were especially elegant, and known throughout St. Petersburg.

A true gem and work of art of the palace is the tiny boudoir of Grand Duchess Maria Pavlovna, decorated in a

The Grand Duchess Maria Pavlovna wearing the uniform of Honorary Chief of the Life-Guard Dragoon Regiment, c. 1914. Photograph by Bulla. [TsGAKFFD SPb]

Mauritanian style, resembling the grandeur of the Alhambra Palace in Granada. The ceiling and walls are covered with stucco decorations, gold-plated and painted with bright colors. This room reminds one of a luxurious Far-Eastern jewelry box and leaves all visitors of the palace in admiration upon entering. The fireplace, situated across from the entrance to the room, is of Italian marble, designed according to the plans of M. Messmacher in the atelier of E. Rudgia and S. Maderni. The clock, in Mauritanian style, produced by Paul Buhre, forms a complete ensemble with the fireplace. Above the fireplace was a portrait of Grand Duchess Helen, the daughter of Vladimir Alexandrovich and Maria Pavlovna; she is portrayed in the costume of a Turkish girl; the artist V.M. Izmailovich.

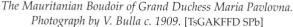

The Mauritanian Boudoir of Grand Duchess Maria Pavlovna.
Photograph by V. Bulla c. 1909. [TsGAKFFD SPb]

The grand staircase of the Vladimir Palace, c. 1893.
Photograph by Bulla. [TsGAKFFD SPb]

In the pointed niche, to the left of the window, there was an exhibit of unique pieces of jewelry, many of which were from the firm of Carl Fabergé.

From 1880 to 1893 many Vladimir Palace rooms were redecorated by the leading Russian architect of the time, Maximilian Messmacher. The ensemble of the Grand Staircase, Grand Duchess Maria Pavlovna's Library, the new Dining Room and the Golden Staircase have been preserved, practically intact, to this day. The flowing turn of the Grand Staircase, with its twelve steps, expertly combined its central landing with the Grand Ballroom. The arch is topped with a medallion of intertwined initials of the owners of the palace. On account of the special lighting designed by M. Messmacher, the staircase itself is seen as one of the most beautiful parts of the interior. The walls are richly adorned with stucco and other decorations on a gold background. Sculptor M.A. Chizhov made special marble statues of Amour, Triton and dolphins, for this staircase.

The "Golden" Staircase connected the New Dining Room with the grand halls of the belle etage. The white marble of its stairs

Architect M.E. Messmacher.
(1842-1906)

Grand Duchess Maria Pavlovna surrounded by her children and grandchildren.
From the left, standing: Grand Duke Andrei Vladimirovich, Prince Nicholas of Greece, Grand Duchess Maria Pavlovna, Grand Dukes Kirill and Boris Vladimirovich. Seated, same order: Princess Marina of Greece, Grand Duchess Helen Vladimirovna, Princess Elisabeth of Greece, Princess Maria Kirillovna, Grand Duchess Victoria Feodorovna and Princess Kira Kirillovna. On the foreground: Princess Olga of Greece.

[Eurohistory Archive]

Grand Duchess Victoria Feodorovna.
[RGAKFD]

The palace of the Grand Duke Kirill Vladimirovich on Nikolskaya Street (presently Glinka Street). Photograph by G. Korneva, 2005.

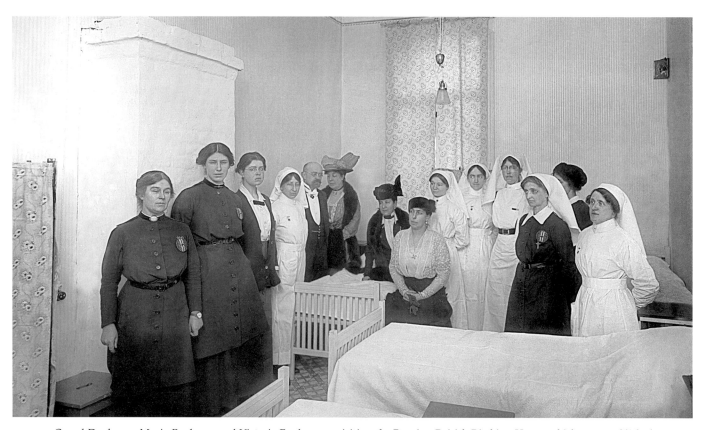

Grand Duchesses Maria Pavlovna and Victoria Feodorovna visiting the Russian-British Birthing Home, which was established in the former palace of Grand Duke Sergei Alexandrovich.
[TsGAKFFD SPb]

Grand Duchess Maria Pavlovna and her son-in-law Prince Nicholas of Greece while staying in Contrexéville. [RGAKFD]

contrasted with the gold decoration of the latticework and the handrails, which were of red oak. The little room before the Small Dining Room is richly decorated in white and gold stucco.

On January 25, 1883 a "historical" costume ball was held in the Vladimir Palace; it served as a prototype for the famous ball of 1903 in the Winter Palace. The writer for the magazine "Vsemirnaya Illustratsiya" described his impressions of the unusual celebration in the Vladimir Palace in this manner: "all of pre-Peter the Great Russia seemed to have come back to life and sent representatives to the ball." Grand Duke Vladimir Alexandrovich greatly appreciated the work of M. Messmacher in doing the preparatory work for this ball and recommended him to his elder brother, Emperor Alexander III. He proceeded to assign the talented architect the task of remodeling the private quarters of the Emperor and his wife at the Anitchkov Palace.

Grand Duke Kirill Vladimirovich had a spacious apartment in his parents' palace, located on the second floor of the Hofmeister Wing (the present address is Millionnaya Street, No. 27). The design and furniture for the apartment was almost entirely provided by the English firm "Maples" during the years 1895–1897. After the death of Grand Duke Vladimir Alexandrovich, his son Kirill and Victoria Feodorovna, having received a pardon from the Emperor, moved with their children back to Russia and settled in their own new palace on Nikolskaya Street, No. 13; they had their furniture moved from their old apartment to their new residence. This English furniture can be seen to this very day, in the rooms of the Kindergarden located at Glinka Street (formerly "Nikolskaya").

Grand Duchess Maria Pavlovna in front of the entrance of her home in Contrexéville, the "Sovereign" Hotel. [Eurohistory Archive]

During the years of the First World War Grand Duchess Victoria Feodorovna actively helped her mother-in-law Maria Pavlovna, who was head of the Main Administration of War Relief in the Petrograd region. She was busy in the establishment of aid stations, workshops, storage units, for the provision of clothing and other goods to wounded and sick soldiers. The first aid transport unit under the patronage of Grand Duchess Victoria Feodorovna became one of the best in Russia.

After the February Revolution the entire family of Grand Duchess Maria Pavlovna was able to leave Russia. Grand Duke Kirill Vladimirovich and

Grand Duchess Maria Pavlovna with members of her entourage inside her rooms at the "Sovereign" Hotel. From the collection of G. Salvini.

The Vladimirovich.
In back, from left: Grand Duke Andrei, Grand Duchess Helen, Grand Duke Kirill and Grand Duke Boris. At front, same order: Grand Duke Vladimir Alexandrovich and Grand Duchess Maria Pavlovna. [Eurohistory Archive]

The Hotel Sovereign, where Grand Duchess Maria Pavlovna often stayed in Contrexéville.
Photograph by Galina Korneva, 2008

The name plate for the street named after Grand Duchess Maria pavlovna, Contrexéville, France.
Photograph by Galina Korneva, 2008.

The bell of the Orthodox Church of Saints Vladimir and Mary Magdalene in Contrexéville. Photograph by G. Korneva, 2008.

The Orthodox Church of Saints Vladimir and Mary Magdalen. From the collection of G. Salvini.

his family moved to Finland during the summer of 1917. There they settled in the town of Borgo, on the estate of Haikko, owned by the von Etter family. Alexander Sebastianovich von Etter was a Kammerherr (Chamberlain) of the Royal Court and from January 22, 1898, was an attendant to Grand Duchess Maria Pavlovna. This is why members of the family of Grand Duke Vladimir Alexandrovich very often visited the villa of Haikko, and would stay there for long periods of time. It was here on August 30, 1917, that Grand Duchess Victoria Feodorovna gave birth to her son Vladimir. For five years the family remained in Finland, later – they moved to Coburg, and after that, they settled in France, on the north coast of Brittany, in the town of St. Briac-sur-Mer. In 1924 Grand Duke Kirill Vladimirovich accepted the title of Emperor of Russia in Exile.

Grand Duke Kirill Vladimirovich and his wife Grand Duchess Victoria Feodorovna were buried in the family crypt of the Dukes of Saxe-Coburg & Gotha, but in 1995, their remains were re-interred in the Grand Ducal Chapel of the Peter and Paul Cathedral in St. Petersburg.

The icon of St. Mary Magdalene in the altar screen of the Orthodox Church, Contrexéville. Photograph G. Korneva, 2008.

During the period of 46 years that she had spent in Russia, Grand Duchess Maria Pavlovna, practically every year, traveled to Europe and "took the cures" in fashionable resorts of Germany and France. The mineral springs at Contrexéville, according to her physicians, were very beneficial to the Grand Duchess, and she would visit this little town often; she would stay at the hotel "Sovereign." Her daughter Helen, with her husband Prince Nicholas of Greece, would join her, as well as representatives of the Russian elite – Princes A.B. Lobanov Rostovsky and F. Yousoupov, General A.N. Sinelnikov, Minister of Foreign Affairs A.P. Izvolsky.

One of the streets of Contrexéville still carries the name of the Grand Duchess Maria Pavlovna.

The altar screen inside the Orthodox Church, Contrexéville
From the collection of G. Salvini.

In February 1909 Grand Duke Vladimir Alexandrovich died suddenly from respiratory complications. In his memory Maria Pavlovna decided to build a Russian Church in Contrexéville and to dedicate it to the patron saints of her late husband and herself – Saints Vladimir and Mary Magdalene.

When she was forced to leave Russia in February 1920, Maria Pavlovna was already deathly ill, and she survived only a few months in exile. On September 6 of the same year her aide, Kammerger Savinsky, officially announced the death of the Grand Duchess. Her remains rest in the church that was built by her. Her son Boris, who died in Paris in 1943, also found his last resting place in this church.

The memorial plaque at the entrance to the
Russian Church in Contrexéville.
Photograph by Galina Korneva, 2008.

The grave of Grand Duchess Maria Pavlovna.
Photograph by G. Salvini.

The Engagement of Tsarevich Nicholas Alexandrovich and Princess Alix of Hesse and by Rhine

*I*n April 1894, during the wedding ceremonies of Victoria Melita and Ernst Ludwig in Coburg, an event occurred that would play a decisive role in the history of Russia and the demise of the Romanov Dynasty – the engagement of Tsarevich Nicholas Alexandrovich and Princess Alix of Hesse and by Rhine.

Alix first met Tsarevich Nicholas Alexandrovich in June 1884 when she came to St. Petersburg for the wedding of her elder sister Ella. Having married the Grand Duke Sergei Alexandrovich, Ella at first remained a Lutheran, and only in 1891, having come to the understanding that Orthodox dogma was closer to her heart, did she convert to Orthodoxy. Perhaps, this occurred under the influence of her husband, who was a devout follower of the Orthodox faith. In April 1894 Alix was helped to make her own important decision about faith by the Grand Duchess Maria Pavlovna, who possessed an uncompromising mind and great diplomatic talent. She had lived in Russia for twenty years, and she understood all too well that it was mandatory for the future Empress to convert to Orthodoxy; she herself had been prepared to do the same, for "governmental reasons."

The numerous guests, representatives of the various reigning houses of Europe, present at the celebrations in Coburg were witness to the couple's engagement, which took place in Schloß Rosenau. Schinkel rebuilt this summer residence of the Dukes of Saxe-Coburg and Gotha in 1806–1817 in a neo-Gothic style. It was at the Rosenau that in 1819 Prince Albert was born – he was destined to be the future consort of Queen Victoria. Here he had spent his childhood. Prince Albert's brother, Duke Ernst II had given the castle as a gift to his nephew

Tsarevich Nicholas Alexandrovich and Princess Alix of Hesse and by Rhine, Coburg, April 20 (May 2), 1894.
Photograph by E. Uhlenhuth. [TsGAKFFD Spb]

Prince Alfred, the husband of Grand Duchess Maria Alexandrovna. The relatively small building, situated amid an English garden, with a serrated front and a high, romantic tower, became the favorite abode of Maria Alexandrovna's family.

She had made many changes in the furnishing of the castle; she had bright paintings hung, which she had brought with her from Malta; she redid the rooms with new furniture, but she had refused to use contemporary styles in the interior design. Cozy rooms, as in days of old, were illuminated with flickering candles, and Russian "rogozhki" (small rugs) replaced old Victorian carpets on the staircases.

Maria Alexandrovna always loved flowers, and would grow them from seeds brought to Germany from Russia. She could be found in her beautiful rose garden early in the morning,

The year is 1894. "April 8th; Friday. It is a glorious, unforgettable day in my life – the day that I was engaged to my dear, beloved Alix. After ten o'clock she came to Aunt Michen's [sic] room, and after a talk with her, we came to a decision. My dear Lord, what a weight off my shoulders."

The diary of Emperor Nicholas II, 1890-1906.

Schloß Rosenau, near Coburg.

From the left: Princesses Beatrice and Alexandra of of Saxe-Coburg & Gotha, Crown Princess Marie and Crown Prince Ferdinand of Romania, Schloß Rosenau, 1894. Photograph by E. Uhlenhuth. [RNB]

View from the terrace of Schloß Rosenau.
Photograph by G. Korneva, 2008.

Princess Beatrice's Tea Tower, Schloß Rosenau.
Photograph by G. Korneva, 2008.

tending to her bushes personally. Very often tea would be taken on a little terrace just in front of the castle, under the shade of an old, overhanging linden tree.

In the picturesque countryside around the Rosenau guests and hosts would take rides on horseback, or go hunting. There, everyone led an idyllic existence.

Sadly, in 1900 Maria Alexandrovna became a widow, but she continued to use the Rosenau as her country home. Later, the family of her youngest daughter, Beatrice, came to live with her. Beatrice had married the Spanish Infante, don Alfonso of Orléans y Borbón.

Emperor Nicholas II at a hunt with relatives.
From the left: Hereditary Prince Alfred of Saxe-Coburg & Gotha, Emperor Nicholas II, Grand Duke Ernst Ludwig
of Hesse and by Rhine, Duke Alfred of of Saxe-Coburg & Gotha, Coburg 1897. [TsGAKFFD SPb]

Tsarevich Nicholas Alexandrovich with his fiancée Princess Alix of Hesse and by Rhine, Schloß Rosenau, April 8 (20), 1894.
Photograph by J. Russel the Younger. [ILN]

A royal gathering at Schloß Rosenau at the time of the engagement of Tsarevich Nicholas Alexandrovich and Princess Alix.
Standing, from left: Prince Henry of Battenberg, Prince Philipp of Saxe-Coburg & Gotha, Crown Prince Ferdinand of Romania, Prince Heinrich of Prussia, Duke Alfred of Saxe-Coburg & Gotha. Grand Duke Paul Alexandrovich, Tsarevich Nicholas Alexandrovich, Kaiser Wilhelm II, Grand Duke Vladimir Alexandrovich, the Duke of Connaught, Prince Louis of Battenberg, Princess Alexandra of Saxe-Coburg & Gotha, the Prince of Wales (Edward VII). Second row, seated, same order: Princess Victoria of Battenberg, Princess Louise of Saxe-Coburg & Gotha, Princess Beatrice of Battenberg, the Duchess of Connaught, the Duchess of Saxe-Coburg & Gotha, Crown Princess Marie of Romania, Princess Alix of Hesse and by Rhine, Grand Duchess Maria Pavlovna, and Hereditary Princess Charlotte of Saxe-Meiningen. Seated on the floor, same order: Princess Irene of Prussia, Princess Beatrice of Saxe-Coburg & Gotha, Grand Duke Sergei Alexandrovich, Princess Feodora of Saxe-Meiningen, Grand Duchess Elisabeth Feodorovna, and Hereditary Prince Alfred of Saxe-Coburg & Gotha.
April 8 (20), 1894. Photograph by J. Russel the Younger. [ILN]

The northern façade of Schloß Rosenau. It was here where the above photograph was taken in 1894.
Photograph by G. Korneva, 2008.

The Grand Duchy of Hesse and by Rhine
Alix, Ernst Ludwig and Elisabeth –
The "Hessian Siblings"

The Grand Duchy of Hesse and by Rhine is situated on the banks of the Rhine and its tributary the Main. The territory of this grand duchy is much smaller than that of its neighbors, Bavaria and Württemberg. However, its political importance among the lower German states was always considerable.

Two Russian Empresses – the wife of Alexander II, Maria Alexandrovna, and the wife of Nicholas II, Alexandra Feodorovna, were born Princesses of Hesse and by Rhine. Both of these Hessian princesses did not sever their ties with their homeland and would come to visit their German relatives quite often.

Because of its mild climate and medicinal springs Hesse became attractive to the Russian elite, the artistic intelligentsia, and even representatives of the middle class.

In 1877 Ludwig IV, the father of Alexandra Feodorovna and Elisabeth Feodorovna, succeeded his uncle Ludwig III. He had married the talented Princess Alice of Great Britain in 1862, thus entering the inner sanctum of Queen Victoria's family. They raised their growing family, from the mid-1860s, inside the New Palace, the construction of which was partly financed with Alice's dowry.

At Ludwig IV's untimely death in 1892, his only surviving son, Ernst Ludwig, who married Princess Victoria Melita in 1894 and ruled the grand duchy until 1918,

The Empress Alexandra Feodorovna, born Princess Alix of Hesse and by Rhine.
[RGAKFD]

Prince Ludwig and Princess Alice of Hesse and by Rhine c. 1867.
[Eurohistory Archive]

succeeded him. Ernst Ludwig was known as a devotee and specialist of art; his wife also had very good taste. In 1897–1898 they had invited the famous English architect Bailey Scott to redecorate the interior of the New Palace. Two years later Ernst Ludwig and Victoria Melita had decided to expand their residence, and, under the direction of Ludwig Hoffman, a mansard wing was added.

Grand Duke Ernst Ludwig was a famous patron of the arts. During the turn of the century, not far from the center of town, he organized an artists' colony. In 1899 Ernst Ludwig invited a group of young artists to Darmstadt – Peter Behrens, Joseph Olbricht, Ludwig Habikh and others. Their "colony" was situated on a hilltop, and was known as "Mathildenhöhe," similar to the Russian artists' colony of Abramtsevo, where talented artists and architects lived and worked. These young people, who later were to become famous masters, created an architectural complex, which to this day is a tourist attraction of Darmstadt. Here at Mathildenhöhe, the Russian Orthodox Church of St. Mary Magdalene was built, according to the plans of the famous Russian architect Leon Benois; the church was richly adorned with mosaics. The famous Russian artist Victor Vasnetsov designed many of its frescoes and mosaics.

After his divorce from Victoria Melita, the Grand Duke of Hesse and by Rhine married a second time. In February 1905 Ernst Ludwig allied his life to a devoted woman, Princess Eleonore of Solms-

The New Palace, Darmstadt.
During the Second World War it was taken over by the Gestapo. An incendiary bomb hit the structure in 1944 and caused major damage to the building. Today the State Theater stans where the New palace used to be.

Princess Alix's bedroom in the New Palace.
[Mathildenhöhe Institute]

Hohensolms-Lich. The couple had two sons, Georg Donatus and Ludwig, both of whom were to have tragic destinies.

Grand Duke Ludwig IV (1837–1892, a nephew of Empress Maria Alexandrovna, was a first cousin to Emperor Alexander III. As mentioned before, in 1862 he became related to the English Royal Family, having wed Princess Alice (1843–1878), second daughter of Queen Victoria. At that time, the family was in mourning for the recent death of the father of the bride, the Prince Consort, and the wedding was relatively quiet, overshadowed by the somber mood clouding the daily life of Queen Victoria and her family.

Senator A.A. Polovtsov remembered Prince Ludwig as a "not too witty person," whose chief passion was taking strolls, both on foot and on horseback. He loved his wife, but could not always understand her spiritual needs and deep intellectual prowess. Princess Alice had received an excellent education, was interested in history, philosophy, theology. She was very religious, and would even dabble in mysticism. The family led a simple and quite life, always busy in the raising of seven children. As a wife, Alice felt frustrated, but not so as a mother, for she relished this role.

The first fifteen years after his marriage, before Ludwig became the ruling grand duke, he, his wife and their children lived in a large, comfortable home in the center of Darmstadt. It

The children of Grand Duke Ludwig IV and
Grand Duchess Alice of Hesse and by Rhine.
From left: Princess Irene, Prince Ernst Ludwig, Princess Victoria holding Princess Marie, Princess Alix (on the floor) and Princess Elisabeth, October 1875. [ILN]

Grand Duke Ludwig IV in fancy dress.
[Eurohistory Archive]

Grand Duchess Alice wearing some of her jewels.
[Eurohistory Archive]

The four Hessian sisters, left to right: Princess Irene, Princess Victoria, Princess Elisabeth and Princess Alix c.
1885. Photograph by Mayall.
[RGAKFD]

The Grand Duchy of Hesse and by Rhine

was near a large park, and not far from the Grand Duke's old residence. When their new home was finished, the family moved to the spacious New Palace, site of both happy and tragic events. Queen Victoria grudgingly helped pay for this palace, much to the urging of her daughter Alice. It was built in 1864–1865, according to the plans of the German architect Conrad Kraus.

Alice devoted much of her time to charity. She established in Hesse a special society to aid in women's education, and during the war, she would help organize aid to soldiers at the front, while personally tending to the wounded.

I glance at you, I marvel every hour:
You are indescribably beautiful!
Oh, there is no doubt, that under
such a wonderful exterior,
There is also a wonderful soul!
There is some sort of mysterious
gentleness and sadness
That fills the depths of your eyes;
Like and angel you are silent,
chaste and pure;
Like a woman you are bashful
and gentle.
Let nothing in this world
Amid all of the many
evils and sadness
Blemish your perfection.
And anyone, who shall
glance at you,
Will praise the Lord,
For having created such beauty.

Konstantin Romanov ("K.R.")
1884

Grand Duchess Elisabeth Feodorovna, née Princess Elisabeth of Hesse and by Rhine, London c. 1887. Photograph by H. Mendelsohn.
[TsGAKFFD SPb]

Tragically, two of the couple's children died before reaching the age of five years. Tragedy, in fact, was always to be a constant in the grand ducal family. Prince Friedrich Wilhelm, Alice's second son, died after falling from an open window in 1873. Then, in 1878, tragedy struck again. The grand ducal children caught diphtheria and Alice personally nursed her family to health. However, her youngest daughter, Marie, did not survive the epidemic and died aged four-and-a-half years old. Then, nearly three weeks later, exhausted by the intensity of nursing her family, Alice died after catching the illness. She was but thirty-five years old.

The Hessian siblings were devastated by the loss of their mother. Wishing to play an important role in their upbringing and education, Queen Victoria often had her daughter Alice's children come to England. They would often pass the summers with their grandmother, and came to love England. The four surviving sisters (Victoria, Elisabeth, Irene and Alix) were not only very close, but they were very protective of their only brother, Ernst Ludwig, whom the family called by his nickname, Ernie.

The death of Grand Duchess Alice brought a sudden end to the childhood of her two oldest daughters. Together with her sister Victoria, Elisabeth (Ella), the second daughter of Ludwig IV and Alice, took upon herself all of the duties of caring for the family. She practically became a mother to her six-year-old sister Alix.

Ella, and her future husband Grand Duke Sergei Alexandrovich (1857–1905), brother of Emperor Alexander III, knew each other since childhood. They met frequently at Schloß Heiligenberg, on the estate of Jugenheim, where Sergei would spend many months with his mother while she visited her brother Prince Alexander of Hesse and by Rhine, the father of the morganatic, but exquisitely married, Princes of Battenberg. Therefore,

Grand Duke Sergei Alexandrovich.
(1857-1905)
Photograph by D. Asikiritov..
Eurohistory Archive]

Grand Duchess Elisabeth Feodorovna and Princess Maria
Alexandrovna Vasilchikova (1859-1934).
Maria Alexandrovna was the daughter of Hofmeister and Director of the Hermitage, Prince Alexander Alexeievich Vasilchikov. She was not only the lady-in-waiting of two empress, but also the friend of Ella, Alix and Ernst Ludwig.
[RGAKFD]

*Interior of one of the main rooms of Grand Duke
Sergei's palace c. 1903. Photograph by K. Bulla.*
[TsGAKFFD SPb]

*The Palace of Grand Duke Sergei Alexandrovich in St. Petersburg.
Located at Nevsky Prospect No. 41, the building was constructed
by Architect F.I. Demertsov in 1799-1800. It was later
remodeled by A. Stakenschneider in 1847-1848.
The figures of the Atlantes were sculpted by D. Jensen.
After the assassination of Grand Duke Sergei Alexandrovich in 1905,
the palace was inherited by his nephew Grand Duke Dmitri Pavlovich.*
[TsGAKFFD SPb]

from early youth Ella and Sergei Alexandrovich were dear to each other. In 1884 Elisabeth, the bride of Grand Duke Sergei Alexandrovich went to St. Petersburg; she brought along her 12-year-old sister, Alix.

That June, the couple's wedding was celebrated in the large chapel of the Winter Palace. The Empress Maria Feodorovna provided the bride with a brilliant dowry. The bride was exquisitely beautiful and all those present remembered for many years what a beautiful scene the wedding presented.

On their wedding day, the young couple proceeded to their own palace, purchased by Grand Duke Sergei Alexandrovich from Prince K.E. Beloselski-Belozersky shortly before their nuptials. It is located in the very center of St. Petersburg on Nevsky Prospekt, No. 41, right across from the

*Interior view from the Lower Dacha, Alexandria Park.
Photograph archives of GMZ "Peterhof."*

Anitchkov Palace, in which the family of Alexander III resided. Empress Maria Feodorovna took an active role in the fate of the Hessian Princess, who had lost her own mother at such an early age. She prepared the dowry

Emperor Nicholas II with his wife, Alexandra Feodorovna, and her sister, Grand Duchess Elisabeth Feodorovna (on the right) c. 1898. Photograph by L. Gorodetsky. [RGAKFD]

for the bride, and on the glorious day of their wedding, the Imperial couple greeted the newlyweds on the staircase of their palace with bread and salt (Russian greeting tradition). Not surprisingly then, Sergei Alexandrovich and Elisabeth Feodorovna, who, was known as Ella in the family, were exceptionally close to Emperor Alexander III, Sergei's brother, and later to Emperor Nicholas II, whose future wife would be Ella's younger sister.

When Ella took Alix with her to St. Petersburg, she had no way of knowing that this journey would determine the fate of her younger sister. It was during the days of Sergei and Ella's wedding that Tsarevich Nicholas Alexandrovich first started to take note of the beautiful and very shy young princess.

Emperor Alexander III and his wife were not particularly happy with their son Nicholas' choice of Alix as a bride. They feared that her religious nature and lack of social grace would pose insurmountable challenges for her in St. Petersburg. They were not to be disappointed.

The unexpected death of Alexander III rushed the decision-making process about the forthcoming wedding and the move of Princess Alix to Russia. The first months after their wedding Nicholas and Alexandra spent in the Anitchkov Palace, not wanting to leave the Dowager Empress Maria Feodorovna alone. Very often, practically several times a week, the two sisters would see each other. They would have breakfast together, go for carriage rides, have tea, meet at family gatherings. During 1895 the interiors of the Alexander Palace and the Winter Palace, as well as the Lower Summer Dacha in Alexandria Park, near Peterhof, were being prepared for the young couple. Elisabeth Feodorovna, having an impeccable sense of artistic taste, became the chief advisor on questions of interior design. In his diary, Nicholas II calls Ella "the creator of their private rooms at the Winter Palace." From childhood, the sisters had a passion for English art, they were well acquainted with furniture of English masters, and because of this, they ordered pieces of furniture not only from Russian suppliers, but also from the popular English company "Maples."

The Coronation of Emperor Nicholas II
and Empress Alexandra Feodorovna

Emperor Nicholas II.
[TsGAKFFD SPb]

The Tsar's throne in the Andreevsky (St. Andrew's) Hall of the Large Kremlin Palace, Moscow, May 1896. Photograph by K. Fisher.
[TsGAKFFD SPb]

"The throne in the Andreevsky Hall is changed for the coronation during every reign. For the coronation of Emperor Nicholas II the throne was redone completely, not only for the change of the initials, but also because it was necessary to expand the seating space on the throne to three: for the Emperor himself, the Empress Alexandra Feodorovna, and the Dowager Empress Maria Feodorovna. As it is known, Their Highnesses are seated on the throne before the procession to the Cathedral of the Dormition, and also upon their return from the cathedral, after the coronation. The Andreevsky Hall has been adorned with this new throne of exquisite artistic work performed by the firm of P.A. Schmidt, who, working on the drawings of the keeper of the Armament Palace, Count A.E. Komarovsky, gave the world this wonderful creation ... The awning is made of gold thread, on which are placed the national emblems (work of A. and V. Sapozhnikovs), the lining is of ermine, work of A.M. Mikhailov, and the wide tasseled edging, created by F.P. Vinogradov, finishes all sides of the fabric, forming the awning. Above the awning there is a canopy, made of wonderful carvings on a single piece of wood (the work of Schmidt). Count A.E. Komarovsky took the inspiration for the motif of the carving from the canopy over the altar table in the St. Nicholas-Nadeyan Church in Jaroslavl. The four corners of the canopy are topped with national emblems, the work of Khlebnikov, and in the middle is the Imperial crown ... The throne has three seats of a muted gold coloring, created by P.A. Schmidt, from the drawings of Komarovsky."

The St. Petersburg Gazette, April 28, 1896.

The Coronation of Emperor Nicholas II

View of the Kremlin from the Moscow River c. 1908. From the collection of M.S. Pariisky. [RGAKFD]

*I*n 1896, when all of Russia gloriously celebrated the coronation of Nicholas II and Alexandra Feodorovna, the "first capital" (or the "first throne city" as Moscow was called) visitors from all over the world traveled to Moscow. The Emperor's uncle, Grand Duke Sergei Alexandrovich, was the Governor-General of Moscow. He held this post from 1891 to 1905. During winter months the Grand Ducal couple would live in the palace on Tverskaya, while most of the summer months they would spend in their estate at Illinskoe.

The palace of the Governor-General of Moscow on Tverskaya Street, c. 1896. Built by Architect M.F. Kazakov, the palace was built in 1778-1782. It was remodeled in 1791. Photograph by L.L. Konasevich.
After its remodeling, the "Tverskoi Government House" became, probably, the largest administrative building in Moscow. It remained as such until the revolution.
[RGAKFD]

A contemporary drawing depicting the coronation of Emperor Nicholas II. To his left are his wife Empress Alexandra Feodorovna and his mother the Dowager Empress Maria Feodorovna, on whom a ray of sunlight shines. To the Emperor's left are Grand Duke Michael Alexandrovich and Grand Duke Vladimir Alexandrovich. Other members of the dynasty are featured throughtout. [Eurohistory Archive]

A contemporary drawing showing Emperor Nicholas II and Empress Alexandra Feodorovna after the coronation. Next to Nicholas II is his uncle Grand Duke Vladimir Alexandrovich, then eldest surviving son of Alexander II.
[Eurohistory Archive]

At the Coronation of Emperor Nicholas II.
Standing from the left: Grand Duchess Vera Konstantinovna, a Page, Grand Duchess Anastasia of Mecklenburg-Schwerin, Grand Duchess Maria Pavlovna, Grand Duchess Helen Vladimirovna, Grand Duchess Elisabeth Mavrikievna, a page, Princess Helen of Saxe-Altenburg.
Seated, same order: Duchess Elsa of Württemberg, Grand Duchess Alexandra Iosifovna and the Duchess of Connaught.
[Eurohistory Archive]

Foreign guests and relatives at the Coronation of Emperor Nicholas II.
Seated from the left: Crown Princess Marie of Romania and the Duchess of Saxe-Coburg & Gotha. Behind them, same order: a Page, Crown Prince Ferdinand of Romania, Grand Duke Ernst Ludwig of Hesse and by Rhine, a Page, the Duke of Saxe-Coburg & Gotha, Grand Duchess Victoria Melita of Hesse and by Rhine, Hereditary Prince Alfred of Saxe-Coburg & Gotha, and a page.

[Eurohistory Archive]

Grand Duchess Elisabeth Feodorovna

*E*lisabeth Feodorovna especially loved the picturesque village of Illinskoe, situated on the banks of the Moscow River. Relatives of the Romanov family would often gather here, while other aristocrats, like the Yousoupovs and Golitsyns, would come and visit from their neighboring estates. From the time of Empress Maria Alexandrovna, Illinskoe had a working farm on its grounds where elite breeds of cattle were raised. Grand Duke Sergei Alexandrovich tried to improve the business of his estate every year. He would purchase Swiss and Holstein cattle, also beautiful purebred horses. He acquired an Arden stallion – the only one of its kind at that time in Russia. There was always something being built on the grounds – a new school, new hot houses, or new aviaries.

Guests and hosts would spend happy hours together at Illinskoe. They would go riding on horseback, go mushroom picking, or would participate in various Russian national holidays.

In 1891 the son of Grand Duke Paul Alexandrovich, Dimitry, was born here. As a result of a complicated labor Paul's young wife Alexandra, born a Princess of Greece, died a few days after giving birth to their son. Her two children, year and a half-year-old Maria, and the newly born Dimitry, had been left without a mother. In 1902, when Grand Duke Paul Alexandrovich entered into a morganatic marriage and was forced to leave the country, Sergei Alexandrovich and Elisabeth Feodorovna became the foster parents to these children. After Grand Duke Sergei Alexandrovich's assassination in Moscow's Kremlin in 1905, his widow made the decision to forsake all social appearances and dedicate her life to aiding the needy. She willed Illinskoe to her niece and nephew, Maria and Dimitry, and dedicated herself to charity work.

To carry out her mission, Grand Duchess Elisabeth Feodorovna purchased property on Moscow's Bolshaia Ordynka Street. There in February 1909, the Martha and Mary Convent was opened. A church was built on the grounds, dedicated to the Pokrov ("Protection") of the Blessed Mother of God, according to the plans of architect A.V. Shchusev. The artist M. Nesterov did the interior design of the church. A state-of-the-art hospital was

Grand Duke Sergei (at the head of the table) with Grand Duchess Elisabeth (to the left of her husband) at tea in the garden of Illinskoe. [RGAKFD]

Of Illisnkoe, Maria Pavlovna the Younger said, "The house was square, made out of old oak. It was not large, with few rooms, and had absolutely no pretensions of a particular style. Throughout the gardens one could find scattered here and there guest cottages, for friends and courtiers. The park was the most charming part of the estate ... The estate provided no income. Quite the opposite, Uncle Sergei spent a lot of money on its upkeep.

Grand Duchess Maria Pavlovna the Younger's Memoirs.

Grand Duke Sergei Alexandrovich and his wife Grand Duchess Elisabeth Feodorovna with Grand Duke Paul Alexandrovich and his children: Grand Duchess Maria Pavlovna and Grand Duke Dimitry (on Paul's lap) c. 1892 Photograph by V. Lapres. [RGAKFD]

Grand Duchess Elisabeth Feodorovna, Abbess of the Martha and Mary Convent c. 1909. [Eurohistory Archive]

also built, together with a pharmacy and an outpatient clinic, a food kitchen for the poor, an orphanage for girls, a parish school and a library. The Grand Duchess herself occupied three sparsely furnished rooms in the abbess' house. These were her study, sitting room and bedroom.

Together with the sisters of the Martha and Mary Convent Elisabeth Feodorovna worked in the hospital, she assisted during surgeries and tended to the seriously ill. She was not afraid of going to the most horrible sections of Moscow, where the poorest and most downtrodden lived. She was often seen at Khitrovka (a very notorious section of town), together with her companion, Sister Barbara. They would walk through brothels, gather orphans, or try to convince parents of letting them take their children, to be raised in their orphanage.

The Grand Duchess did not leave Russia even during the terrible years of the revolution, although she was offered the opportunity to do so several times. In April 1918 Elisabeth Feodorovna was arrested and sent to Siberia. There, together with her devoted assistant Sister Barbara, and several other members of the Imperial family, Ella was assassinated during the night of July 17/18. The Romanov prisoners had been living in the local school at Alapaievsk. From there they were

The Grand Duchess Elisabeth Feodorovna's sitting room in the Mary and Martha Convent and House of Good Works. Photograph from 1914.

taken to a mineshaft and thrown into the dark, damp hole. To ensure themselves that the deed was done, the killers, all local Communists, also threw grenades down the mineshaft. Ella, Sister Barbara, three sons of Grand Duke Konstantin Konstantinnovich, and Grand Duke Sergei Mikhailovich, who was shot for protesting the evening's actions, died as martyrs. In 1992 the Archbishops Council of the Russian Orthodox Church beatified Grand Duchess Elisabeth Feodorovna and her assistant, Sister Barbara, as saints.

In Jerusalem, in the Garden of Gethsemane, according to the plans of the Russian architect David Grimm, an Orthodox cathedral was built, dedicated to St. Mary Magdalene. Her sons built the church in memory of Empress Maria Alexandrovna; the consecration took place in 1888. The official representative from Russia was Grand Duke Sergei Alexandrovich, who, at the time, was the Chairman of the Imperial Palestine Society. His wife brought as a gift to the church holy items – the Holy Bible, the chalice, with its necessary coverings.

In the crypt located under the church, the remains of Grand Duchess Elisabeth Feodorovna and her assistant Sister Barbara, found their last resting place. Sister Barbara had refused to leave the side of her abbess, even though this means certain death.

The monument to Grand Duchess Elisabeth Feodorovna, erected on the grounds of the Martha and Mary Convent in 1990. The monument was unveiled by Patriarch Alexei II. It was sculpted by V. Klykov. Photograph by G. Korneva.

Children in the orphanage of Grand Duchess Elisabeth Feodorovna. From the magazine "Stolitsa i Usad'ba," (1916). [The Capital and the State]

The Church of St. Mary Magdalene in Jerusalem, c. late 1880s. Photograph by Bonfis. [IIMK RAN]

Russia and the Grand Duchy of Hesse and by Rhine

A ll four Hessian sisters, when they attained adulthood, were married and had to leave their parental home and settled faraway. In 1884, Victoria became the wife of her cousin Prince Louis of Battenberg and moved to England, where he served in the Royal Navy. They vacationed at his estate, Heiligenberg, near Darmstadt. Ella and Alexandra Feodorovna tied the knot with Russia, while Irene became the wife of her cousin Heinrich of Prussia and moved to Northern Germany. Heinrich, the second son of German Kaiser Friedrich III married Irene in 1888. The sisters would happily visit each other's homes, but the main place of their mutual visits remained Darmstadt, where the ruler was their brother, Grand Duke Ernst Ludwig.

Architect Joseph Maria Olbrich.
(1867-1908).

In 1899–1901, in the park atop a hill, the "Mathildenhöhe," the "House of Ernst Ludwig" was built, according to the plans of Architect Joseph Maria Olbrich, who ten years later critics would call "one of the twelve apostles of contemporary architecture." There was an atelier in the "house" where seven talented artists, sculptors and architects worked in this creative "colony." They were all invited there by the artistic Grand Duke. The house still commands an imposing view; its wide

A panoramic view of the Mathildenhöhe. To the left is the "Wedding Tower," while to the right is the Church of St. Mary Magdalene.
Photographby by Galina Korneva.

Entrance gate to the house of Architect J.M. Olbrich. Photograph by Galina Korneva.

Portal in the front of "Grand Duke Ernst Ludwig's House." Photograph by Galina Korneva, 2008.

staircase leads to a massive portal in the form of the Greek letter "omega." It is flanked by two huge statues representing Adam and Eve, and created by the sculptor Ludwig Habikh. Gold ornaments, made according to the designs of Olbrich, surround the doorway inside the portal; it is complimented by a bronze figure of the goddess of Victory.

In 1901 the first international art exhibit was organized in the Mathildenhöhe colony, which paved the way towards a new direction in art – the Jugendstil. The Grand Duke invited artists from other countries to participate, including Russia – among them the sculptor Paolo Trubetskoy, the artists Alexander Benois, Michael Vrubel, Valentin Serov, from the society known as "Mir Iskusstva" ["The World of Art"]. The exhibition was a great success, and the names of the Darmstadt artist colony became famous all over the world. The colony started to be considered as one of the leading centers for new development in the art style, known in Russia as "Moderne." At the invitation of Grand Duchess Elisabeth Feodorovna Architect Olbrich soon participated in an art exhibition in Moscow.

The "House of Ernst Ludwig" (1899-1901), by Architect J.M. Olbrich. [Deutsche Kunst und Decoration]

Fountain in front of Olbrich's house. Sculptor Ludwig Habikh. [Deutsche Kunst und Decoration]

The gem of the architectural complex at Mathildenhöhe, to this very day, is the Russian Orthodox church of St. Mary Magdalene, with its gold onion domes. It was constructed in 1897 on a plot of land, given as a gift to Nicholas II from Grand Duke Ernst Ludwig. Earth was brought from Russia to Darmstadt and placed under the foundation of the church. Emperor Nicholas II and Empress Alexandra Feodorovna were present at the consecration ceremonies two years later, together with the Grand Duke of Hesse and by Rhine and his wife Victoria Melita. The foundation stone was "covered with gold leaf and had the initials of the Royal Couples etched in the stone." The Russian architect Leon Benois developed the plans for this church in memory of Empress Maria Alexandrovna, a Hessian by birth. For the interior and the design of the façades mosaics were predominantly used. The most noted images were done according to the designs of Victor Vasnetsov and created in the studios of V.A. Frolov, who was famous for his work on the Cathedral of the "Savior-on-the-Blood" in St. Petersburg. V. Vasnetsov also designed the mosaics on the frontons of the steps into the "Savior-on-the-Blood," whose architectural style is very similar to the entrance portals in the church of St. Mary Magdalene. Nicholas II donated 310 thousand rubles of his own money for

Architect L.N. Benois.
(1856-1928)

The fronton of the Church of St. Mary Magdalene,
with the mosaic by V. Vasnetsov.
Photograph by G. Korneva.

The fronton of the "Savior-on-the-Blood" in St. Petersburg.
This mosaic is also by V. Vasnetsov.
Photograph by G. Korneva.

The Greek newlyweds, Prince Andreas and Princess Alice of Greece. Their wedding in 1903 was to occasion of a large royal gathering in Darmstadt.
[Eurohistory Archive]

the construction of the church in Darmstadt. The Duchess of Saxe-Coburg and Gotha donated the one-tiered carved altar screen, made in dark oak, and which previously was located in the private church in Clarence House, her London home. Another German, Timothy Neff, the court artist of Nicholas I, painted nine of the icons, while David Grimm, the Russian architect of German origin, worked out the design for this altar screen. Empress Alexandra Feodorovna embroidered in gold thread the light blue covering of the "analoy" (lectern). One of the main holy items of the cathedral, the icon of Our Lady of Kazan, used to belong to Grand Duchess Elisabeth Feodorovna. The bells were forged in a foundry on the outskirts of St. Petersburg, and marble for the construction of the church was brought from the South of Russia, the Caucasus. On September 26 (October 8), 1899 the court Protopresbyter (main priest) Ioann Ianyshev, in the presence of the Imperial Couple, the Grand Dukes Kirill, Boris and Andrei, and the family of Grand Duke of Hesse and by Rhine, consecrated the new church. At the culmination of the construction Leon Benois received the honorary title of "Architect of the Imperial Court."

In 1903, once again, many relatives traveled to Darmstadt – among them there were representatives of the ruling houses of Russia, Greece, Prussia, Hesse and England, among many others. The happy event

The consecration of the Church of St. Mary Magdalene, September 26, 1899.
Emperor Nicholas II and his wife, along with her brother and his wife, were present.

Guests at the wedding of Prince Andreas of Greece and Princess Alice of Battenberg, New Palace, Darmstadt, October 1903.
Back row, from left: Prince Heinrich and Princess Irene of Prussia, Princess Victoria of Battenberg, Princess Marie of Erbach-Schönberg, Grand Duke Paul Alexandrovich, Queen Alexandra of Great Britain, Queen Olga of Greece, Grand Duchess Maria Pavlovna the Younger, Grand Duchess Vera Konstantinovna, King George I of Greece, Grand Duke Dimitry Pavlovich, Prince Friedrich Karl of Hesse, Prince Christopher of Greece, Grand Duke George Mikhailovich, Grand Duchess Maria Georgievna, Emperor Nicholas II, Crown Prince Constantine of Greece, Princess Victoria of Wales, Crown Princess Sophie of Greece and Princess Margarete of Hesse. Front row, same order: Grand Duke Ernst Ludwig of Hesse and by Rhine, Prince Nicholas of Greece, Grand Duchess Helen Vladimirovna, Prince George of Battenberg, Grand Duchess Tatiana Nikolaevna, Princess Elisabeth of Hesse and by Rhine, Grand Duchess Olga Nikolaevna, Princess Louise of Battenberg, Grand Duchess Anastasia Nikolaevna, Empress Alexandra Feodorovna, Grand Duchess Maria Nikolaevna, Grand Duchess Elisabeth Feodorovna and Prince George of Greece. [ILN]

Darmstadt's Reinstrasse. In the distance one can see Louisenplatz, with a 33 meter high column in honor of Grand Duke Ludwig I c. 1894. [ILN]

was the wedding ceremonies for Prince Andreas of Greece and Princess Alice of Battenberg, the eldest niece of Ella and Alexandra Feodorovna. The wedding ceremony took place on October 8th inside the Russian church at Mathildenhöhe. This alliance once again intertwined the Hessians and the Romanovs since the bride's parents belonged to this family, while the groom's mother was none other than the former Grand Duchess Olga Konstantinovna.

During the autumn of the same year little Princess Elisabeth died unexpectedly while visiting her Russian cousins at Skierniewice, their Polish hunting lodge. The only surviving child of Grand Duke Ernst Ludwig and Victoria Melita, who divorced in 1901, Elisabeth was the last binding tie shared by this disparate couple. Although her death was a great loss to both parents, it also meant that they were now finally free to rebuild their lives.

In February 1905 Ernst Ludwig married a second time, his bride being Princess Elenore of Solms-Hohensolms-Lich. In honor of this event architect Olbrich erected a 48-meter column on the hill at Mathildenhöhe, called the "Wedding Tower," and destined to become the dominant site of this architectural ensemble. This elevated brick building was topped with five feather-like extensions; its construction was completed in 1908. The unusual stepped semicircle fronton turns the thin tower into a building-sculpture, and, according to the intention of Ernst Ludwig, was supposed to resemble a five-fingered hand, extended towards the heavens. The tower, seven floors high, contained several rooms for the Grand Duke's enjoyment, among them a large hall, several rooms for relaxation for the Ernst Ludwig and his wife, and, on the very top, an observation platform. A beautiful view opened out on the capital city of the Grand Duchy, and the villas situated on the neighboring hillsides, most of which had been built by architects invited to Darmstadt by Ernst Ludwig.

The opening of the first international exhibition at the Mathildenhöhe, Darmstadt, 1901. [Deutsche Kunst und Decoration]

A vase and silver candlesticks designed by H. Christiansen. [Deutsche Kunst und Decoration]

Even before the opening of the first international exhibit, which took place in Mathildenhöhe in 1901, Ernst Ludwig had built eight villas next to his home, most of them according to the plans of Joseph Olbrich. They were supposed to be part of the exhibit called "Ein Dokument Deutscher Kunst" ["a Visual Representation of German Art"]; they demonstrated the unity of architecture, sculpture, interior design and landscaping. In the planning of the villas everything was examined to the minutest detail, starting with the overall plan of the building, to the design of the windows and doorways, to the banisters, the iron gates, pieces of furniture, china.

Among the new buildings were the private houses of the architects J.M. Olbrich and P. Behrens, the sculptor Ludwig Habikh, the artist Hans Christiansen, the furniture maker Julius Glückert, and also the building where the furniture produced at his factory was displayed. One cannot find a similar town in the "moderne" style anywhere in Europe.

The house of artists Hans Christiansen, a J.M. Olbrich creation.
[Deutsche Kunt und Decoration]

The dining room inside Hans Christiansen's house.
[Deutsche Kunst und Decoration]

The house of P. Behrens at the Mathildenhöhe. Behrens was the architect desponsible for its creation. [Deutsche Kunst und Decoration]

Behrens' atelier inside his house.
[Deutsche Kunst und Decoration]

Grand Duke Ernst Ludwig and his daughter Princess Elisabeth. [Eurohistory Royal Photo Collection]

The next exhibit in Darmstadt, prepared by the "colonists" of Mathildenhöhe, took place in 1904, and this time the artists wanted to show sample buildings, pieces of furniture and household items which could be purchased by members of the middle class. Similar exhibits took place right up to the beginning of the First World War, after which the group of architects and artists of Mathildenhöhe ceased its activities.

The Hessin siblings gather just before the war. From the left: Princess Irene of Prussia, Grand Duke Ernst Ludwig, Grand Duchess Elisabeth Feodorovna, Princess Victoria of Battenberg and Empress Alexandra Feodorovna. [Eurohistory Archive]

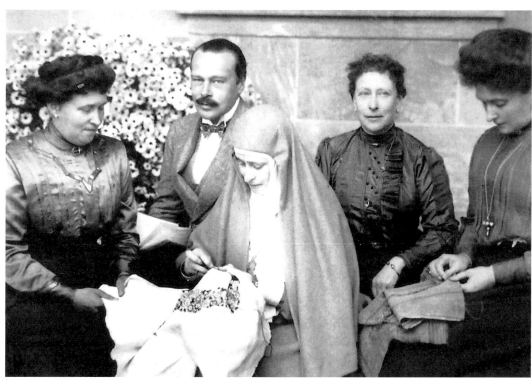

Grand Duke Ernst Ludwig and Grand Duchess Elenore with their sons, Hereditary Grand Duke Georg Donatus and Prince Ludwig, Wolfsgarten c. 1913.
[Eurohistory Archive]

Today a museum is located in the former house of Grand Duke Ernst Ludwig; its collections tell the story of the history of this artists' colony, as well as the achievements of its members, all deeply influential in the "moderne" style.

Peter Behrens, who started working as an architect in 1899 at the Mathildenhöhe, is remembered as one of the founders of contemporary industrial architecture and design. From 1907 Behrens started to work as a consultant for the firm of Allgemeine Elektrische Gesellshaft (AEG – the "General Electric Company"). For the first time in history everything in a building was designed in one style, not only the production facilities and offices, but also the furniture, the catalogues, the exhibition stands, the advertising on the streets of the town, the overall image of the firm's production and its packaging. Due to his work at AEG Peter Behrens was able to create his own artistic signature, easily recognized in the consequent work of this Master. He is considered the pioneer of industrial design.

In Behrens' workshop, future world-renowned architects began their professional careers – among them: Le Corbusier, Gropius and Mies van der Rohe.

Architect Peter Behrens.
(1868-1940)

The dining room in Behrens' house, with the white-lacquered furniture he designed.
[Deutsche Kunst und Decoration]

In 1911 Peter Behrens received the prestigious order to design the new building of the German Embassy in the Russian capital. It was to be erected on one of the central squares of St. Petersburg – St. Isaac's Square. The architect was able to create a mighty building, which complemented the architectural ensemble of the square.

The neo-classical interiors of the Embassy – the vestibule, the grand staircase, and the halls, were decorated with delicacy and grandeur. In the grand enfilade on the second floor, movable doors divided the halls, and, if necessary, the halls could easily be transformed into one large room. The Throne Room, all in marble, could become part of the Prussian Hall, which opened out on St. Isaac's Square. Unfortunately, in 1914, when the First World War began, this building became the target of angry crowds and vandals. The sculpture grouping on the roof of the German Embassy, for example, was torn down and demolished. The war disrupted the ties shared by both countries and their ruling dynasties. Their shared history was forgotten as diplomatic relations between Russia and Germany ceased to exist for years to come.

The German Embassy,
St. Petersburg c. 1913.

Russia and Germany During the Reigns of
Emperor Nicholas II and Kaiser Wilhelm II

*I*n August 1898 the thirty-year-old Emperor Nicholas II approached the governments of different nations with a proposal concerning disarmament. At that time, the Russian Ministry of International Affairs sent out an appeal to representatives of all nations accredited in St. Petersburg. It included an invitation to call an international conference to discuss the threat to peace caused by the arms race then raging among European powers. The leading nations of Europe supported this idea, and consequently a peace conference at The Hague was opened on the day of the Emperor's birthday, May 6 (18), 1899 – 109 delegates from 26 nations of the world participated.

The Conference at The Hague was a tremendous achievement for Russian diplomacy and an important milestone in international law, although many of the questions that were raised at the meeting were never really settled. There were several documents signed at this forum that would later become the basis for future international conventions on human rights.

Members of the Russian delegation at the Hague Conference. In the center of the first row is Actual Privy Counselor de Stahl, head of the delegation. Photograph by B. Matushevsky. [TsGAKFFD SPb]

*Bosch House at the Hague. From the "Strand Magazine."
Photograph by Gunn & Stuart, 1899.*

In 1911 the 15th anniversary of the coronation of Emperor Nicholas II was celebrated. The famous jeweler Carl Fabergé, while working on the design for his traditional Easter egg gift, decided to adorn it with nine miniatures, showing the main events during the reign of Nicholas II. One of them is called the "Palace of Peace at the Hague" (Bosch's house), where the conference had taken place in 1899.

During the reign of Nicholas II a contemporary, as well as a close relative, occupied the German Imperial throne, Kaiser Wilhelm II. The cousin of both Empress Alexandra Feodorovna and her husband, Wilhelm II (1859–1941) was the eldest son of Kaiser Friedrich III and Empress Victoria, eldest daughter of Queen Victoria. Wilhelm II came to the throne in 1888; that year was called "the year of three Kaisers." During that relatively short period of time, after Kaiser Wilhelm I passed away in March, first his son came to rule, and after ninety-nine days,

The "Fifteen Anniversary" egg by Fabergé was created to commemorate the 1896 coronation of Nicholas II. [Archive of V. Skurlov]

The Reings of Nicholas II and Wilhelm II

"Emperor Nicholas II had more meetings with Wilhelm II than with anyone else. The Kaiser was an extremely nervous person, sometimes he even appeared on the verge of hysterics – he had the ability of making everyone lose his wits, anyone that he came in contact with ... The Emperor was always worried after his meetings with her German cousin ... As far as the Empress is concerned ... she always had a headache, whenever she was to have lunch or breakfast with Wilhelm II ... During personal contacts she was always at the edge of correctness: she followed the rules of etiquete, and that was all ..."

A.A. Mosolov, "At the Court of the Last Emperor." An excerpt from the section titled "Meetings with Foreign Monarchs."

Kaiser Wilhelm II at the Rosenau on the day of the engagement of Tsarevich Nicholas Alexandrovich and Princess Alix of Hesse and by Rhine, April 20, 1894. Photograph by J. Russell the Younger. [ILN]

Friedrich III was succeeded by his son Wilhelm II: father, son and grandson all reigned in 1888. Baron Ludwig Knorring, the Secretary of the Russian Embassy in Berlin, later characterized the attitude of Kaiser Wilhelm II towards Russia in the following manner: "When ... Crown Prince Wilhelm of Prussia was kneeling in front of the death bed of his grandfather, the last words of this great Emperor to him were to continue to support the best possible relations with Russia. And Emperor Wilhelm proceeded to fulfill this promise, given as the Heir to the Throne to his dying grandfather." However, when it came to matters diplomatic, the impetuous Wilhelm II was an utter failure.

Soon after he ascended the throne Wilhelm II traveled to St. Petersburg to visit Emperor Alexander III. The next year a meeting of the heads of state took place in Berlin. The German Kaiser and the Russian Emperor would visit each other and often participate in the review of troops. When the Tsarevich Nicholas Alexandrovich came of age, Wilhelm II was among the honored guests at the Winter Palace, and later, after Nicholas II came to rule, he would continue to visit Russia, much to the annoyance of many of his Romanov cousins.

In 1881, Wilhelm married Princess Augusta Victoria of Schleswig-Holstein-Sonderburg-Augustenburg (1858–1921). She was a granddaughter of Princess Feodora of Leiningen, the half-sister of Queen Victoria, Wilhelm's English grandmother. Starting in 1882, and over the following decade, the couple had six sons and one daughter. However, the Hohenzollern children practically had no contact with the children of the Russian Emperor Nicholas II. While the Kaiser's eccentric and unstable character may have had a role in this, the truth is that the children of Emperor Nicholas II were much younger than the children of Kaiser Wilhelm II. Relations between both couples were always distant and cold, this being

Kaiser Wilhelm II and his wife, Empress Augusta Victoria, in 1907. [ILN]

the result of Alexandra Feodorovna's dislike of her Prussian cousin.

Notwithstanding the fact that the personal relations of the families of Nicholas II and Wilhelm II were not that warm, Germany and Russia continued developing numerous common projects in the areas of science, industry and culture. But probably most impressive was the influence of German doctors and medical specialists on the Russian health system.

For the longest time the words "German" and "doctor and pharmacist" were practically synonymous in Russia. Among the private physicians of Russian tsars were such men as Laurence Blumentrost, who tended to Tsar Alexei I, son of Michael I, while his son was the physician to Peter I; Nicholas Arendt was the physician-in-ordinary to Emperor Nicholas I; life-obstetrician Dimitry Ott and others were also greatly respected by the Imperial family. At the end of the 19th century, as a result of the initiatives of various Germans and the support of Imperial family, Russia became a leader in the field of medicine.

Among the brilliant organizers of new scientific thought was Dimitry Oskarovich Ott (1855–1929). To this day his

The Empress Friedrich, surrounded by her family, at home in Schloß Friedrichshof in 1898.
In back, from left to right: Prince Friedrich Karl and Princess Margarete of Hesse, Crown Prince Constantine of Greece, Prince Maximilian of Baden, Crown Princess Sophie of Greece, Princess Victoria and Prince Adolph of Schaumburg-Lippe. At front, same order: Princes Maximilian and Friedrich Wilhelm of Hesse, Princes George and Alexander of Greece, the Empress Friedrich and Princess Helen of Greece. [TsGAKFFD SPb]

The new building of the Clinical Birthing and Gynecological Institute (Mendeleev Line No. 3). At present time it serves as the Research Institute of Birthing and Gynecology and is named after Professor D.O. Ott. (1959) Photograph by N. Naumenko.
[TsGAKFFD SPb]

A group of medical personnel at the Clinical Birthing and Gynecological Institute. At center (in the second row, seventh from the left) is Professor D.O. Ott. St. Petersburg – Photograph by K. Bulla.
[TsGAKFFD SPb]

name is tied to the first, not only in Russia, but also in the whole world, obstetric and teaching institution. The new building on Vasilievsky Island in St. Petersburg, where the Imperial Clinical Birthing and Gynecological Institute was moved, was one of the leading institutions of its kind at that time. According to the architect Leon Benois, who developed the design of the building with Professor Ott, its "equipment and furnishings were brought to the ultimate point of comfort, almost to a point of luxury: everything was extremely simple, but it could be compared to the best hotels in the West. And as far as medical and surgical equipment were concerned – everything was ordered from the best

The Oldenburg Palace in St. Petersburg, Dvortsovaya Naberezhnaya (Palace Embankment) No. 2. [TsGAKFFD SPb]

foreign firms." An organ was installed in the main auditorium, so that, as Doctor Ott would say, "a person in need of solace could find relief, his somber thoughts would be blown away, and his soul would be uplifted."

Among members of the Romanov Dynasty, the Russian branch of the Dukes of Oldenburg became known for their support of the establishment of medical institutions, for their work in the area of education, and also for their charitable work. They were beholden to Russia, to whom they were "tied by their very soul."

Duke Peter of Oldenburg (1812–1881) – the grandson of Emperor Paul I, received his education in Württemberg, where he lived with his mother, Queen Catherine, who, after the death of her husband, was married a second time to King Wilhelm I of Württemberg. In 1830 Peter entered military service in Russia, and was signed into the Preobrazhensky Guard regiment. His uncle, Emperor Nicholas I gave as a gift to the Peter, a large palace in the capital. It was located on the Dvortsovaya Naberezhnaya, next to the Summer Garden. However, in four years time the young Lieutenant General left the military and would continue his career in the areas of education and community service. The Imperial School of Law, founded by him in St. Petersburg in 1835, became the first school in Russia where young lawyers and jurists were trained. Duke Peter of Oldenburg spent almost a million rubles for the establishment of this school.

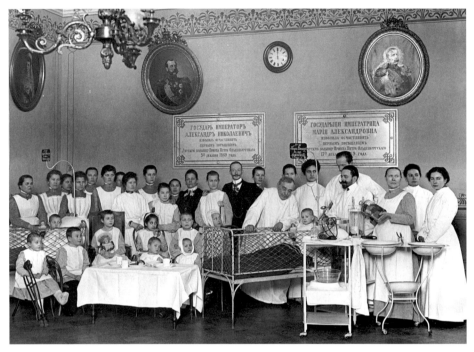

Karl Rauhfus (standing at the bedisde of a child) in the Children's Hospital of Duke Peter of Oldenburg. Photograph by K. Bulla. [TsGAKFFD SPb]

During a half century of service to Russia, Duke Peter of Oldenburg also founded the Women's Institute named for Princess Theresa of Oldenburg, in honor of his wife, the former Princess Theresa of Nassau. He also founded the Orphanage of His Highness Prince P.G. Oldenburg, the Children's Hospital, the Obukhov, Mariinsky and Petropavlovsky hospitals. For seventeen years, he headed the Executive Office for the Institutions of Empress Maria, created by his grandmother Empress Maria Feodorovna, Emperor Paul's consort. Duke Peter's commendable career came to a sudden end in 1881, when pneumonia took his life.

In recognition of his charitable work, in 1889 a monument placed in front of the Mariinsky Hospital paid respect to Duke Peter's life. The monument was to serve as evidence "to future generations that the contemporaries of the Duke were able to understand and to value his unrelenting and bountiful service to good works and education." The sculptor I.N. Schröder represented the late Duke Peter as a tall figure in a General's parade uniform of the

Children from the Orphanage of Duke Peter of Oldenburg and sisters of mercy surround the monument to Duke Peter outside the Mariinsky Hospital. The photograph was taken on the centennial anniversary of his birth. Photograph by K. Bulla. [TsGAKFFD SPb]

Preobrazhensky regiment; at the base of the monument bas-reliefs told the story of his many good deeds. However, in 1929, the next generation thought otherwise. At the command of the Narcompros (the Peoples Commissars of Education), the monument was removed and melted down. The destruction of the monument was motivated by the following false accusation, "Prince Oldenburg was famous, but not rich, and having chosen a "profession" of establishing charitable institutions, he successfully pilfered from them." At about this time, the family crypt of the Oldenburgs was also destroyed. The Militia Academy, which was located on the territory of the former Troitsa-Sergius ["Trinity and St. Sergius"] Monastery, turned the pantheon of these famous Russians into a parade ground.

Duke Alexander Petrovich of Oldenburg. (1844-1932) [TsGAKFFD SPb]

However after decades of being forgotten, the Oldenburg name is once again taking its rightful place in Russian history.

Alexander – the second son of Peter and Theresa of Oldenburg, was born in 1844 in St. Petersburg and was entered into the Preobrazhensky regiment from birth. In 1869 the Imperial family and its various branches, gathered to celebrate the wedding of Alexander Petrovich and Eugenia Maximilianovna, daughter of Grand Duchess Maria Nikolaevna and Duke Maximilian of Leuchtenberg. After the wedding ceremonies in the Winter Palace, the newlyweds settled in the Oldenburg palace next to the Field of Mars. Duke Alexander Petrovich fought in the Russo-Turkish War of 1877–1878. General N.A. Epanchin remembered his service, "throughout the entire campaign he comported himself in a truly Spartan manner; he did not have a carriage, he always rode horseback, he did not have a private cook and other comforts of home

Attendants at the International Convention of Physicians, concerned with experimental medicine, in the garden of the Institute. Duchess Eugenia of Oldenburg is in the light suit – St. Petersburg, 1912. [TsGAKFFD SPb]

The Chemical Building complex of the Institute of Experimental Medicine. Leningrad c. 1932.[TsGAKFFD SPb]

Duke Alexander Petrovich and Duchess Eugenia Maximilianovna of Oldenburg c. 1869. [Eurohistory Archive]

Duchess Eugenia Maximilianovna and her son Duke Peter Alexandrovich of Oldenburg. [Eurohistory Archive]

... The Prince [sic] was of noble character, not capable of any intrigues ..." However, his contemporaries found him to be on the verge of madness and rather eccentric.

Following in his father's footsteps, Alexander Petrovich was very active in charitable programs. At his initiative, and as a result of his funding and energy, the Imperial Institute of Experimental Medicine in St. Petersburg became a reality. During the First World War Alexander Petrovich was in charge of sanitation and evacuation of army personnel, and he was also the Head of the Russian Red Cross. The surgeon S.R. Mirotvortsev described the inspection trips of Alexander Petrovich in the following manner, "As soon as it was heard that Prince Oldenburg was coming, preparations would immediately begin in all of the hospitals: they would clean the courtyards, the basements and sheds, they whitewashed the wards, painted the beds, and all of this because of the forthcoming inspection of the hospital .... I would accompany him during such visits, and I must say, that he was thoroughly unforgiving whenever any sanitary-hygienic norm was not followed in the hospital, he would become a raging storm." In 1916 Alexander Petrovich was awarded a unified portrait of three Emperors – Alexander II, Alexander III and Nicholas II, with a diamond-studded frame.

When the Bolsheviks came to power in Russia, Alexander Petrovich, together with his paralyzed wife, fled to Finland, where in 1915 he had purchased a summer home called Rantalinna in Imatra. He was able to take with him two Rolls Royce automobiles, a boat and many valuables. The Oldenburg family lived in Finland until 1922, when they left to settle in France. Today, a hotel is located in the former Oldenburg summer home; many pieces of furniture and wedding gifts, given to Eugenia Maximilianovna and Alexander Petrovich by the Shah of Persia and the King of Egypt, are lovingly displayed there. Alexander Petrovich died in France in Biarritz in 1932. He survived both his wife and their only son, Peter Alexandrovich.

One can only hope that the great name of Alexander Oldenburg will once again take its lawful and respected place in Russian history.

The Grand Duchy of Mecklenburg-Schwerin

Grand Duchess Anastasia Mikhailovna (1860-1922). [RGAKFD]

At the beginning of the 1890s the rulers of three sovereign German realms enjoyed very close familial ties to the Romanovs – Saxe-Coburg and Gotha, where Maria Alexandrovna was married to Duke Alfred; the Grand Duchy of Hesse and by Rhine ruled by the brother of the future Empress Alexandra Feodorovna; and the Grand Duchy of Mecklenburg-Schwerin, ruled by the husband of Anastasia Mikhailovna, Friedrich Franz III, who was also the brother of Grand Duchess Maria Pavlovna. Other lesser-known German connections were provided by the wife of Konstantin Konstantinovich, Elisabeth Mavrikievna, who was born a Princess of Saxe-Altenburg, as was her mother-in-law, Alexandra Iosifovna. Whilst the wife of Grand Duke Nicholas Nikolaevich was born a Duchess of Oldenburg.

The Mecklenburgs (Schwerin and Strelitz) were the only Western European dynasty of Slavic origin. Their ties with the House of Romanov started in the beginning of the XVIII century, when Karl Leopold of Mecklenburg (1678–1747) married the niece of Peter I, Tsarevna Catherine Ioannovna (1692–1733). The second time the ruling family of Mecklenburg became related to Russian rulers was in 1799 when the 15-year-old daughter of Emperor Paul I, Helen (1784–1803) married the Hereditary Prince Friedrich Ludwig of Mecklenburg-Schwerin (1778–1819). However, since Helen Pavlovna died still rather young in 1803, her offspring did not have strong ties to Russia. She died at Schloß Ludwigslust, a beautiful country palace that had belonged to her husband's family for generations. Helen Pavlovna is buried in a mausoleum in the grounds where her remains rest for eternity.

The region of Mecklenburg was located in Northern Germany, along the Baltic Sea, and was comprised of two grand duchies – Mecklenburg-Schwerin and Mecklenburg-Strelitz. The combined territory of the two Grand Duchies was sixteen thousand square kilometers; Mecklenburg-Schwerin comprised thriteen thousand square kilometers and two fifiths of this land was the private property of the Grand Duke. The population at that time was around five hundred thousand, with the predominant number of inhabitants belonging to the Lutheran faith.

*Grand Duchess Anastasia Mikhailovna and her fiancé Hereditary Grand Duke Friedrich Franz
of Mecklenburg-Schwerin. Photograph by Yatergulielmi (Palermo).* [RGAKFD]

The Grand Duchy of Mecklenburg-Schwerin

"The elderly Princess of Prussia, Alexandrine, sister of Wilhelm I and Grand Duchess of Mecklenburg-Schwerin, whom we called Grandmother, lived in a small castle in Schwerin. She was always very kind to us and spoke a meticulous French of the XVIII century. Grandmother was the daughter of King Friedrich Wilhelm III of Prussia and his famous beautiful wife, Queen Louise, Princess of Mecklenburg-Strelitz. Friedrich Wilhelm and Queen Louise had several other children, among them: Emperor Wilhelm I and Empress Alexandra Feodorovna, wife of Nicholas I. Once grandmother gave a grand dinner in our honor, and, even though she was well into her eighties and was paralyzed, she was rolled into the dining room in a wheel chair, so as to participate in the event personally. We were still rather young at the time, but Grandmother was dressed in full evening attire, with jewelry, and she wore the familial Order of the Romanovs; she also had her traditional fan in her hands. She was the ultimate example of self-discipline and finesse, so characteristic of the previous century."

Grand Duke Kirill Vladimirovich, "My Life in Russia's Service.

Dowager Grand Duchess Alexandrine of Mecklenburg-Schwerin. [RGAKFD

In the second half of the XIX century, members of the Mecklenburg-Schwerin Dynasty twice became related by marriage to members of the Russian Imperial Family. The third son of Emperor Alexander II, Grand Duke Vladimir Alexandrovich, on August 16 (28), 1874 married Marie (1854-1920), the only daughter of Grand Duke of Friedrich Franz II Mecklenburg-Schwerin and his first wife, the former Princess Augusta Reuß. Upon marrying Vladimir she took the Russian name Maria Pavlovna. As a result of visits with his sister in St. Petersburg, Hereditary Grand Duke Friedrich Franz, established a new dynastic tie with the House of Romanov when he met and proposed marriage to Grand Duchess Anastasia Mikhailovna in 1878. Their wedding took place in St. Petersburg in January 1879. The young couple soon moved to Schwerin, where they settled in the Marienpalais, a smaller palace in the grand ducal capital.

The Marienpalais, Schwerin. Photograph by M. Shott, 1998.

The Mikhailovich – The Family of Grand Duchess Anastasia Mikhailovna

Grand Duchess Olga Feodorovna.
(1839-1891)
[Eurohistory Archive]

"Being a part of the Baden family, having married at a rather young age to a Russian Grand Duke, when they settled in Tiflis [present day Tbilisi, Georgia], *she reigned there for 18 years; she had found in her husband an obedient fulfiller of all her desires ... she was of an extremely sharp, natural mind, but with a lack of any substantial education ... Olga Feodorovna very soon became the recipient of overall disdain. She would do no harm to anyone, but, being very self willed, she would quickly judge and remark, and in this way, very naturally, created many enemies among those people for whom their own egotistical wishes would stand above anything else."*

Diary of State Secretary A. Polovtsov.

Grand Duke Michael Nikolaevich.
(1832-1909)
[Eurohistory Archive]

The Ballroom in the New Mikhailovsky palace. Photograph by K. Bulla.
[TsGAKFFD SPb]

The Mikhailovich – The Family of Grand Duchess Anastasia Mikhailovna

The wedding of Grand Duke Michael Nikolaevich with Princess Cäcilie Auguste of Baden took place in St. Petersburg in 1857. When she converted to Orthodoxy, the bride received the name of Olga Feodorovna. After the birth of her first son, Nicholas, her daughter Anastasia, and her second son, Michael, the family moved to the Caucasus, where the Grand Duke was assigned as Governor General in 1862. This was the first time that a member of the Imperial Family was given this position. Surrounding himself with people knowledgeable with local traditions and customs, he, according to Sergei Witte, managed very well in this very difficult position. Governing the Caucasus was no easy task. In two years' time he was able to send the following telegram to his brother Emperor Alexander II: "I have the honor to congratulate Your Highness with the end of the Caucasus War ..." In the Caucasus Michael Nikolaevich promoted the same reforms that were being passed in Russia: the liberation of the serfs, reforms in the military and in the judiciary system. In Tiflis, the family settled in the palace of the Governor General, built in the 1830s. While living in Georgia, the couple was blessed with four more sons, one after the other. Having been raised in relative freedom, as compared to other royal children their age, the Mikhailovich truly loved the Caucasus and hoped that they would be able to stay there forever.

In 1869 Grand Duke Michael Nikolaevich announced the creation of the "Special Executive Offices of the Mineral Springs in the Tiflis Region" and turned his attention to the springs at Borzhomi. A park was created around the springs, while bathhouses were erected. The Emperor visited his brother in the Caucasus in 1871, and as a sign of gratitude for the wonderful time spent there, and the successful activities carried out by Michael Nikolaevich, he granted the Grand Duke lifetime mayoral rights to Borzhomi. The spa continued to

Grand Duchess Anastasia Mikhailovna and her brother
Grand Duke Alexander Mikhailovich. [RGAKFD]

"Our sister, Anastasia Mikhailovna, had a very special position in our family. We all loved this tall, dark haired young lady; she was the favorite of our father. Whenever we would speak to her, we imaged ourselves her faithful knights, ready to fulfil any wish the lady of hearts would desire ... We were passionately jealous of each other, and our hearts ached when the Grand Duke of Mecklenburg-Schwerin arrived, to become acquainted with his future bride ... His appearance threatened to make us lose the object of our deepest affection, the one person to whom we outpoured our innermost souls."

Grand Duke Alexander Mikhailovich, "Memoirs."

thrive, and in the picturesque mountain valley along the Kura River new parks sprang up, together with new palaces, health centers, electrical stations, and even a factory for bottling "Borzhomi" mineral water. For a hundred years the Olga Bridge, named in honor of Grand Duchess Olga Feodorovna, spanned the Kura River.

The Palace of Grand Duke Michael Nikolaevich in Borzhomi. [IIMK RAN]

After the assassination of Emperor Alexander II on the Ekaterininsky Canal, Grand Duke Michael Nikolaevich was called to St. Petersburg and named Chairman of the State Council. From that time on his entire family lived in a gigantic palace on the Dvortsovaya Naberezhnaya, in a luxurious palace, built by an architect of German origin, Andreas (Andrei Ivanovich) Stackenschneider.

The six sons of Grand Duke Michael Nikolaevich were home schooled, and all were prepared for a career in the military. Sergei followed in his father's footsteps and became, in the words of Minister of the Armed Forces A.F. Rödiger, "an outstanding army artillery man," knowing to the minutest detail the workings of field artillery. Alexei lived for only nineteen years. He could not recover from a bout with pneumonia, just as he was completing his studies at sea and died while recovering in Italy. In 1909 George was promoted to Lieutenant General; however, being an artist at heart, he also worked very hard as the Director of the Russian Museum, named for Emperor Alexander III, in St. Petersburg. The eldest son, Nicholas, also had the rank of General, but was world famous as a historian. Their second son, Michael, gave Michael Nikolaevich and Olga Feodorovna the most worries. He was a brilliant officer, loved by all in St. Petersburg high society, and a great admirer of the fairer sex; in 1891, with-

The Palace of the Governor General of the Caucasus, Grand Duke Michael Nikolaevich, in Tiflis. From the magazine Vsemirnaya Illustratsiya, 1894.

The Mikhailovich – The Family of Grand Duchess Anastasia Mikhailovna

"Up until the age of fifteen my upbringing could be compared to military service in a regiment. My brothers Nicholas, Michael, Sergei, George and I lived as if in barracks. We slept on thin metal beds with the skimpiest of mattresses, placed on wooden boards ... We would be awakened at 6:00 AM, we had to jump out of bed immediately ... say our prayers, standing on our knees in front of the icons, then we would take a cold bath. Our breakfast consisted of tea, bread and butter. Everything else was strictly forbidden, so that we would not become accustomed to luxury."

Grand Duke Alexander Mikhailovich, "Memoirs."

Grand Duke Michael Nikolaevich and Grand Duchess Olga Feodorovna surrounded by their sons.
Standing, from the left: George Mikhailovich (1863-1919), Sergei Mikhailovich (1869-1918), Alexander Mikhailovich (1866-1933). Seated, same order: Alexei Mikhailovich (1875-1895) and Nicholas Mikhailovich (1859-1919). Three of them were to fall victims to the Bolshevik terror. [RGAKFD]

out his parent's approval, and, worse yet, without the permission of the Emperor, he married the granddaughter of Alexander Pushkin, Countess Sophie von Mehrenberg. Michael Mikhailovich was forced to leave Russia and spent most of his life in England and France. The only son of the Grand Ducal couple, who not only had a successful career, but also was the father of many children, was Alexander.

Throughout the entire history of the House of Romanov, the only Romanov to marry a Grand Duchess instead of a foreign princess was Alexander Mikhailovich. He married Xenia Alexandrovna, the eldest daughter of Emperor Alexander III. Their wedding took place in July 1894, in the Church of Apostles Peter and Paul in the Large Peterhof Palace. The next year Xenia gave birth to a daughter, Irina, who married Prince Felix Yousoupov, and after her Xenia, just like her in-laws, had six sons.

Alexander and Xenia lived in St. Petersburg in a palace on the Embankment of the River Moika, No. 106. During the middle of the 1850s the owner of a one-story stone townhouse on this property was Her Serene Highness Princess Maria Vasilievna Vorontsova, née Trubetskaya. In order to remodel her newly acquired building she invited an architect well known to the Imperial Court, Ippolit Monighetti; according to his plans, the townhouse acquired a second floor, a new entrance with a grand staircase appeared facing the embankment and, in front of the main façade – a stone terrace with a balustrade. Before the wedding of Grand Duchess

Tsarevich Nicholas Alexandrovich and his sister Grand Duchess Xenia Alexandrovna, Gatchina Palace.
[RGAKFD]

Grand Duchess Xenia Alexandrovna.
(1875-1960)

Xenia, the townhouse was purchased for one million rubles, and another 500 thousand was soon spent on remodeling the interior. N.V. Sultanov and N.I. Roshefor did this; they created grand reception rooms, as well as private apartments, styled with the greatest of taste and rich decoration. In 1897– 1899, Nicholas Sultanov planned the creation of a private chapel, in pure Russian style; it was dedicated to Blessed Xenia and St. Alexander Nevsky. When Emperor Nicholas II ascended the throne, he issued an edict, according to which the palace was granted to his sister, Grand Duchess Xenia Alexandrovna, "as a gift, for eternal and hereditary ownership ... with all other property contained therein."

In this palace Grand Duke Alexander Mikhailovich acquired a unique library collection, primarily of books about the navy. Before the October revolution the collection contained over twenty thousand volumes. The Grand Duke's interest in the navy was not by chance. In 1902, having the rank of Rear-Admiral, the Grand Duke was head of the Chief Executive Offices of the Commercial Fleet, created at his own initiative. He had a wide knowledge of naval military matters, and some of his projects were ahead of their time. Alexander Mikhailovich is by right called the founder of Russian military aviation.

Grand Duke Alexander Mikhailovich.
This photograph was taken while he visited the USA in 1893.

158

The Mikhailovich – The Family of Grand Duchess Anastasia Mikhailovna

The Palace of Grand Duchess Xenia Alexandrovna on St. Petersburg's Moika Embankment, No. 106. The initial structure was built by Monighetti in the 1850s. The palace was later remodeled in the 1890s by architects N.V. Sultanov and N.I. de Roshefor.

A view of the interior of the palace church inside the reisdence of Grand Duchess Xenia Alexandrovna. It was consecrated in 1908. [TsGAKFFD SPb]

Alexander Mikhailovich's large family would spend the summer months on the southern Crimean coast at Ai-Todor, an estate belonging to the Grand Duke. A new, Smaller Palace, planned out in the "moderne" style by architect Nicholas Krasnov, was built specifically for the seven children.

After the abdication of Emperor Nicholas II and his brother Michael, the family of Grand Duke Alexander Mikhailovich, along with his mother-in-law, the Dowager Empress Maria Feodorovna, was placed under house arrest in Ai-Todor, Crimea. It was from here in 1919 that Maria Feodorovna and her daughter Xenia Alexandrovna (accompanied by most of her sons),

A balalaika orchestra performing in the Palace of Grand Duchess Xenia Alexandrovna. Both Xenia and her husband, Alexander Mikhailovich, were talented balalaika players and can be seen in this image. [RGAKFD]

departed Russia never to return. Alexander Mikhailovich had left several months before had traveled to Paris to be present at the Versailles peace conference.

At the present time descendants of Grand Duke Alexander Mikhailovich and Xenia Alexandrovna live in many nations of the world.

From the left: Princess Marie of Greece, Grand Duchess Xenia Alexandrovna and Grand Duke Alexander Mikhailovich.
[Eurohistory Archive]

The children of Grand Duke Alexander Mikhailovich and Grand Duchess Xenia Alexandrovna.
From the left: Prince Nikita Alexandrovich (1900-1974), Prince Dimitry Alexandrovich (1901-1980), Princess Irina Alexandrovna (1895-1970), Prince Rostislav Alexandrovich (1902-1978), Prince Feodor Alexandrovich (1898-1968), Prince Andrei Alexandrovich (1897-1981) and Prince Vasili Alexandrovich (1907-1989).
[Eurohistory Archive]

The Mecklenburg-Schwerin Relatives of
Grand Duchess Anastasia Mikhailovna

After he ascended the throne in 1883, Friedrich Franz III, his wife Grand Duchess Anastasia Mikhailovna and their family moved into the ancestral castle of the Grand Dukes of Mecklenburg-Schwerin.

On a picturesque island on the large Schwerin Lake a fairy tale castle appears, with its numerous towers and turrets, and golden domes; its history started over one thousand years ago. It was built on the spot of an ancient Slavic military post. In 1160 Prince Niklot, the first Duke in the House of Mecklenburg, besieged the fortress on the island. In the XIV-XVII centuries a larger castle was built here, and it became the official residence of the House of Mecklenburg-Schwerin.

Monument to Grand Duke Friedrich Franz II sculpted by L. Brunov. Photograph by T. Cheboksarova, 1998.

The Castle in Schwerin. It was remodeled in 1844-1857 by Architect G.A. Demmler. From the magazine "Vsemirnaya Illustratsiya," 1874.

In the middle of the XIX century, Grand Duke Friedrich Franz II decided to completely remodel the ancient castle, which, by this time, had come to ruin. To do so, he asked the Court architect Georg Adolph Demmler, student of K.F. Schinkel, to develop the design, taking as a model the château of Chambord on the Loire. Although the construction was very well planned, it still took more than ten years to complete the grandiose job. Grand halls, decorated in the style of the times, are, for the most part, still intact today, and can be viewed as a museum exhibition. The family of the Grand Dukes had a rich collection of works of art and furniture. Their collection of Dutch masters is considered third in the world. Very valuable, also, is the collection of porcelain and china; among the pieces one can find gifts that were given by the Romanov family – work of the Imperial Porcelain Factory.

In 1893 a bronze equestrian statue of Friedrich Franz II was erected in the park near the ancestral castle of Schwerin. The Grand Duke is in the parade uniform of a Field Marshal, with all regalia, including the cross he received from Kaiser Wilhelm I for commanding Mecklenburg troops in the Franco-Prussian War of 1870–1871. Sculptor Ludwig Brunov placed bas-reliefs on the pedestal of the statue depicting the main events in the life of

The Throne Room in Schwerin Castle, with portraits of Grand Duke Friedrich Franz II and his first wife Augusta.

The bas-relief "The Grand Entrance of the Grand Duke of Mecklenburg Schwerin on June 14, 1871," located on the pedestal of the monument to Friedrich Franz II. Photograph by M. Schott, 1999.

The central railroad station in Schwerin c. 1910.

the Grand Duke. One of them shows the opening of a new university in Rostok in 1870, while another shows the meeting of the victors in Schwerin on July 14, 1871. His son, the Hereditary Grand Duke, saw battle when he joined with Friedrich Franz on the battlefield. They are located in the center, on horseback, surrounded by their relatives, one of whom is the Dowager Duchess Alexandrine, facing the viewer, and on her left hand, with the garland of flowers, is the her granddaughter Maria, the future Grand Duchess Maria Pavlovna.

The family of Friedrich Franz III would spend just a few months of the year in the ancestral Schwerin castle. Due to the illness of the Grand Duke the couple could be in Schwerin only during the mild summer months and the beginning of autumn. It was at this time that they organized official receptions and gave balls at the castle. In the fall, the Grand Duchess Anastasia, together with her husband and three children, would move to the French Riviera, to Cannes, where they had a home, the Villa Wenden. The name of the villa refers to the highest award of the two grand duchies (Schwerin and Strelitz), known as the Order of the Wendishen Crown. It was established on May 12, 1864 by the then ruling Grand Dukes – Friedrich Franz II and Friedrich Wilhelm.

The Villa Wenden is located on a high cliff, overlooking the sea. Of neo-classic style with a German touch, the

The Mecklenburg-Schwerin Relatives of Grand Duchess Anastasia Mikhailovna

Grand Duke Friedrich Franz II.
(1823-1883)
[Eurohistory Archive]

Grand Duchess Augusta.
(1822-1862)
[Eurohistory Archive]

building constructed in 1889, rises on a garden terrace sustained by a spectacular peripheral wall. This work of art is remarkable, like the wrought iron gates closing the accesses of the property. The Villa Wenden is the first residence in Cannes equipped with electricity. A winter residence, the villa served as the place of the winter retreat. In the front of the villa, from the plaza surrounded by palm trees, guests would walk up a staircase, covered by a red carpet, to a spacious hall, where on the right hung a portrait of Grand Duchess Anastasia, in full height, painted by the English artist Hubert von Herkomer. From a large salon with three windows one could enter into a covered veranda, where there was a wonderful view on to the sea, the mountains, and the quai. The villa was surrounded by a luscious garden. Rose bushes, white and red, were planted at the edges. The Grand Duke, an extremely hospitable and elegant man, also a gifted storyteller, played a very important role in the life of this resort town. Any member of European royalty, who would come to Cannes, always visited the Grand Duke and his wife. The most frequent guests at the Villa Wenden were relatives from Russia – Anastasia's brothers Grand Dukes Nicholas Mikhailovich and Michael Mikhailovich with his wife Countess de Torby, owners of the nearby Villa Kazbeck. Anastasia's father, Grand Duke Michael Nikolaevich, who greatly enjoyed the French Riviera, was also a frequent visitor.

The Grand Duchess of Mecklenburg-Schwerin had to hide from everyone her husband's terrible illness, a skin disease that caused him constant agony, and forced Friedrich Franz III to take painkillers often. He also suffered from asthma, a condition that forced the poor man to seek warmer climates. Her Hofmeisterine (Chief Lady-in-Waiting) Baroness Louisa von Reibnitz remembers: "only contacts with the outside world would bring back strength to Anastasia, after which she, like a ray of sunshine, could enter her ill husband's room."

Grand Duchess Anastasia Mikhailovna had a very willful, independent character that in more than one opportunity got her in deep trouble. Her dislike of Schwerin gained her the ire of her husband's government, while her private conduct brought her scandal. Anastasia loved gambling and spent with abandon; she was always elegantly dressed, with style, she wore fabulous jewels, and she would attract attention in any social situation. Her greatest enjoyment was sports. She played tennis extremely well, and she even participated in international tournaments. Not far from the hunting lodge Gelbensande in Mecklenburg she had a tennis court installed, and she would invite famous tennis stars to instruct her in the sport, and to instill the same love of sport in her children.

Duke Johann Albrecht of Mecklenburg-Schwerin.
[Eurohistory Archive]

Gelbensande, a hunting owned lodge of the Grand Dukes of Mecklenburg-Schwerin. The foundation stone was laid by Grand Duke Michael Nikolaevich on May 1, 1885.

Friedrich Franz III was a devoted husband and father. Life had not been easy for him, his illness being the culprit for much of his physical sufferings. In April 1897, sensing himself in need of fresh air, the ailing Grand Duke walked on to the balcony of Villa Wenden, and having lost his sense of balance, fell from the second floor. It was a fatal fall. This unfortunate accident was a reason why his demise came earlier than expected.

When he inherited the grand ducal throne, Friedrich Franz IV was only 15-years-old. The government of Schwerin could not countenance Anastasia Mikhailovna, who was unpopular with her husband's subjects, serving as regent for her son,. Instead this responsibility fell on the shoulders of Duke Johann Albrecht, a younger brother of Grand Duke Friedrich Franz III.

Schloß Willigrad, the residence of Duke Johann Albrecht of Mecklenburg-Schwerin.

Schloß Wiligrad, the country residence of Johann Albrecht was located 15 kilometers from Schwerin on the shore of Schwerin Lake. This castle was built in 1896–1898 at the personal expense of Johann Albrecht. It was one of the last residences built by the Mecklenburg-Schwerins. Located in a picturesque setting, Wiligrad was surrounded by some 210 hectares of forest.

During the years of the Regency, the life of Grand Duchess Anastasia changed drastically. She continued to have the use of several rooms in Schwerin Castle, but, whenever she would

The Mecklenburg-Schwerin Relatives of Grand Duchess Anastasia Mikhailovna

Grand Duchess Anastasia Mikhailovna.
(1860-1922)
[Eurohistory Archive]

Wedding photo of Grand Duke Friedrich Franz IV of Mecklenburg-Schwerin and Princess Alexandra of Cumberland,
[Eurohistory Archive]

return to the grand ducal capital, she would more often stay in Gelbensande, another country estate, or Schloß Ludwigslust. The Regency ended in 1901, and her son Friedrich Franz became the ruler of Mecklenburg-Schwerin. A few years later he married Princess Alexandra of Cumberland, the niece of Empress Maria Feodorovna, strengthening his ties to the family of Emperor Nicholas II.

In 1897, not long before his death, Friedrich Franz III had blessed his eldest daughter Alexandrine's choice to marry Prince Christian of Denmark, the eldest son of Crown Prince Frederik, a brother of Empress Maria Feodorovna. After the wedding, celebrated in Cannes, Christian and Alexandrine settled in Copenhagen. They were also given Marselisborg Castle as a country residence.

Schloß Ludwigslust, the country residence of the Grand Dukes of Mecklenburg-Schwerin, where Friedrich Franz II was born, as well as of some of his children, among them Grand Duchess Maria Pavlovna. The rite of baptism of the grand ducal children would take place in the Golden Hall of the palace.

The Church of St. Olga, with the belfry, in Mikhailovka. Architect D.I. Grimm.
Photograph by D. Bianki.
[From a Private Collection]

The belfry of the Church of St. Olga
in Mikhailovka.
[IIMK RAN]

With Alexandrine's departure, Grand Duchess Anastasia was left in the company of her youngest daughter Cecilie, named after her Russian grandmother, Grand Duchess Olga Feodorovna. Every year, during a period of seven years, the Dowager Grand Duchess Anastasia of Mecklenburg-Schwerin, together with her daughter, would come for a summer visit to her Russian relatives. Her father, Grand Duke Michael Nikolaevich, owned an ancestral estate on the Peterhof road, where the family loved to spend the summer months.

The idea of turning the road from St. Petersburg to Oranienbaum into a chain of beautiful Grand Ducal estates belongs to Emperor Nicholas I. On the instructions of the Emperor, property was purchased along the Gulf of Finland for five of his children – huge tracts of land were acquired in Strelna for Konstantin, the territory of the future Mikhailovka for Michael, in Znamenka land for Nicholas; the heir and Tsarevich, was given a

The Palace of Mikhailovka on the Peterhof road c. 1900.
[IIMK RAN]

The Mecklenburg-Schwerin Relatives of Grand Duchess Anastasia Mikhailovna

The gardens of the Mikhailovka Palace. A view of the "Dolphin" fountain in the little courtyard in front of the embroidery room of Grand Duchess Olga Feodorovna. Photograph c. 1900. [IIMK RAN]

"In St. Petersburg at the train station we were greeted by the father, brother and other relatives of Anastasia. They would hug each other so strongly, her face was simply radiant when she finally found herself in her homeland, surrounded by her family. A special train brought us to Mikhailovka. This was the palace of Michael Nikolaevich. This large building is surrounded by terraces and veranda, so that from any point in the building on the first floor one can exit into the park. The Grand Duchess settled into her large, well created rooms, where she had spent her childhood. A very beautiful view opens out from the windows. During her stay in Mikhailovka, the Grand Duchess would not have any large public receptions. Anastasia would very often visit with other members of the Imperial Family, especially the Tsar and his wife, who, during the summer months, led a very secluded lifestyle in Alexandria ..."

Louise, Baroness v. Reibnitz-Maltzan, "Gestalten vom letzten Zarenhof und andere personliche Begegnungen," 1928.

personal summer residence, "Sobstvennaya Dacha," and in Sergievka a romantic villa was built for Grand Duchess Maria.

Several outstanding architects took part in the creation of the "Mikhailovka" estate – A. Stackenschneider, I. Charlemagne, and G. Bosse. The summer palace complex has an exterior not usual for St. Petersburg buildings. The inspiration for this project was ancient Roman and Renaissance villas, with numerous sculptural decorations. The Grand Palace with a corner tower and overhanging turrets was connected via open galleries with the asymmetrical Smaller Palace. On the first floor of the Grand Palace one finds the grand reception halls, as well as the private apartments of the Grand Duke and his wife, on the second floor – rooms for the children and their teachers.

The interiors were designed by Bosse, and are striking in their unique and multi-faceted decor. Around the palace one can find seven fountains, vine covered pergolas, and picturesque walkways.

Even before the completion of the main building during the summer of 1861, Architect David Grimm was already planning the construction of a church. In three years time a small brick building, in a "Russian-Byzantine" style was built, and it was dedicated to St. Olga, the heavenly protector of the lady of the estate, Grand Duchess Olga Feodorovna. David Grimm's planning was considered to be so successful, that he was later called to design two churches abroad: the Cathedral of the Raising of the Cross in Geneva, and St. Mary Magdalene Cathedral in Greece, on the island of Crete.

As a rule, the Dowager Grand Duchess Anastasia with her daughter would come to Russia from Germany on Grand Duke Alexei Alexandrovich's private yacht the "Svetlana." The voyage would take only several days. They were usually met in Kronstadt by the commanding Admiral of the Russian Navy, Grand Duke Alexei Alexandrovich, where the guests would transfer to a smaller vessel, and under sail, come to Peterhof. Emperor

Tsarevich Alexei Nikolaevich at the age of two-years, Peterhof 1906. Photograph taken by a security officer. [ILN]

Nicholas II would have a private audience in honor of his August relatives, which would usually include a breakfast with only close family members present. Very often Cecilie and her mother would return to Germany from Russia on the Imperial yacht, the "Standart."

Several special celebrations, in which she had the honor of participating remained in the memory of the young Cecilie: the wedding of Grand Duchess Olga Alexandrovna and Duke Peter of Oldenburg in Gatchina, the wedding of Grand Duchess Helen Vladimirovna and Prince Nicholas of Greece in Tsarskoe Selo, the baptism of Grand Duchesses Maria, Anastasia, and the Tsarevich Alexei Nikolaevich. He was born in 1904 in the Lower Dacha at Peterhof, his parent's summer home. The baptism of the Tsarevich took place on the morning of August 11 (24), in the majestic church of the Grand Peterhof Palace.

Emperor Nicholas II wrote in his diary: "It was such a wonderful day ... the rite of baptism started at 11:00 am. I was later told that little Alexei was very quiet. Olga, Tatiana and Irina, together with other children, were present at an Imperial Procession for the first time, and they stood throughout the long ceremony excellently. The main "Receivers" [Godparents] were Maman and uncle Alexei."

According to Cecilie's memoirs, a swallow once flew into her room in Mikhailovka. The young lady considered this a very good omen. Shortly thereafter, a courier arrived at the summer residence of Grand Duke Michael Nikolaevich. It was sent from the German Embassy and contained a marriage proposal from Crown Prince Wilhelm of Prussia for Cecilie. Their wedding took place in Berlin on May 24 (June 6), 1905. Representing Russia at the celebrations were Grand Dukes Michael Alexandrovich, Nicholas Mikhailovich and Grand Duchess Maria

The Church Pavillion at the Grand Peterhof Palace. Photograph by K. Bulla. [TsGAKFFD SPb]

Emperor Nicholas II and Tsarevich Alexei Nikolaevich.
[TsGAKFFD SPb]

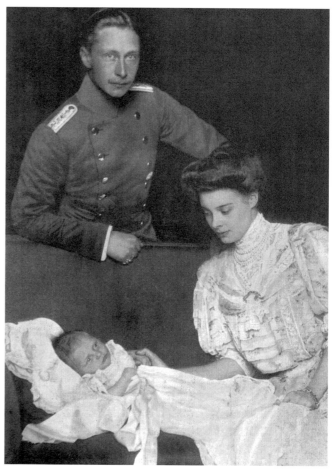

Grand Duchess Anastasia Mikhailovna and her daughter Cecilie.
[Eurohistory Archive]

Crown Prince Wilhelm and Crown Princess Cecilie with their first-born son, Wilhelm, 1906. [Eurohistory Archive]

Pavlovna the Elder. That day Berlin presented the young bride with 80,000 glorious roses, with which they decorated the wedding route and the interior of the church.

On July 1906 Cecilie gave birth to a son, her first born, and he was baptized in the Hall of Mirrors of the New Palace in Potsdam; this event was of grand European importance. Representing the House of Romanov were Grand Duke Vladimir Alexandrovich with his wife, Cecilie's aunt. The celebration is depicted in a picture by Wilhelm Pape, which hangs in the private apartments of Crown Princess Cecilie in the summer residence at Cecilienhof.

In 1911 Cecilie and her husband visited Russia. At that time the building of the German Embassy was being remodeled, and German diplomats had signed an agreement on the leasing transfer of the former palace of Grand Duke Alexei Alexandrovich for the temporary use by the embassy. Count Pourtàles gave a dinner in honor of the Crown Prince and his wife. Cecilie remembers that it was most pleasant to find herself once again in the palace of Grand Duke Alexei, which she and her mother had visited often, when she would come to Russia as a child.

After their first born, Wilhelm (1906–1940), Crown Prince Wilhelm and his wife had three more sons, Prince Louis Ferdinand (1907–1994), Hubertus (1909–1950) and Friedrich (1911–1966), and a daughter Princess Alexandrine Irene (1915–1980). Kaiser Wilhelm II ordered that an English style cottage be built for their family in Potsdam, not far from the Jungfernsee Lake. This spacious summer home became the last residence built by the Hohenzollerns. The building is of red brick, and in it one finds fachwerk (timberframe) construction from oak; Architect Paul Schultze-Naumburg designed it in 1914–1917. Crown Princess Cecilie, whose name was given to the new palace, settled into her apartments only in August 1917, and this was where her sixth

Grand Duchess Anastasia Mikhailovna, Crown Princess Cecilie of Prussia and Princes Wilhelm, Louis Ferdinand and Hubertus.
[Eurohistory Archive]

Crown Princess Cecilie of Prussia with her brother Grand Duke Friedrich Franz IV and his wife Grand Duchess Alexandra.
[Eurohistory Archive]

child was born, Princess Cecilie (1917–1975). However, the quiet blissful life of the august couple was cut short in 1918, when Kaiser Wilhelm II was forced to abdicate the throne. His son Crown Prince Wilhelm gained Cecilienhof as his private property in 1926, and the family continued to reside there until 1945. It was then that the Palace of Cecilienhof became famous as the location of the Potsdam Conference.

Cecilienhof Palace. Built by Architect Paul Schultze-Naumburg

Russia and Denmark

Denmark is a relatively small European country, both in territory and in population. Towards the second half of the XIX and the beginning of the XX century, every year it was the meeting place of the rulers of the most powerful countries on earth, as Tsars, Kings and Emperors traveled to Denmark with members of their families. It was here that the Russian Emperor Alexander III, the Prince of Wales, the King of the Hellenes, the King of Sweden, and even the dreaded Kaiser Wilhelm II, as well as many other crowned rulers, came to visit the King Christian IX and Queen Louise of Denmark. There were days when in the summer residence of Fredensborg 80 members of royal families would sit down to dinner, and they were all dynastically related. It would seem that during friendly dinner conversation one could easily solve intergovernmental problems, but, according to eyewitness accounts of the aide to the Greek Court, Michael Onou, "there was an unstated rule among monarchs, who were all so closely related, not to discuss politics at the dinner table." The atmosphere of informal conversation, the possibility to forego strict rules of etiquette, and the hospitality of the Danes, made King Christian IX a very attractive host. Their home filled with this polyglot menagerie, it was not surprising that the Danish Royal Couple was known as the "Father and Mother-in-law of Europe."

In 1863 Christian eldest daughter, Alexandra, married the Prince of Wales. That same year Prince William of Denmark, Christian's second son, was chosen as the new monarch of Greece. By year's end even Christian had succeeded to the Danish throne. Three years later Dagmar, the second daughter of King Christian IX and Queen Louise, left her dear Denmark to build a life in mysterious and tantalizing Russia. She said goodbye to her childhood and to the joyful abandonment of youth. In doing so, she left a country where the ruler and his subjects did not feel distanced from one another; where everyone lived simply and peacefully, as one large family. On September 26, 1866, Dagmar first set foot on Russian soil to become betrothed of the Heir to the throne, Tsarevich Alexander Alexandrovich. She would spend more than half a century in Russia and for thirteen years she, alongside her husband, would be at the head of a vast and mighty nation. Together they would have a family, where feelings of humanity and kindness, support, trust and understanding would prevail. They lived in luxurious palaces in St. Petersburg, Gatchina, Tsarskoe Selo, and Peterhof; very often they would visit the Crimea.

Today, many of these palaces have been transformed into beautiful museums, where many of the objects collected by Empress Maria Feodorovna and Emperor Alexander III have been preserved.

The dynastic ties established by Maria Feodorovna's siblings, not only benefited Denmark, but also established closer links between Russia and those countries. Not only was her brother the King of Greece, but also her sister would eventually become the Queen Consort of Great Britain. Maria's eldest brother, Frederik VIII, succeeded their father in 1906 and ruled until his death six years later. Thyra, Maria Feodorovna's youngest sister, married the exiled Duke of Cumberland and with him had six children, three of whom established important dynastic ties to Baden, Mecklenburg-Schwerin and Prussia. Later, a daughter of Prince Valdemar, Christian IX's youngest child, married a brother of Empress Zita of Austria. One can only begin to image what the Romanov's dynastic ties would have looked like had there been no Russian Revolution.

Empress Maria Feodorovna.
(1847-1928)
Photograph by Levitsky. [RGAKFD]

King Christian IX and Queen Louise of Denmark.
[Eurohistory Archive]

The Family of King Christian IX
The Amalienborg Palace

King Christian IX (1818–1906), by birth, was a member of the youngest branch of the Glücksburg line of the Oldenburg dynasty, which had ruled in Denmark from the XV century. The sixth child in the large family formed by Duke Friedrich Wilhelm of Schleswig-Holstein-Sonderbug-Glücksburg and Landgravine Luise of Hesse-Kassel, he was left without a father at the age of thirteen. His uncle, King Frederik VI of Denmark, himself childless, took an active role in the life of the fatherless young boy – he considered the Christian as his own son, and helped him obtain an excellent education.

Two lines of Danish royal descendants were joined on May 26, 1842, when Christian married his cousin Louise of Hesse-Kassel. The grand ceremony took place in the palace of Brockdorf at Copenhagen's Amalienborg Palace. The bride's mother was Charlotte of Denmark, a first cousin of Frederik VI, as well as a sister of his successor, King Christian VIII, who succeeded on the Danish throne in 1839. The young couple settled in a four-story stone townhouse, decorated with a yellow façade, on Amaliegade, No. 18. They lived in this house until 1863; it was here that five of the couple's six children were born. The Yellow Palace, as the building was called, did not have many servants, as the parents did not possess much of a fortune to speak of. Consequently, the princes and princesses had to perform many of the household chores themselves.

The Yellow Palace.
Photograph by G. Korneva, 2005.

King Christian IX (1818-1906).
[GARF]

Queen Louise (1817-1898), née Hesse-Kassel.
[RGAKFD]

The Marble Cathedral in Copenhagen. From the magazine "Vsemirnaya Illyustratsiya," 1894.

A bas-relief with an image of philanthropists Karl and Laura Tiegen, at the Marble Cathedral. Photograph by G. Korneva, 2005.

At the London Conference in 1852, the question of the Danish succession was solved when Prince Christian was proclaimed the Heir to the Throne. The following year the Danish Parliament confirmed this decision. A decade later, when King Frederik VI died childless, Christian IX became the King of Denmark. His family moved into the royal residence at Amalienborg.

The short street of Frederiksgade, going through the central axis of Amalienborg, ends on one side with a high-domed Marble Cathedral, covered with tin sheets – this is the Frederiks Kirche. This edifice, with a façade of white marble and a classical portico, was built according to the plans of the Danish architect Ferdinand Meldahl. The cathedral was under construction for almost half a century. In memory of the 300th anniversary of the reign of the Oldenburg dynasty, King Frederik V laid the cornerstone on December 29, 1749. According to the original plans of Court Architect Niels Eigtved, the building was to surpass the famous cathedral of St. Peter's in Rome in its grandeur and the richness of its decor. But Eigtved passed away in 1754 and the work was continued by the French Court architect Nicolas Henri Jardin. However, after the death of Frederik V in 1766, when Denmark was going through difficult times, the construction of the Marble Cathedral was paused. By that time only the foundation of the grand façade was completed. The construction planks were disassembled, the granite sold. It was a century later, in 1874, that one of the richest men in Denmark, director of a bank and owner of several large commercial and trading enterprises, Karl Frederik Tietgen decided to complete the construction of the marble cathedral through his personal funding and to give it as a gift to the city of Copenhagen. In total, the cost of the cathedral for all contributors was around 1.6 million krone, of which Karl Tietgen provided 900 thousand.

On August 19, 1894 the consecration of the cathedral took

The palace of Christian IX in Amalienborg. Photograph by F. Danielsen. [TsGAKFFD SPb]

place, in the presence of King Christian IX, Queen Louise and members of their family.

The palace complex of Amalienborg in Copenhagen became the official residence of the Danish Kings after the fire of 1794, when serious damage occurred to the royal residence of Christiansborg. In contrast to the grand palaces of St. Petersburg, which belonged to the House of Romanov, Amalienborg consists of four stand-alone manors. The Court Architect of King Frederik V built them during the celebration of the 300th anniversary of the Oldenburg reign, in 1749. All four manor houses resemble each other, they are three-storied structures of a light colored stone, constructed by architect Niels Eigtved; he had built similar structures for rich aristocratic families, whose names are still remembered in Copenhagen: Schack, Brockdorff, Levetzau and Moltke. Together with the side structures, the buildings form a large eight-pointed square. In the center of this square an equestrian monument was placed in 1771, in memory of the founder of this complex, King Frederik V. The young Princess Dagmar used to live in the former Schack Palace on the southern side, together with her parents, brothers and sister from 1863 until the year when she left for Russia. She would often visit her relatives in Denmark, and when in Copenhagen would stay at this palace.

Prince Valdemar and Princess Thyra, the youngest siblings of Princess Dagmar of Denmark. [RGAKFD]

The family of King Christian IX and Queen Louise consisted of six children, three sons and three daughters. They were: Frederik (1843-1912), William (1845-1913), Valdermar (1858-1939) and daughters Alexandra (1844-1925), Dagmar (1847-1928) and Thyra (1853-1933). When Dagmar left Denmark in 1866, her younger brother was eight years old, her sister Thyra – thirteen. All of the children were very close to each other, but Dagmar, usually sought the company of her elder siblings, and her closest relations were with her brother William and her sister Alexandra. In 1863 Willie, as William was called within the family circle, was selected as the new King of Greece, and Alexandra married the eldest son of Queen Victoria, Albert Edward, and left for England. Dagmar was very unhappy about their departure. She was allowed to visit her sister Alexandra and her husband the following autumn. And very soon she was to meet a young man who would win her heart, from the very first glance.

View on to the Torvaldsen Museum on the island of Slotholm, Copenhagen c. 1900. [IIMK RAN]

Princess Dagmar of Denmark, c. 1864.
Queen Louise sent this photograph of her daughter to Emperor Alexander II.
Photograph by I. Petersen.
[State Hermitage Museum]

"*The future Heir to the Throne seems to be most promising. His appearance is most appealing. He resembles, for the most part, his father, but has many traits of his grandfather. His facial features are correct and harmonious, his eyes blue, very much alive; his hair is light and shortly cut. Nicholas Alexandrovich is a happy, cordial person, with a meek and obedient character. For his age he knows quite a lot, and his intellect is very developed. He has brilliant talents. He is extremely conscious of others, has a vibrant imagination and is very eager to learn.*"

From the notes of J.K. Grott, governor and tutor of the Tsarevich.

*Tsarevich Nicholas Alexandrovich.
(1843-1865).
[TsGAKFFD SPb]*

Princess Dagmar
& Tsarevich Nicholas Alexandrovich

Tsarevich Nicholas Alexandrovich, the eldest son of Empress Maria Alexandrovna and Alexander II, was born on September 8, 1843, in the Imperial countryside retreat known as Tsarskoe Selo, in the outskirts of St. Petersburg. The best teachers of the nation took part in his education and upbringing, a great future was expected for him. Everyone who would come in contact with the Tsarevich would remark about his excep-

Tsarevich Nicholas Alexandrovich and his fiancée Princess Dagmar of Denmark, 1864.
[Eurohistory Archive]

tional kindness and charm. Within the Imperial Family, Nixa, as Nicholas was called, enjoyed great popularity.

During his childhood Nicholas would spend the summer months with his brothers in Tsarskoe Selo, where he enjoyed sailing, playing various games; very often together with their parents they would take carriage rides to the neighboring town of Pavlovsk.

A very important part in the upbringing of the royal children were trips abroad, and, in 1863, escorted by his courtiers the Tsarevich took a trip around many Russian cities, in order to learn about the various corners of this nation, which, in a few years time, he was expected to rule. The following year his parents decided that it was time for him to visit European nations, and to understand for himself, what were the advantages and disadvantages of living under different political systems. In his message upon his son's departure Emperor Alexander II

A panoramic view of Tsarskoe Selo circa early 1900s. Postcard from the collection og G.V. Dvas.

wrote: "Much will seem attractive to you, but upon closer observance you will come to understand that not everything is worthy of being copied ... we always need to retain our own national traits, our own imprint on the world, and woe be to us, if we should shy away from this ... however, this should in no way make you indifferent, or any less interested in that which is curious and outstanding in any nation or region."

There was also another reason for this trip – his parents recommended that the Tsarevich Nicholas make a stop at Copenhagen and turn his attention to the second daughter of Christian IX, Princess Dagmar, who, by that time, had already turned seventeen.

Bernstorff Palace. Photograph by F. Kretzmeyer. [IIMK RAN]

Russia and Europe

When Tsarevich Nicholas came to Denmark, the Royal Court was at their summer residence in Bernstorff.

The estate, located some ten kilometers from Copenhagen, came into the ownership of Dagmar's father in 1852, after he was declared the Heir to the Throne. Here, in the middle of the XVIII century Johann Ernst Bernstorff, Minister of Foreign Affairs during the reign of King Frederik V, had ordered that an elegant stone mansion be built, one of the first buildings in the country decorated in the neo-classical style. The master of this project was the French Court architect Nicolas Henri Jardin. The estate had belonged to the Bernstorff family before 1812; it was later purchased by King Christian VIII and from 1852 to 1906 was one of the Danish monarchs' preferred country residences. After the death of Christian IX, Bernstorff went to his son Prince Valdemar, who raised his large family in this beautiful palace.

Bernstorff profited greatly when from the 1760s onward a shady, picturesque park, landscaped in a romantic style, surrounded it. Hundreds of oak trees had been planted there, together with linden trees and birches. It was here that Dagmar felt the first yearnings of mutual affection. Tsarevich Nicholas, during a walk in the park, had confessed his love to the Princess and had offered his hand in marriage. When the young people returned to the house, they announced their engagement. Photographs of Dagmar soon appeared in St. Petersburg in the windows of fashionable stores, and the citizens of the city very eagerly bought portraits of the attractive bride of the Heir to the Throne.

In 1888 a little "Swedish House" was built next to the central building of the estate at Bernstorff. Queen Louise bought it at a Scandinavian exhibit, in which some Russians had also participated. Famous jewelers, furniture makers and other masters of the trade had come to Denmark. As a result, out of 399 non-Scandinavian participants there were 225 Russians. According to the Lady-in-Waiting of Grand Duchess Anastasia of Mecklenburg-Schwerin, the mother-in-law of the future King Christian X of Denmark, "the Imperial Family would stay in a cute, little Swedish House, if they were staying in Bernstorff for a short period of time. Alexander III, Ruler of All of Russia, had spent his most blissful days here."

Queen Louise and her daughter Princess Dagmar.
[RGAKFD]

A view of the "Swedish House" purchased by Queen Louise in 1888. In this photo the Danish Queen is seen at the entrance to the house, while several of her grandchildren stand in front of the house. Photograph by F. Danielsen.
[TsGAKFFD SPb]

Princess Dagmar and Tsarevich Nicholas Alexandrovich

The "Swedish House," having lost some of its wooden lacework decorations, can still be seen in the Bernstorff Park to this day.

The young couple said goodbye to each other in Denmark in October 1864. In just a month's time, while in Italy, the Tsarevich Nicholas Alexandrovich felt the first symptoms of a serious disease. At his doctor's suggestion he moved to Nice at the end of December, where his mother, Empress Maria Alexandrovna, was taking the cure. There, at the Villa Bermont, on the shores of the azure sea, a tragedy was to take place. A young man, just a half a year ago full of energy and with the highest of hopes, with each passing day would dwindle away, succumbing to torturous and indescribable pain. In great agony, the night of the 11th to the 12th of April 1865, he died of spinal meningitis. During the last days of his life his closest relatives and friends gathered at his bedside: his parents, his brothers Alexander, Vladimir and Alexei, Queen Louise of Denmark, her son the Crown Prince Frederik, and totally lost in grief, Princess Dagmar. Being together at the bedside of the dying Heir to the Throne, Nicholas, his younger brother Alexander, who had a sincere love for his brother, and his "orphaned" bride, shared their grief ever more sharply.

The earthly remains of the Tsarevich were transported to St. Petersburg and interred in the Cathedral of SS. Peter and Paul in the Peter and Paul Fortress. During one of the memorial services the Lady-in-Waiting of Empress Maria Alexandrovna, Alexandra Tolstoy suggested that a letter be sent to the grieving bride of the Tsarevich. An "address," with words of condolences, together with a "cross and a Holy Bible, exquisitely decorated" with lapis lazuli, were sent to Dagmar, "as a small expression of the emotions felt" by the ladies of the court.

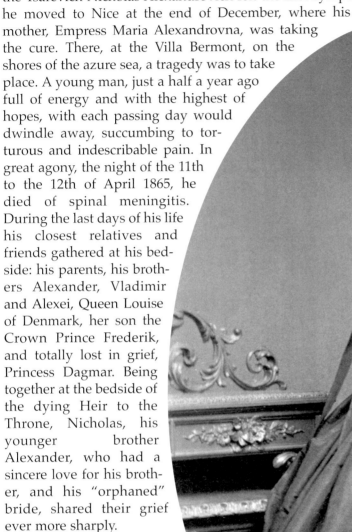

Princess Dagmar of Denmark,
Copenhagen (1864).
[GARF]

The Villa Bermont in Nice was purchased by Emperor Alexander II, and on the spot of the room where the Tsarevich had died; a small Byzantine-styled chapel was later erected. Russian Court artist Timothy Neff decorated the interior. The municipal authorities of Nice named the nearest street in memory of "Nixa" – "Tsarevich Boulevard." On April 12, 1868, on the third anniversary of Tsarevich Nicholas' death, when the consecration of the new chapel took place, his brothers Tsarevich Alexander Alexandrovich and Grand Duke Vladimir Alexandrovich were present to witness the solemn event.

In later years Empress Maria Feodorovna came to the Côte d'Azur many times. In 1896 she had spent the winter there with her children George, Michael and Olga. The priest to the Imperial Family, Protopresbyter Sergei Liubimov, at that time the chief priest at the Church of Sts. Nicholas and Alexandra on Longchamps Street in Nice, told the Empress of the wishes of the Russian community to have a new church constructed. The Dowager Empress supported this idea and agreed to head the construction committee. Her son, Emperor Nicholas II had decided to donate the plot where the Villa Bermont had previously stood. In 1912, in memory of the first betrothed of Maria Feodorovna, the new Cathedral of St. Nicholas was consecrated in Nice. It was most colorful in its decoration, reminiscent of Moscow cathedrals of the XVII century; the architect was Michael Preobrazhensky.

The chapel of St. Nicholas in Nice, erected on the spot where Tsarevich Nicholas Alexandrovich had died. Architect D. Grimm. [IIMK RAN]

The Engagement of Princess Dagmar
& Tsarevich Alexander Alexandrovich

Dagmar took the death of her future bridegroom with great difficulty, and her relatives were worried about her. However, Emperor Alexander II did not dispense with the idea of establishing family links with the Danish Royal House. He had a great attachment to the young princess, and Dagmar herself, during the past year had become accustomed to the idea that her future was tied to Russia; their joint sorrow had made her even closer to Nixa's parents. It was at this time that Dagmar received a letter from Emperor Alexander II, in which he expressed a hope that she could still become a member of their family.

In the beginning of 1866 a serious talk took place between the Emperor and his son Alexander, who had unexpectedly become the Tsarevich. Alexander Nikolaevich was infatuated with the Lady-in-Waiting to the Empress, Maria Mestchersky; he even had dreams of marrying her. But, in the end, his sense of duty was to prevail. Maria was sent away from Russia and married in Paris Prince Paul Demidov, dying early in 1868.

According to the orders from his father, the Tsarevich set off on a journey on the Imperial yacht, the "Standard," to Denmark, with the intention of proposing marriage to Princess Dagmar. His brother Grand Duke Vladimir, his close friend Vladimir Baryatinsky, previously the adjutant to Tsarevich Nicholas Alexandrovich, and Count Boris Perovsky accompanied him on this voyage. The honored guests from Russia

Tsarevich Alexander Alexandrovich and his fiancée Princess Dagmar of Denmark, 1866.
[GARF]

187

were met with great pomp and ceremony in Denmark. King Christian IX himself and members of his court greeted them on the quay. Great numbers of Danish citizens watched as the Grand Dukes Alexander and Vladimir, together with the King of Denmark, made their way to the summer residence of Fredensborg, located on the banks of the large Lake Ezrum, approximately 50 kilometers to the north of Copenhagen.

Danish architect Johan Cornelius Krieger built the main building of the Fredensborg palace complex, which resembled a Tuscan villa, at the request of King Frederik IV in 1720–1722. This monarch, who was known by

his contemporaries as the "builder-King," very often would come visit this picturesque forest domain and would stop at a hunting lodge, which had been erected in memory of the end of the Northern War, and was called "Fredensborg," or the "Castle of Peace." In 1724–1726 a winter garden wing, church, still well preserved to this day, and a cavaliers' residence for courtiers were added to the eastern side of the small single-storied building. Closer to the main entrance, on the other side of the palace, J.C. Krieger erected a Chancellors' House in 1731. Later, according to the plans of architect Niels Eigtved four more wings were added.

Fredensborg Palace.
[TsGAKFFD SPb]

Grand Duke Vladimir Alexandrovich with His sister-in-law Dagmar's youngest siblings: Princess Thyra (who married the Duke of Cumberland) and Valdemar (who married Princess Marie d'Orléans.
[RGAKFD]

The Engagement of Princess Dagmar and Tsarevich Alexander Alexandrovich

Panoramic view of Copenhagen – View on to the Vedstranden.
[IIMK RAN]

In was in this summer residence of the Danish Royal Family that the engagement of Tsarevich Alexander and Princess Dagmar took place.

News of the engagement was met with great joy both in Denmark and in Russia. Present at the celebratory dinner in Fredensborg were Alexander's younger brothers Vladimir and Alexei, who shared in their brother's happiness. Dagmar received from her groom and his parents a beautiful necklace of diamonds, pearls and emeralds; Vladimir gave his older brother a rather unusual gift – Alexander received a necktie with red and white stripes, the colors of the Danish national flag.

On the day following the engagement announcement the Tsarevich and his brothers went to Copenhagen to the Russian Embassy to pray at the Russian Orthodox Church on Laksegade Street, No. 6, where a priest well known to them greeted them, Father Ioann Rozhdestvensky. They had known him since childhood – Father Ioann had been their catechism teacher and had served in the Small chapel of the Winter Palace in St. Petersburg.

During this trip Alexander spent another two weeks in Denmark. The Court photographer Georg Emile Hansen took many photographs

Tsarevich Alexander Alexandrovich at Fredensborg Palace.
First row, at bottom: Grand Duke Vladimir Alexandrovich, Princess Thyra, Queen Louise. Second row: Landgraf Wilhelm of Hesse-Kassel, Prince Julius of Schleswig-Holstein-Sonderburg-Glücksburg, Princess Dagmar, Tsarevich Alexander Alexandrovich, Prince Valdemar, King Christian IX and Crown Prince Frederik. [TsGAKFFD SPb]

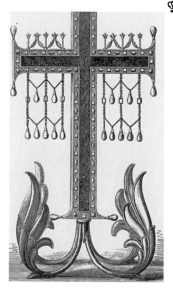

The cross brought from Denmark to Russia by Dagmar; it was presented to her by Russian women as a token of support during her grief upon the death of Tsarevich Nicholas Alexandrovich.

Made by the Court Jeweler K. Michelson out of lazurite and decorated with 22 pearls, in a dual golden frame. It was modeled after the "gleaming cross" with the words "with this you shall conquer" on a painting of the IX century. According to legend, this cross appeared to Emperor Constantine before battle and brought him a great victory.

From the magazine "Illustreret Tidende," 1865.

of the happy faces of the bride and groom, their relatives and other guests of the Royal family.

During her separation from her intended Dagmar studied the Russian language and the Law of God, as she continued her preparations for converting to Orthodoxy. Her studies were carried out under the guidance of Father Ioann Ianyshev, a professor of religion at the University of St. Petersburg, who in 1865–1866 served in

The Large Peterhof Palace, c. 1913.
[TsGAKFFD SPb]

The Engagement of Princess Dagmar and Tsarevich Alexander Alexandrovich

the Orthodox churches of Berlin and Wiesbaden. He was a famous proselytizer, who later became the private chaplain of Emperor Alexander III and his son Nicholas II.

Dagmar arrived in Peterhof on September 24, 1866. When the Danish Princess stepped off of the boat, she was amazed by the large amount of people who had come to greet her at the quay. Soon the grand arrival into the city of St. Petersburg of the "highly honored bride of the Tsarevich" followed. A golden parade coach, harnessed with eight beautiful horses, brought Dagmar and Empress Maria Alexandrovna to the Kazan Cathedral, considered the familial cathedral of the House of Romanov, wherein the miracle-working icon of Our Lady of Kazan was kept; this icon was in a cover of gold, encrusted with 1,432 raw diamonds, 1,665 cut diamonds and 638 rubies. From the time of Tsar Mikhail Feodorovich, first of the Romanov Dynasty, this icon was considered the protector of the royal family.

On October 12 a very important event took place in Dagmar's life – she was brought into the Orthodox faith. The rite of myrrh anointment took place in the Large Palace Church of the Icon of the Savior Not-Made-By-Hands in the Winter Palace; upon receiving communion Dagmar was declared Maria Feodorovna.

Danish citizens, who at that time resided in Russia, gave the bride of the Tsarevich an enamel plate with a picture of her favorite places in Denmark – Fredensborg, Amalienborg and the Yellow Palace on Amaliegade No. 18, where she was born.

Tsarevich Alexander Alexandrovich with his wife Tsarevna Maria Feodorovna and their firstborn child, Grand Duke Nicholas Alexandrovich. Alexander and Martia named their son after their beloved "Nixa," whose death had brought them together.
[Eurohistory Archive]

Tsarevich Alexander Alexandrovich
& Tsarevna Maria Feodorovna

Early in the morning of October 28, 1866, the citizens of St. Petersburg heard cannon fire from the walls of the Peter and Paul Fortress. The ceremonial cannonade announced the start of the wedding festivities of Heir to the Russian Throne with the Princess of Denmark. The marriage, the wedding dinner and ball all took place in the luxurious Winter Palace. At the same time a grand celebration was also being held in the Danish capital. The citizens of Copenhagen were radiant with joy. The festivities went on all day in the Tivoli Gardens, and in the evening a colorful fireworks display lit up the sky, while the streets were bedecked in Russian and Danish flags. A formal dinner was hosted at Christiansborg – in the halls of the Ratusha (City Council) there was a ball, at which the parents of Grand Duchess Maria Feodorovna (the name Dagmar from here onward would adopt) received numerous congratulatory wishes. Meanwhile, in St. Petersburg the happy newlyweds left the ball riding a golden carriage and headed to the Anitchkov Palace; it was the decision of the Imperial Family that the Anitchkov become the residence of the Heir to the Throne.

The Anitchkov Palace was built at the request of

A view of the Anitchkov Palace from the side of the Nevsky Prospect. Photograph from the 1880s.
[TsGAKFFD SPb]

Grand Dukes Nicholas and George Alexandrovich.
[Eurohistory Archive]

Tsarevna Maria Feodorovna and her two eldest sons, Nicholas and George Alexandrovich. [RGAKFD]

Empress Elisabeth Petrovna, daughter of Peter the Great, and given as a gift to her "favorite" courtier, Count Alexei Razumovsky. Notwithstanding that the building was located in the central part of the city, very close to the Nevsky Prospect, it still retained the charm of a suburban estate, and its owners could feel themselves both at the center of a tumultuous city life, and also in the quiet corner of a shady park. The palace's main façade faced the Fontanka River. It took over two centuries to be completed. On its construction worked some of the most famous architects, artists and other masters of St. Petersburg – Mikhail Zemtsov, Francesco Bartolomeo Rastrelli, Ivan Starov, Karl Rossi, Ippolit Monighetti, Andreas Stackenschneider, and Maximilian Messmacher.

The Anitchkov Palace had come to change owners several times throughout its history. In order to prepare it for the arrival of Grand Duke Alexander Alexandrovich and his wife, during the 1860s much remodeling work was performed. By time the new owners moved in, the palace church be completely redone. On December 26, 1866, the church was consecrated in the name of St. Alexander Nevsky. The interior resembled the richly decorated palaces of Moscow. The two rows of columns were faced with faux marble of a red color, the ceilings and arches decorated in gold.

The Anitchkov Palace was the favorite home of Maria Feodorovna during her entire life in Russia. The mistress of the house had decorated her living rooms and boudoir in her own taste; she kept her most

Grand Duchess Xenia Alexandrovna on a swing. Photograph by V. Iasvoin.
[GMZ "Petergof"]

precious possessions here: everything brought from her native Denmark, and those things purchased during her travels in Russia. Maria Feodorovna had impeccable taste, she had a passion for drawing, and anything she possessed became a work of art. Of special importance was her collection of jewelry and decorations, among which were the gifts received from her husband and her son, Emperor Nicholas II, the famous Easter eggs of the world-renowned St. Petersburg jeweler Carl Fabergé.

Alexander Alexandrovich also developed a passion for collecting. A special "museum," created according to the plans of Ippolit Monighetti, was started in the Anitchkov; it contained paintings, sculptures, antiques from glass and crystal, majolica, silver pieces and rare books. The art collection alone counted around 800 canvases, and was unique in the fact that contained works of Danish masters, like K. Blokh, K. Neiman, K. Sorensen, H. Hansen, and others.

Throughout the decades she spent in Russia, Empress Maria Feodorovna never lost contact with Denmark and tried to help, in any possible way, Danish entrepreneurs whenever they came to St. Petersburg. She would meet with specialists, striving to establish contacts with Russia, even in Copenhagen. Her contemporaries recounted how in 1866 Maria Feodorovna had started a list to which she would add the names of Danish citizens, who had turned to her for aid and support. One of the most enterprising Danish businessmen who had obtained very profitable accounts in Russia was K.F. Tietgen.

Karl Frederik Tietgen (1829–1901) was a famous Danish entrepreneur, banker and philanthropist. He was the eldest son in the large family of a furniture maker Johan Frederik Tietgen. He learned the banking trade first in Denmark, where private financing firms were just starting to appear, and later in England, where he went in the 1850s. At age 26 Karl Tietgen married Laura Jorgensen, and they lived together for many years. In 1857 he had started his career as the manager of a private bank; rather quickly he became prosperous and was able to open several new companies. He played an important role in the industrialization of Denmark, in the

The church of St. Alexander Nevsky in the Anitchkov Palace.
[TsGAKFFD SPb]

The private museum of Alexander III in the Anitchkov Palace.
From the magazine "Khudozhestvennye sokrovishcha Rossii," 1903.
[The Art Treasures of Russia]

Tsarevich Alexander Alexandrovich and Tsarevna Maria Feodorovna

Tsarevich Alexander Alexandrovich, with his wife and brother, surrounded by members of his Court.
Sitting (left to right): Hofmeisterine Princess Julia Kurakina, Tsarevich Alexander Alexander Alexandrovich,
Tsarevna Maria Feodorovna, Grand Duke Alexei Alexandrovich, Lady-in-Waiting Alexandra Kurakina,
unidentified man. Standing (same order): Hofmarschal Vasiliy Zinoviev, art instructor Alexei Bogolubov,
law instructor Konstantin Pobedonostsev, unidentified man, Leib-Surgeon Gustav Hirsch, Feodor Ohm
(Maria Feodorovna's secretary), Adjutant Paul Kozlov, c. 1869. [IIMK RAN]

development of telegraphy, and also in shipbuilding. He financed the laying of railroad lines and the construction of a port on the western part of the country, in Esbia. So great was the contribution of this person to the prosperity of Denmark that on the hundredth anniversary of his birth a commemorative medal in his honor was established, and the very first one was bestowed upon King Christian X. Over 79 years only 19 people were honored with this rare medal, among who are the philanthropists Mærsk Mc-Kinney Møller and Lars Kann-Rasmussen.

In June 1865 in Paris Christian IX and Alexander II ratified the agreement, which states: "... the Emperor of Russia and ... the King of Denmark, wishing to aid in the establishment of an underwater telegraph line between their nations ... obligate themselves to connect the above-mentioned telegraph line to their telegraph networks..." On June 1, 1869, under the direction of K.F. Tietgen the "Greater Northern Telegraph Society" was formed, and it received exclusive rights to transmit telegraph communications between Russia and Europe. This Danish company played a role in the Russian market for a long time. With the support of Maria Feodorovna, it was Tietgen who received the concession for the laying of cables from Vladivostok to Nagasaki and Shanghai. The realization of this project brought great income to both countries.

Karl Frederik Tietgen was also the owner of the shipbuilding yards in Copenhagen. In 1890 one of them was privileged to fulfill an important order from Alexander III, the building of the Imperial yacht, the "Standart." Yachts such as these can only be described as "floating" palatial residences. In size and in level of comfort they would equal any summer palace. In planning a yacht the architect needed to consider the special circumstances of court life and to provide spacious, but at the same time intimate, rooms for all members of the family, as well as members of the court, general reception rooms and meeting rooms for members of other reigning monarchs. The "Standart" was conceptualized for a crew of over 350 people. The interior of the cabins was ordered from the studios of the Danish architect Ludwig Monberg. Different types of wood were utilized for the cabin interiors – cherry, walnut, Karelian birch, oak, maple and buk. Accessorized with the latest technical advances of the times, the yacht was the pride and joy of the Russian fleet, and contemporaries considered it to be, easily, the most beautiful in the world.

A family gathering at Bernstorff Palace, c. 1892.
Back row, standing, from left: Prince George of Greece with his hands on the shoulders of his uncle Prince Valdemar of Denmark; King Christian IX of Denmark and his daughters Empress Maria Feodorovna of Russia and the Princess of Wales; Queen Louise of Denmark; Queen Olga of Greece; Prince Nicholas of Greece; Princess Maud of Wales; Tsarevich Nicholas Alexandrovich and Tsar Alexander III of Russia (visibly troubled by his health as he is the only one seated on a chair). On the steps (same order): The Duchess of Cumberland with her children Prince Ernst August and Princess Alexandra of Hannover; Prince Christopher of Greece (with hat); Princess Olga, Prince Christian and Prince Georg Wilhelm of Hannover; Grand Duchess Olga Alexandrovna of Russia; Princess Victoria of Wales; Grand Duke Michael Alexandrovich of Russia.
[Eurohistory Archive]

Karl Frederik Tietgen.
(1829-1901)

The nose decoration of the Imperial Yacht "Standart," c. late 1890s.

The gala ceremony of the commencement of work occurred in Copenhagen in October 1893. Emperor Alexander III, Empress Maria Feodorovna, with their children, the English Princesses Victoria and Maud boarded a steamboat and set off for the large Refsgalsk shipbuilding yards. A reporter for the magazine "Vsemirnaya Illustratsiya" described the event as follows: "Here, in the main dock, in the morning, the blessing of the keel with holy water had already occurred. At the dock of the main wharf a grand tent had been erected; Their Highnesses were greeted by the highest dignitaries of the city, by members of the Russian embassy, by the commanders of Russian vessels standing at port, by the directors of the wharves, and by other consultants, with Mister Tietgen at the head. The sound of the Russian national anthem could be heard. As the August guests approached, Mr. Tietgen had the honor of giving the Russian Empress a grand bouquet of violets, and to the Grand Duchess Xenia Alexandrovna a bouquet of white and red roses. The Emperor was dressed in a parade Admiral's uniform, with the ribbon of the Danish Order of the Elephant. His Imperial Majesty, when he and the Empress approached the keel of the ship to be constructed, desired to remove his hat and to place in the previously blessed opening in the metal keel a silver plate, which was later sealed with a steel cover. The Emperor had desired to hammer in the first nail, with a special silver mallet. The Empress hammered the second nail, while the Tsarevich the third ...

The burial plot of Carl Frederik and Laura Tietgen, Lungby Church.
Photograph by Galina Korneva, 2008.

and the following by other August guests present ... At the end of the ceremonies, at which all workers at the wharves and their families were permitted to attend, the August guests departed back to their ship, the "Polar Star," surrounded by cries of jubilation from the dock workers, the sounds of music, and a cannonade."

The Danish jeweler A. Dragsted created the silver plate for the "Standart".

Tsar Alexander III.
A studio photo by "Levitsky and Son" from the early 1890s. [GARF]

Tsarevich Alexander Alexandrovich and Tsarevna Maria Feodorovna

Empress Maria Feodorovna c. 1881.
Photograph by A. Pazetti. [TsGAKFFD SPb]

Gatchina – The Residence of
Emperor Alexander III and His Family

Having succeeded after the assassination of his father in 1881, Alexander III made the decision to leave the capital, and to take up permanent residence with his family in Gatchina Palace. The palace complex is an extremely picturesque location approximately fifty kilometers from St. Petersburg; for a long time it was famous for its crystal clear lakes and dense woodlands. From 1765 it belonged to the "favorite" of Catherine II, Gregory Orlov. The Empress' courtier, who possessed great personal wealth, invited the leading Italian architect Antonio Rinaldi to create a grandiose ensemble, including a Romantic style palace and an English park with numerous pavilions, islands, marble sculptures.

After the death of Count Orlov in 1783 Catherine II gave Gatchina, with its attached villages, as a gift to her son Paul. The Grand Duke was glad for the opportunity to turn the settlement into his own "little country," including his own personal army, where he felt himself as ruler. By decree of Emperor Paul I Gatchina was granted the status of a city, with its own coat of arms.

A view from the plaze in front of Gatchina Palace c. early 1900s.
[TsGAKFFD SPb]

The move from the Anichkov Palace to a suburban residence did not initially please Maria Feodorovna, who enjoyed the balls and social pleasures of St. Petersburg court life. However, she later came to appreciate the solitude and peace of Gatchina. The quite little town was also well loved by the Imperial children, especially the younger ones, Michael and Olga. As a rule the family spent their autumn and winter months here.

The Imperial couple took up residence in the tiny rooms on the entresol floor of the Arsenal Block. Prince Vladimir Mestchersky, who was an early friend of Alexander III, when he first visited Maria Feodorovna in her study, was amazed by the simplicity of the decor: "I ... came into a very small room, where I found the Empress in such surroundings, where there was not the minutest sign of luxury, and where it was difficult to imagine to find a Russian Empress." The children's rooms in the Arsenal Block were similarly plain in their furnishings. They had metal beds with mattresses, bentwood chairs, and on the walls there was a myriad of small alcoves with an entire exhibition of little Easter eggs, which were given to the girls as gifts every Easter.

Gatchina became so dear to the Imperial couple that in their letters they even started to call the little house that they had purchased in 1880s in Denmark, not far from the Fredensborg Castle, their "miniature Gatchina."

On May 24, 2007, a permanent exhibit was opened in the Gatchina Palace-Museum called "The Personal Rooms of Emperor Alexander III." The subtitle to the exhibit are the words from the memoirs of Count S.D.

Gatchina Palace

Sheremetiev: "Here in total simplicity lived and ruled a person who had no desire for the burdens of grandeur of this century, a person of great moral purity and strength."

The parks surrounding Gatchina Palace were established in the XVIII century. They cover a large territory, around 700 hectares, including many reservoirs. In the middle of the park one finds the White Lake, with wonderfully clear water. Its special beauty is due to the natural and man-made islands of various shapes and forms. A pavilion built in 1792 and dedicated to Venus decorates one of them, with the poetic name of Island of Love. Its construction was modeled on a romantic corner of the grounds belonging to the French Prince de Condé.

Members of Alexander III's family loved to spend time in their own Private Garden, go for walks in the parks, amid the box woods and correctly pruned trees, and gaze at the Italian sculptures of the XVIII century.

Gatchina attracted members of the Imperial family with the possibility of hunting in the dense forests. It was here that during the reign of Alexander II official Court Hunts took place. In order to accommodate a large number of forest wardens, dog keepers and other necessary personnel, not far from Gatchina in Marienburg a special "Jaegermeister" (Hunt Master) Village was built according to the plans of Georg Gross; eventually it would contain 62 new houses.

The family of Alexander III on the terrace that opened to their Private Garden at Gatchina. From left: Maria Feodorovna, Alexander III, George Alexandrovich, Nicholas Alexandrovich, Michael Alexandrovich and Xenia Alexandrovna.
[TsGAKFFD SPb]

A porcelain cup with a picture of the Kaiser Villa on exhibit at Gatchina Palace.
[GMZ "Gatchina."]

The bedroom of Alexander III and his wife in the Arsenal Block of Gatchina Palace. [GMZ "Gatchina."]

A view of Gatchina Palace and the Echo Grotto from the Silver Lake.
Photo atelier of "Kudryatsev & Company." [GMZ "Gatchina."]

The Venus Pavillion, by Architect V. Brenna.
[IIMK RAN]

The houses for the gamekeepers were constructed of raw logs, on a stone foundation, and were richly decorated in carvings; wooded carvings of moose and deer, with real antlers, graced their frontons. Each house had its own plaque with gold letters, announcing the owner: "His Highness's Trapper," "The Chief Footman," "The Arms Carrier," "His Highness's Physician."

At the request of Alexander III in the center of the village a church was built in "Russian style" and dedicated to the Protection of the Virgin Mary. On November 20, 1888, in the presence of the Imperial Family, it was consecrated. The planning of the church was done by the famous St. Petersburg architect David Grimm.

Many famous artists represented the Jaegermeister Village on their canvases. Among them are the court artists of three emperors, Mihaly Zichy, Nicholas Sverchkov, Alexei Savrasov, and others. In honor of the 100th anniversary of the establishment of the Jaegermeister Corps, which was celebrated in 1896, one of the houses in the Jaegermeister Village was converted into a museum, which existed up until 1917.

Alexander III and Maria Feodorovna walking around the tables, where
peasants, members of the Tsar's Hunt, are being fed, c. 1892.
Photograph by Konalski, Spala. [RGAKFD]

The Arsenal Hall at Gatchina Palace, c. 1940.
Photograph by M.A. Velichko. [GMZ "Gatchina."]

Gatchina Palace

Laurits Tuxen.
(1853-1927)

Tuxen's famed group portrait of King Christian IX and Queen Louise of Denmark with ther family. At center are the Danish monarchs with their son Valdemar and his sister Thyra, Marie d'Orléans, holding her daughter Alexandra. To Christian IX's left are Alexander III, Maria Feodorovna and their youngest son Michael Alexandrovich. Next to the Tsar are his brothers-in-law Crown Prince Frederik of Denmark and King George I of the Hellenes, followed by Princess Alexandra and Queen Olga of Greece. Seated in front of Frederik is his wife, Crown Princess Louise with their daughter Princess Ingeborg. To the left of the painting, seated, is the Prince of Wales with his eldest son Albert Victor (Eddie) and his wife Alexandra, herself the eldest daughter of the Danish monarchs. [Eurohistory Archive]

In 1884 the court artist of Christian IX, Laurits Tuxen (1853–1927) spent several months at Gatchina. He had received the choice assignment of making parade portraits of members of the Danish Royal family in connection with the twentieth anniversary of the reign of King Christian IX and his wife Queen Louise. During his visit to Gatchina, the artist was to make preliminary drawings of Empress Maria Feodorovna and her family. Tuxen, by this time, had a substantial education as an artist. He had graduated from the Danish Royal Academy of Art, and also had spent time studying in France. At the beginning of his career the young artist was supported by the Danish "King of Beer," Karl Jacobsen, who in 1879 had ordered the artist to paint for him copies of the works of Titian and Raffael.

In his memoirs, published in Denmark in 1927, Tuxen described what it was like to work at Gatchina. Empress Maria Feodorovna and her children Michael, Xenia and Olga would pose for him several times, but Alexander III did this only once. The artist recounted: "He came to me in a parade uniform, asked what pose to take, and for an hour stood in one position, without moving. I worked as fast as I could, and as a result, when the Emperor asked to look at my sketch, he broke out in a huge laugh."

The Empress, during one of her sittings, asked Tuxen why he never walked in the park, and having learned that he was not allowed to leave the premises, she commanded that a pass be issued to the artist so he could walk through the palace grounds. Once, while taking a walk, on a small bridge Laurits Tuxen met the Russian Emperor.

This episode, which became the subject of social rumors, the court artist of the King of Denmark remembered in the following manner: "I greeted the Emperor, and having put my hat back on my head, asked, could he

Grand Duchesses Xenia and Olga Alexandrovna.
[RGAKFD]

please pose for me once again. "We shall see." Came the response.

Later I learned that I had committed a major faux pas by replacing my hat in the presence of the Emperor. A new session was out of the question, and the newspapers ran reports about my offensive behavior. That which might have been allowed in Fredensborg, the Emperor of Russia did not permit in his country."

In 1886 work on the group portrait comprised of 32 members of royalty was completed, and the huge canvas, measuring five by seven meters, was exhibited at a special viewing in Charlottenborg, the residence of Crown Prince Frederik. During the first two days, some twenty thousand people came to see the painting. It brought great fame to the Court Artist, and also many orders. At the present time the original painting can be found in the Representative Hall of Queen Margrethe II in Christiansborg Palace, Copenhagen.

Grand Duke Michael Alexandrovich with his dog next to the bridge by the White Lake in Gatchina Palace park, c. late 1880s.
[TsGAKFFD SPb]

The Visits of Emperor Alexander III and His Family to Denmark

For Easter 1890, Emperor Alexander III gave his usual surprise gift to his wife. For the sixth year in a row he ordered for Maria Feodorovna an Easter egg from the jewelry atelier of Carl Fabergé. The never-ending imagination of the famous jeweler this time expressed itself in a pink egg, covered in semi-transparent enamel, in the style of Louis XVI. His new work of art Fabergé decorated with applications of gold laurel leaves, encrusted with little belts of diamonds. Emeralds shone in the crisscrossing. The egg stood on a very delicate gold tripod, and a sapphire, the beauty of which was underscored by a tiny ring of twinkling diamonds, topped the cover of its little "jewelry chest."

Although the outside decoration was of exquisite beauty, the true miracle of this work of art was contained inside. Ten mother of pearl sections held for the eye of the beholder miniature images of the fondest memories in the heart of Maria Feodorovna.

European society of the 1890s was familiar with the residences of the Danish King and the Russian Emperor, and these images appeared on the surprise section of the egg. On two side sections were pictures of the yachts the "Polar Star" and the "Tsarevna" floating on a brilliant sea; these were the yachts on which Alexander III and Maria Feodorovna would make their voyages.

A year after their marriage Grand Duke Alexander Alexandrovich and his wife made a visit to Denmark, and from that time on their visits to her relatives became regular, almost yearly, events. Totally charmed by the friendly atmosphere and the warm receptions, the young couple always strove to spend part of the summer months visiting with Christian IX. Alexander III and all members of his ever-growing family thoroughly enjoyed time spent in Copenhagen; it was here, according to the words of Grand Duchess Olga Alexandrovna that they "felt like ordinary people." As a rule they would set out on their journey to Denmark on the Imperial yacht. Members of Court would accompany the couple, and for a few days the yacht would become home, with

The 1890 Easter created in the workshop of Carl Fabergé, with its surprises – the small screens, 2.5 centimeters in height, with miniatures by Konstantin Kryzhitsky, depicting the favorite residences of Empress Maria Feodorovna: Bernstorff, the Kaiser Villa at Fredensborg, Fredensborg Palace, Amalienborg Palace, Kronborg Palace, the Cottage at Peterhof and Gatchina Palace. Photograph from the archives of V. Skurlov.

all necessary facilities. Grand Duchess Olga Alexandrovna would remember, "We were allowed to take on board several of our household pets, but not our rabbit or our wolf cub ... the yacht took on the appearance of Noah's ark. There were two cows on the deck. The trip took exactly three days, and Maman thought that we should not go without our fresh milk."

In Denmark members of the Royal Family and personnel of the Russian Embassy made preparations for the visit of the esteemed guests from Russia. Maria Feodorovna's relatives waited eagerly for the arrival of the Imperial family. As soon as the Imperial yachts sailed past the island of Bornholm, the King was sent an immediate telegram, announcing the arrival of his guests. Having received the message, Christian IX, together with his sons, would go on board the Royal yacht "Dannebrog" and it would set out to sea. Queen Louise accompanied by her Court would go to the dock in her carriage. Very often, during the summer months, King George I of Greece and his sister the Princess of Wales, accompanied by their families, would also be visiting. They would all come to the dock to participate in the grand meeting of their relatives from Russia.

After their arrival on Danish soil, members the ruling Houses of Europe would take a trip by railroad to the town of Helsingor. This little

A view of Konborg Castle. [IIMK RAN]

Grand Duke Michael Alexandrovich and his sister Grand Duchess Olga Alexandrovna on the deck of the Russian Imperial yacht. A young sailor accompanies them. With them is the Imperial family's dog, who traveled everywhere with them.

Empress Maria Feodorovna in the early 1880s.
Photograph atelier of "Levitsky and Son." [GARF]

The Russian Embassy on Copenhagen's New Royal Square.
Photograph by I. Danielsen. [TsGAKFFD SPb]

King Christian IX and Queen Louise of Denmark.
[RGAKFD]

settlement became famous to the world under the name of Elsinor, being the main location of Shakespeare's tragedy "Hamlet."

The ancient castle of Kronborg stands high on a cliff; it was erected in the 16th century at the command of Danish King Frederik II. The main decoration of the castle, one of the best examples of Danish national architecture, is the high central tower, the Buglers' Tower. The silhouette of this tower announces to approaching ships their proximity to the nation of Denmark.

In 1891 the main building of the railroad station at Helsingor was deemed to be not appropriately imposing as the greeting place of the Russian Tsar; so, it was totally remodeled. A marble staircase now leads to the second floor, where on both sides of the entrance doors of dark oak stand the figures of stone lions, with the Danish coat of arms in their paws. Through these doors one can enter into the Tsar's Room. These apartments for the August couple were decorated in gold-leafed leather wallpaper, dark oak paneling, a fireplace with the Royal Crown above it, and a large brass chandelier.

The garden by the Western façade of Fredensborg Palace. [TsGAKFFD SPb]

The Visits of Emperor Alexander III and His Family to Denmark

While days were filled with many informal activities that led to many a shenanigan and countless anecdotes, evenings were a formal affair. Christian IX and Louise enjoyed hosting their various visiting relatives to formal dinners, like the one pictured here. This particular evening affair took place in the Cupola Hall in 1889, and among those present one can see Alexander III and Maria Feodorovna, her brother Frederik and their sister Alexandra of Wales, among many others. [TsGAKFFD SPb]

In the Cupola Hall, Fedensborg.
Seated at center is Queen Olga of Greece with Grand Duchess Xenia Alexandrovna and Princess Victoria of Wales flanking her. Leaning on Olga is her son Andreas, while her niece Louise of Denmark sits on the floor. Standing are: Princess Maud of Wales, Princess Marie of Greece and Queen Louise of Denmark, c. late 1880s. [RGAKFD]

Emperor Alexander III and Maria Feodorovna, as a rule, spent the better part of their stay in Denmark in the summer royal residence of Fredensborg.

Even today, Fredensborg is still considered to be the summer residence of the Danish monarch. During the days when the Royal family is in residence, a gala changing of the guard is performed daily on the eight-pointed square by the entrance gate.

The largest room in the palace is the Cupola Hall, with a height of 27 meters; its floor consists of black and white marble plates. It is here that grand receptions and dinners are held, with a multitude of important guests. The Russian Imperial family would stop in the apartments next to the large Cupola Hall. The windows in these rooms face the park, with its wonderful view of the walkways leading to Lake Ezrum. The central room is the White Hall, also known as the Park Hall; this was the favorite of Alexander III. A description of its interior decor has been preserved in the account of the Danish journalist Valdemar Zeger: "... the living room also served as a working study for the Emperor; this was a large room furnished with white and gold-encrusted furniture, with light blue fabric. There were many paintings of Dutch masters on the walls, as well as a portrait of Catherine II. The mantelpiece had a bust of the grandfather of the Emperor; the walnut desk was covered in green

Queen Louise with her daughters Alexandra of Wales and Maria Feodorovna on a ride in the park of Fredensborg. [RGAKFD]

Prince Valdemar of Denmark with his sisters Alexandra and Maria Feodorovna. [RGAKFD]

King Christian IX and Queen Louise's daughters: Maria Feodorovna, Thyra of Cumberland and Alexandra of Wales. [Eurohistory Archive]

cloth, like the armchairs, and they were in stark contrast with the other furniture, but the Emperor liked this desk very much, and he always kept a record of the dates he visited Denmark in the drawer." It was in this very room, the Park Hall at Fredensborg Palace, that in 1880 the Danish Court artist Laurits Tuxen depicted the members of the Royal family for their group portrait.

A beautiful park was created around the palace at Fredensborg. French architect Nicolas Henri Jarden designed it in 1760s baroque style. According to the plans of this master on the western side of the palace there was a so-called "Marble Garden." In the 19th century the parks were expanded, new straight walkways and romantic twisting alleyways appeared. In 1883 a Russian journalist wrote, "The main attraction of the park is the so called "Valley of Normans," which contains some 70 statues out of sandstone. They are very delicate in their design and illustrate the most original national costumes of all the nationalities which had inhabited, and still inhabit, the nation of Denmark."

A multitude of guests from different European countries would pass the time here, riding horses, playing games, or going on picnics. Emperor Alexander III would often appear in the walkways of the park, surrounded by children. Grand Duchess Olga Alexandrovna remembers that, "My father was very prone to all sorts of pranks. Sometimes he would take us to muddy ponds in search of baby frogs, sometimes to the fruit orchards of Apapa (Grandfather) to steal apples .... Papa would participate in all of our games, and because of him we

The small garden on the Island of Roses in the park at Fredensborg.
Photograph by F. Danielsen. [TsGAKFFD SPb]

From left: Prince Valdemar of Denmark, Prince George of Greece, Tsarevich Nicholas Alexandrovich, Prince Nicholas of Greece and Prince Christian of Denmark, c. 1893.

The bust of Alexander III in Fredensborg Park. Photograph by Galina Korneva, c. 2008.

The Russian Pavillion in the park of Fredensborg Palace.
[TsGAKFFD SPb]

Vladimir Rat'kov-Rozhnov.
(1834-1912)

would sometimes be late for meals, but no one would reproach us ... The three weeks spent in Denmark would provide a real respite for him. I had the impression that inside the adult man a young scamp of a boy continued to exist."

The visits of the Imperial family to Fredensborg were considered to be real holidays for the local citizens. The first day after their arrival the quiet streets of the village would fill with merriment, store merchants and little shops would display their best wares, and journalists would try to catch glimpses of members of the royal families in public.

After the death of Alexander III, Danish citizens living in the environs of Fredensborg took up a collection and erected a monument in his memory, created by the Danish sculptor N. Nilsen. On the pedestal one can still see engraved the dates of the first and the last visit of the Emperor to this royal summer residence: "1866–1893."

From the windows of the Park Hall there was a beautiful view on to the Russian Pavilion. At the suggestion of

The Kaiser Villa at Fredensborg.
Photograph by Galina Korneva, c. 2008.

Alexander III's study at the Kaiser Villa. From "Vserminaya Illustratsiya, 1899."

Visits of Emperor Alexander III and His Family to Denmark

St. Petersburg philanthropist Vladimir Rat'kov-Rozhnov, the pavilion, in which the Russian exhibit was housed during the Scandinavian Fair of 1888, was given as a gift to King Christian IX. This exhibit was organized to mark the 25th anniversary of his reign, and, as a result of the support of Empress Maria Feodorovna, many famous Russian masters participated. The success of those who had presented their wares, jewelers and silver

smiths – Carl Fabergé, Michael Grachev, Paul Ovchinnikov, textile producers – the brothers Sapozhnikov, and furniture maker Roman Meltser, was so great that, paying no attention to established traditions, they were all elevated to the rank of "Suppliers to the Court of Denmark." At the end of the exhibition Vladimir Rat'kov-Rozhnov offered King Christian IX to move the Russian pavilion, at his own expense, to any place that the King would desire. The building was reassembled in the park at Fredensborg on a greater scale and was very beautifully furnished. For his grand gesture in 1888 Vladimir Rat'kov-Rozhnov was bestowed with the Large Cross of the Order of Dannebrog.

The Park Hall in Fredensborg Palace.
Photograph by F. Danielsen. [TsGAKFFD SPb]

Even though Emperor Alexander III had a desk in the Park Hall of the palace, the presence of so many relatives would often distract him from his work. He needed to work on government business in the quiet of his study. Because of this, in 1885 the Russian Emperor decided to purchase a small house, constructed of native rock and brick, situated on a high crag not far from the central entranceway of Fredensborg Palace. This small, cozy house, decorated with carvings, with little balconies and a mezzanine, local Danes called "Kaiser Villa," and the street on which it was located – "Kaiser Lane." On one of the windows of the miniature winter garden to this day one can see etched in the Cyrillic alphabet the word "Niki," this was written using a diamond, by the son of Alexander III, the future Emperor Nicholas II.

In 1892 Denmark celebrated the golden wedding anniversary of the Royal Couple. On May 14 (26) the weather was absolutely perfect in Copenhagen. The Russian

The changing of the guard at Fredensborg Palace.
Photograph by Galina Korneva, c. 2000.

Embassy, located on New Royal Square, was bedecked in red cloth on the cornices, with fresh flowers on the windows. For this exceptional event many relatives of Christian IX and Queen Louise gathered in Copenhagen. They were all present at the church service at the Slotkirche – the Royal Chapel, and a festive procession followed in the streets of the Danish capital: "after the carriage of the King and Queen of Denmark came the carriage of Emperor Alexander III, dressed in the uniform of the Danish Life-Guard Regiment, with Empress Maria Feodorovna. Following them were the Heir and Tsarevich Nicholas Alexandrovich, members of the Russian Court, the King of the Hellenes, in a Danish admiral's uniform, the Queen of Greece with their

The triumphal arch built on Heibro Square to celebrate the Golden Wedding Anniversary of Christian IX and Louise of Denmark, 1892. [RGAKFD]

children and members of their court, the Prince of Wales and his wife Alexandra, with their children and members of their court, the Danish Crown Prince and his wife Louise with their children, the Duke of Cumberland and his wife Princess Thyra and their children, Prince Valdemar and Princess Marie with their children, Archduke Franz Ferdinand of Austria with his courtiers, the representative of the German Emperor, Prince Albert of Schleswig-Holstein-Glücksburg, Prince Carl of Sweden, the brothers of the King of Denmark and others." On that day the Heir of the Danish Throne gave a dinner for 100 people; there was a special gala performance at the Royal Theater. In the evening, the streets of the city were illuminated and at ten o'clock in the evening the ships in the harbor were ablaze in fireworks. The procession to the royal palace at Amalienborg consisted of 100,000 people. The artisans of Copenhagen presented the Royal Couple with a golden carriage.

For their Golden Anniversary all of the children, daughters-in-law, sons-in-law and grandchildren presented King Christian IX and Queen Louise with two gold-covered silver goblets for chilling wine, made by the master Julius Rappoport and other jewelers of the House of Fabergé. The goblets had the names of the 48 gift givers engraved on them, and their handles were in the form of elephants, symbols of happiness, and also reminiscent of the highest state award in Denmark, the Order of the Elephant.

Crowds outside the Amalienborg Palace congratulating King Christian IX and Queen Louise on their Golden Wedding Anniversary. [RGAKFD]

Queen Louise of Denmark.
(1817-1898)

Empress Maria Feodorovna

& Her Siblings

I n 1892 during the grand celebrations for their Golden Wedding Anniversary, the Royal Couple was especially pleased that all of their children could travel from across Europe and spend some time together in Denmark.

From the moment he had ascended the throne, Christian IX was greatly assisted in governmental affairs by his twenty-year old eldest son. In 1863 Frederik was at Oxford University, but it was necessary for him to return to Denmark as the Crown Prince and to commence participating in the work of the State Council; the following year he was able to show his military talents during a trying time for Denmark. For the duration of the war with Prussia and Austria, Crown Prince Frederik took upon himself the duties of Inspector General of the army. Two years later, Frederik accompanied his younger sister Dagmar to Russia, had supported her during her first weeks in a strange country, and was present at her wedding to the Heir and Tsarevich Alexander Alexandrovich.

Frederik had the title of Crown Prince for 43 years and ascended the throne in January of 1906, at the age of sixty. In 1869 the Crown Prince married a very rich bride, Princess Louise of Sweden. The newlyweds settled

A royal gathering around King Christian IX and Queen Louise, 1892.
Standing (left to right): Princess Maud of Wales, Crown Princess Victoria of Sweden, Prince Carl of Denmark, King Christian IX, King George I of the Hellenes, Tsarevich Nicholas Alexandrovich, Tsar Alexander III, Crown Prince Frederik of Denmark, Prince Hans of Schleswig-Holstein, Crown Princess Louise of Denmark, Crown Prince Gustav of Sweden, Princess Victoria of Wales, Sprincess Marie of Greece, Prince Valdemar of Denmark. Seated (same order): The Princess of Wales, Queen Louise, Empress Maria Feodorovna, Grand Duke Michael Alexandrovich. On the ground (from left): Prince Andreas of Greece, and Princess Thyra, Princess Ingeborg and Prince Harald of Denmark. [TsGAKFFD SPb]

King Frederik VIII of Denmark.
(1843-1912)
[RGAKFD]

in the Brockdorf Palace at Amalienborg, which in 1906 became known as Frederik VIII's Palace. The summer residence of Crown Prince Frederik's family was the palace of Charlottenlund. Both of these palaces were noted for their comfort and impeccable furnishings. Crown Princess Louise had great artistic talents and very good taste. Her handsome dowry allowed the young couple to be independent and to purchase articles of luxury and works of art. It is well known that at the Paris World's Fair in 1900 they purchased a collection of multi-layered glass from the French master of the "moderne" Emile Halle. In the couples' palaces there were collections of silver and other applied arts.

Charlottenlund Palace was constructed for the sister of King Christian VI, Charlotte Amalie, in 1731–1733 and named in her honor. The remodeling of the building was performed under the direction of architect Johan Cornelius Kriger. In 1880 the Crown Prince's family assigned architect Ferdinand Meldahl to substantially enlarge the residence. Two wings were added to the main building, as well as a dome with a lantern on top. The palace changed from its baroque style to one reminiscent of the French Renaissance, especially its façade.

In the second half of the 17th century an expansive park was created around the palace, with many ponds and over four hundred different kinds of plants. When the palace was owned by Charlotte Amalie there were baroque-styled parterres in the park, and these framed with neatly trimmed trees and bushes. In the 1880s Crown Prince Frederik and his wife, reflecting the changing fashions of the times, gave the wonderful park a new appearance, transforming it into a landscaped English garden.

The Palace of Frederik VIII at the Amalienborg, Copenhagen.
Photograph by Galina Korneva, 2008.

The family of Frederik and Louise consisted of eight children – four sons and four daughters: Christian (1870–1947), Carl (1872–1957), Louise (1875–1906), Harald (1876–1949), Ingeborg (1878–1958), Thyra (1880–1945), Gustaf (1887–1944) and Dagmar (1890–1961). The Crown Prince's eldest sons – Christian, the future King Christian X of Denmark, and Prince Carl, who in 1905 was declared the King of Norway, with the name of Haakon VII, were both born in Charlottenlund. Queen Louise continued to live in Charlottenlund until her death in 1926.

The eldest daughter of Christian IX and Louise, Alexandra, was born in 1844 in Copenhagen's Yellow palace the family home. From her childhood everyone around her considered the young lady to be extremely beautiful, and Alexandra was able to keep this beauty right up until the last days of her life.

On March 10, 1863, Princess Alexandra made a spectacular marriage to the Prince of Wales, Albert Edward ("Bertie"), Queen Victoria's eldest son and heir. The wedding ceremony took place in Windsor Castle. The young Princess of Wales was well loved by the British due to her kindness, dedication to charity and love of her family. Alexandra was an excellent equestrian; she enjoyed music and photography, and loved to dance and ice skate. For the celebration of the Golden Anniversary of her arrival in England, Alexandra requested that the anniversary be marked by the sale of roses in London. The funds collected were used to finance the various charities the Dowager Queen supported. In her honor, the celebration became known as the "Alexandra Rose Day." Noble ladies and volunteers, to raise money for hospitals, orphanages and clinics, sold handmade flowers, put together by disabled persons. The fundraising continues to this day and Princess Alexandra, The Honourable Lady Ogilvy, the Dowager Queen Alexandra's

Crown Prince Frederik and his wife Louise with their four eldest children. Behind Louise are Christian and Carl. In her lap is Harald and leaning on her is Louise. Photograph by Hansen, 1877. [TsGAKFFD SPb]

great-granddaughter and namesake is the current President of the Alexandra Rose Day.

Sandringham House became the main country residence of the Prince and Princess of Wales. It was here that

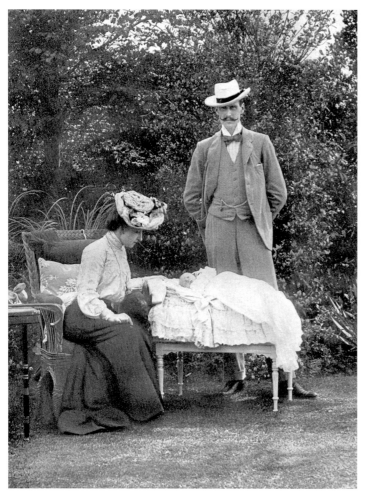

Prince Carl of Denmark and his wife, and first cousin, Princess Maud of Great Britain, with their baby son Alexander. Two years later Carl became King Haakon VII of Norway. Photograph by Ulaf, 1903. [ILN]

they were happy, and saw their family grow. Alexandra preferred to live here after the death of her husband, and it was in this large mansion that she herself died in 1925. In London, before succeeding his mother in 1901, the Prince of Wales lived at Marlborough House.

During the first eight years after their marriage, Princess Alexandra and Bertie, his family nickname, saw the arrival of three sons and three daughters: Albert Victor (1864–1892), George (1865– 1936), the future King of Great Britain, Louise (1867–1931), Victoria (1868–1935), Maud (1869–1938), and Alexander (b./d. 1871). Alexandra devoted a lot of time and effort to raising her children and enjoyed immensely her relations with them, but she disregarded their education.

The closest person to the Princess of Wales was her younger sister Dagmar. The warm relationship that the two sisters had in Denmark, they were able to preserve throughout their entire lives. Not having the possibility to see each other, they exchanged letters constantly, sending with them photographs of their children and extended relatives. With the passing of time Queen Alexandra and Empress Maria Feodorovna had amassed thousands of pages of correspondence written in Danish, the language in which the two sisters had conversed since childhood.

In June 1873, Tsarevich Alexander Alexandrovich and his wife Tsarevna Maria Feodorovna came to London on an official visit. They stayed in England for almost two months, and the sisters were happy to be able to see each other, making every attempt not to be separated. They made a pact to dress alike, every day. This little prank they repeated again at a later time. Photographs taken in Denmark, Russia and other countries have captured the friendly sisters always dressed in the same attire. During their stay in England the children of Maria

The Park Hall and Louise's boudoir in Charlottenlund Palace. From the magazine "The Queen," 1894.

Charlottenlund Palace.

The Prince of Wales, who in 1901 succeeded as King Edward VII.
[RGAKFD]

The Princess of Wales, born Princess Alexandra of Denmark.
[RGAKFD]

Feodorovna became very close to their Wales cousins. Everyone could not help but notice how Nicholas and George resembled each other.

In January of the following year the Prince of Wales and his wife visited Russia. Bertie and Alexandra came to St. Petersburg to attend the wedding of his younger brother Alfred to Maria Alexandrovna, the sister of Tsarevich Alexander Alexandrovich. The honored guests stayed at the Anichkov Palace and at the Alexander Palace in Tsarskoe Selo, where eleven rooms were specially prepared for them. The British Ambassador to Russia, Lord August Loftus, noted that the center of everyone's attention those days were the two sisters, "glowing in their rare beauty and simply beaming with joy from being together."

Sandringham, the country residence of the Prince and Princess of Wales.
Photograph by Bedford Lemer, "The Strand Magazine," 1893.

Tsarevich Alexander Alexandrovich with Tsarevna Maria Feodorovna and her sister Alexandra, the Princess of Wales. This image dates from the early 1870s and shows the two sisters wearing identical dresses. [RGAKFD]

Empress Maria Feodorovna and Her Siblings

The third daughter of King Christian IX and Queen Louise, Princess Thyra, was also born in Copenhagen's Yellow Palace. When the little girl turned nine, her elder sister Alexandra married the Prince of Wales, during that same year her brother Willie was invited to become the King of Greece. Three years later, Princess Dagmar would also leave Denmark and settle in Russia. In this way, young Thyra became the closest relative to the rulers of four European nations – Denmark, Russia, Greece and England. Her brother Frederik was many years her senior, and it was only with Prince Valdemar, five years her junior, that Thyra could share childhood games. All three daughters of Queen Louise were considered to be pretty, but without a doubt the most beautiful was Alexandra. Contemporaries also noted the quick wit and attractiveness of Dagmar; as far as Thyra was concerned, people first spoke of her outgoing nature and her kindness. All three Danish Princesses were taught to play the piano; Alexandra and Thyra were considered to be the most talented.

At the age of seventeen Thyra experienced her first big love. She was enamoured with a Hussar officer, First-Lieutenant Vilhelm Frimann Marsher, who was twelve years her senior. When Queen Louise realized that her daughter was with child, in order to avoid scandal, she took Thyra away. During this journey, Thyra delivered a daughter. The baby's father was forbidden from seeing his beloved, and in January 1872 he committed suicide; Thyra learned of this tragedy only a half year later.

While resting in Rome with her sister Alexandra and her husband Bertie in 1872, Thyra met the man who would be her future husband, Ernst August. He was the son of the blind King Georg V of Hannover and his wife, the former Princess Marie of Saxe-Altenburg). On his mother's side Ernst August was the nephew of the Grand Duchess Alexandra Iosifovna. Thyra and Ernst were mutually attracted to each other, but due to political reasons the marriage was postponed for six years since it was feared that an alliance between a Danish princess and the Heir to Hannover, a dynasty dethroned by the Hohenzollerns, would upset Germany. The wedding finally took place on December 21, 1878, at Christiansborg palace in Copenhagen. Earlier that year, after the death of his father, Ernst August took the title of the Duke of Cumberland. The newlyweds spent their honeymoon in Fredensborg, and later settled in Upper Austria, in Gmunden Palace, the summer residence of the son of the King of Hannover.

A miniature portrait of Empress Maria Feodorovna placed inside a heart-shaped frame made by Master Michael Perkhin.
This was given in 1905 by Maria Feodorovna to her sister Thyra of Cumberland. Sotheby's Auction House Catalogue, November 24, 2008.

The Princess of Wales with her two eldest sons, Albert Victor and George, 1866.
[RGAKFD]

A Fabergé bell, Master Michael Perkhin.
From the Anichkov Palace Collection.

Queen Louise and some of her children.
Seated are Maria Feodorovna and Prince Valdemar. Behind them are:
Queen Louise, the Princess of Wales and Princess Thyra.
[RGAKFD]

A photograph of Princess Thyra, who in 1878 became the Duchess of Cumberland as the wife of the Heir to Hannover. She was born in 1853 and died in 1933. Photograph by Hasen & Weller. [RGAKFD]

Here the couple spent the first years of their married life, until their own home Cumberland Castle was built in a nearby park. Christian IX and his wife visited their youngest daughter often. In the autumn of 1889 Prince Sergei Volkonsky came to Cumberland Castle and wrote the following account about the mistress of the castle, "She was totally beguiling. The mother of many children, she herself remained childlike, someone not of this world; she gave the impression of having invisible wings on her shoulders ... In the huge hall, where two grand pianos stood, there was also a large sofa, where, after dinner, the father and his children would play, bounce around, slide down, jump up and down, and the whole room would resound with their screams. Above all of this bustle Princess Thyra and I would play on the two pianos."

Thyra and Ernst August had six children: Maria Louise (1879–1948) – she was named in honor of Ernst August's mother and Thyra's mother; in 1900 she became the wife of Max of Baden; Georg Wilhelm (1880–1912), he was named in honor of Thyra's eldest brother and died in an automobile accident; Alexandra (1882–1963), she had the same name as Thyra's sister; in 1904 she became the wife of Grand Duke Friedrich Franz IV of Mecklenburg-Schwerin, the son of Grand Duchess Anastasia Mikhailovna; Olga (1884–1958), named after her Russian aunt, the Queen of Greece; Christian (1885–1901), who died of appendicitis, was named in honor of his maternal grandfather; and Ernst August (1887–1953), named in honor of his father. In 1913 he married Princess Victoria Louise of Prussia, the only daughter of Kaiser Wilhelm II.

Maria Feodorovna's youngest sibling was Prince Valdemar. He remained in Denmark and served in the navy. In 1886 Valdemar married Princess Marie d'Orléans (1865–1909), the eldest daughter of the Dukes of Chartres (Robert and Françoise), and niece of the claimant to vacant French throne, the Count of Paris. Valdemar had a peculiarly close friendship with his nephew Prince George of Greece. Still, he and Marie did manage to pro-

An interesting royal gathering showing Prince Valdemar of Denmark and his nephew Prince George of Greece.
From left: Princess Margrethe, Princess Marie Bonaparte (George's wife), Prince Erik, Prince Valdemar, Prince Aage, Prince George of Greece (note his hand holding on to Prince Valdemar), Prince Viggo and Princess Marie c. 1908. [Eurohistory Archive]

duce five children: Aage (1887–1940), Axel (1888–1964), Erik (1890–1950), Viggo (1893–1970), and Margrethe (1895–1992), who married Prince René of Bourbon-Parma (1894–1962), a brother of Empress Zita of Austria-Hungary. Of the sons only Axel married equally, his wife being Princess Margaretha of Sweden, eldest daughter of his own cousin Princess Ingeborg of Denmark. Valdemar's wife was a very unique princess who loved joining the fire brigades to help fight fires in Copenhagen. She was a talented artist as well. Marie and her brother-in-law Alexander III were very close friends and she tended to bore him with political talk. Princess Marie died unexpectedly in 1909. Her husband survived her thirty years. When after the Russian Revolution Maria Feodorovna settled in Denmark, Valdemar was a constant visitor to his sad sister. He died in 1939.

Among Valdemar's and Marie's descendants is Queen Anne, wife of King Michael I of Romania, himself the great-grandson of both Grand Duchess Maria Alexandrovna (Duchess of Saxe-Coburg & Gotha and Edinburgh) and of Grand Duchess Olga Konstantinovna, better known as Queen Olga of Greece.

Prince Valdemar and Princess Marie of Denmark.
[Eurohistory Archive]

Important Events in the Life of
Emperor Nicholas II

Because of the success of the "Fredensborg portrait" Laurits Tuxen became famous not only at home, but also in other European countries. In 1887 Queen Victoria invited the Danish artist to Windsor Castle to put on canvas members of her family who had gathered to celebrate her Golden Jubilee.

On the portrait, which he painted while in England, Tuxen depicted 55 relatives and guests of the Queen, and received very high praise for his work from his client. In 1894 Queen Victoria, who herself was unable to go to Russia, offered Tuxen the opportunity to go to St. Petersburg to paint the wedding of her granddaughter the Princess of Alix of Hesse and by Rhine and Emperor Nicholas II.

Queen Victoria was also very fond of photographs. In the photo albums of Queen Victoria there were many photographs of her children and grandchildren, made during the happy moments, whether it was their visits to her Court or their weddings. Such photographs would also appear in English periodicals, magazines and newspapers, such as the Illustrated London News and The Queen. As a rule, they were accompanied with articles describing the wedding dress of the bride, the gifts received, and her illustrious dowry. When, in 1894, Queen Victoria set out to Coburg, where she was scheduled to attend the wedding of her grandchildren Grand Duke Ernst Ludwig of Hesse and by Rhine and Princess Victoria Melita of Saxe-Coburg & Gotha, she invited Court Photographer James Russell to accompany her on this journey; his numerous photographs, made during the wedding celebrations, became treasured pieces in family albums of European rulers, and also appeared

Tuxen's spectacular painting depicting the wedding of Emperor Nicholas II and Empress Alexandra Feodorovna.
Standing around the Imperial couple were, among others: King Christian IX, the Dowager Empress Maria Feodorovna with her daughters Xenia and Olga, the Prince of Wales, the Duke and Duchess of Saxe-Coburg & Gotha, the King and Queen of Greece, Grand Dukes Vladimir, Sergei and Alexei Alexandrovich, Grand Duke Michael Alexandrovich, among many others. [Eurohistory Archive]

Important Events in the Life of Emperor Nicholas II

The Iconostas (Altar Screen) of the Large Church in the Winter Palace c. 1903. [TsGAKFFD SPb]

Tsarevich Nicholas Alexandrovich with his bride Princess Alix of Hesse and by Rhine, Coburg – April 14 (26), 1894. Photo by Uhlenhuth, Coburg. [Eurohistory Archive]

on the pages of newspapers and magazines, describing this wedding, as well as the engagement of Tsarevich Nicholas Alexandrovich and his beloved Alix of Hesse and by Rhine.

In the Russian Imperial Family, during the second half of the 19th century, it was not customary to photograph the bride and groom in their wedding attire. This was basically tied to church traditions: orthodox rites and the interiors of churches were only illustrated on canvases or in watercolors, not on photographs. That was why on November 14 (26), 1894, in the front side pew of the Large Church of the Icon of the Savior Not-Made-By-Hands inside the Winter Palace, together with the choir, one could see the artists Ilia Repin, Mihaly Zichy and Laurits Tuxen. These three talented artists busily drew the important

A view of the Palace Enbankment and the Winter Palace, St. Petersburg 1900. Photography by K. Bulla. [TsGAKFFD SPb]

event they witnessed and later transferred their vision into canvas.

The wedding of Nicholas and Alexandra was an extraordinary event for Russia – for the first time in the history of the Romanov Dynasty an Emperor was getting married, not an Heir to the Throne, a Tsarevich. The wedding took place on the birthday of Dowager Empress Maria Feodorovna, and for that day only mourning for Emperor Alexander III was lifted. In his memoirs the Danish artist described the ceremony in the church in

225

the following words, "The newlyweds stepped on to a pale pink carpet. Each had a candle in their hands. The priests, three on each side, were around the small gilded analogion, "a lectern or slanted stand on which icons or the Gospel Book are placed for veneration by the faithful."

The bride – her back completely straight, with her head slightly bowed, appeared as a most beautiful creation in the works of Luini and Leonardo, with her face lit by the candle from underneath; the diamond tiara, the dark blond curly hair above her forehead, a single curl flowing down to her bosom, her shoulders uncovered, her mantle of gold cloth, with an ermine lining, her dress of silver brocade ....

Standing along a wall is King Christian IX, who had traveled from Copenhagen to support his grandson. To the right of King Christian XI are the Dowager Empress Maria Feodorovna, Grand Duchess Olga Alexandrovna, the Princess of Wales, Queen Olga of Greece, [the Duchess of Saxe-Coburg & Gotha, Grand Duchess Alexandra Iosifovna, and many others]. Olga Alexandrovna had some lace on her dress, the others were simply in white [court dresses] ... I was totally inebriated with joy and can hardly recall another time when the beauty of the moment so engulfed me. The beautiful bride, the entrancing singing of the choir, the brilliancy of colors, the flickering of the candles and the gold cloth."

The Danish artist was allowed to work in the Large Church and in the Malachite Hall of the Winter Palace, and inspired by the beauty he remembered, was able to complete his masterpiece in just two months. Nicholas II

Grand Duchess Maria Pavlovna posing in the studio of artists E. Liphart for her official portrait, assigned to the Academy of Art. St. Petersburg, 1909-1910. Photograph by K. Bulla. [TsGAKFFD SPb]

I. Repin's painting illustrating the marriage of Nicholas II and Alexandra was presented to them in 1910. This can be attested in the following excerpt from a letter regarding the presentation of two paintings – "The Marriage of the Tsar" to the by the painter – to Grand Duchess Maria Pavlovna and to the Emperor:

*"May 6, 1910 – Kuokkola Station of Finnish Railroad.
Your Imperial Highness!
We, the association of Traveling Exhibits, will be eternally grateful, if you, and His Imperial Majesty will accept from us this small gift, as a symbol of gratitude for the enormous support of artists, and for Your intercession with His Imperial Majesty, the building on Mikhailovsky Square of the exhibition hall for art and sculpture ... "*

Member of Your Imperial Highness's endowed Imperial Academy of Art, Ilia Repin.

was so pleased with Tuxen's creation, that he paid him £900 Sterling and ordered a copy made to give as a gift to his mother, the Dowager Empress Maria Feodorovna. Today this painting can be seen on display at the State Hermitage Museum, where in September 2006, during the days of the reburial of Maria Feodorovna, an exhibition titled "The Court Artist Laurits Tuxen" was held.

A year after his ascending the throne, Nicholas II decided to create in the Mikhailovsky Palace, purchased by the state treasury from the descendants of Grand Duchess Ekatherina Mikhailovna, a Museum of Russian Art named in memory of his father, Emperor Alexander III. The grand opening of the museum took place on March 7, 1898. The initial basis of its collection was the works of art acquired by representatives of the Imperial Family.

The Russian Museum, named after Emperor Alexander III, and former home of Grand Duke Michael Pavlovich and his descendants, c. 1900.

Grand Duchess Maria Pavlovna, the President of the Academy of Art, in 1910 expressed the desire to build in St. Petersburg an exhibition center called the "Palace of Art." Two years later the Academy of Art was given a plot of land, next to the Mikhailovsky Palace, on the side of the Ekaterininsky Canal embankment. Only one problem was left unsolved – where to obtain the huge sum of money, over one million rubles, necessary to complete the project, according to the plans of the Rector of the Academy of Art, Leon Benois. In February 1913 St. Petersburg and Moscow bankers were able to collect just such an amount, in time for the celebration of the 300th anniversary of the reign of the Romanov Dynasty. The donors asked Nicholas II to designate the goal and recipient of these funds. And although the Emperor was advised to spend the money on other matters, he preferred to support the proposal of Grand Duchess Maria Pavlovna. In a few months the decision was finalized, and during the summer construction of the exhibition hall was start-

The Benois Wing of the State Russian Museum in St. Petersburg. Architect L. Benois. Photograph by Galina Korneva, 2001.

ed; it became known as the Benois Wing. During the festive laying of the corner stone, the first bricks of the foundation were laid by Emperor Nicholas II and Grand Duchess Maria Pavlovna.

At the present time the Benois Wing houses a large exhibition of Russian art from the beginning of the 20th century – the time when the Russian school of art became well known throughout the world.

Before their wedding, Emperor Nicholas II and Alexandra Feodorovna, when he was in St. Petersburg, resided with his mother at her home, the Anichkov Palace. Not wishing to leave the Dowager Empress Maria Feodorovna alone in her grief, the young couple decided to settle in the same rooms at the Anichkov Palace that Nicholas, when Tsarevich, had previously occupied. At the same time from the end of 1894 plans were being made regarding the remodel of the suite of rooms the young Emperor's family would use in the Winter Palace. These rooms were located on the second floor of the northwestern wing, and from their windows a wonderful view opened out on to the vast Neva River and the Admiralty buildings. At the suggestion of the

The bedroom of Nicholas II and Alexandra Feodorovna in their suite of rooms at the Winter Palace. [GMZ "Peterhof"]

Folding icons given by Elisabeth Feodorovna to her sister Alexandra on her wedding day to Nicholas II. In the center are the icons of Our Lady of Kazan and the Savior-Not-Made-By-Hands. On the sides are the heavenly protectors of the Imperial couple, St. Nicholas and St. Alexandra. From the magazine "Vemirnaya Illustatsiya, 1894.

The Cathedral of the Feodorov Icon of the Mother of God, built in honor of the Tercentennary of the Romanov Dynasty. St. Petersburg. Architect S. Krichinsky.

Grand Duchess Elisabeth Feodorovna the plans for the interiors were to be prepared by St. Petersburg architect Alexander Krasovsky. N. Nabokov did designs for the furniture. On December 30 of the following year (1895), the Imperial Family, together with their two-month old baby daughter Olga, left the Alexander Palace in Tsarskoe Selo and moved into their new rooms at the Winter Palace; their rooms were blessed with holy water on that same day.

On the first day of the New Year, 1896, Emperor Nicholas II wrote in his diary, "We slept well and arose rather early ... At 11:00 the formal Procession commenced. For the first time we performed the New Year entrance side by side ... We had lunch together, then in the evening we hung our icons in the new alcove for them in the bedroom."

Among the icons which hung in the sleeping quarters of the Imperial Couple in the Winter Palace, two were very special – the Savior Not-Made-By-Hands and the Feodorov Icon of the Mother of God; it was with these icons that Their Imperial Highnesses were blessed on the day of their Imperial Wedding. They were painted in oil on wood, and were encrusted with jewels. During the celebrations of the 300th Anniversary of the Romanov Dynasty a decision was made to build a cathedral dedicated to the Feodorov Icon of the Mother of God in St. Petersburg; a collection was made throughout the entire country, and members of the Imperial family donated a substantial amount of money. Nicholas II donated 25 thousand rubles for the construction of the cathedral. The President of the Academy of Art Grand Duchess Maria Pavlovna, in addition to the 25 thousand rubles donated, had decided to also order at the Mosaic Department

*The miracle-working Feodorov Icon
of the Mother of God.*

*View of the Ipatiev Monastery from the banks of the Kostroma River.
Kostroma Gubernia (Region), 1913. Photograph by K. Bulla.* [TsGAKFFD SPb]

of the Academy an image of the Savior Not-Made-By-Hands, and to have it placed above the entrance to the memorial cathedral. Knowing about the two icons that were always in the sleeping chamber of the Tsar and Tsarina – the icon of the Savior was painted by the artist Victor Vasnetsov – Maria Pavlovna requested Nicholas II in July of 1912 to allow for a copy of the image to be made.

The stone, two-storied cathedral was erected on the grounds of the Feodorov Monastery of the Nizhny Novgorod diocese. The altar table of the lower church was consecrated in the name of the patron saint of St. Petersburg, St. Alexander Nevsky. The upper church was consecrated in the name of the Feodorov Icon of the Mother of God; this cathedral could serve up to two thousand people, and it was exceptional in its decoration. The firm of P. Olovianishnikov, owner of factories in Moscow and Yaroslavl, and a trading house in St. Petersburg, ordered a marble altar table for the cathedral, as well as silver holy items and a huge "grand panikodilo" (central chandelier), 6.5 meters in width, made out of light bronze, in the shape of the "Monomakhs Cap" (the crown of early Russian Grand Dukes – trans. note). The Emperor's Court had donated to the cathedral a silver alcove for the holy sacraments, the Corps of the Guard – had copies made of the

*Restoration of the frescoes in the Ipatiev Monastery –
May 1913. Photograph by K. Bulla.* [TsGAKFFD SPb]

holy items in the Ipatiev Monastery. The façade of the cathedral was faced with white rock from the town of Staritsa. On the north side there was a four-meter high icon of "The Protection of the Virgin Mary over the Imperial House." The Feodorov Icon of the Mother of God, made according to the design of Chekhonin, was specially created in the maiolica studio of Peter Vaulin. Over the entranceway was the icon of the Savior Not-Made-By-Hands donated by Grand Duchess Maria Pavlovna, made in mosaics and copied from the work of Victor Vasnetsov.

It was not by accident that the second icon with which the newlyweds Nicholas and Alexandra were blessed on their wedding day was the Feodorov Icon of the Mother of God. This miracle-giving icon was known in

Emperor Nicholas II and his wife Alexandra Feodorovna exiting the Trinity Cathedral in the Ipatiev Monastery immediately after the service of gratitude praising the Lord for the 300th Anniversary of the Romanov Dynasty, 1913. Photograph by K. Bulla. [TsGAKFFD SPb]

Russia from the 12th century. According to tradition, the parents of Alexander Nevsky blessed him with this icon before his wedding with a Polotsk Princess. Not long before his death Grand Duke Alexander, who was later called "Nevsky," took monastic vows before this icon in the Gorodets Monastery. For some time the exact location of the icon was not known, but at the end of the 1250s the icon was miraculously found again in Kostroma, and it appeared to Alexander Nevsky's younger brother Vasiliy. The icon was placed in the monastery of St. Feodor Stratelates; it was from here that it became known as the "Feodorov" icon. Prince Vasiliy Yaroslavovich built the Uspensky ("Dormition") Cathedral in Kostroma, where the icon was housed up until 1929.

The next important event tied with this icon occurred on March 14, 1613. That year in the Holy Trinity Cathedral of the Ipatiev Monastery of Kostroma, the Abbess Martha blessed her 16-year-old son Michael to become Tsar with this icon. Thus, the first member of the Romanov Dynasty ascended the throne of Russia, and from that time on the Feodorov icon of the Mother of God was to become highly revered by the ruling family. In May 1913, when the celebrations of the 300th Anniversary of the House of Romanov took place, Emperor Nicholas II, together with members of his family, visited the ancestral home of the Romanov family, the lands around Kostroma. On the morning of May 19, the steamship "Mezhen" smoothly approached the Imperial dock, where the Emperor and his family were greeted by numerous relatives, including those who had arrived from Germany: the Dowager Duchess of Saxe-Coburg & Gotha and the Dowager Grand Duchess of Mecklenburg-Schwerin. From here the procession of colorful coaches moved towards the Ipatiev Monastery; in front of the Green Tower, Archbishop Tikhon greeted the Imperial family together with representatives of the senior clergy. The correspondent for the newspaper "Kostromskaya zhiz'n" ("Kostroma Life") recounted the event as follows, "The cinema cameras started to crackle, as the Imperial cortege approached the monastery. The sounds of the national anthem could be heard. By the tower gate the court coaches stopped. Their Highnesses ... kissed the Feodorov icon and proceeded into the Trinity Cathedral ... After the liturgy Their Highnesses viewed the restoration works; the guide for the Imperial family was the artist and architect D.V. Mileev. Upon exiting the cathedral Their Highnesses took a tour of the Romanov Boyar Palace."

During the Imperial visit to Kostroma in the month of May 1913, the foundation was laid of the memorial statue dedicated to the 300th Anniversary of the House of Romanov. The decision to create the main monument for the tercentenary event in this city was made long before the anniversary celebrations; in 1911 the Imperial Academy of Art reviewed some of the works submitted in the competition for its implementation. The honor

Important Events in the Life of Emperor Nicholas II

In May 1913, Emperor Nicholas II, the Imperial Family and distinguished guests, attended an important celebration in Kostroma to commemorate the 300th Anniversary of the House of Romanov. [TsGAKFFD SPb]

of producing this grand monument fell to sculptor Amandus Adamson, famous by that time for his work in Sevastopol (the monument to the "Sunken Ships"), in Reval (the monument to the armored ship "Rusalka"), and for other works in St. Petersburg. The artist had the idea of reproducing in bronze the figures of several Tsars, Minin, Pozharsky, Susanin, all encircling a granite tower with a canopy, on top of which would be a two-headed eagle. The overall image of the monument recalled one of the towers of the Moscow Kremlin. The location of the monument was to be next to the Kostroma Kremlin on a cliff over the Volga River.

On May 20, the religious procession ("Krestny Khod") started out from the Uspensky Cathedral of the Kremlin to the spot where the new monument would be located. Nicholas II himself placed the first brick for the

Sculptor Amandus Adamson. (1855-1929) [TsGAKFFD SPb]

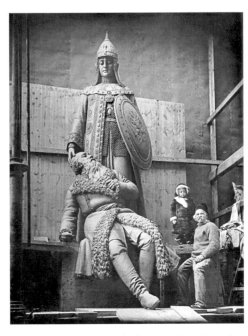

Adamson sculpting the figures of Russia and Susanin. [TsGAKFFD SPb]

231

foundation; he then spoke to the sculptor and examined the three large figures already created by that time – the statue of "Russia," "Tsar Mikhail Feodorovich" and "Ivan Susanin."

The following year saw the beginning of the First World War, and then came the revolution. Not surprisingly, the monument was never completed. On the pedestal so grandly situated on the bank of the Volga today stands the totally disportionally huge (15 meter high) figure of Lenin; and the Uspensky Cathedral in the Kostroma Kremlin, where the miracle-working icon, the protector of the House of Romanov, used to be kept, has been destroyed, at the command of the Bolsheviks. They destroyed not merely the cathedral, but Nicholas II himself and other members of the Imperial Family fell victims to their brutality.

Another cathedral of great importance to the family of Nicholas II was consecrated in the name of the Feodorov Icon of the Mother of God. It was constructed in the environs of the Russian capital before the First World War.

In 1905, Nicholas II and his wife decided to make their permanent residence at the Alexander Palace in Tsarskoe Selo. The Imperial couple had spent the first months of their honeymoon in this palace. It was there where the Tsarevich Nicholas Alexandrovich was born in 1868. Nicholas II wrote in his diary on November 30, 1894, "My contentment is without bounds. It is so hard to leave Tsarskoe, which has become so dear to the two of us; for the first time since our wedding we were totally alone, and lived completely heart to heart (in the original Russian "soul to soul" – trans. note)." It was at this time that the newlyweds started to plan how to remodel their private rooms in the right wing of the palace; in September of the following year they spend several months there. The favorite room of the entire family was the Mauve Boudoir of the Empress Alexandra Feodorovna, that she furnished in a Victorian style with furniture imported from Maples in London.

The monument to Lenin in Kostroma. Photograph by Galina Korneva, 2007.

The original model of the monument dedicated to the 300th Anniversary of the House of Romanov in Kostroma. Sculptor A. Adamson. [TsGAKFFD SPb]

Important Events in the Life of Emperor Nicholas II

Not far from the Alexander Palace were the quarters of His Imperial Majesty's Combined Infantry Regiment, created by Alexander III for the protection of the Imperial Family in 1881. Located close to the Egyptian Gate at the entrance to Tsarskoe Selo, the Combined Regiment had requested several times from the Emperor permission to build its own cathedral. Finally, in 1908 Nicholas II agreed to their request, selected a location for the cathedral, and donated 150,000 rubles for its construction. The Tsar's Cathedral was erected, modeled on the Annunciation Cathedral in the Moscow Kremlin; it was consecrated on August, 1912 and named after the Feodorov Icon of the Mother of God. There were three tent-shaped entrances with high staircases; this enabled everyone – the Imperial Family, the clergy and the military to be at the proper place at once. The Imperial entrance was adorned with a gold-leafed two-headed eagle. Over the main western entrance there was a huge mosaic panel with the image of the Feodorov Icon. In the lower part of the cathedral, at the request of the Empress, and built by funds donated by her personally, there was a "cave" church, with many frescoes; here, especially during the weeks of Great Lent, Alexandra Feodorovna liked to pray.

Ancient icons from the 16th–17th centuries, in richly ornamented special cases, were kept here; there were also numerous rare holy ritual items, and wonderful icon cloths, embroidered with gold and silk thread.

The Family of Emperor Nicholas II.
Right to left: Grand Duchess Olga Nikolaevna, Emperor Nicholas II, Empress Alexandra Feodorovna holding Tsarevich Alexei Nikolaevich, Grand Duchess Tatiana Nikolaevna. Sitting on the floor: Grand Duchess Maria Nikolaevna (in front of Tatiana) and Grand Duchess Anastasia Nikolaevna (holding her father's hand).
St. Petersburg, 1904. Photograph by Boissonas & Eggler. [TsGAKFFD SPb]

In 1904 arguably the happiest moment in the life of Nicholas II's family took place – on July 30 (August 12), the long awaited Heir and Tsarevich, Alexei Nikolaevich, was born. The little boy arrived into this world in Peterhof, in the Lower Summer Dacha (Lower Dacha), where, since 1895, Empress Alexandra Feodorovna and her husband would rest practically every summer.

The Lower Summer Dacha was built for Tsarevich Nicholas Alexandrovich according to the plans of architect Anthony Tomishko. It was blessed on June 16, 1886. After their wedding in 1894 Nicholas II and his wife decided to prepare for their first summer season in Russia, and had the Lower Summer Dacha remodeled to

The Tsar's Cathedral dedicated to the Feodorov Icon of the Mother of God (Feodorovskaya Icona, c. 1912. Architect V. Pokrovsky. Photograph by K. Bulla. [TsGAKFFD SPb]

The Alexander Palace in Tsarskoe Selo. Fragment of a lithograph based on a drawing by Meyer, c. 1840.

include residential rooms. The large, urgent order for preparation of furniture was received by St. Petersburg architect Roman Meltzer. The Management of the Peterhof Palace required from the firm of Meltzer that the order be fulfilled "by Imperial Decree for the new palace in Alexandria" in a time frame of "no later than May 20, 1895." By the onset of the first warm days of summer everything was ready. Furniture from polished Karelian birch stood in the study of Alexandra Feodorovna, the bedroom had furniture from mahogany, and for the study of His Imperial Majesty a special desk – "a writing desk of carved walnut" according to Meltzer' drawings, with a padded leather desk cover.

Peterhof – the Imperial summer residence – is as old as St. Petersburg. Starting from the first quarter of the 18th century this was where members of the House of Romanov liked to spend part of their summers with their families. The luxurious Grand Palace rooms would be made ready for very important guests, representatives of the ruling Houses of Europe.

During Nicholas I's reign, not far from the "Versailles on the bank of the sea," architect Adam Menelas, a Scott by nationality, built a cottage in the manner of the most beautiful villas on the outskirts of

The Mauve Boudoir in the Alexander Palace, c. 1914.
[TsGAKFFD SPb]

Important Events in the Life of Emperor Nicholas II

London. This adorable little manor home in a Neo-Gothic style Nicholas I gave as a gift to his wife, and in her honor, the Romanov family "dacha" (or summer house) was called "Alexandria." From that time on the little cozy palace was passed on from one generation to the next, and in 1894 its owner became the Dowager Empress Maria Feodorovna.

Empress Alexandra Feodorovna and Tsarevich Alexei Nikolaevich, c. 1906. [ILN]

Every summer numerous relatives from abroad would come to visit Russia. Maria Feodorovna was especially pleased whenever her parents would come, and also her elder sister Alexandra, accompanied by her daughters. Very often Alexander III's only sister, the Duchess of Edinburgh, Maria Alexandrovna, would stay at Alexandria. The greatest number of guests, and the most boisterous crowds, would be present during the "Greek gatherings" – these would be the family of Queen Olga and her husband King George I. Olga Konstantinovna and Maria Feodorovna were close in age, and in their attitude towards life, and they were able to pass along their bonds of sincere and loving friendship to their children, particularly to Princess Marie of Greece and her first cousin Grand Duchess Xenia Alexandrovna, who were always very close friends. In the future their friendship continued when they both married sons of Grand Duke Mikhail Nikolaevich. The Greek Royal Family most often stayed at the Konstantin Palace in Strelna, the residence of Queen Olga's parents.

The family of Nicholas II would very often go on vacation to Europe. As a rule, they would travel on Imperial

The Lower Dacha in Alexandria.
[TsGAKFFD SPb]

Nicholas II's study in the Lower Dacha in Alexandria. Photograph by K. Bulla. [GMZ "Peterhof"]

The Imperial Family with their Greek Royal cousins at the Cottage Palace in Alexandria, c. 1889.
Standing in back (left to right): King George I of the Hellenes, Empress Maria Feodorovna, Queen Olga of Greece, Prince Nicholas and Princess Alexandra of Greece, Grand Duchess Xenia Alexandrovna, Crown Prince Constantine and Princess Marie of Greece. At front (same order): Grand Duchess Olga Alexandrovna, Emperor Alexander III and Grand Duke Michael Alexandrovich. [RGAKFD]

yachts. Emperor Nicholas II would come to his closest relatives to Denmark aboard the Imperial yacht "Standart." Alexander III ordered the vessel to be built at a Danish shipyard; the yacht was put to sea in 1896. The official launch was done in the presence of the Danish Royal family, headed by Crown Prince Frederik. However, by the time the ship was finished, Alexander III had been dead by nearly two years.

The decor of the yacht was in a strict English style, no gold leaf or stuccowork. Everything was made for the ultimate comfort of the Imperial passengers and their guests. The Emperor, Empress, and the Dowager Empress all had their own private suites, consisting of a living room, bedroom and bathroom. On the same floor were located the dining room, a salon, the Grand Duchesses' cabins and the officers' quarters.

In the mess hall, right in the middle, there was a large dining table, across from which there was a buffet, and alongside that a piano. In one corner there would be several soft armchairs, and above them, under glass, a silver mallet, with which Alexander III had driven in the first nail into his "Standart." A library bookcase was also present. On the bulkhead there was a large portrait of the first owner of the yacht, as well as photographs of other Imperial family members, given as gifts to the officers of the vessel.

On the lower deck were the children's rooms. Nicholas II was pleased that the new "Standart" had utilized furniture and silver utensils from his old yacht – "Derzhava" ("the Realm"). A new china service for the yacht, including 1,625 pieces of china and 1,190 pieces of glassware, were made at the Imperial Porcelain and Glass Works of St. Petersburg.

The Imperial family and its Court would settle in the large rooms, and right next to them were the cabins of the officers and servants. Also, on the lower deck were the rooms for the musicians of the brass band and the balalaika orchestra.

In September 1896, the "Standart" set sail for England and France. That year was the beginning of twenty years of service of the world's most beautiful Imperial yacht. During its stops in European nations it was like an "island of Russian soil" – on its decks the most glamorous receptions were held, while many important diplomatic meetings occurred. There was probably not a single major European leader who did not set foot on the deck of the "Standart."

In 1902 while anchored off Reval, Kaiser Wilhelm II visited the "Standart", and six years later in the same port city the family of Nicholas II entertained King Edward VII of Great Britain. In June 1912, in

The study of Empress Maria Feodorovna in the Cottage Palace in Alexandria.
[GMZ "Peterhof"]

Reval, the German Kaiser visited Nicholas II onboard the "Standart" one last time. The Kaiser's white and gold yacht, the "Hohenzollern" was smaller in size than the "Standart," and Wilhelm II was quite open in his

The younger children of Alexander III – Xenia, Michael and Olga at the Cottage Palace. [RGAKFD]

The Princess of Wales and her niece Princess Marie of Greece at the Cottage Palace. [GARF]

The Imperial Family onboard the Imperial Yacht "Standart." Finland, 1906. Photograph K. E. von Gan & Go. [RGAKFD]

Tsarevich Alexei Nikolaevich with young balalaika players on the deck of the "Standart." Photograph K. E. von Gan & Go. [RGAKFD]

admiration of the Russian Emperor's yacht. The pair met one last time in 1913 when Nicholas II attended the wedding of Kaiser Wilhelm II's daughter to Ernst August of Hannover, Duchess Thyra of Cumberland's youngest son.

The Imperial yacht was so dear to Emperor Nicholas II that he even had his dining room in the Lower Summer House at Alexandria made to be an exact copy of the yacht's interior.

During the Great War, the "Standart" was kept in dry-dock. After the revolution, sadly, the Communists, who ordered it stripped down and turned the one-time unique sailing marvel into a minelayer, also destroyed the "Standart." Later it became a training ship before being scrapped in 1963 off Tallinn, Estonia.

Emperor Nicholas II and Kaiser Wilhelm II onboard the "Standart." Reval, July 24, 1902. Photograph K. E. von Gan & Go. [RGAKFD]

The mess hall on the "Standart."

The Dowager Empress Maria Feodorovna

The year 1906 proved to be a pivotal one for the Danish Royal Family. That January, Christian IX, after a long and successful reign that began in challenging times in 1863, passed away. Her brother, King Frederik VIII, who was to reign over Denmark for six short years, succeeded the Dowager Empress Maria Feodorovna's beloved late father.

With the passing of Christian IX, his daughters Alexandra and Maria Feodorovna purchased the Villa Hvidore not far from Copenhagen, on the shore of the Eresund. The villa was built in Italian style in 1871–1872, according to the plans of architect Johan Schreder. The beautiful mansion, surrounded by fruit trees and flower gardens, stands on a small promontory overlooking the sea. From the grand terrace of the snow-white two-storied building, and also from its balcony decorated with caryatids, one has a marvelous view of open waters. Having bought the summer residence, Maria Feodorovna and Alexandra took to remodeling it with great joy. They selected the fabric for the wallpaper, they ordered furniture from the firm "Waring and Gillow" in London, they invited interior design specialists from England, and very soon the cozy house took on the appearance of an English cottage. From the expansive white hall, with gold leaf decoration, a double-lane staircase led to the rooms of the second floor. On the first floor were located two living rooms, one for each of the sisters, a study, with two separate writing desks and book cases, a billiard room and a dining room, covered in vines and greenery on trellises. Here, among the grand pots with tropical plants, the sisters liked to dine, enjoying the view of

Empress Maria Feodorovna surrounded by her children.
From the left: Grand Duke Michael Alexandrovich, Grand Duchess Xenia Alexandrovna, Empress Maria Feodorovna with her youngest child Grand Duchess Olga Alexandovna, Grand Duke George Alexandrovich and Tsarevich Nicholas Alexandrovich.
[Eurohistory Archive]

the sea, which could be seen through the widely opened glass doors, leading on to the terrace. For assistance, for looking after all of the houseplants and the voluminous gardens the sisters hired a gardener from England.

Maria Feodorovna and Alexandra had their rooms filled with photographs of people dear to them, as well as countless souvenirs and their favorite books. Maria Feodorovna's bedroom also had many holy icons. In order to underscore their particular affection to Hvidore, the mistresses of the house had placed an inscription above the fireplace in the billiard room with the saying, "East, West, home is best." They both signed it. Since one of the

*The Villa Hvidore, an image from the collection of
T. Ladyzhenskaya-Meiners.*

*Queen Alexandra and Maria Feodorovna in the billiard room at
Hvidore, c. 1907. Photograph by Mary Steen.* [ILN]

ladies was the Dowager Empress of Russia and the other the Queen of Great Britain, this quote took on a much deeper meaning.

In September 1907, when Maria Feodorovna and Alexandra first settled in their new seaside residence, they had the flags of both England and Russia raised. At Hvidore, only their closest relatives and friends visited the sisters.

Now that Maria Feodorovna had her own house in Denmark, she would go to England in the spring, and in the fall she and Alexandra would spend time in Hvidore. In 1914, while she was visiting her sister, the Dowager Empress learned about the onset of war between Russia and Germany. She gathered her belongings in a hurry, said goodbye to the Royal Family and set off for St. Petersburg on an express train. She traveled through France and Belgium, crowds cheered her train as it passed villages readying for war, but this ended when she reached

*The study shared by Alexandra and Maria Fedorovna at Hvidore.
From the collection of T. Ladyzhenskaya-Meiners.*

*From left: Dowager Empress Maria Feodorovna, King George of
the Hellenes, Queen Alexandra and King Frederik VIII of
Denmark in the garden of Hvidore, 1907.* [ILN]

The Dowager Empress Maria Feodorovna with her daughter Grand Duchess Olga Alexandrovna in her boudoir at the Anichkov Palace. [RGAKFD]

the German capital. On July 22 (August 4) Dowager's train entered the station at Berlin, where the Russian Ambassador Sergei Sverbaev awaited her on the platform. He warned her that traveling further was out of the question since Germany had closed the lines to Russia. Not wanting to appeal to the Kaiser, who did not bother to send anyone to greet the Dowager Empress, her train waited at the station for a solution to the impasse. The crowds grew noisier, louder, more menacing. Some windows on the train were broken and little did Maria Feodorovna know that only the fear of international outrage prevented the Kaiser from ordering her arrest. Finally, Count Mirbach, an official from the Foreign Ministry, told the Dowager Empress that due to Russia's dec-

The Duchess of Cumberland, Dowager Empress Maria Feodorovna and Queen Alexandra. [Eurohistory Archive]

At Hvidore Maria Feodorovna and Alexandra pose with their pet dogs. [Eurohistory Archive]

The Dowager Empress Maria Feodorovna and Grand Duchess Olga Alexandrovna surrounded by nurses at their hospital in Kiev, c. 1916.
[GMZ "Peterhof"]

laration of war, she would have to head out of Germany. It was necessary then to detour to neutral Denmark. Once at Hvidore, where she stayed for a short visit, Maria Feodorovna ordered that her most valuable possessions be moved to Christian IX's Palace at Amalienborg. From Copenhagen Maria Feodorovna, and the large retinue that had joined her since arriving in France, sailed to Malmo, from where they boarded a train to Stockholm. Eventually, after driving to the Swedish-Finnish border near the Arctic Circle, the Russians, after some further delays, were able to board an old Imperial train. On July 27, after many difficulties and nine days of journey, the Dowager Empress finally reached the Russian capital.

Life in the Anichkov Palace changed drastically. Maria Feodorovna had some of the rooms in the palace transformed into a home for wounded soldiers; in the dining room, she and ladies of St. Petersburg society would prepare bandages and gift packages, or sort clothing and linens for field hospitals. During just one year clothing and foodstuffs needed at the front were sent out from the warehouses of the Anichkov Palace totaling over 1,246,567 roubles. The Dowager Empress had ordered that hospitals be opened in Minsk, Kiev, Tbilisi, as well as a sanitarium in the Crimea for officers recovering from wounds. She herself paid for two military hospital trains for 100 and 400 wounded.

In May 1916 Maria Feodorovna went to Kiev, as she did often. She would always visit the Main Hospital, where the chief trustee was her daughter Olga. Here Grand Duchess Olga, side by side with medical personnel, would spend days tending to the wounded, assisting with operations, and serving in the wards. She was tireless and worked around the clock, as did several other ladies of the Imperial Family. Once in Kiev, Maria Feodorovna felt that her presence was of great help there and stayed longer than expected. The Dowager Empress had no idea that she had left behind her beloved Petrograd, as St. Petersburg was then known, forever.

October 27, 1916, was the 50th anniversary of the wedding of Maria Feodorovna and the late Alexander III. This day was extremely joyous for the Dowager Empress – she was visited by her darling son Nicki and the Tsarevich Alexei. That fall also saw a very

The military hospital train of the Dowager Empress Maria Feodorovna on the platform of the Nikolaevsky Station, St. Petersburg. Photograph by K. Bulla.
[TsGAKFFD SPb]

The Dowager Empress Maria Feodorovna

Members of the Danish Embassy.
Seated from left: Ambassador Skavenius, Secretary and Commercial Attaché
M.V. Langberg and Attaché Ove de Kaas.
From the magazine "Stolitsa i Usad'ba," 1914. [The Capital and the State]

*The building in which the Danish Embassy as located at
Petrograd's No. 11 Millionaia Street.
Photograph by Galina Korneva, 2004.*

happy event in the life of Grand Duchess Olga. Earlier in 1916, she was finally granted permission from the Emperor to divorce Duke Peter of Oldenburg, a marriage that had caused Olga much unhappiness. In November, in a little suburban church, she was married to her beloved partner of many years – Colonel Nikolai Kulikovsky. Grand Duke Alexander Mikhailovich remembered that, "This was an exclusively quiet, almost secret, wedding: the bride, the groom, the Dowager Empress and I, two nurses from the Red Cross and four officers from the Akhtyrsk Hussar Regiment, whose patron was the Grand Duchess herself."

Her mother's love took precedence over implications of dynastic duties, and having blessed her daughter in this dynastically unequal marriage, Maria Feodorovna felt sincerely happy for her, even though she always treated Kulikovsky coldly. These joyous moments were soon to be replaced by terrible trials and tribulations, which were to rain upon the entire Romanov family, and all of Russia.

On March 2, 1917, Emperor Nicholas II was forced to abdicate the throne. He soon after decided to also abdicate in the name of his son. The Romanov Dynasty no longer ruled over Russia and uncertain times overcame its members. At the end of the month, and by order of the Provisional Government, the Dowager Empress, Olga Alexandrovna and her husband Colonel Kulikovsky, and Alexander Mikhailovich were moved from Kiev to the

*Anna (1889-1962), the wife of
Ambassador Skavenius.*

*The living room in the Skavenius residence.
From the magazine "Stolitsa i Usad'ba," 1914.* [The Capital and the State]

243

Crimea. At the same time Grand Duchess Xenia Alexandrovna and her sons were also able to flee Petrograd to their estate Ai-Todor. Red Army officers placed all of them under house arrest, and with each passing day their troubles and fears only increased. In March 1918 the Danish Ambassador to Russia Harold Skavenius reported to his government that any day "gangs of Bolshevik sailors" can at any moment murder all members of the Romanov family, "The Dowager Empress, her two daughters and her son-in-law are in extremely dangerous circumstances, without money, and undergoing great difficulties." The nephew of Maria Feodorovna, King Christian X, and her brother, Prince Valdemar, sent telegrams to Skavenius in Petrograd asking for his help. They insisted that the journey out of Russia for Maria Feodorovna be organized as soon as possible. Being a man of great personal valor, the Skavenius started actively organizing the return journey of the former Danish princess back to her homeland.

Harold Skavenius came from a famous Danish family, representatives of which had brought fame to Denmark as ministers, diplomats, entrepreneurs, members of the world of culture and the arts. Having served as consultant to the Danish Embassy in St. Petersburg for six years, Skavenius spoke Russian fluently. In January 1909 he married Anna Sophie Stensen, and in 1913 they settled in an apartment on St. Petersburg's prestigious Millionnaia Street, No. 11.

C. A. Koefoed in the steppes of Siberia, c. 1911
The Koefoed family archives.

C. A. Koefoed with his wife Elisabeta Petrovna
(née Obiedova) and their daughter Nina.
The Koefoed family archives.

It was here that Harold Skavenius had moved some of the furnishings from his Danish estate Gjorslev, where he had spent his childhood. He invited a cook and several other servants to come with him to Russia to help run his household. The Danish Ambassador was known for his unusual courage, his correctness, and a deep sense of duty. His wife remembered in her memoirs how once, during the autumn of 1917 some soldiers were beating up a passerby right under the windows of their apartment. Not being a man of great physical strength, the Ambassador, without a second thought, ran outside to help the unfortunate Russian stranger, fought off the attackers, and gave the man refuge in the Danish mission.

Harold Skavenius did everything possible to help the Imperial Family. The Ambassador visited the Grand Dukes who were taken prisoner, tried to obtain their release, and risking not only his reputation, but also even his life, attempted to save members of the House of Romanov from injustices brought upon them by the Bolsheviks. It was at the initiative of Skavenius that a representative of the Danish Red Cross, Karl Krebs, was sent to Maria Feodorovna in the Crimea. Krebs was a nephew to Andrei Andreevich Koefoed. He had hidden in his belt one million rubles, to be used to obtain the release of the Romanovs, and also 50,000 rubles and a basket of provisions for Maria Feodorovna.

From 1916 to 1920 Carl Andreas Koefoed (1855–1948) worked at the Danish Embassy defending the rights of Austro-Hungarian prisoners of war. He, like his benefactor, Empress Maria Feodorovna, had spent more than

"When we were all running around without our heads, and did not know what to do, in order to save the situation, Koefoed, at his own expense, would travel around the countryside and do the one thing that was necessary. His name shall be written in gold letters in the history of Russia."

Prince B. A. Vasilchikov, Chief of Land Use and Agriculture (1906-1908) in the cabinet of Prime Minister Stolypin.

C. A. Koefoed on this 83th birthday, 1935.
The Koefoed family archives.

fifty years in Russia. He shared with his new country not only a period of great success and development, but also all of the trials of the revolution. In Russia, Carl Andreas was known as Andrei Andreevich; he not only spoke Russian impeccably, but he even wrote his scientific dissertations in this language. Here he had a family, and in 1892 he even became a Russian citizen.

At the beginning of his career Andreas Koefoed was helped by the Danish Ambassador, Camerger Kier, who was able to obtain the support of Maria Feodorovna. With the help of her recommendation, Koefoed received a position in the Dvoriansky ("Nobility") Bank in 1881; working as an appraiser, unexpectedly for himself, he became very interested in the problems of communal ownership. From August 1901, under his own initiative, he commenced work on breaking up communal property into private ownership, and in this he found his life's work. Koefoed was one of the initiators and a very active participant in the reforms of Prime Minister Stolypin. More than a fifth of the land privatized for peasants in Russia was realized under his direction. He even wrote a small pamphlet, in very comprehensible Russian, about the problems of a rational distribution of land to peasants, which was printed in more that half a million copies, and sold out in a matter of months.

It would seem that it was not by chance that the lives of Koefoed and his similarly minded friend, the reformer Stolypin, had crossed. Supported by the Prime Minister, Andrei Andreevich was able to defend his principles, and reach real, practical results; he also rose on the career ladder – by the beginning of the First World War he already had the rank of State Advisor and was a member of the Council of Ministers of Agriculture.

The Dowager Empress Maria Feodorovna and Queen Olga of Greece at Hvidore. Photograph by Z. Mengden. [GARF]

During the difficult days of the revolution Koefoed had to change his citizenship one more time, and become a Dane once again. Carl Andreas traveled across all of Siberia, was even accused of being a spy and spent several months in a Tobolsk concentration camp. From 1924 C.A. Koefoed worked in Moscow as a consultant to the Danish Embassy on questions of agriculture, and only in 1930, when Stalin destroyed the peasantry, especially the successful peasants, Koefoed returned to his homeland. When this extraordinary human being turned 90, he published a book of memoirs titled "Fifty Years in Russia," the pages of which are filled with the deepest love for his second homeland.

After many different schemes to free the Romanovs, the Dowager Empress and her daughters and their families managed to survive the revolution and to escape Russia. In April 1919 Maria Feodorovna, accompanied by a large retinue, left the Crimea on HMS Marlborough, sent to retrieve her by King George V, her beloved nephew, who had failed to save the Tsar and hi family. After spending time in England in the company of her sister Alexandra, Maria Feodorovna finally arrived in Denmark, where she would live her last years.

The Kulikovskys. From the left: Tikhon, Grand Duchess Olga Alexandrovna, Guri and Nikolai. From the collection of T. Ladyzhenskaya-Meiners.

King Christian X of Denmark and his wife Alexandrine, a granddaughter of Grand Duke Michael Nikolaevich. [GARF]

The Dowager Empress Maria Feodorovna

In Copenhagen Maria Feodorovna settled at Hvidore, and in the autumn, when the weather got cold, she moved to Amalienborg, where her living style upset her nephew Christian X, who at times proved most unkind to his Russian aunt. From 1920 onward, she would spend most of her time in her villa. The Dowager Empress, whose life had been passed in huge, luxurious Russian palaces, ended her life in a small residence, resembling a typical manor home. This was the only spot on earth that still belonged to Maria Feodorovna; it became very dear to her, and she was often heard to exclaim, "I love Hvidore – it is mine!"

On the eve of Easter 1920, after the most trying circumstances, Olga Alexandrovna and her husband Nikolai Kulikovsky, with their very young sons Tikhon and Guri, finally reached Denmark. Timothy Yashchik, the faithful chamber-cossack of Maria Feodorovna, sent by her to Rostov, helped the family in overcoming the very difficult journey. The once luxurious court of the Russian Empress in Hvidore had now turned into a small circle of close friends and loyal servants. Maria Feodorovna was extremely generous and tried to help all, who had remained devoted to her. Olga's family stayed near Maria Feodorovna until her last days. Olga Alexandrovna had loved to draw, even as a young child, and during her stay in Denmark she painted many scenes around her, or, from memory, would paint things dear to her: Russian churches, snow covered fields and villages. Her watercolors with scenes of Hvidore, the gardens surrounding the house and the flowerbeds, have been saved.

The bedroom of the Dowager Empress Maria Feodorovna at Hvidore; she died in this room.
From the collection of T. Ladyzhenskaya-Meiners.

Maria Feodorovna received constant attention and help from her Danish relatives, first and foremost from Prince Valdemar, who would visit his elder sister almost every day. In exile, the main source of income for Maria Feodorovna were the funds allocated to her from the English Royal Family, who after her death paid handsomely for her jewels. She also received support of Danish entrepreneurs whom the Dowager Empress had once helped in Russia. Among them, were the Director of the Main Northern Telegraph Society, Christian Skavenius, and the Director of the East-Asian Company, Hans Niels Andersen.

During the beginning of October 1928 the Dowager Empress Maria Feodorovna became very ill. Both her daughters, Xenia and Olga, stood vigil at her bedside. Maria Feodorovna died in Hvidore on October 13. News of her death immediately became known all around Copenhagen and throughout Europe. On the following day her obituary was printed in the Danish newspaper "Nationaltidende." It ended with the words: "Denmark is today mourning her wise and courageous daughter."

On the morning of October 16 the coffin with her body was brought to the Russian Orthodox Church of St. Alexander Nevsky on Bredgade Street. Alexander III built the church in the 1880s mostly from donations by the Imperial Couple. It was here, in this Russian church, that the body of Maria Feodorovna lay in state for people to come and say their farewells. On top of the coffin there were two flags – the white and light blue Russian naval flag of St. Andrew, and the red and white flag of Denmark.

Russia and Europe

The funeral services for the Empress took place on October 19. Metropolitan Evlogii came to Denmark from Paris especially for them. Many leading figures from various European countries came to say their farewell to the last Russian Dowager Empress – kings from Denmark, Norway, Belgium, and officials from other nations were in attendance as well. There were representatives from the House of Romanov and Maria Feodorovna's many relatives. Her personal priest, Father Leonid Kolchev said the following in his eulogy, which, today, seems like a prophecy, "The Good Lord did not allow you to see here, on earth, that joyful moment, but from way on high, from beyond, things will be clearer. And that day will come, You will see … churches and cathedrals, filled with people, free to profess their faith, free to ardently pray, You will hear the tolling of bells, and You will see Your people, victorious in truth and faith." At the end of the service the priest came up to the casket, fell on his knees, bowed and said: "To you, our Tsaritsa, I kneel to the ground, from all of the people of Russia."

Empress Maria Feodorovna was interred in Roskilde Cathedral, in the burial vault of the Danish Kings. Many years passed, and the words of her personal priest, Father Leonid Kolchev finally came true. The day arrived when the churches of a new Russia have, "become filled with free and faithful believers," victorious in their truth and faith.

Finally, in 2006 an important event occurred, both for Russia and for Denmark – the remains of the Dowager Empress Maria Feodorovna were laid to rest in St. Petersburg's Cathedral of SS Peter and Paul, where all Russian Emperors are buried, and where, for more than 100 years her beloved husband, Emperor Alexander III, has rested in peace. This event was meant to correspond to the 140th anniversary of the first arrival of the then Tsarevich's bride, Danish Princess Dagmar, to Russia. On the evening of Friday, September 22, in the crypt of the chapel of Christian IX, at

Princess Maria Ladyzhenskaya exiting the gates of Hvidore on the day the Dowager Empress died. From the collection of T. Ladyzhenskaya-Meiners.

Roskilde Cathedral, an Orthodox service was held; present were clergy from the Russian Orthodox Church, a delegation from Russia headed by the Minister of Culture Alexander Sokolov, members of the House of Romanov, Danish and Russian diplomats.

The Church of St. Alexander Nevsky in Copenhagen, consecrated on August 28 (September 9), 1883. From the magazine "Vsemirnaya Illyustratsiya," 1883.

Father Leonid Kolchev (on the right) in the garden of Hvidore. From the collection of T. Ladyzhenskaya-Meiners.

The Dowager Empress Maria Feodorovna surrounded by memories at Hvidore, November 1924.
[Eurohistory Archive]

The lying-in-state of the Dowager Empress Maria Feodorovna in the Church of St. Alexander Nevsky, Copenhagen – October 19, 1928. From the collection of T. Ladyzhenskaya-Meiners.

Members of the clergy, participants at funeral procession on the day of the internment of the Dowager Empress's remains. From the collection of T. Ladyzhenskaya-Meiners.

The farewell ceremony for the remains of Maria Feodorovna continued in Copenhagen. The coffin, covered with the Imperial standard – a black two-headed eagle on a gold background, was placed on a special funeral cortege. With a military escort of members of the Hussars Guard Regiment, the procession proceeded past the most memorable sites in the life of Maria Feodorovna. Then the body of the Dowager Empress was brought to the harbor. With a military salute and under the sounds of the Danish national anthem, a combined Russian-Danish guard of honor carried the coffin on to a Danish ship, the "Esbern Snare," which set sail for Russia.

On September 26, 2006, a small ship brought the remains of Empress Maria Feodorovna to Peterhof, and, like 140 years before, anxious Russian citizens gathered on the banks of the gulf. There was an honor guard at the quay, a military band, descendants of the House of Romanov, officials, dignitaries from

Royal mourners attending the funeral of the Dowager Empress Maria Feodorovna, Roskilde Cathedral.
From the left: Prince Aage of Denmark, Grand Duke Kirill Vladimirovich, Grand Duke Dimitry Pavlovich, the Duke of York (King George VI), Prince George of Greece, Prince René of Bourbon-Parma, King Haakon VII of Norway, Prince Valdemar of Denmark, Grand Duke Friedrich Franz IV of Mecklenburg-Schwerin, Crown Prince Frederik and Prince Harald of Denmark, Duke Ernst August of Brünswick-Lüneburg (profile) and Crown Prince Gustav Adolf of Sweden. [Eurohistory Archive]

Russia and Denmark, present to greet the coffin. Six Danish Royal Guards and six Russian military men, wearing the historic uniform of one of the regiments of which Empress Maria Feodorovna was the "chief," brought the coffin on to Russia soil. There was cannon salute from Kronstadt; the fountains of Peterhof threw their waters into

The Dowager Empress Maria Feodorovna

The Danish Royal Family.
Crown Princess Mary and Crown Prince Frederik, Prince Consort Henrik
and Queen Margrethe II. [Scanpix – Jens Norgaard Larsen]

*The coffin containing the remains of the Dowager Empress being
carried out of Roskilde Cathedral, September 2006."*
[Scanpix – Keld Navntoft]

the sky. For three days Russian citizens could come and say their farewells to the Empress, whose Son and His Family, have already been canonized as Saints. The funeral ceremonies completely repeated the route taken, many years before, by the young 18-year-old Princess Dagmar.

In the main cathedral of St. Petersburg – St. Isaac's – the Illustrious Patriarch of Moscow and All of Russia, Alexei II, served the Divine Liturgy. The voices of the best singers filled the enormous cathedral. Bowing their heads, members of the Danish Royal Family – Crown Prince Frederik and his wife Princess Mary, fifty-nine descendants of the House of Romanov, and many other important officials, all said farewell to the remains of the Dowager Empress. From St. Isaac's the procession moved to SS Peter and Paul Cathedral. From that day on, the remains of Empress Maria Feodorovna lie next to her beloved husband, Emperor Alexander III, and daily an unending mass of mourners walk by, both Russians and visitors. The Dowager Empress is now, and forever, back in the northern capital that for half a century she called home.

*Representatives of the clergy and Governor Valentina Matvienko saying
their farewells to the body of Maria Feodorovna. [Photograph by Panov]*

*Ragnar Backström, Langinkoski Museum Director, visits Maria
Feodorovna's grave, SS Peter and Paul Cathedral. [Private]*

251

Russia and Greece

Queen Olga of Greece (1851-1926).
[RGAKFD]

During the end of the 19th and the beginning of the 20th centuries, relations between Greece and Russia were determined by the close dynastic ties shared by the their ruling families. For over fifty years King George I reigned over Greece, his consort being the former Grand Duchess Olga Konstantinovna. Three of the children of the Royal Couple (Alexandra, Nicholas and Marie) were also closely tied to Russia, where they found spouses. The descendants of King George and Queen Olga are now found in many of Europe's ruling and former ruling dynasties, including: the Dukes of Edinburgh and Kent, King Constantine II of the Hellenes, Queen Sofía of Spain, King Michael I of Romania, Crown Prince Alexander of Yugoslavia, Prince Alexander and Princess Elizabeth of Yugoslavia, Margrave Max of Baden, Fürst Philipp of Hohenlohe-Langenburg, Duke Amedeo of Aosta, Count Hans-Veit of Toerring-Jettenbach, Archduchess Helen of Austria, and renowned royal author Prince Michael of Greece, among many others. Both the Prince of Wales and the Prince of Asturias, heirs to the thrones of Great Britain and Spain, respectively, are descendants of the august Royal Couple.

In March 1863, seventeen-year-old Prince William, the second son of future King Christian IX of Denmark and of his wife Louise, née Hesse-Kassel, ascended the Greek throne with the name of George I. The country's first modern-era king, Otto I, had been overthrown the year before. Emissaries were sent from Athens to various European capitalks, including Copenhagen. It was there where they found Prince William to whom the Greek Constitutional Assembly made a formal offer of the throne of the Hellenes.

Earlier, William's oldest sister, Alexandra, had married the Prince of Wales, Queen Victoria's eldest so and heir. This dynastic alliance only enhanced the ties that William would bring to Athens. It is worth mentioning, that the major powers (England, Russia and France) approved the decision of the Greek Constitutional Assembly, for after all William of Denmark becoming the new Hellenic Majesty would not affect the balance of power in the continent. He was both a dependable and a safe choice to start a new dynasty in Greece.

George I arrived in Piraeus, the port near Athens, in October 1863. Soon after, he took the oath of allegiance to the constitution and readily took up his many responsibilities. Finding a bride, in fact, was among the new King's most pressing quests for after all Greece needed a new dynasty. A direct heir, which King Otto had never had, would only strengthen the dynasty's future.

The main residence of the Greek Royal Family was a rambling and drafty palace built in the 1830s according to the plans of German architects F. Gertner and L. Klenze. It was built accross Sintagma (Constitution) Square in the center of Athens. The palace is still there, even though the monarchy no longer exists. The Greek Parliament now occupies the building. With the passing of time, George I acquired other picturesque residences, including a country estate named Tatoi, outside of Athens, and a palace on the beautiful Ionian island of Corfu. It was in these three residences where George and Olga raised their large family, who remain until today, among the most original, well-connected, and well-known of royal figures.

The Konstantinovich – The Family of
Grand Duchess Olga Konstantinovna

When the question arose about choosing a bride for 22-year-old King George I, he traveled to St. Petersburg in the hopes of receiving a positive response to his proposal to Grand Duchess Olga Konstantinovna, the favorite second cousin of Tsarevich Alexander Alexandrovich. It was very desirable that the King of the Hellenes join the Romanov family, since this would mean a strengthening of ties between the two nations. As if that were not a strong enough reason, it would be highly advantageous for Greece. Another positive point for this dynastic union was the fact that in both countries, Greece and Russia, the predominant religion was Orthodoxy. Luckily, this marriage was determined not merely by dynastic considerations – King George was very much in love with the young Olga.

Grand Duchess Olga Konstantinovna – the eldest daughter of Grand Duke Konstantin Nikolaevich – was born at Pavlovsk in 1851. By that time Konstantin Nikolaevich was a 24-year-old Rear Admiral and had experience as a statesman and a naval officer. His father, Tsar Nicholas I, had made the decision that Konstantin would serve in the navy. At the age of four the little boy already had the title of Admiral-General and had been assigned the "Chief" of the Guard Equipage. His love of the sea grew, due very much to the influence of his teacher, the explorer of the Arctic Ocean and future Admiral, Feodor Litke. In later years, Konstantin Nikolaevich would remark that, "I was attached to naval matters not simply because of my sense of duty, but because of my deep devotion to this man." The Grand Duke was a man of many talents – he enjoyed literature,

Grand Duke Konstantin Nikolaevich.
(1827-1892) [TsGAKFFD SPb]

The King of the Hellenes and the Konstantinovich.
In the back, left to right: Grand Duke Nicholas Konstantinovich, Grand Duchess Olga Konstantinovna, King George I, Grand Duchess Alexandra Iosifovna. At front, same order: Grand Duke Konstantin Konstantinovich, Grand Duke Vyacheslav Konstantinovich and Grand Duke Dimitry Konstantinovich.

Photograph by K. Bergamasko, 1867. From the collection of B. Ianush.

possessed musical skills, he played the cello, the piano and the organ; he would even, sometimes, accompany the famous composer A. Rubinstein.

When it was time for Konstantin to find a wife, he headed to Germany, a journey traditionally undertaken by Romanovs wanting to marry. There, he found a young princess who lived in Altenburg. Konstantin's marriage to Grand Duchess Alexandra Iosifovna, née Princess Alexandra of Saxe-Altenburg, took place in 1848. Two years later their first child was born, a son named Nicholas in honor of Konstantin Nikolaevich's father. Being close in age, Olga and Nicholas were raised together and particularly enjoyed romping and playing in the picturesque corners of the park in Pavlovsk.

In 1777 Empress Catherine II gave the village of Pavlovsk as a gift to her only son Paul when his first child, the future Tsar Alexander I, was born. Because of the impeccable taste of the Grand Duke and his wife Maria Feodorovna, a wonderful palace and park complex arose on the banks of the River Slavianka, which can be enjoyed by all to this very day. Realizing the wishes of Paul Petrovich and Maria Feodorovna fell upon several architects – Charles Cameron, Vincenzo Brenna, Andrei Voronikhin, and a specialist in park landscaping, Pietro Gonzago. His talent, and the many years of labor of Russian masters, created in Pavlovsk a unique ensemble, which absolutely amazes one by its harmony of nature and man made creations; the collection of works of art from Russia and Western Europe is also unequalled.

After the death of Tsar Paul I, Maria Feodorovna lived for another 27 years. The palace at Pavlovsk remained her favorite residence. The Dowager Empress continued to decorate the interi-

The throne room inside Altenburg Palace.
[IIMK RAN]

The ramparts heading up to Altenburg Palace.
[IIMK RAN]

or, build new pavilions in the park, grow flowers, collect rare plants, and also look after the needs of the local residents. She willed her "favorite child" to her youngest son, Michael, hoping that he would never become Emperor, and that the palace would not be remodeled according to the latest whims of the time. That is exactly what happened. Her heirs took much care that the ensemble she so meticulously created, remained intact, just as it was in the 18th century.

The summer residence of Pavlovsk came into the possession of Olga's father soon after his marriage, as a result

A reception room at Altenburg Palace.
[IIMK RAN]

of the death of the former owner, Grand Duke Michael Pavlovich. Members of Grand Duke Konstantin Nikolaevich's family would spend the first half of their summers here; they lived rather simply and a bit apart from the social scene. They did not have any grand receptions, balls or loud entertainment. In the early hours of the morning the Grand Duke would work in his study and very often fellow naval officers would visit him.

Every once in a while other members of the Imperial Family would come from Tsarskoe Selo to visit. Special close ties were evident between the owners of Pavlovsk and Tsar Alexander II and his son Tsarevich Nicholas Alexandrovich, "Nixa." Konstantin Nikolaevich supported his older brother in the passing of his greatest reforms. He was one of the first to liberate his serfs, and from 1860 on he was head of the Committee for Peasant Affairs. The Grand Duke had also passed several major changes in the Department of the Navy; one outstanding reform was the creation of a fleet of steamships. The early death of his nephew, Nicholas Alexandrovich, was a great personal loss to him. In the park, in an amphitheater on the high banks of the

A reception room at Altenburg Palace.
[IIMK RAN]

The courtyard of Pavlovsk Palace.
[Author's Collection]

The rooms of Grand Duchess Olga Konstantinovna, c. 1900.
[GMZ "Pavlovsk"]

Slavianka River, where "Nixa" used to enjoy spending his time, the Grand Duke had placed his nephew's portrait, above a pedestal with a statue to the goddess Flora and a memorial marble plaque.

It was at Pavlovsk where the Grand Duke spent his last years; he was paralyzed and bound to a wheel chair. He died in there during the night of January 12 to 13, 1892, and was interred in the SS Peter and Paul Cathedral.

The beautiful palace and park of Pavlovsk were tied not only to Olga's early days of childhood, but also to her entire life. She would come here to visit her closest relatives; it was here that she was to spend the first days of the revolution.

Grand Duke Konstantin Nikolaevich's family would spend the winter months in their town residence in St. Petersburg, the Marble Palace. The vast building belonged to him; the famous Italian architect Antonio Rinaldi built it in the 18th century. The palace's façades and its interior decorations are all made of different types of marble – white, grey and pink. Empress Catherine II had intended to give this palace as a gift to her

The Marble Palace, St. Petersburg, early c. 1900s.
Photograph by K. Bulla. [TsGAKFFD SPb]

The Louis XVI-style living room in the Marble Palace.
[IIMK RAN]

favorite, Gregory Orlov; however, the Count never lived there. From 1849 the Marble Palace had the name of its owner, the Konstantinovsky Palace. It was here that the family of Konstantin Nikolaevich and Alexandra Iosifovna would organize amateur productions, have musical salons with the participation of members of the House of Romanov; the most famous literary figures and composers would be invited to attend. When the Grand Duke published a literary journal titled "The Naval Collection," such famous authors as I. Goncharov, V. Dal', A. Ostrovsky and the poet A. Maikov were included. Peter Iliich Tchaikovsky wrote, that not a single one of his operas would have been produced on the Russia stage, if it had not been for the support of Grand Duke Konstantin Nikolaevich. It was not surprising, that Olga Konstantinovna had received a wonderful education in her parental home; she loved Russian poetry, music, and history.

After the death of Konstantin Nikolaevich the Marble Palace belonged to his widow, Alexandra Iosifovna, but in actuality, its owner was their son, Grand Duke Konstantin Konstantinovich. He was a very gifted poet, and he kept company with the leading literary figures of Russia, who would very often be guests at the palace.

Grand Duchess Olga Konstantinovna. Photograph by P. F. Baier. [RGAKFD]

The Konstantinovich, c. 1863.
In back, from left: Grand Duke Konstantin Konstantinovich, Grand Duchess Alexandra Iosifovna, Grand Duke Nicholas Konstantinovich and Grand Duches Olga. On the floor: Grand Duchess Vera Konstantinovna and Grand Duke Dimitry Konstantinovich. *Photograph by P. F. Baier.*

The elder children of Grand Duke Konstantin Nikolaevich and Grand Duchess Alexandra Iosifovna: Vera Konstantinovna, Nicholas Konstantinovich and Olga Konstantinova. [RGAKFD]

Queen Olga of Greece

When King George I came to St. Petersburg in the spring of 1867, his younger sister, who had come to Russia just half a year before, joyously greeted him. Tsarevna Maria Feodorovna and her husband, the Tsarevich Alexander Alexandrovich, put forth all efforts to ensure that George and Olga would marry. Pyotr Alexandrovich Valuev, Minister of Internal Affairs of Russia, wrote in his impressions of the newly-weds in his diary, "The King of the Hellenes in a Russian general's uniform, the Queen, merely a child, over-burdened with a diadem and mantle."

Some time around the end of the 16th and the beginning of the 15th century B.C., the Greek capital was named in honor of the goddess of wisdom and honest warfare, Athena. Legend has it that the goddess gave the city an olive tree as a gift, and her adversary, Poseidon, the god of the sea, a source of water. The gods preferred Athena's gift, and gave her power over the city. Athenian glory finally came to an end in the 15th century, when the Turks, who demolished many of the ancient buildings and turned the once mighty city into a big village, overran Athens.

The revival of Athens started after the victory of the Greeks in their fight for independence from the Ottoman Empire. As a result, in 1832 Greece was declared a new European nation and her borders were officially delineated. Later that year, in August, the Greek National Assembly agreed with the opinion of the leading nations of Europe and elected as their King 17-year-old Prince Otto of Bavaria (1815–1867), who, in February 1833, during a grand celebration ascended the throne of Greece with the name of Otto I. The young monarch declared

Tsarevna Maria Feodorovna (seated on the floor) with her brother King George I and his wife, the former Grand Duchess Olga Konstantinovna. Photograph by Levitsky.
[RGAKFD]

Athens the capital and gave architects the directive to develop a new general plan of the city. Otto I chose as his residence the Royal Palace built in 1834–1835 by the German architects F. Gertner and L. Klenze. Leo von Klenze was the Court Architect to King Ludwig I of Bavaria, Otto I's father, and had by that time built many buildings in Munich – the most famous of these are the Royal Residenz, the Pinakoteka, and the Odeon Concert Hall.

The Royal Palace in Athens was built on a hill, from which there was a beautiful view of the Parthenon and the central streets of the city, these radiated out from the square on which the palace was located. In 1844 from his balcony, King Otto I, according to the will of the Greek nation, declared a constitution limiting the rights of the monarch. From that day on the square became known as Sintagma (Constitution) Square. At the present time it is the administrative and tourist center of Athens, and the former Royal Palace houses, as previously mentioned, the nation's Parliament.

During the reign of King Otto I and his wife Amalie, who was from the Oldenburg family, a new city center was formed and many new buildings arose in a neoclassical style, giving the Greek city a decidedly European look. The most notable of these buildings include the Academy of Science, the University and the National Library.

After the wedding of George and Olga, which was most elaborately celebrated in St. Petersburg on October 15, 1867, the young couple left for Greece. One of the baggage trunks of the 16-year-old new Queen of Greece was filled with her dolls. But soon her childhood games and pastimes were replaced by the care of royal children: the Greek Royal Family was to have eight children, one after the other, five sons and three daughters, one of whom, Olga (her mother's namesake) did not live long.

In Athens, the building of the Academy of Science was designed by Danish architect Theophile von Hansen, who was also responsible for building the grandiose complex of the Parliament buildings in Vienna. The project was started in 1859, and construction of the Academy of Science continued for almost thirteen years. The central part of the building consists of a portico with six Ionic columns. Two huge statues are located on both sides, one of Athena, and one of Apollo the – staircase leading to the central entrance is decorated with statues

A gold stamp, in the form of a plummet, given as a gift by Olga and George to his sister Prince Thyra, as a memento of their wedding. The stamp opened to reveal a surprise, photos of the Royal Couple. Sotheby's Auction House Catalogue, November 24, 2008.

A panorama of Athens, with a view of the Old Palace on Sintagma Square. [IIMK RAN]

of famous Greek philosophers – Plato and Aristotle. In the vestibule the statue of Venetian Baron Sinas, a great benefactor and founder of the Academy, greets visitors.

When he ascended the Greek throne, George was only 18-years old. Such a responsibility, which an experienced, elderly person would rarely take upon himself, the young man accepted with no qualms. When his father and old King Frederik VII, agreed with the idea that a Danish Prince would become the King of Greece, the young man was studying at the cadets school and getting ready to follow one of his childhood dreams, a naval career. He had to abandon his dreams, leave his parents and homeland, and totally immerse himself in the duty of serving a nation that had invited him to rule. As King of the Hellenes, George I was to dedicate his life to the Greek nation.

The first thing the young King did upon his arrival in Athens was start learning the language of his new homeland, and for the next four years, wanting to grow strong roots, he did not leave Greece. In 1867 he visited Russia, from where he returned together with his young wife, Grand

King George I and Queen Olga with her sister Grand Duchess Vera Konstantinovna, c. 1870. Cabinet photograph by Bergamasco. [Eurohistory Archive]

Duchess Olga Konstantinovna. The newlyweds settled in the royal residence on Sintagma Square. The palace was a cumbersome building, with a white marble portico in the center of the main façade; it was situated on a hill, rising above the city. Although rather laconic in its exterior, it still gave the impression of a sleeping giant. During state ceremonies guests would enter through the main gate and arrive in an expansive vestibule with massive stone pylons and a grand staircase. Here they would see an enfilade of huge halls, situated along the entire façade.

The private apartments of the King were located on the first floor. George I's love of the sea was reflected in the furnishings. In the long, not too wide room, which he used as his study, models of ships were found under glass cases, which the children loved to admire. In the neighboring large living room, finished in walnut, the family would gather for meals. The dining table stood in a corner, and in the center of the room, on a large oval table, covered in green cloth, there were neatly illustrated folios. After meals, the King would usually read newspapers and journals: the "Graphic," the "Illustrated London News," and his particular favorite, "Punch."

An enfilade of seven rooms on the second floor were assigned to Queen Olga: three living rooms, a small library, a room for arts and crafts (embroidery, knitting, etc …), a bedroom and a dressing room. In the corner living room, with windows overlooking the park and the palace square, the family would have breakfast. Here again, the table was on the side, by the wall, and in the middle of the room was a piano, with notes on the stand. There were little tables everywhere, covered with albums filled with photographs of relatives, intermingling with marble busts, palm trees and vases with flowers. In the middle of each wall was a painting depicting an important moment in Greek history; on one wall there was a large portrait of King Otto I. In one corner of the room, right by the window, there was a slightly elevated floor with garden furniture. When breakfast was over, the King would usually sit by the window and enjoy the view of the shady park, or look over the Parthenon through a pair of binoculars. In the park, which was created by Queen Amalie, George I and members of his family had planted many palm trees, umbrella pine trees, or flowers. One of their contemporaries described this park as a, "mantle, beautifully embroidered with precious stones … of exquisite handicraft, falling graciously from the "shoulders" of the majestic palace, the center of modern Athens."

Athens – both in ancient times and the contemporary one – is a city of white marble, reflecting the golden rays of the sun, with sharp spots of dark-blue shadows … On the day of my arrival to Athens, when we were traveling from the port city of Piraeus, all along the Long Walls, and later, when we arrived in modern Athens, opening up like a fan from Acropolis, blinded by the shining sun and the grandeur of the panorama, I was sure that I would never in my life see anything of comparable beauty."

"Royal Palaces and Parks."
London, 1916.

A panoramic view of Athens. [IIMK RAN]

The children enjoyed spending time in their Mother's cozy library, where they could leaf through beautifully illustrated volumes, bound in leather with gold leafed pages. During her first years in Athens, when the young queen did not yet know the Greek language, and being homesick for her homeland, she would order from Russia many books by her favorite authors. She particularly enjoyed the works of M. Lermontov, and had compiled a unique collection of excerpts of the author's poems and prose; it was comprised of 365 pages, and was called "From Day to Day." From childhood, Queen Olga, just like George I, was interested in the navy, and she had accompanied her Admiral father on many ships. Her living rooms had hundreds of photographs of ships and other naval memorabilia, given to her as gifts from seamen. In the long, narrow gallery, where ladies would sit while awaiting their audiences with the Queen, along the walls stood bronze busts of Emperors from the Romanov Dynasty.

In her own private rooms Olga Konstantinovna had many icons. A Russian Orthodox chapel was built on the top floor of the palace, where the choir, with singers chosen by the Queen, sang Russian Orthodox hymns.

The royal children grew up in a warm and gentle atmosphere, one in which access to their parents was easy and informal. Whenever free from his duties of state,

Tall, straight-backed and elegant, to the end of his days he had a great stature. Whether in regular suit, or a naval uniform, which he always wore with great pride, he was always something more than a King, he was a gentleman. Wherever he was, no matter what he was doing or saying, he was always true to his own credo, which for him was "Noblesse oblige."

From "My Fifty Years," the memoirs of Prince Nicholas of Greece.

265

George I would spend time with his family, which, with each passing year, was becoming more numerous. He had been accustomed from childhood to the simple surroundings of the Yellow Palace in Copenhagen, and he tried to instill in his own children a sense of independence and cleanliness, which he himself enjoyed.

Princes Nicholas and Christopher have left behind memoirs that illustrate very accurately the lifestyle of the Royal Family in Athens. The youngest of Queen Olga's children, Christopher, compared the palace to a, "huge cardboard box" and noted that, "It was totally devoid of any frivolous comforts ... The rooms had oil lamps, hanging from the ceilings or standing on the tables, in the most unusual places. They would give off a very strong odor and light blue smoke would emanate from them, which made one's eyes teary ... There was only one bath, and I do not believe that anyone ever used it. Water faucets, if, on the rare occasion, one could open them, would stream forth a very thin spring of water, in which one could find little bits of dead fishes and other strange living organisms ... That was why every morning servants would bring into the rooms zinc basins of water, in which my brothers and I were supposed to take cold baths. Usually I would be lying in my warm bed waiting my turn, and would think to myself, that if I were king, I would abolish such bathing in my entire kingdom. But a servant would come and drag me out of bed.

.... In wintertime, when the strong rains, having washed away the dust from the streets, would turn into torrents, the palace would become unbearably cold. The wind whistled everywhere, raising little whirlwinds in the rooms, it would howl in the corridors and swirl in the living rooms. There were fireplaces in some rooms, and in some – tiled heating units, but they would get so hot, that on one side one could be "fried," but on the other side, one shivered with cold."

However, notwithstanding the discomfort, the children remembered very fondly all of their games and various amusements, which quite often, were lead by their father. It was very easy to talk him into being at the head of a column of bicyclists, riding at top speed in the corridors, surrounded by uninhabited rooms, or spiraling around the columns in the huge ballrooms.

It is not difficult to imagine the contrast of the simple life of Athens to the luxury of the Russian Court. Christopher, who was born twenty years after the firstborn, Constantine, often visited Russia with his mother. For this young boy a trip to St. Petersburg was the epitome of "true happiness." In Sevastopol, the Imperial train, with its elegant cars, comfortable sleeping quarters and a dining car, would usually meet Queen Olga – "everything was reminiscent of a fairy tale, not at all resembling the primitive trains in Europe."

The New Royal Palace on Sintagma Square.
[IIMK RAN]

The Greek Royal Family, c. 1887. Clockwise from top: Crown Prince Constantine, Princess Alexandra, King George I, Prince Andreas, Princess Marie, Queen Olga, Prince Nicholas, Prince George. [RGAKFD]

Prince Christoper of Greece (1888-1940).
[GARF]

At every station where the Imperial train stopped, officials, who gave her various gifts – flowers, fruits, and sweets ... greeted Queen Olga on the platform After three splendid days of travel the Queen and her children usually arrived in Pavlovsk, where they would be joyously greeted by numerous relatives; first of all the children would find themselves in the arms of their Grandmother, Grand Duchess Alexandra Iosifovna. In her youth she would amaze her contemporaries by her similarity to Mary Stuart, and to the end of her life she retained her beauty and her stature. She was particularly proud of her "wasp waist" and her tiny feet; according to her grandson, Christopher, she would not remove her corset and her slippers, even at night.

A sitting saloon wagon on the Imperial train.
[TsGAKFFD SPb]

The family of Konstantin Nikolaevich would usually spend the spring months in Pavlovsk, but in the middle of the summer they would move to their residence on the Peterhof Road, in Strelna, the palace that had belonged to the Grand Duke since 1831.

It was in this palace, which became known as the Konstantinovsky Palace, that the future poet Konstantin Konstantinovich was born (he would sign his poems simply "K.R."), as well as his brother Dimitry. After she became a widow, the vast palace belonged to Grand Duchess Alexandra Iosifovna for over twenty years.

In the last few years, and after a major restoration and remodeling project, the Konstantinovsky Palace has become a museum and the official residence of the Russian President.

Queen Olga, when she visited her parents,

The southern façade of the Konstantinovsky Palace, c. early 1900s.
[IIMK RAN]

The Marble Hall in the Konstantinovsky Palace.
[IIMK RAN]

One of the rooms in the Konstantinovsky Palace.
[IIMK RAN]

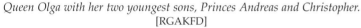

Queen Olga with her two youngest sons, Princes Andreas and Christopher.
[RGAKFD]

Grand Duchess Alexandra Iosifovna in 1896.
Photograph by Studio Rumbler-Wirbelauer. [GARF]

would usually spend July with her children in Strelna, and very often would meet the Imperial Family, who would be resting not far away on the banks of the Gulf of Finland in Alexandria. Having left Russia as a sixteen-year-old, she would very often recall the happy days of childhood spent at Alexandria, neighboring on the grand Peterhof Park. The Cottage and the Farm Palace, where the then Heir to the Throne, Tsarevich Alexander Nikolaevich (Olga's uncle) resided, had left an indelible imprint on the young Grand Duchess. When she settled in Greece, the Queen was thus intent on creating for herself a little corner of peace that would remind her of her childhood memories of Russia. Her husband met this idea with approval and thus Tatoi came to be.

In 1871 the King of the Hellenes purchased a small estate some 24 kilometers from Athens. Once, when the fields were being ploughed, a stone plaque was unearthed, with the word "Tatoi" on it; this was the name of an ancient

Grand Duke Konstantin Konstantinovich and his wife Grand Duchess
Elisabeth Mavrikievna host their Imperial cousins at Pavlovsk. With them are
the Dowager Empress and Empress Alexandra Feodorovna.
[Grand Duchess Helen's Collection – Eurohistory Archive]

*The Farm Palace in
Alexandria, Peterhof,
c. 1894.
Photograph b y
P. I. Babkin.
[IIMK RAN]*

fortress in Sparta, and this was the name given to the new summer residence of the Royal Couple. In 1886 the King laid the cornerstone for a two-storied house; it was to be in a neo-Gothic style with plans coming from Russia. However, George I's summer palace ended up being very spacious, with rooms set aside for every member of the family, except for the Crown Prince, and the most beautiful and largest rooms were the private apartments of the Royal Couple. There were flowerbeds surrounding the house, apple and cherry trees on the slopes. Peacocks roamed on the walkways of the park. Wine was made from grapes grown in Tatoi, and wine experts deemed it of the highest quality. In front of one of the façades of the palace one can still see today a sculpture by Eugene Lansere called "The Tsar's Falconer," which was called by the Greeks "the Russian cos-

*The Palace of Tatoi.
[IIMK RAN]*

A visit to Bernstorff, Denmark.
King George I and Queen Olga were frequent visitors to Denmark, where they would spend long periods in the company of his parents and their extended relations. This image from the early 1890s pictures Queen Louise of Denmark, King George I and Queen Olga and his sister Alexandra, the Princess of Wales.
[Grand Duchess Helen's Collection – Eurohistory Archive]

sak." Every year the Birthday and the Namesday of Queen Olga were celebrated in Tatoi, even when she herself was not present. These days were festive not only for the children of the Greek Royal Couple, but also for the soldiers of the garrison, the workers and peasants who lived in countryside around the summer palace. Early in the morning a military band arrived in Tatoi from Athens and would march around the palace three times. Ladies-in-waiting would come to the residence from the capital. At ten o'clock in the morning members of the family and guests would gather in the square before the palace and would proceed to the little church of St. Elijah, located in a forest on a little knoll not far from the house. Standing around the church would be soldiers from the Tatoi garrison and the elite Greek Guards, in their colorful uniforms of short white skirts, red caps with long black tassels, white tights and brown leather shoes with huge pompoms. And in the evening there would be a street fair with dancing, singing, and all types of food, "al fresco."

King George at Tatoi. From left: Prince Nicholas, King George, Grand Duchess Maria Georgievna (George's daughter), Grand Duchess Helen Vladimirovna (Nicholas's wife) and Grand Duke George Mikhailovich.
[Grand Duchess Helen's Collection – Eurohistory Archive]

Crown Prince Constantine of Greece
(1868-1923)

In 1889 the eldest son of the Royal Couple, Crown Prince Constantine (1868–1923) married Princess Sophie of Prussia (1870–1932), a sister of German Kaiser Wilhelm II. On her mother's side Sophie was the first cousin of Princess Alix of Hesse and by Rhine, the future Empress Alexandra Fedorovna of Russia. After she married Constantine, Sophie converted to Orthodoxy. Wilhelm II, Sophie's brother, was upset by this and announced that for three years his sister was banned from Germany.

Tsarevich Nicholas came from St. Petersburg for the wedding of his cousin. In his letter to his mother from Athens on October 20, 1889 he wrote, "On the 15th, Sunday, one could not ask for better weather. Actually, it was even too warm. At ten thirty everything was ready; Uncle Willie [the King of the Hellenes] himself helped us get into the carriage. Aunt Alix [Alexandra, Princess of Wales, sister of George I], Uncle Valdemar [Prince of Denmark, brother of George] and I were together in the fifth carriage; the Greeks were on horseback, escorting the golden coach with Aunt Olga [the Queen of Greece] and Sophie. We went to the cathedral and back in the same order. Tino's [Crown Prince Constantine's] best men were George, Nicky [Princes of Greece] and I; Heinrich [of Prussia, the bride's brother], Eddie [the Duke of Clarence, the eldest son of Alexandra, Princess of Wales, cousin of both the groom and bride] and George [the future King of Great Britain, George V] held the crown over the bride's head. Right after we returned to the palace we went to the private chapel of Uncle Willie, where the priest said a quick prayer and gave a short sermon. After that the family, totally

King Constantine I of the Hellenes. (1868-1923) [Eurohistory Archive]

King Constantine and Queen Sophie surrounded by their children.
In back, from left: Prince Paul, Prince Alexander, Crown Prince George, Princess Helen. At front, same order: Queen Sophie, King Constantine I and Princess Irene. [Eurohistory Archive]

famished and dying of thirst from the heat, went to breakfast. At seven in the evening there was a celebratory dinner where Uncle Willie and Wilhelm [the German Kaiser] made toasts. The following day I was present at the "baise-main" [the rite of "kissing the hand"] in the Throne Room; Sophie was dressed in a Greek costume, which looked very well on her. In the evening there was a family dinner in the residence of the newlyweds. "Apapa" [Christian IX] said a few kind words. At ten we all went with Aunt Olga to the Russian church for a service; "Apapa" and "Amama" [Louise] also joined us for the prayer of Thanksgiving. All of our sailors were present ... In the evening there was a grand ball for 3,000 people, which was started by a polonaise from the opera "Life for the Tsar" ... Notwithstanding the awful heat, everyone was in parade dress."

A special palace was built in Athens for the Crown Prince and his wife. The German architect Ernst Ziller was given the order to construct a building for the newlyweds, in neo-Classical style, at the end of the royal park. King George I did not wish the palace to resemble one of the grand residences of Europe, he preferred that it resemble an estate of the Greek nobility. The light-colored, pleasant three-story building, which became known as the "Crown Prince's Palace," was built in 1891–1897. Between the windows of the second floor there are heraldic symbols and the Greek letters "K" and "S," the beginning letters of the names Constantine [Konstantinos] and Sophie. The decoration of the façades and

Queen Sophie of Greece.
(1870-1932) [Eurohistory Archive]

the interiors of the palace show the influence of the Danish architect T.E. Hansen. In 1901 a fire destroyed a large part of the Old Royal Palace, and the family of George I moved into the Crown Prince's Palace, which at that time became the official Royal residence. That same year an addition was built: a grand White Hall. After the fatal shots fired in Thessaloniki in 1913, when George I was assassinated and his son Constantine

ascended the throne, the palace was his official residence. This remarkable architectural sight can still be seen in Athens – it is now the Presidential Palace.

Constantine and Sophie had six children: sons George II (1890–1947), Alexander I (1893–1920) and Paul I (1901–1964) — they all, in turn, were to become the King of the Hellenes; and three daughters: Princess Helen (1896–1982), who was married to Crown Prince Carol of Romania, Irene (1904–1974), who married the Duke of Aosta, and Catherine (1913–2007), who married an English commoner, Mr. Richard Brandram.

The Crown Prince's Palace, Athens.
Photograph by K. Kaurinkoski, 2010.

Prince George of Greece
(1869-1957)

The second son of the King George was named in honor of his father. Even as a young boy Prince George was very muscular and had great strength. He had started his service in the Greek navy, and, like his parents, loved the sea. He had a close friendship with the Tsarevich Nicholas Alexandrovich of Russia. In 1890–1891, when the Russian Heir to the Throne had set out on a long voyage to the East on the frigate "Memory of Azov," his first stop was in sunny Greece. He visited with his relatives for ten days, and with Prince George accompanying him, left that hospitable country; in three days time the ship was already docking at Port Said.

During their stay in Japan in 1891 an incident that nearly cost the life of the Tsarevich shocked the Russian and Greek royals – a fanatic samurai warrior tried to kill Nicholas Alexandrovich, wounding him on the head with a sword. The attack occurred so quickly that everyone was in total shock. Only George kept his wits and was able to knock down the attacker, thus saving the Tsarevich's life.

The following year the cousins met again in Denmark for the Golden Anniversary of their Grandmother and Grandfather – King Christian IX and Queen Louise. During the celebrations in Bernstorff a famous European entertainer, Madame Felice Bentley, was invited to show

Prince George and his brother Crown Prince Constantine.
[RGAKFD]

Tsarevich Nicholas Alexandrovich and his traveling companmions.
Seated, left to right: The Russian Ambassador to Greece, artist N. N. Gritsenko, unidentified man, Tsarevich Nicholas Alexandrovich, Prince George of Greece, an unidentified man, E. N. Volkoff. Standing, same order: Colonel Dzheridze, unidentified man, Mr. Harding, Doctor V. K. von Rambakh, Sergeant N. Wilkins, Prince V. S. Kochubei, Prince N. D. Obolensky, Prince E. E. Ukhtomsky, Captain Grivers.

The traveling royals on top of the pyramid of Cheops.

The Church of St. Maria Magdalene, Crete.

The quay at the Port of Piraeus.
[IIMK RAN]

*King George and Queen Olga's three oldest sons.
From left: Crown Prince Constantine, Prince Nicholas
and Prince George, c. 1879.* [Eurohistory Archive]

Prince George and Princess Marie of Greece.
[RGAKFD]

the guests some unusual tricks. She first asked Russian Emperor Alexander III, famous for his herculean strength, to put on the floor a cue stick that she held in her open palms. When he was unable to do so, Madame Bentley requested the same from the Greek "Hercules" Prince George. Although George surpassed the Emperor both in size and in height, he was also unable to lower the cue; he only broke it. The lady entertainer, who had amazing powers, from that day forth carried with her the broken cue, and recounted the story to everyone. This was described in detail in 1893 in the then popular English journal "Strand Magazine."

As a result of demands from European nations, in 1898 Turkey agreed to grant autonomy to the island of Crete. Russia supported the candidacy of Prince George as the High Commissioner of the island, and in that same year the Greek Prince settled in Crete.

The new ruler of Crete, Prince George, chose as his residence the small seacoast town of Chania. When the question arose of building a small private Orthodox church, Queen Olga helped her son, both with advice and with funding. Thanks to her plans for the future cathedral on Crete, the contract to design the building was given to Russian architect David Grimm. On the eve of Christmas 1902 the church was consecrated in honor of St. Equal-to-the-Apostles Maria Magdalene. Members of the Royal Family were present at the festive service, along with Russian officers. Russian artists painted four of the central icons with a gold background in the single-tiered altar screen.

In 1907, Prince George married a very truy unique woman, Princess Marie Bonaparte. She was both immensely rich, as one of the heirs of the Casino de Montecarlo, founded by his maternal grandfather, and a follower of Sigmund Freud and psychoanalysis. George and Marie had a very peculiar marriage, one that respectedhis special friendship with his uncle Valdemar of Denmark. George and Marie were married for fifty years and had two children, Peter (1908-1980) and Eugenie (1910-1989).

Queen Olga's Charities

When she moved to Greece, Queen Olga did not sever ties with her homeland and its traditions. Grand Duke Kirill Vladimirovich once commented that for Olga Konstantinovna, "Russia remained her ideal, throughout her life." From the very first days she was in Athens, the Queen wished to establish a hospital that would serve as an example for institutions of its kind for the entire Near East. Young Olga was supported in this goal by several family members, among them her uncle, Emperor Alexander II, and other Romanovs, who set aside the necessary funds. The Annunciation Hospital in the center of Athens opened to serve the city's population. Queen Olga herself worked long hours in that hospital, tending to the sick, without a second thought of being exposed to various diseases. Largely in part to the generosity of G. Averov, a rich Greek from Egypt, who provided the Queen with the necessary funding, as a gift for her silver wedding anniversary, in 1896 Olga was able to open a Rehabilitation Center for young boys, having taken upon herself the duties of founder and patron.

Very often, the Royal Palace was visited by officers and sailors from Russian ships anchored at Piraeus harbor, which served as a Mediterranean base for the Russian navy. As a sign of gratitude Russian sailors called the Queen of the Hellenes, "the mother of the Russian Navy."

Queen Olga of Greece.
[Eurohistory Archive]

Ships at harbor in Piraeus, Athens.
[IIMK RAN]

The quay at the Port of Piraeus.
[IIMK RAN]

In 1890 from her own personal funds, Queen Olga built a hospital for Russian sailors in Piraeus; an Orthodox church, consecrated in honor of St. Equal-to-the-Apostles Olga was on the grounds. Sailors who died far away from home would be buried not far from the hospital, and very soon a cemetery was attached to the hospital, also carrying the name of the Greek Queen. It was here where many of those people who were forced to leave their homeland as a result of the upheavals of 1917 found their final resting place. These events are immortalized in the shape of a huge stone with a naval anchor and Orthodox cross, and the words, "The Russian cemetery of the Association of Russian Emigres in Greece, founded by Her Majesty the Queen of the Hellenes, Olga Konstantinovna." For Olga Konstantinovna, as for all Russian Grand Duchesses, charitable activities were of the utmost importance. Having been raised in the traditions of the Orthodox Church, and, after marriage, being in a country where Orthodoxy was the main religion, Queen Olga not only supported existing cathedrals, but she also often allocated her own personal funds for the building and decoration of new churches. She also did much in helping the poor and homeless. She participated in the building of a church affiliated with the Annunciation Hospital in Athens. Icons for the altar screen were specially ordered by the Queen, who paid for everything and who selected as the artist Sophia Prosalenti; she had painted the icons for the private palace chapel in the Queen's summer residence of Tatoi.

The consecration of the Memorial Cathedral "Savior-upon-the-Waters," in St. Petersburg, July 1911. Photography by K. Bulla. [TsGAKFFD SPb]

During her many visits to her homeland Queen Olga would participate in major events of great importance for Russia. In 1879 Emperor Alexander II appointed his niece Olga as "chief" of the Second Naval Guardian Equipage. Also, as mentioned before was very fond of naval matters for after all her father the creator of the Russian steam vessel fleet. She did everything possible to help her regiment, especially if any problems arose. It is known that in 1909 the Queen of the Hellenes donated 10,000 rubles for aid to needy lower level officers. After the tragedy of the Russo-Japanese War of 1904–1905 a decision was made to erect in St. Petersburg a cathedral "as an inspiration to future victories and for the resurrection of the nation's fleet," and, most importantly, in memory of all fallen sailors. On the altar there was supposed to be a large mosaic of Christ "Walking upon the Waters."

A fragment of the mosaic left intact
after the demolition.

The altar image in "Savior-upon-the-
Waters." Mosaic by N. Bruni.

"Glory to Russia,
Our pride and our love,
For your valor,
For your suffering and
your blood
With our sorrow we honor
you,
And with your admiration!"

K.R. (Grand Duke Konstantin
Konstantinovich of Russia).

As a result, the cathedral became known as the "Savior upon the Waters." By order of Emperor Nicholas II the duty of Head of the Special Committee for gathering donations fell upon Queen Olga. Her brother, Grand Duke Konstantin Konstantinovich, President of the Academy of Science, was Head of the Construction Committee.

As directed by the mother of Olga Konstantinovna, Grand Duchess Alexandra Iosifovna, her court took it upon itself, on a purely voluntary basis, to carry on the correspondence and to keep a record of tens of thousands of documents. The budget for the cathedral was supposed to be 278 thousand rubles; however, within a year's time around 300 thousand rubles had been collected. Members of the Construction Committee also worked as volunteers, and, trying to economize wherever possible, kept a strict count of every ruble spent. Volunteers also performed many other types of work on the cathedral, and when searching for laborers, native Russian specialists were given preference. This is seen in a document found in the archives of the State Russian Federation: "The Construction Committee of the cathedral in memory of sailors who lost their lives during the Japanese War, inspired by their wish to fulfill the sacred duty which fell upon them through the labor of Russian masters, after a review of all submitted proposals, has attested, that it accepts the report of construction engineer S.N. Smirnov, on allocating the work of covering the mosaic cupola of the cathedral and the dome supporting it be given to V.A. Frolov, owner of the mosaic studio affiliated with the Academy of Art; V.A. Frolov successfully completed the assignment."

During the consecration ceremony of the "Savior upon the Waters," Olga Konstantinovna put a St. George's cross into the foundation stone. All members of the Imperial Family were present at the ceremony, which took place on July 31, 1911. The walls of the cathedral were covered with icons from ships, as well as plaques with names of all those lost during the war, from Admirals to sailors, a total of 12,000 names.

On March 8, 1932, during the terrible times of religious persecution, the beautiful cathedral was ruthlessly demolished, since it "stood in the way" of construction of a shipbuilding yard. After the demolition, the entire quay was covered in pieces of bricks and mortar. By some miracle the image of Christ the Savior was saved; it was part of the altar knave, weighing almost a ton, and it was found in the depths of the neighboring canal. In 1990 a fund was established in the hopes of reconstructing the cathedral; thousands of documents on its history have been found, including almost all of the original documents of the first Construction Committee. Even the original plans, thought to have been lost, have been located. In 1995 a group of enthusiasts, working totally on a voluntary basis, for the Committee of Restoring the "Savior upon the Waters," came upon a real discovery: in the storage areas of the Russian Museum were located the main mosaics of the cathedral. And one can only hope that the day will come when over the waters of the grand Neva River one will again see the white walls and the golden domes of a restored memorial cathedral.

Prince Nicholas of Greece and
Grand Duchess Helen Vladimirovna

The children of Queen Olga greatly enjoyed visiting their Russian relatives. In Russia they would always find surprises prepared for them by their grandmother, Grand Duchess Alexandra Iosifovna, they could enjoy the company of children their own age, their cousins with whom they could share games and pranks. They met rather often, in Copenhagen, or Athens, or St. Petersburg; the children of the King of Greece became very close to their Russian relatives, and three of them even found their fated loves in Russia.

Nicholas (1872–1938), the third son of Queen Olga, married Grand Duchess Helen Vladimirovna (1882–1957). Her contemporaries very often commented upon the charming beauty of the daughter of Grand Duke Vladimir Alexandrovich and Maria Pavlovna the Elder; her deep, penetrating eyes would be compared to stars. Prince Felix Yousoupov remembered, "For a long time I was in love with Grand Duchess Helen Vladimirovna ... Her beauty simply mesmerized me. I knew no other eyes as charming. She would beguile absolutely everyone." Helen would always be dressed in the best fashions of the most famous Parisian couturiers, her parents constantly spoiled her, buying for their little girl unique dolls, and later, the

Grand Duchess Helen Vladimirovna and her dolls.
[TsGAKFFD SPb]

The Vladimirovich in Tsarskoe Selo. From left: Grand Duchess Helen Vladimirovna, Grand Duke Kirill Vladimirovich, Grand Duchess Maria Pavlovna and Grand Dukes Andrei and Boris Vladimirovich. [TsGAKFFD SPb]

Grand Duchess Helen Vladimirovna and Prince Maximilian of Baden. Photograph by Gorodetsky.
[RGAKFD]

Prince Nicholas of Greece and Grand Duchess Helen Vladimirovna

The Vladimir Villa in Tsarskoe Selo. Photograph by Galina Korneva, 2000.

most beautiful jewelry. One of the favorite spots on this earth for the Grand Duchess was Tsarskoe Selo. Here in the palace of her parents on Sadovaya Street she was born, here she spent her childhood and youth. Helen was an avid participant in the games and activities of her older brothers, and sometimes these games could become a little violent. Kirill Vladimirovich once wrote, "Our adorable suburban estate in Tsarskoe was built in the Catherine style of the end of the 18th century. It was surrounded by a garden and pond, which we called "the Lake," because it seemed so huge to us ... When we were little, we would be taken for rides in a sailboat, when we became older, we would go alone in row boats." The family would spend the greater part of the year in Tsarskoe. Usually the Grand Duke and his family would arrive here from St. Petersburg in early spring, and would return to the capital at the end of December, just in time for the winter ball season. Grand Duke Vladimir Alexandrovich and his wife would set the tone for St. Petersburg high society. From childhood Helen was used to the most luxurious settings, surrounded by great works of art.

Once when she was resting in Cannes with her mother, Grand Duchess Helen Vladimirovna met one of her distant relatives, a grandson of Grand Duchess Maria

Wedding photograph of Prince Nicholas of Greece and Grand Duchess Helen Vladimirovna of Russia.
[Grand Duchess Helen's Collection – Eurohistory Archive]

281

Nikolaevna, Prince Maximilian. He was the son of Ludwig Wilhelm of Baden and Maria Maximilianovna, née the Duchess of Leuchtenberg. The handsome, intelligent and elegant young man totally conquered Helen's heart. The young people were engaged in 1898, but a few months later, their relationship fell apart. Eventually, Prince Maximilian married the elder daughter of Duchess Thyra of Cumberland, the sister of Empress Maria Feodorovna, and Helen was to find a future in Greece.

The wedding of Prince Nicholas of Greece and Grand Duchess Helen Vladimirovna took place on August 16, 1902, on the feast day of the Feodorov Icon of the Mother of God, in the private chapel of the Large Palace in Tsarskoe Selo. That day was also the 28th wedding anniversary of Helen's parents. Vladimir Alexandrovich was the cousin of Olga Konstantinovna, so the groom was the bride's second cousin. Many relatives of the newly-weds came together in St. Petersburg for the occasion, and there were representatives from the ruling houses of Europe. The Dowager Grand Duchess of Mecklenburg-Schwerin, Anastassia Mikhailovna, came to her niece's wedding with her son Grand Duke Friedrich Franz IV of Mecklenburg-Schwerin and her daughters Alexandrine and Cecilia, who had barely turned sixteen. This was Cecilia's first trip to Russia for such a pompous occasion, and in her memoirs she gave a very detailed accounting of the event and her impressions.

After the grand Procession of the Imperial Family at the Catherine Palace, and the ball, started with the tradi-tional "polonaise," the newlyweds, Emperor Nicholas II and both Empresses in their parade coach started out towards the palace of Grand Duke Vladimir Alexandrovich in Tsarskoe Selo. For their daughter's wedding Helen's parents had ordered decorations and attire from the most famous masters of Europe: one diamond tiara from the House of Gustav Bolin cost 33 thousand rubles. Charles Worth made the gowns in Paris, and pieces of furniture were purchased from the English firm "Maple." Right on the eve of the wedding the master silver-smith Louis Aucock arrived especially from Paris to bring pieces of the Grand Duchess' dowry.

Notwithstanding the fact that Helen had been acquainted with Prince Nicholas from early childhood, and that their marriage had been met both in Russia and in Greece with great joy, the fact that she would have to move to a different country was not an easy matter for the Grand Duchess. She wrote, "The thought of leaving my

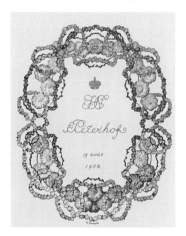

An invitation to a performance in honor of the wedding of Grand Duchess Helen Vladimirovna and Prince Nicholas of Greece.

Grand Duchess Helen Vladimirovna and Prince Nicholas of Greece, Tsarskoe Selo, c. 1902. Photograph by Gorodetsky.

A golden platter presented as a gift to the newlyweds by the citizens of Tsarskoe Selo.

Prince Nicholas of Greece and Grand Duchess Helen Vladimirovna

A view of the island of Corfu. [IIMK RAN]

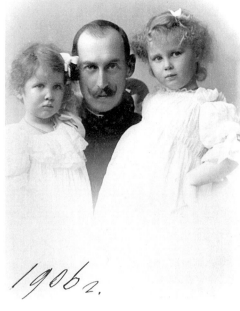

1906₂.

Prince Nicholas of Greece and two of his daughters, Olga and Elisabeth, 1906. Photograph by Bohringer.

ancestral home is simply tormenting me, but I am trying, as much as I can, not to show this, so that I do not upset Nicky."

It was difficult for Helen to become accustomed to the simple surroundings in the Royal Palace, and to the quiet, unhurried atmosphere of life in Athens. During the first months of marriage she found great support in letters from the Dowager Empress Maria Feodorovna. In responding to one of these from Athens on January 7 (20), 1903, Helen thanked the Dowager Empress for the adorable broach from the House of Fabergé that she had received as a Christmas gift, and also recounted, "My darling Nicky simply flooded me with gifts. I am slowly beginning to get accustomed to my new home, although it still seems strange to live in this new palace." That same year Helen and Nicholas became happy parents.

Their daughter, who was born in Tatoi, they named Olga, in honor of her grandmother. A nurse was brought from Russia, and she helped Olga during her labor. Grand Duchess Maria Pavlovna ordered many gifts for her granddaughter in London, and personally went to Athens to visit her daughter, and to see her first granddaughter. In the next few years, little Olga had two sisters, Elisabeth and Marina; that last delivery nearly cost Helen Vladimirovna her life. Marina arrived into the world with a loud yell in the newly built Nikolaevsky Palace in Athens. This building was named after the Prince Nicholas, and was a gift to his cousins from Emperor Nicholas II. The palace was noted for its various comforts – the building had cold and hot running water, there were several bathrooms, and in each of these special hot pipes on which to dry towels. The Royal Couple lived here happily right up until 1917, the year of the revolution in Greece.

Helen's brother, Grand Duke Kirill Vladimirovich, served in the Imperial navy, and every time his ship would come to port in Piraeus, he would visit Queen Olga, and also his sister, in her "wonderful house in Athens."

Helen and her husband, and their three daughters, visited Russia often, especially after her father's death in 1909. She would visit her beloved Tsarskoe Selo, where the Greek family would always have separate quarters waiting for them. Prince Nicholas, a gifted artist, also greatly appreciated the beauty and tranquility of Tsarskoe Selo; he left for posterity not only his paintings, but also memoirs, written in an exemplary literary language.

Grand Duchess Helen also often saw her relatives at various European resorts. The year after they were married she and her husband came to Contrexéville to visit her mother, who was going through a cure at this small French resort. Maria Pavlovna enjoyed Contrexéville immensely and she eventually purchased a home there.

After the Greek revolution of 1917 the family of Nicholas and Helen were forced to leave their native land. Moving from one European city to the next, they would stay at various hotels; it was greatly due to Nicholas' artistic talent that they were able to overcome material discomforts. Paintings signed by "Nicholas le Prince," sold at a good price. In 1920 the couple was able to return to Athens, to their beloved Nikolaevsky Palace, but, alas, not for long. In 1923 they rented their estate to the huge hotel "Grand Bretagne," and Nicholas and Helen moved to Paris. When the political situation in Greece changed once again, they again returned to Greece. Here, in the "Grand Bretagne," on February 8, 1938, Nicholas died; he whispered before his death: "I am happy to die in my homeland, in my beloved country." He was buried in the royal residence of Tatoi.

Grand Duchess Helen Vladimirovna stayed and settled in Athens. She was to live a long life, going through a lot of torment, seeing all of the suffering that befell upon Russia and Greece. She was a benefactor of the Russian community and performed much charitable work. In 1954, thanks to her help, the cupola atop the Byzantine Church of the Holy Trinity in Athens was restored; this church is located not far from the Royal Palace – the "Old" Palace. Queen Olga would very often come to this church; this was where the icons, given as gifts to the Queen from Russian sailors, were kept.

The daughters of Helen and Nicholas, noted for their beauty and impeccable manners, all made brilliant marriages. In October 1923, Princess Olga (1903–1997) wed Prince Paul (1893–1976), the future Regent of Yugoslavia; Princess Elisabeth (1904–1955) became the wife of German Count Karl-Theodor zu Toerring-Jettenbach

The Italian Embassy in Athens, formerly the Nikolaevsky Palace. Photograph by K. Kaurinskoski, 2010.

The Church of the Holy Trinity, Athens.

At Tatoi, Prince Nicholas and Grand Duchess Helen Vladimirovna enjoy a private moment with Queen Olga. [GARF]

G. de Pernau, phot.-éditeur.   *Contréxéville.* – S. A. la Princesse Hélène à la Buvette.

Grand Duchess Helen Vladimirovna in Contrèxeille, France, 1903.

(1900–1967); the youngest daughter Princess Marina (1906–1968) married Prince George, the Duke of Kent, in a huge ceremony celebrated in London in November 1934 and attended by countless royals from Great Britain and cross Europe. This was perhaps one of the last great gatherings of royalty before the outbreak of war.

Marina of Kent moved to London, where her closest friend became Grand Duchess Xenia Alexandrovna, who happened to be first cousin to both her parents. Xenia and her children, especially the family of Nikita, had very close and warm relations with Helen Vladimirovna's daughters. All of them, during the terrible years of the Second World War, were very worried about Helen, who had stayed behind in Athens, and who experienced great discomfort and sacrifice during the Second World War. Grand Duchess Helen Vladimirovna, who was very popular with her Greek relations, died in 1957 of a heart attack and was buried next to her husband in Tatoi.

Standing in back, from left to right: Grand Duchess Helen Vladimirovna, Grand Duke Michael Nikolaevich and Grand Duchess Maria Pavlovna. At front, same order: Grand Duke Paul Alexandrovich, Prince Nicholas of Greece, Grand Duke Michael Alexandrovich, Emperor Nicholas II, Grand Duke Vladimir Alexandrovich and Grand Duke Peter Nikolaevich
[Grand Duchess Helen's Collection – Eurohistory Archive]

Princess Alexandra of Greece and Grand Duke Paul Alexandrovich

The eldest daughter of King George I and Queen Olga, Princess Alexandra (1870–1891), married Grand Duke Paul Alexandrovich, youngest son of Emperor Alexander II. Grand Duke Paul Alexandrovich met his young cousin, and future wife in Greece. He had spent several summer seasons in that country's warm climate in the hopes of improving his lungs. In 1888 King George I was celebrating the 25th anniversary of his reign, and Paul came to Greece once again, this time with his brother Sergei and his wife Elisabeth Feodorovna; they wanted to congratulate their relatives. It was at this time that Paul proposed to Alexandra and received the approval of her parents.

Grand Duke Paul Alexandrovich (1860–1919) – was the sixth son in Emperor Alexander II's family. Even though he was three years younger than Sergei, both boys studied and played together. Paul and Sergei remained very close all of their lives. Paul, the last child in the Imperial family of Alexander II, was everyone's favorite. In the 1870s, when Empress Maria Alexandrovna's days were darkened by betrayal, obvious to all, the boy very rarely left his mother's side. She would take her daughter Maria and her two youngest boys with her often on trips abroad. In Hesse, her homeland, Maria Alexandrovna would stay at Heiligenberg Castle, the country estate of her

Grand Duke Paul Alexandrovich and his wife Grand Duchess Alexandra Georgievna. [Eurohistory Archive]

The children of King George and Queen Olga: Alexandra, Marie, Constantine, Nicholas and George. [RGAKFD]

Grand Duke Paul Alexandrovich and his father-in-law King George of the Hellenes. [RGAKFD]

favorite brother Prince Alexander. Here her children played with their relatives, among them was Princess Elisabeth of Hesse and by Rhine, who was very close in age to the Russian siblings. Both brothers were infatu-ated with her, but Princess Elisabeth chose as her mate Grand Duke Sergei Alexandrovich.

Grand Duke Paul suffered a terrible tragedy in his early youth – right after the death of his mother in 1880, his father was assassinated by a terrorist bomb just months later. The young man continued to live in the Winter Palace and served in the elite Hussars Regiment. From the middle of the 1880s and for a period of many years his faithful and dedicated servant was Alexei Volkov. He remembered, "Grand Duke Paul Alexandrovich did not possess a very even character. At times he could be rather brusque and hot-tempered, but for the most part he was very kind, especially to people who were in any way dependent on him. He himself was not very talkative and led a simple, rather solitary, life; in many ways his illness progressed because of this. Doctors were very apprehensive about his health, on account of the development of his tuberculosis."

Before his marriage to Princess Alexandra of Greece, the Grand Duke purchased a palace on St. Petersburg's English Embankment from Nadezhda Polovtsova, daughter of the Court banker, Baron Alexander Ludwig Stieglitz. He was considered to be the wealthiest person in the capital, and he had ordered in the end of the 1850s that a palace be built; plans were made by the architect to the Imperial Court Alexander Krakau – the cost was an astronomical more than three million rubles. According to the wishes of Baron Stieglitz, the artist Luigi Premazzi made watercolor sketches of the interiors decorated in various artistic styles.

Having bought the palace, Paul Alexandrovich invited the architect Maximilian Messmacher to remodel

Rising above Athens is the most famous monument of ancient civilization, the Acropolis – Its name means "the top of the city."
Here one can still see the ancient temples of the Parthenon and the Erechtheion, as well other building dating back to the 5th Century B. C.
Photograph from the early 1900s. [IIMK RAN]

The Erechtheion – Temple of Athena and Poseidon-Erichthonius in the Acropolis.
The stone caryatids, holding the temple's roof, are the most well known symbols of the Acropolis. In ancient times, the Erechtheion was the central temple, where rituals having to do with the adoration of Athena were performed. According to legend, the Acropolis was built on the site where Athena and Poseidon battled for domination of the city.
Photograph from the early 1900s. [IIMK RAN]

The Palace of Grand Duke Paul Alexandrovich, English Embankment No. 68. "Vsemirnaya Illustratsiya," 1889.

some of the rooms. A shield with the initials of Paul Alexandrovich was placed above the entrance. The work did not touch the showcase rooms located in the "belle etage," among which one finds the luxurious White Living Room with caryatids, connected to the Ball Room by a triple arcade.

It was in this beautiful palace that nineteen-year-old Alexandra Georgievna settled in St. Petersburg in 1889. The couple was married on June 17. The day before, "the triumphant arrival of Princess Alexandra Georgievna, the August intended bride" of Grand Duke Paul Alexandrovich into the capital of Russia took place. The following day was the festive wedding. Official participants were, "Their Imperial Majesties Alexander III and Maria Feodorovna, Their Royal Majesties George I and Olga Konstantinovna," the brothers of the bride, her sister Princess Marie, the sister of the groom, Maria Alexandrovna, Duchess of Edinburgh, and other members of the Romanov Family, present in St. Petersburg at the time.

The wedding of the brother of Emperor Alexander III was celebrated according to strict protocol, established for important state figures – this included cannon salutes, a marriage ceremony in the Large Church of the Winter Palace, as well as an official dinner and a ball in the luxurious rooms of the main Imperial residence. After the ball, the newlyweds were driven in a parade coach to the palace of Grand Duke Paul Alexandrovich on the English Embankment, where they were met (according to Russian tradition) with bread and salt held by Grand Duke Vladimir Alexandrovich and his wife Maria Pavlovna.

The Church of St. Alexandra in the Palace of Grand Duke Paul Alexandrovich, St. Petersburg, c. 1890s. [IIMK RAN]

Princess Alexandra of Greece and Grand Duke Paul Alexandrovich

The young couple participated with great joy in all of the social activities of the capital. The smart, lively and quick-witted Alexandra was accepted with warmth by all of her relatives in St. Petersburg. There was no end to the balls, receptions and picnics. Paul liked to act on stage and took part in family productions presented by members of the Romanov family; he was particularly good in the roles of successful lovers. The season of 1889–1890 saw the production of "Tsar Boris" on the stage of the Hermitage Theatre; Paul Alexandrovich played Christian, the Prince of Denmark. The performance, according to Prince Michael Volkonsky was, "brilliant, especially for the eyes." In the palace on the English Embankment special historically correct costumes were prepared for the "Prince of Denmark and his Court"; each cost some 700 rubles to produce. As a special request the Hermitage even allowed the use of some authentic museum pieces; during the performance "Tsar Boris" was presented with a saddle encrusted with turquoise and other precious stones.

The marriage of Paul and Alexandra was very successful, but, unfortunately, not long-lasting. In 1890, Alexandra Georgievna gave birth to a daughter, Maria Pavlovna the Younger. In January of the following year Grand Duke Sergei Alexandrovich was appointed by the Emperor as Governor-General of Moscow, and during the summer Paul and Alexandra came to visit him and his wife at their estate,

Grand Duke Paul Alexandrovich, c. late 1870s.
[RGAKFD]

In back, from left: Prince Nicholas, Prince George, Crown Prince Constantine and King George I. Front row, same order: Princess Marie, Queen Olga, Grand Duke Paul and Princess Alexandra, c. 1888.
[Eurohistory Archive]

Grand Duchess Alexandra Iosifovna.
Portrait given as a gift to Grand Duke Paul by Grand Duchess Alexandra Iosifovna one year before his wedding to her granddaughter and namesake. The autograph reads, "To my dear grandson Paul! Grandmother Alexandra, 1888.
[RGAKFD]

289

Grand Duke Paul Alexandrovich with his children Maria and Dimitry. [Eurohistory Archive]

Illinskoe. Grand Duchess Alexandra was already expecting her second child, but continued to participate in all of the games and other entertainment of her young relatives. Once, when she jumped from the bank into a boat, she tripped and fell, the impact causing premature labor. It was a difficult birthing that left Alexandra Georgievna exhausted. Although weak, the mother seemed to be headed to full recovery. However, tragedy soon struck and Alexandra Georgievna's health took a turn for the worst. The doctors could not save her life, but the little newborn, Dimitry Pavlovich, was kept alive. Paul was left a widower with two young children. Later on, when he entered an unequal marriage, Grand Duke Sergei Alexandrovich and his wife Ella took over raising the two motherless children, Maria and Dimitry.

Alexandra, who had just turned 21 years of age, was buried in Peter and Paul Cathedral in St. Petersburg; however, during Soviet times "in 1939 the remains of Alexandra Georgievna, born a Greek Princess, were sold, for currency, to Greece, and moved to that country for burial." She was reburied in the Greek Royal family's burial grounds at Tatoi. Nonetheless, her memorial sarcophagus with a plaque and the name of Alexandra Georgievna can still be seen in the SS Peter and Paul Cathedral today.

Grand Duke Paul Alexandrovich in fancy costume.
[IRGAKFD]

Grand Duchess Alexandra Georgievna in fancy dress.
Photograph by Bergamasco. [RGAKFD]

Grand Duke Dimitry Pavlovich and his sister Grand Duchess Maria Pavlovna the Younger, 1903.
[RGAKFD]

Princess Marie of Greece and
Grand Duke George Mikhailovich

The youngest surviving daughter of King George I and Queen Olga, Marie (1876–1940), also married a first cousin of her mother's, Grand Duke George Mikhailovich (1863–1919). Marie was born in Athens, and her childhood was spent in her parents' palace in the capital and in Tatoi, with seasonal visits to Corfu. As the other children of King George I, she had received an excellent education and was especially fond of drawing. As a little girl she would often visit Russia with her mother, and her very close friend was Grand Duchess Xenia Alexandrovna, who was just one year older than her cousin. According to her older brother Nicholas, their father had brought up the children not only with a deep sense of Greek nationalism, but also the conviction that they were always to serve Greece. As a result, Marie was very closely tied to her country, and this love of homeland she was to carry with her throughout her life.

Her first serious love Marie experienced in Greece, and she started to hope about the realization of her dream – to marry a Greek and to remain in her homeland. However, her intended was not of Royal blood, and her parents were against this union ("mesalliance," as it was called). In 1896 Grand Duke George Mikhailovich

"This was a very dear compassionate and kind person, always ready to give a helping hand and to provide needed support. The Grand Duke was never interested in, nor participated in politics. His interests first and foremost were concentrated on his family ... "

Count D. I. Tolstoy, Director of the State Hermitage Museum.

came to Athens to formally propose to Marie. Although she did not have any deep feelings for him, the twenty-year-old Princess agreed reluctantly. The engagement took place on March 23, 1896. However, the wedding would take place a long four years later, as Marie tried to avoid marrying George by any means she could. In the end, she ran out of time and on May 12, the Marie and George Mikhailovich were married. At the request of the bride, and with the approval of the Russian Emperor, the celebrations took place in Greece, in King George I's residence "Mon Repos" on the island of Corfu. Her nephews, dressed in white sailor suits, the future kings of Greece George II and Alexander I, carried the bride's veil. Not long before the wedding the Grand Duke was in Rome, where, according to the reminiscences of Princess Maria Baryatinskaya, he lived only with the thought of his upcoming nuptials and was "constantly buying the most expensive gifts ... to prove to Marie his great love, when they will finally be married." At that time George Mikhailovich was already 37 years old. Grand Duke Mikhail Nikolaevich traveled to Corfu for the wedding of his son. Present also were sailors from Russian ships of the Mediterranean fleet. When she moved to St. Petersburg Grand Duchess Maria Georgievna (as Marie became known there) found it very hard to get used to the severe northern climate. She was

Princess Marie of Greece and Grand Duke George Mikhailovich

A beautiful cabinet card depicting the Greek Royals and their Mikhailovich cousins.
Standing in back, from left: Prince Nicholas, Crown Princess Sophie, Crown Prince Constantine, Prince Andreas and Princess Marie.
Seated: Prince George, Grand Duke Michael Nikolaevich, Queen Olga and King George I, and Grand Duke George Mikhailovich.
On the floor is Prince Alexander of Greece, second son of Constatine and Sophie. [Grand Duchess Helen Collection, Eurohistory Archive]

extremely happy to spend summers in the Crimea, which always reminded Marie of her beloved Greece.

George Mikhailovich was born not far from Tiflis, where his father served as Viceroy of the Caucasus. Up until the age of 18, George Mikhailovich was brought up in an atmosphere of strict discipline, under the watchful eyes of his teachers, who tried to make the boys, "good Christians and faithful servants of the Tsar and Russia." His younger brother Alexander recalled that, "once at the dinner table, in answer to the question "Who would you like to become when you grow up?" George timidly answered, "I would like to become a portrait artist." His words were met with a somber silence by all present, and George understood his mistake only when the waiter, serving dessert to all the guests, passed him right by, and the wonderful raspberry ice cream did not appear on his plate."

As with all the boys in the Romanov family, George was to have a military career, but it did not become his main goal in life. He injured his leg, and in this way, George Mikhailovich could not completely dedicate himself to the military. From an early age, the Grand Duke was interested in history, art, and could draw very well. He showed a great interest in becoming a collector as well. In 1895, three years before the opening of the Russian Museum named in honor of Alexander III, he was appointed its Head. At that time it was decided to build an addition to the Mikhailovsky Palace, which would have a special wing in which to house a Memorial Hall for Alexander III, the patron of Russian art. The huge building, with a ceiling made of crystal panes, richly decorated in pink marble, was supposed to demonstrate the might and power of a multinational Empire. Along the perimeter of the gallery there were 28 marble monolith columns, each weighing 24 tons. On the relief, 96 meters in length and 1.87 meters in height, there are 183 figures, each representing a different ethnic

The first Council of the Russian Museum.
Seated, from left: M. P. Botkin, Grand Duke George Mikhailovich, V. F. Svinjin.
Standing, same order: A. A. Teviashov, Albert N. Benois, P. A. Briullov.

nationality of Russia. The memorial room was constructed only from native Russian materials, using Russian firms and masters of the trade. Inside, there was a monument to Alexander III, three and a half meters in height, with a pedestal of jasper, according to the model of sculptor M. Kharlamov. Another monument to the Tsar, whose collection had laid the foundation for the Russian Museum, was placed on the grand entrance staircase.

The Grand Duke's name was also tied to the establishment of a numismatics collection at the Russian Museum. George Mikhailovich was an avid collector from a very early age, when he started to purchase old coins at the Armenian bazaar in Tiflis. In time, his collection of Russian Imperial coins would have no equal in the world, and its description was contained in thirteen volumes.

There is a portrait of the Grand Duke, painted by Valentin Serov, in the Radischev Museum in Saratov. George Mikhailovich was the august patron of this art gallery, established by the gifts of

A holiday in Tiflis – fragment from a frieze in the Memorial Hall of Alexander III. Sculptors M. Kharlamov and V. Bogatyrev.

The grand staircase of the Russian Museum named in honor of Emperor Alexander III, decorated for the festive arrival of Grand Duke George Mikhailovich upon his return from Greece after his wedding in 1900.
"Khudozhestvennye Sokrovishcha Rosii."

artist Alexei Bogolubov, the grandson of Radischev. At the present time, the name of someone who did so much for Russia is returning to the pages of our nation.

After they moved to Russia, Maria Georgievna and George Mikhailovich settled in St. Petersburg. The summers they would spend in Mikhail Nikolaevich's estate, Mikhailovka, on the Peterhof road; here their two daughters were born – Nina (1901–1974) and Xenia (1903–1965). In 1869 Mikhail Nikolaevich had purchased for his wife Olga Feodorovna the estate "Ai-Todor" (St. Feodor), located on the southern coast of the Crimea. After the death of the Grand Duchess in 1891 the huge estate was willed to their son Alexander Mikhailovich, husband of Xenia Alexandrovna. Later on, he had passed along a portion of the estate to his brother George, who named his new estate "Harax," in memory of an ancient fortress that once stood on the tip of "Ai-Todor." In 1904 the Grand Duke's family invited the architect Nicholas Krasnov to design a new building, according to his own plans, and to create a surrounding park. Grand Duchess Maria Georgievna wanted to have a palace, "in a contemporary Scottish style, made from local limestone." This type of building reminded her of her parent's villa in Tatoi. Whenever she visited her aunt, Queen Alexandra of Great Britain, Maria Georgievna would always admire the quality of decor and the furniture from the English firm "Maple." This she also saw in the Royal residence at White Lodge. When the time came to decorate her own residence at Harax, the Grand Duchess ordered roofing tiles from

Grand Duke George Mikhailovich and Grand Duchess Maria Georgievna, 1900. [Eurohistory Archive]

England, English silverware, and also textiles for her wallpaper and furniture.

In 1908, the construction of a church was completed; it was dedicated to the Feast day of the Transfiguration

Grand Duke George Mikhailovich.
[Eurohistory Archive]

Grand Duchess Maria Georgievna and her daughters Nina (on the left) and Xenia, c. 1908.

Harax, the Crimean estate of Grand Duke George Mikhailovich. Architect N. P. Krasnov. From the magazine "Zodchiy" (Architect), 1913.

and to St. Nina. It was made from local limestone and its appearance reminds one of Georgian and Armenian churches. Above the entrance there is a mosaic representation of the Icon of the Savior Not-Made-By-Hands a copy of the icon by Simon Ushakov, found in the log cabin of Peter I in St. Petersburg. In 1905 Nina, then only four years old, became ill with diphtheria, and she was saved by an operation performed in Bad Homburg on the Feast day of the Transfiguration of Christ. That was why the church was dedicated to this holiday. The Yalta architect Nicholas Krasnov considered the palace of Harax and its neighboring church to be one of his greatest achievements.

In the summer of 1914 Grand Duchess Maria Georgievna and her two daughters were in England when the First World War began. It was a trial separation since Marie and George Mikhailovich's marriage was under considerable stress. Against her husband's will, Marie decided to remain in England, even passing on an invitation from the Dowager Empress to join her retinue on their long trek back to Russia. Marie and her daughters were never again to set foot in Russia, nor would they ever see George Mikhailovich alive again. During the war, the Grand Duchess established a hospital in Harrogate and kept very busy with various charitable activities.

Grand Duke George Mikhailovich was arrested in 1918 simply because he was a member of the Imperial family. Having learned that her husband and his relatives had been taken to prison, Maria Georgievna did everything possible to try to arrange their release. She asked for this from Queen Alexandrine of Denmark, as well as the Kings of Great Britain, Norway and Spain, even the Pope in Rome was approached in Maria Georgievna's efforts to save her husband. The Dowager Grand Duchess of Mecklenburg-Schwerin, Anastasia Mikhailovna, also tried to help her brothers Nicholas, George and Sergei, all prisoners of the Bolsheviks.

Thanks to the actions of the Ambassador of Denmark, Harold Skavenius, a prison visit to the four Grand Dukes held in Petrograd was arranged. The entire fall of 1918 the Ambassador and his wife visited the prisoners, and a secret exchange of letters between them and their close relatives was arranged. George Mikhailovich was totally aware that death awaited him – how full of courage are his words, "I am not afraid, since my soul is clear, and with the help of God, I shall die in peace."

Grand Duke Nicholas Nikolaevich and Grand Duke George Mikhailovich, c. 1910s.
[RGAKFD]

Tragic End of an Era –
The Final Years

On a dark, cold night on January 24, 1919, according to the decree of the Presidium of the VChK (Vserossiyskaya Chrezvychaynaya Komissiya [the All-Russian Emergency Commission]), without any trial or investigation, inside the walls of the SS Peter and Paul Fortress four Grand Dukes were assassinated – Paul Alexandrovich, the brothers Nicholas and George Mikhailovich, and Dimitry Konstantinovich. They were guilty of absolutely nothing, except for the fact that they had served their country with dignity. On their way to their execution in the Trubetskoy Bastion, where a grave had already been dug for them, walking past the SS Peter and Paul Cathedral the Grand Dukes removed their headgear and crossed themselves. They met their fate with dignity and amazing self-control. Nothing is known of what happened to their bodies. For many years, during Soviet rule, this criminal act was left silenced. It was as if these four innocent men had simply banished. A decision for a full rehabilitation of the Grand Dukes was only made in the 1990s. In 2004, inside the Grand Ducal Chapel of the SS Peter and Paul Cathedral, where they would have been buried with honor had not the normal path of Russian history been thrown off track, a memorial plaque of white Carrara marble was placed with their names engraved on it.

The Russian Revolution was not the only tragic event that affected the lives of the Romanovs and their European relations. The 20th century brought some very difficult trials for Greece as well. In 1913, in Thessaloniki, King George I was shot by a madman, he, who all of his life had served his country. For the half century that he was its ruler, Greece witnessed major changes. Athens was transformed from a provincial town into a well-planned capital city with over 2.5 million inhabitants. At that time, the capital of the Hellenes was considered to be one of the most democratic cities of Europe. Titles were not used, and if the Royal children happened to be on the streets, they were simply called by name, with no title of "Your Highness." There were no class distinctions during official receptions or court balls in Athens. In the rooms of the Royal residences one could hear many different languages. The youngest Royal son, Christopher, wrote in his memoirs, "Since

An aerial view of the SS Peter and Paul Fortress. Across the River Neva one can see the Winter Palace and the cupola of St. Isaac's Cathedral.

Russia and Europe

Father was a Danish Prince and a King of Greece, and Mother was Russian, it was always difficult to choose a language in which to converse in our family. We, the children, spoke in Greek to each other, and with our parents we spoke English. And they, amongst themselves, would speak German. As he grew older, Andreas stubbornly spoke only Greek. Nicholas' wife, Grand Duchess Helen spoke English with us, but with my mother she spoke Russian. Both Helen and Alice, the wife of my other brother Andreas, took lessons in Greek. As a result each of us could easily converse in five or six languages. Probably we inherited our ability to speak in different languages from my Mother. When she had come to Athens, she did not know a single word of Greek, but after a year she was already easily conversing in her new language."

During the reign of King George I, the Greeks were finally able to solve a problem, which had been put before them from the seventh century B.C. – to dig a canal through the Isthmus of Corinth, separating the Peloponnesian Peninsula from the mainland. These technological achievements greatly reduced the time needed to travel from the Eastern to the Western side of the country. The first attempt to do this was not completed because of the differences in sea levels between the Aegean and Ionian Seas; there was worry that the project would lead to massive flooding of land. In the year 67 AD the Roman Emperor Nero commanded that the problem be solved. Six thousand slaves started to dig a canal through the thick limestone; but Nero's death put a stop to this expensive proposition.

Work on the Corinth Canal began in earnest in 1881. It took twelve years to lay the foundation for its course, six kilometers in length, 24 meters in width, and eight meters in depth. Since the sides are naturally built, their height reaches 75 meters. Once completed, the time needed for ships to make their way around the Peloponnesus was shortened by 400 kilometers, thus saving both time and fuel, while making it easier for trade and commerce to succeed. Greek banker and philanthropist Andreas Singru provided the funds needed for this project. Today one of the central streets of Athens carries his name.

Grand Duke Paul Alexandrovich.
[Eurohistory Archive]

Grand Duke George Mikhailovich.
Photograph by P. Zhukov. [GARF]

"Paul was handsome, well natured, completely happy in his morganatic marriage, not interested in the least but in the monarchy or in power ... The total ineptitude of this slaughter should be absolutely clear even to the most blood-thirsty communist."

Grand Duke Alexander Mikhailovich

"I am more than at peace, and nothing can upset me anymore. God has granted me courage and my heart has come together ... I have decided that if I am to be shot, I will refuse to have my eyes tied, because I want to see the rifle that will kill me."

From a letter from the Grand Duke to his wife.

The Tragic End – The Final Years

A person famous for his charitable work both in Greece and in Russia was Dimitry Georgievich Benardaki (1799–1870). He was born in the merchant family of George Benardaki, who had become a Russian citizen in 1784. Dimitry was very smart, and had an excellent education. He was always impeccably dressed in the latest European fashion; he was very outgoing and could always find people who agreed with him. The large fortune amassed by the Benardakis was due to the sale of wine. He would charm the Minister of Finance, from whom profitable orders could be won, with the words, "A Russian cannot live without his vodka, it is his elixir, his water of life, his universal medicine: it warms one during freezing temperatures, it helps fight the dampness, it gives solace in grief, and happiness in joy."

Any profits that Benardaki earned he would invest in the purchase of real estate and in stocks of other companies. Because of his intelligence and endless energy the Tugboat and transport factory that he had built in 1849 in Nizhny Novgorod had become a leading enterprise – "The Sormovo Plant", which made metal ships. Having purchased all of the stock, in 1860 Benardaki became its sole owner. The first iron smelter in Russia was set up here, and metal put out by the plant was considered to be the best in the country.

By the end of his life, the successful entrepreneur owned houses, land, and even the entire island of Gutuev in St. Petersburg; he had estates in eight regions of Russia, two gold mines and two potential gold veins.

The Greek community of St. Petersburg turned to Benardaki, the richest and most famous Greek in Russia, for help in building a Greek church in St. Petersburg. Benardaki donated a large sum of money for its construction. According to the plans of architect Roman Kuzmin the church of St. Dimitry of Thessaloniki was constructed; it was of purely "Byzantine style," and it was an added architectural treasure to the city. In 1865, in the presence of the Greek Ambassador and members of the Greek community the central part of the cathedral was consecrated. Five years later, the charitable philanthropist died in Wiesbaden; for the first time in history the

Grand Duke Dimitry Konstantinovich.
Photograph by A. Pazetti. [GARF]

Grand Duke Nicholas Mikhailovich.
Photograph by E. Clare. [GARF]

"Grand Duke Dimitry Konstantinovich, because of his shy nature, was not that well known in Russia, although he possessed some very rare qualities. He never played any political role ... He was well-rounded, intelligent, and an interesting conversationalist ..."

General A. A. Mosolov, Head of the Chancellery of the Minister of the Court

"A person with an excellent education, unusually gifted, and an exceptional lover of work, he had a wonderful career as a scientist. From 1892 Nikolai Mikhailovich was the Chairman of the Russian Geographical Society; he also had a Doctorate of Philosophy from the Berlin University, and from 1915 – a Doctorate of Russian History from Moscow University ..."

Grand Duke Gabriel Konstantinovich.

The Family of King George I and Queen Olga. Standing, from left: Prince Nicholas, Princess Marie, Crown Princess Sophie, Crown Prince Constantine, Prince Andreas. Seated, same order: King George I holding Prince Alexander (future King Alexander I), Queen Olga, Prince George (future King George II), Prince George with Princess Helen and Prince Christopher, c. 1899. [Eurohistory Archive]

Emperor himself greeted the coffin with the body of the merchant at the train station. With a special decree of Emperor Alexander II, "as an exception, and in view of his outstanding good deeds" it was permitted to inter the body in a sepulcher beneath the altar of the church. But his heart, according to his last will and testament, Dimitry Benardaki had asked be transported to Greece and buried there. In 1962 the Greek church was blown up, to make room for the construction of a large "October" Concert Hall, the grave with the remains of hereditary nobleman, honorary citizen of St. Petersburg, Dimitry Benardaki, was opened, and in it were also found his biography and six photographs.

The assassination of George I was the first in a series of tragic events to fall upon the Greek Royal family. Constantine I ascended the throne while his country was still at war with other Balkan nations. Then a year later, the First World War divided Europe and forced each ruler to make a choice. Constantine, who was married to a Prussian Princess, was no great sympathizer of Kaiser Wilhelm II. However, Greece having just ended its involvement in the Balkan conflict, Constantine knew his country was not ready to enter another war. This did not sit well with some politicians and the warring countries. France was particularly miffed by Constantine's choosing to remain neutral. Finally, in June 1917 Constantine was forced to abdicate and to pass the crown not to Crown Prince George, who was accused of pro-Berlin sympathies simply because he had done military training in Potsdam, but to his next son, Prince Alexander (1893–1920). It is tragic indeed to know that

A view of the Corinth canal. [GARF]

Dimitry Egorovich Benardaki.
(1799-1870)

The Benardaki House on Nevsky Prospect No. 86, St. Petersburg. [TsGAKFFD SPb]

even though they were accused of being German-sympathizers, the Greek Royal family had always been quite open in its predilection for England.

Constantine left for Switzerland, where he soon became ill; his mother Olga Konstantinovna was in Russia when the First World War began. She decided to stay there during the conflict and was very active in charitable causes. Olga was in Russia when revolution toppled the Tsar and only left in May 1918 to be with her eldest son. She was able to leave the country, in the grasp of war and revolution, only with the aid of the Danish Red Cross.

Two years later, the young King Alexander I died unexpectedly after a rabid little monkey bit him. Only the grandmother of the dying King, Olga Konstantinovna, was allowed to enter the country; upon his death she was declared the Regent of Greece. Later Constantine I returned to the Greek throne, but not for long. Greek politicians had taken the country into another military conflict in Asia Minor. A war King Constantine inherited, but did not start. He, with the aid of his sons and brothers, tried his best to assure Greece of a victory. Their efforts proved unsuccessful and the exhausted Constantine was forced off the throne one last time. In September 1922, accompanied by most members of the Royal Family, Constantine left Greece never to return alive. He died a broken man while in Palermo, Sicily, in January 1923. George II succeeded his father as King

A panoramic view of Corinth Harbor and the entrance to the canal.

*After the victorious Balkan Wars, King Constantine I received a marshal's baton at an official ceremony
celebrated in Athens. In this photo taken that day, we see various members of the King's family. From the left: Grand Duchess Helen
Vladimirovna, Prince Nicholas, Prince Christopher, Princess Helen, King Constantine I, Grand Duke George Michaelovich of
Russia, Prince Andreas and Crown Prince George. (c. 1913)* [Eurohistory Archive]

Three widows in Imperial Russia during the Great War.
From left: Grand Duchess Elisabeth Mavrikievna, Queen Olga of Greece and Grand Duchess Maria Pavlovna. [Eurohistory Archive]

of the Hellenes, but his reign did not last long either and by 1924 he was forced to leave the country and spend more than a decade in exile in London.

Olga Konstantinovna passed her last years in Rome, with her youngest son Christopher. The death of the Russian Grand Duchess, who had been the Queen of Greece for half a century, occurred in Italy in 1926. She was 75 years old. The unstable political situation in Greece did not allow for the internment of the Greek Royal Family in Athens. In the crypt of the Orthodox church of the Nativity of Our Lord and of St. Nicholas the Wonderworker in Florence, the grave of Constantine I was placed in 1925, and then in 1926 – that of his mother, Queen Olga; finally in 1932 – that of Queen Sophie. And only in 1936 their earthly remains were removed and brought to the royal burial plot in Tatoi.

The university buildings in Athens.
[IIMK RAN]

The last years of Olga Konstantinovna's life were filled with tragedy. Her sister Vera died suddenly, after a life filled with ailments, in 1912. Then King George I was assassinated in 1913. Two years later, Grand Duke Konstantin Konstantinovich fell victim to heart disease, while Russia was in the middle of war. In 1917, not only was Constantine I ousted, but also earlier in the year the unthinkable happened – Russia's mighty Tsar was forced to abdicate, thus bringing to a sad end three hundred years of Imperial rule. War and revolution devastated Russia and ripped apart the Romanov Dynasty. Between 1918 and 1919 eighteen Romanovs were executed by the blood-thirsty Bolsheviks, among them Olga's last surviving brother, four first cousins and several nephews, includ-

The Church of St. Dimitry of Thessaloniki on Greek Square, St. Petersburg.
Architect R. Kuzmin.

ing three sons of Konstantin Konstantinovich. These victims included Emperor Nicholas II, Alexandra Feodorovna and their five children. They also included Michael Alexandrovich, Elisabeth Feodorovna and Prince Vladimir Pavlovich Paley, Grand Duke Paul Alexandrovich's talented poet son. Those Romanovs that managed to escape Russia did so with very little material wealth and their exile was to be a far cry from the life of plenty they were once accustomed to living. Queen Olga's own Russian fortune was lost to the Revolution, her last years made comfortable by aid received from those closest to her. She lived a life complete, but one in which she also experienced great sorrow and unimaginable loss. Yet, Olga Konstantinovna remained the keel of her family and a beloved figure to her Greek subjects. Her death brought about the closing of a sad and tragic chapter not just in the history of the Greek Royal family, but also in that of the Romanov Dynasty.

King Constantine I was exiled in 1917. The Greek royals settled in a hotel in Switzerland and waited for events in Athens to settle down. This image was taken during that time. From left: Princess Irene, Queen Sophie, Princess Anastasia (the former Mrs. Leeds), Prince Christopher, King Constantine I, Queen Olga, who had returned from Russia in May 1918. Seated: Crown Prince George and Princess Helen. [Eurohistory Archive]

The Surivors Gather in Denmark – Queen Olga of Greece traveled to Denmark where she reunited with her sister-in-law the Dowager Empress Maria Feodorovna, who by then had escaped Russia and settled at Villa Hvidore. [Eurohistory Archive]

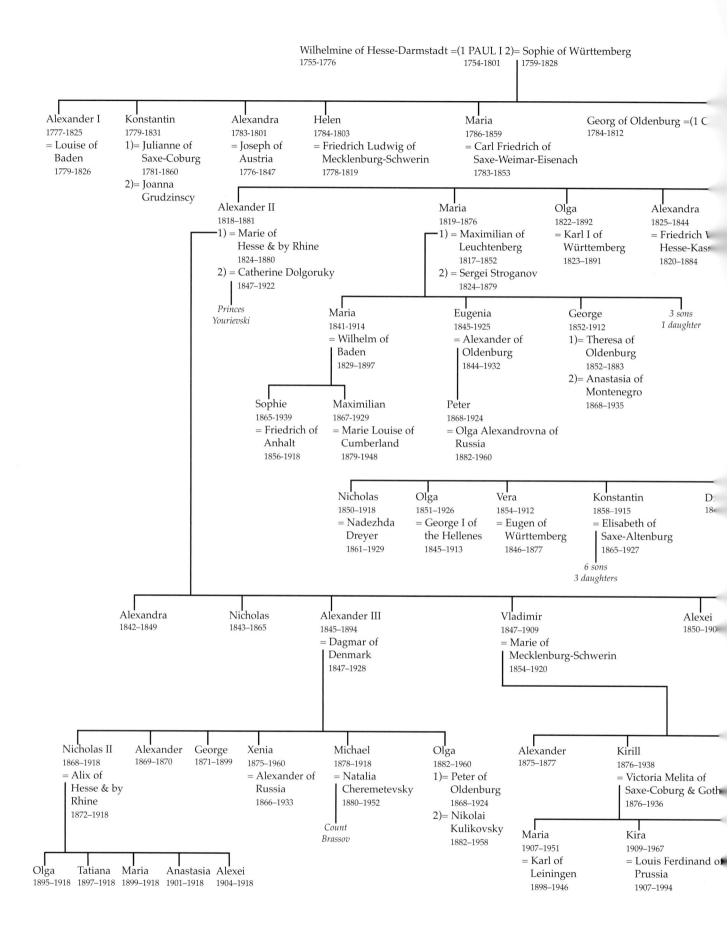

Wilhelmine of Hesse-Darmstadt =(1 PAUL I 2)= Sophie of Württemberg
1755-1776   1754-1801 | 1759-1828

Alexander I   Konstantin   Alexandra   Helen   Maria   Georg of Oldenburg =(1 C
1777-1825   1779-1831   1783-1801   1784-1803   1786-1859   1784-1812
= Louise of   1)= Julianne of   = Joseph of   = Friedrich Ludwig of   = Carl Friedrich of
Baden   Saxe-Coburg   Austria   Mecklenburg-Schwerin   Saxe-Weimar-Eisenach
1779-1826   1781-1860   1776-1847   1778-1819   1783-1853
                     2)= Joanna
                     Grudzinscy

                          Alexander II   Maria   Olga   Alexandra
                          1818–1881   1819–1876   1822–1892   1825–1844
                          1) = Marie of   1) = Maximilian of   = Karl I of   = Friedrich V
                          Hesse & by Rhine   Leuchtenberg   Württemberg   Hesse-Kass
                          1824–1880   1817–1852   1823–1891   1820–1884
                          2) = Catherine Dolgoruky   2) = Sergei Stroganov
                          1847–1922   1824–1879

                          Princes   Maria   Eugenia   George   3 sons
                          Yourievski   1841–1914   1845–1925   1852–1912   1 daughter
                                                   = Wilhelm of   = Alexander of   1)= Theresa of
                                                   Baden   Oldenburg   Oldenburg
                                                   1829–1897   1844–1932   1852–1883
                                                                                                   2)= Anastasia of
                                                                                                   Montenegro
                                                                                                   1868–1935

                                   Sophie   Maximilian   Peter
                                   1865-1939   1867-1929   1868-1924
                                   = Friedrich of   = Marie Louise of   = Olga Alexandrovna of
                                   Anhalt   Cumberland   Russia
                                   1856-1918   1879-1948   1882-1960

                          Nicholas   Olga   Vera   Konstantin   D
                          1850–1918   1851–1926   1854–1912   1858–1915   18
                          = Nadezhda   = George I of   = Eugen of   = Elisabeth of
                          Dreyer   the Hellenes   Württemberg   Saxe-Altenburg
                          1861–1929   1845–1913   1846–1877   1865–1927

                                                                               6 sons
                                                                               3 daughters

          Alexandra   Nicholas   Alexander III   Vladimir   Alexei
          1842–1849   1843–1865   1845–1894   1847–1909   1850–190
                                             = Dagmar of   = Marie of
                                             Denmark   Mecklenburg-Schwerin
                                             1847–1928   1854–1920

  Nicholas II   Alexander   George   Xenia   Michael   Olga   Alexander   Kirill
  1868–1918   1869–1870   1871–1899 1875–1960   1878–1918   1882–1960   1875–1877   1876–1938
  = Alix of   = Alexander of   = Natalia   1)= Peter of   = Victoria Melita of
  Hesse & by   Russia   Cheremetevsky   Oldenburg   Saxe-Coburg & Goth
  Rhine   1866–1933   1880–1952   1868–1924   1876–1936
  1872–1918   2)= Nikolai
                                                                            Kulikovsky
                                       Count   1882–1958   Maria   Kira
                                       Brassov   1907–1951   1909–1967
                                                                                              = Karl of   = Louis Ferdinand o
  Olga   Tatiana   Maria   Anastasia   Alexei   Leininger   Prussia
  1895–1918 1897–1918 1899–1918 1901–1918   1904–1918   1898–1946   1907–1994

The Russian Imperial Family

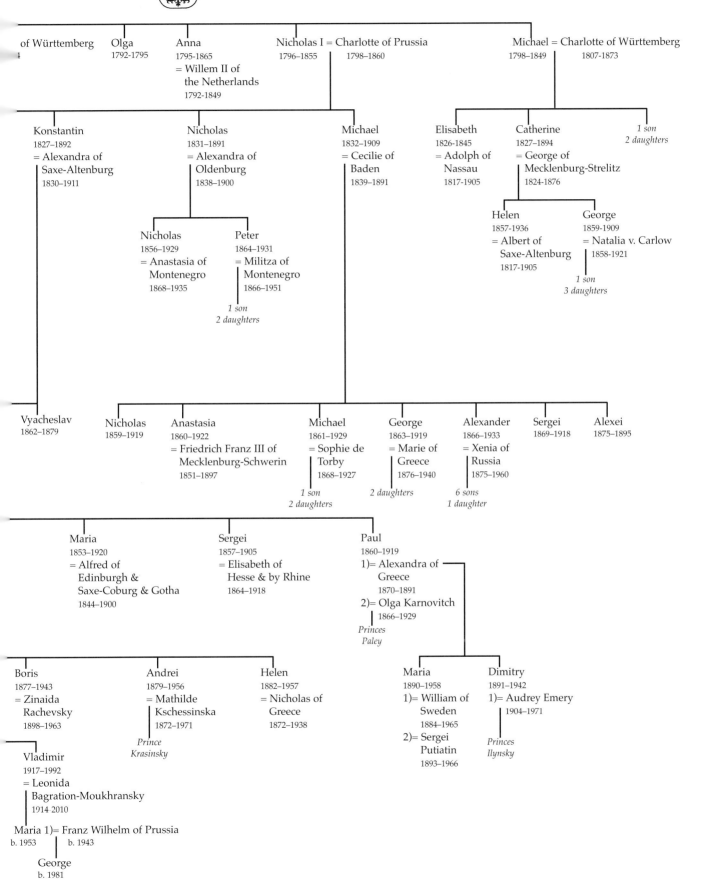

of Württemberg

Olga
1792-1795

Anna
1795-1865
= Willem II of
the Netherlands
1792-1849

Nicholas I = Charlotte of Prussia
1796–1855   1798–1860

Michael = Charlotte of Württemberg
1798–1849   1807-1873

Konstantin
1827–1892
= Alexandra of
Saxe-Altenburg
1830–1911

Nicholas
1831–1891
= Alexandra of
Oldenburg
1838–1900

Michael
1832–1909
= Cecilie of
Baden
1839–1891

Elisabeth
1826-1845
= Adolph of
Nassau
1817-1905

Catherine
1827–1894
= George of
Mecklenburg-Strelitz
1824-1876

1 son
2 daughters

Nicholas
1856–1929
= Anastasia of
Montenegro
1868–1935

Peter
1864–1931
= Militza of
Montenegro
1866–1951

Helen
1857-1936
= Albert of
Saxe-Altenburg
1817-1905

George
1859-1909
= Natalia v. Carlow
1858-1921

1 son
2 daughters

1 son
3 daughters

Vyacheslav
1862–1879

Nicholas
1859–1919

Anastasia
1860–1922
= Friedrich Franz III of
Mecklenburg-Schwerin
1851–1897

Michael
1861–1929
= Sophie de
Torby
1868–1927

George
1863–1919
= Marie of
Greece
1876–1940

Alexander
1866–1933
= Xenia of
Russia
1875–1960

Sergei
1869–1918

Alexei
1875–1895

1 son
2 daughters

2 daughters

6 sons
1 daughter

Maria
1853–1920
= Alfred of
Edinburgh &
Saxe-Coburg & Gotha
1844–1900

Sergei
1857–1905
= Elisabeth of
Hesse & by Rhine
1864–1918

Paul
1860–1919
1)= Alexandra of
Greece
1870–1891
2)= Olga Karnovitch
1866–1929

*Princes
Paley*

Boris
1877–1943
= Zinaida
Rachevsky
1898–1963

Andrei
1879–1956
= Mathilde
Kschessinska
1872–1971

Helen
1882–1957
= Nicholas of
Greece
1872–1938

Maria
1890–1958
1)= William of
Sweden
1884–1965
2)= Sergei
Putiatin
1893–1966

Dimitry
1891–1942
1)= Audrey Emery
1904–1971

*Prince
Krasinsky*

*Princes
Ilynsky*

Vladimir
1917–1992
= Leonida
Bagration-Moukhransky
1914 2010

Maria 1)= Franz Wilhelm of Prussia
b. 1953   b. 1943

George
b. 1981

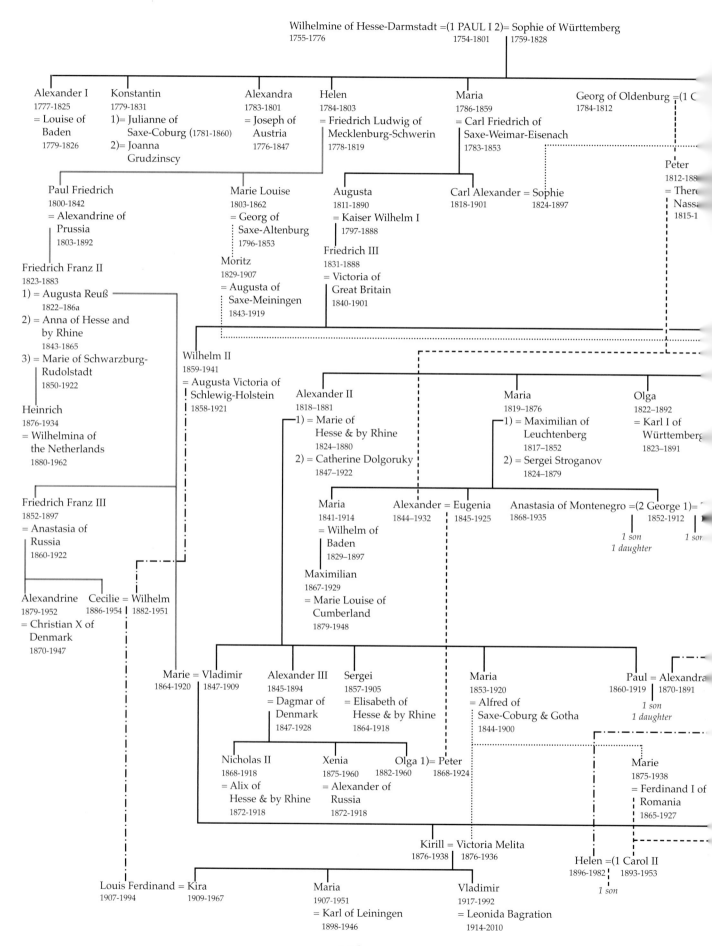

Wilhelmine of Hesse-Darmstadt =(1 PAUL I 2)= Sophie of Württemberg
1755-1776   1754-1801 | 1759-1828

Alexander I   Konstantin   Alexandra   Helen   Maria   Georg of Oldenburg =(1 C
1777-1825   1779-1831   1783-1801   1784-1803   1786-1859   1784-1812
= Louise of   1)= Julianne of   = Joseph of   = Friedrich Ludwig of   = Carl Friedrich of
Baden   Saxe-Coburg (1781-1860) Austria   Mecklenburg-Schwerin   Saxe-Weimar-Eisenach   Peter
1779-1826   2)= Joanna   1776-1847   1778-1819   1783-1853   1812-188
                     Grudzinscy   = There
                                                                                                                                          Nassa
                                                                                                                                          1815-1

Paul Friedrich   Marie Louise   Augusta   Carl Alexander = Sophie
1800-1842   1803-1862   1811-1890   1818-1901   1824-1897
= Alexandrine of   = Georg of   = Kaiser Wilhelm I
Prussia   Saxe-Altenburg   1797-1888
1803-1892   1796-1853
                                    Moritz   Friedrich III
Friedrich Franz II   1829-1907   1831-1888
1823-1883   = Augusta of   = Victoria of
1) = Augusta Reuß   Saxe-Meiningen   Great Britain
    1822-186a   1843-1919   1840-1901
2) = Anna of Hesse and
    by Rhine
    1843-1865   Wilhelm II
3) = Marie of Schwarzburg- 1859-1941
    Rudolstadt   = Augusta Victoria of   Alexander II   Maria   Olga
    1850-1922   Schlewig-Holstein   1818–1881   1819–1876   1822–1892
                       1858-1921   1)= Marie of   1)= Maximilian of   = Karl I of
Heinrich   Hesse & by Rhine   Leuchtenberg   Württemberg
1876-1934   1824–1880   1817–1852   1823–1891
= Wilhelmina of   2)= Catherine Dolgoruky   2)= Sergei Stroganov
the Netherlands   1847–1922   1824–1879
1880-1962
                                                Maria   Alexander = Eugenia   Anastasia of Montenegro =(2 George 1)=
Friedrich Franz III   1841-1914   1844–1932 1845-1925   1868-1935   1852-1912
1852-1897   = Wilhelm of
= Anastasia of   Baden   1 son   1 son
Russia   1829–1897   1 daughter
1860-1922
                                                Maximilian
Alexandrine   Cecilie = Wilhelm   1867-1929
1879-1952   1886-1954 | 1882-1951   = Marie Louise of
= Christian X of   Cumberland
Denmark   1879-1948
1870-1947
                          Marie = Vladimir   Alexander III   Sergei   Maria   Paul = Alexandra
                          1864-1920 | 1847-1909 1845-1894   1857-1905   1853-1920   1860-1919 | 1870-1891
                                                = Dagmar of   = Elisabeth of   = Alfred of   1 son
                                                Denmark   Hesse & by Rhine   Saxe-Coburg & Gotha   1 daughter
                                                1847-1928   1864-1918   1844-1900
                                                Nicholas II   Xenia   Olga 1)= Peter   Marie
                                                1868-1918   1875-1960   1882-1960 1868-1924   1875-1938
                                                = Alix of   = Alexander of   = Ferdinand I of
                                                Hesse & by Rhine Russia   Romania
                                                1872-1918   1872-1918   1865-1927

                                                            Kirill = Victoria Melita
                                                            1876-1938 | 1876-1936   Helen =(1 Carol II
                                                                                            1896-1982 | 1893-1953
                                                                                                 1 son
Louis Ferdinand = Kira   Maria   Vladimir
1907-1994   1909-1967   1907-1951   1917-1992
                                      = Karl of Leiningen   = Leonida Bagration
                                      1898-1946   1914-2010

The Russian Imperial Family
The German and Greek Descendants of Tsar Paul I

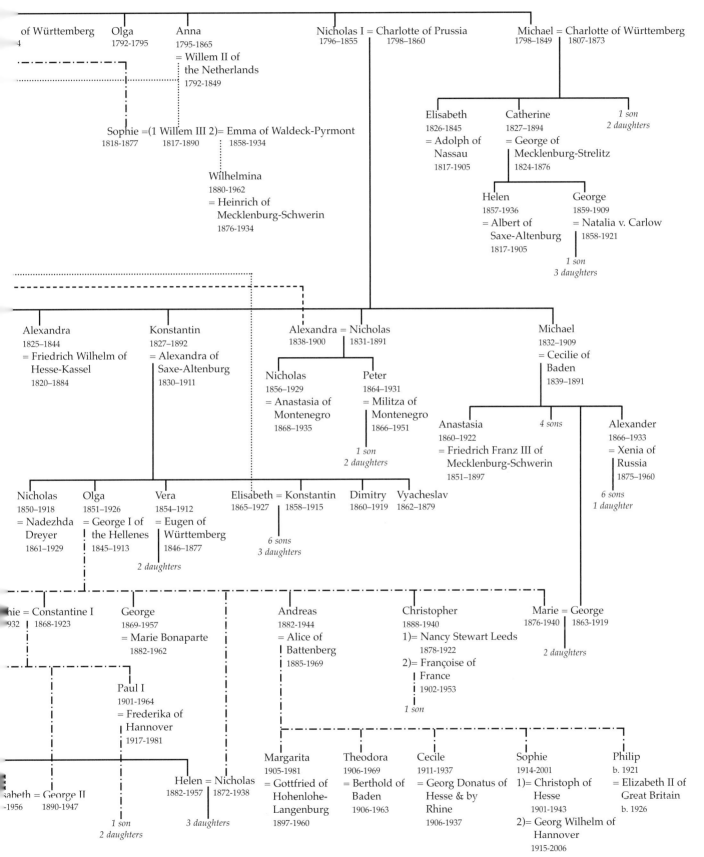

of Württemberg   Olga
1792-1795

Anna
1795-1865
= Willem II of
the Netherlands
1792-1849

Nicholas I = Charlotte of Prussia
1796–1855   1798–1860

Michael = Charlotte of Württemberg
1798–1849   1807-1873

Sophie =(1 Willem III 2)= Emma of Waldeck-Pyrmont
1818-1877   1817-1890   1858-1934

Elisabeth
1826-1845
= Adolph of
Nassau
1817-1905

Catherine
1827–1894
= George of
Mecklenburg-Strelitz
1824-1876

1 son
2 daughters

Wilhelmina
1880-1962
= Heinrich of
Mecklenburg-Schwerin
1876-1934

Helen
1857-1936
= Albert of
Saxe-Altenburg
1817-1905

George
1859-1909
= Natalia v. Carlow
1858-1921

1 son
3 daughters

Alexandra
1825–1844
= Friedrich Wilhelm of
Hesse-Kassel
1820–1884

Konstantin
1827–1892
= Alexandra of
Saxe-Altenburg
1830–1911

Alexandra = Nicholas
1838-1900   1831-1891

Michael
1832–1909
= Cecilie of
Baden
1839–1891

Nicholas
1856–1929
= Anastasia of
Montenegro
1868–1935

Peter
1864–1931
= Militza of
Montenegro
1866–1951

1 son
2 daughters

Anastasia
1860–1922
= Friedrich Franz III of
Mecklenburg-Schwerin
1851–1897

4 sons

Alexander
1866–1933
= Xenia of
Russia
1875–1960

6 sons
1 daughter

Nicholas
1850–1918
= Nadezhda
Dreyer
1861–1929

Olga
1851–1926
= George I of
the Hellenes
1845–1913

Vera
1854–1912
= Eugen of
Württemberg
1846–1877

2 daughters

Elisabeth = Konstantin
1865–1927   1858–1915

Dimitry
1860–1919

Vyacheslav
1862–1879

6 sons
3 daughters

hie = Constantine I
932   1868-1923

George
1869-1957
= Marie Bonaparte
1882-1962

Andreas
1882-1944
= Alice of
Battenberg
1885-1969

Christopher
1888-1940
1)= Nancy Stewart Leeds
1878-1922
2)= Françoise of
France
1902-1953

1 son

Marie = George
1876-1940   1863-1919

2 daughters

Paul I
1901-1964
= Frederika of
Hannover
1917-1981

sabeth = George II
-1956   1890-1947

Helen = Nicholas
1882-1957   1872-1938

1 son
2 daughters

3 daughters

Margarita
1905-1981
= Gottfried of
Hohenlohe-
Langenburg
1897-1960

Theodora
1906-1969
= Berthold of
Baden
1906-1963

Cecile
1911-1937
= Georg Donatus of
Hesse & by
Rhine
1906-1937

Sophie
1914-2001
1)= Christoph of
Hesse
1901-1943
2)= Georg Wilhelm of
Hannover
1915-2006

Philip
b. 1921
= Elizabeth II of
Great Britain
b. 1926

Bibliography

1. *Alexander III.* In "Gosudarstvennye Deyateli Rossii Glazami Sovremennikov." [Russian Statesmen Russia in their Contemporaries Opinions]. St. Petersburg, 2001.
2. Alexander, Grand Duke of Russia. *Once a Grand Duke.* Royalty Digest Reprint, 2000.
3. *Alice. Grand Duchess of Hesse.* London, 1884
4. "Anichkov Dvoretz – Pamyatnik Rossiiskoi Istorii" [Anichkov Palace as the Memorial to Russian History]. St. Petersburg, 1997.
5. Annenkova, E. and Yu. Golikov. "Printsy Oldenburgskie v Peterburge" [Princes of Oldenburg in Petersburg]. St. Petersburg, 2004.
6. Antonov V. and A. Kobak. "Russkie khramy i obiteli v Evrope" [Russian Churches and Monasteries in Europe]. St. Petersburg, 2005.
7. Astakhovskaya, S. and A. Shukurova. "Gatchinsky Dvorets. Stranitsy istorii Muzeya" [Gatchina Palace. From History of the Museum]. St. Petersburg, 2007.
8. Bachman, G. "Herzogin Marie und Herzog Alfred. Coburg zwischen Russland und England am Ende des 19. Jahrhunderts." Coburg, 1994.
9. "Baden–Baden. Russishe Kirche." München, 1995.
10. Barty, King H. *Maples. Fine Furnishers.* London, 1992.
11. Baryatinskaya, M. "Moya russkaya zhizn" [My life in Russia]. 1870–1918. ?., 2006.
12. Battiscombe, Georgina. *Queen Alexandra.* 1969.
13. Beéche, Arturo E. (Editor & Publisher). *The Grand Duchesses.* Eurohistory, 2004.
14. Belyakova, Zoia. "Velikiy knyaz' Aleksey Aleksand rovich. Za i protiv" [Grand Duke Alexei Alexandrovich. Pro and Contra]. St. Petersburg, 2004.
15. Belyakova, Zoia. "Velikie knyaz'ya Nikolaevichi v vysshem svete i na voine" [Grand Dukes from the Niklaevichi branch of Romanovs among the elite and the fields of war], St. Petersburg, 2002.
16. Benckendorff, Count Paul. *Last Days at Tsarskoe Selo.* London, 1927.
17. Benois, Alexander. "Moi vospominaniya" [My Memoires]. 2 vol. M., 1980.
18. Bing, Edward. *The letters of Tsar Nicholas and Empress Marie.* 1937.
19. Bogdan, A. "Doch' i sestra imperatorov" [Daughter and sister of Emperors, Grand Duchess of Edinburg and Saxe-Coburg & Gotha]. St. Petersburg, 2011.
20. Bogolyubov, A.P. "Zapiski Moryakakhudozhnika" [Notes of Sailorpainter]. "Volga" 1996, No. 2, 3.
21. Bramsen, Bo. *Huset Glücksborg.* 2 vol. 1975.
22. Broitman, L., Krasnova E. "Bol'shaya Morskaya ulitsa" [Bol'shaya Morskaya street]. SPb., 2005.
23. Buchanan, George. *My Mission to Russia and Other Diplomatic Memoires.* Boston, 1923.
24. Buchanan, Meriel. *The Dissolution of an Empire.* London. 1932.
25. BW. *Russian Court Memoires* (by a Russian). 1914–1916. L. 1917.
26. Chavchavadze, David. *The Grand Dukes.* Atlantic International Publications, NYC, 1990.
27. Cheboksarova, T. and J. Heusler. "O pervoi "nauchnoi ekskursii" studentov Elektrotekhicheskogo instituta v Germaniyu v kontse 1897 – nachale 1898 goda" [On the first "scientific tour" of students from the Electrotechnical Institute to Germany at the end of 1897 – beginning of 1898]. Nemtsi v Rossii. St. Petersburg, 2011. Pp. 381–396.
28. Cheboksarova T. and Korneva G. *Empress Maria Feodorovna' Favorite Residences in Russia and in Denmark.* St. Petersburg, 2006.
29. Cheboksarova T. and Korneva G. "Kejserinde Marija Fjodorovnas Yndlingsresidenser i Rusland og Danmark" [Empress Maria Feodorovna' Favorite Residences in Russia and in Denmark]. St. Petersburg, 2008.
30. Christie's auction catalogues.
31. Christopher, Prince of Greece. *Memoirs.* London.

32. "Chronik des 19 Jahrhundert." Berlin, 2006.
33. Clark, W. *Hidden Treasures of the Romanovs.* 2009.
34. *The Correspondence of the Empress Alexandra of Russia with Ernst Ludwig and Eleonore, Grand Duke and Duchess of Hesse. 1878–1916.* Kleinpenning, Petra H. (Ed.). 2010.
35. "Daniya i Rossiya – 500 let" [Denmark and Russia – 500 years]. Moscow, 1996.
36. "Danmarks Kongeslotte." Copenhagen, 1969.
37. Dehn, Lili. *The Real Tsaritsa.* London, 1922.
38. Demicheva N.N. and V.I. Akselrod. "Zodchie i Stroiteli Anichkova Dvortsa" [Architects and Builders of Anichkov Palace]. St. Petersburg, 1994.
39. "Deutshe Kunst und Illustration." 1901.
40. Dieterich, S. "Württemberg und Russland." 2003 .
41. "Dnevniki imperatora Nikolaya II." [Diaries of Emperor Nicholas II]. Moscow, 1991.
42. "Dnevniki imperatora Nikolaya II. 1894–1918." [Diaries of Emperor Nicholas II. 18941918]. vol. 1. 1894–1904. Moscow, 2011.
43. "Dnevniki imperatritsi Marii Feodorovny" [Diaries of Empress Maria Feodorovna]. Moscow, 2005
44. Effern, R. "Russische Wege." Baden-Baden. 2000
45. Effern, R. "Trekhglavyi orel. Russkie gosti v Baden-Baden." [Three-headed eagle. Russian guests in Baden-Baden]. Krasnodar, 2004.
46. «L'Eglise Orthodoxe Russe Saint Nicolas et Saint Alexandra.» Nice, 1959.
47. Epanchin, N. "Na sluzhbe trekh imperatorov" [At the Service for Three Emperors]. Moscow, 1996.
48. Fabergé, T., Gorynya, A. and V. Skurlov. *Faberge i peterburgskie yuveliry* [Faberge and jewelers from Pe tersburg]. St. Petersburg, 1997.
49. Fabergé T., Proler, L. and Skurlov, V. T*he Fabergé Imperial Easter Eggs.* London, 1997.
50. Fedorchenko, V. "Rossiiskiy Imperatorskiy Dom i evropeiskie monarkhi" [The Russian Imperial Family and Monarchs from the European Countries]. Moscow–Krasnoyarsk, 2006.
51. Ferrand, J. "Noblesse Russe: Portraits." 6 vols. Paris. 1985–1996.
52. "Frauen Zeitung," 1870–1907.
53. Geyrot, A. "Opisanie Petergofa. 1501–1868" [Description of Peterhof. 1501-1868]. St. Petersburg, 1868.
54. Grützner G?nter, Ohlen Manfred. "Schloss Cecilienhof und das Kronprinzenpaar." Berlin, 1991.
55. Habsburg-Lothringen, Geza von. *Fabergé: Treasures of Imperial Russia.* The Link of Times Foundation, 2005.
56. Haider, Edgard. "Verlorene Pracht. Geschichten von zerstörten bauten." 2006.
57. Haiko, Peter, Iezzi, Caterina and Renate Ulmer. "Joseph Maria Olbrich." Institut Mathildenhöhe, Darmstadt, 2006.
58. Hall, Coryne. *Little Mother of Russia.* London, 1999.
59. Hall, Coryne. *Our Dear Miniature Gatchina.* Royalty Digest, Oct. 2000.
60. Hall Coryne – Driver, Senta. *Hvidøre. A Royal Retreat.* Rosvall Royal Books, 2012.
61. Heusler J. "Karl Vinkler i ego khudozhestvenno stroitel'noslesarnyi zavod" [Karl Winkler and his Fac tory]. "Istoriya Peterburga" [History of Petersburg], 2007, No. 4 (38). Pp. 32-40.
62. "Illustrated London News." 1890–1911. (ILN).
63. "Imperator Alexander III. Imperatritsa Maria Feodorovna" [Emperor Alexander III. Empress Maria Feodorovna]. Catalogue of exhibition. St. Petersburg, 2006.
64. "Imperator Alexander III i Imperatritsa Maria Feodorovna" [Emperor Alexander III and Empress Maria Feodorovna]. Collected Papers of Scientific Conference in GMZ «Gatchina». St. Petersburg, 2006.
65. "Imperator Alexander ? i Imperatritsa Maria Feodorovna. Perepiska" [Emperor Alexander III and Empress Maria

Feodorovna. Correspondence]. Moscow, 2001.
66. "ImperatritzaMariaFeodorovna.Zhizn'isud'ba." [Empress Maria Feodorovna. Life and Destiny]. Catalogue of Exhibition. St. Petersburg, 2006.
67. *Imperial and Royal Presents.* London. 24 Nov. 2008. The Sotheby's Auction House.
68. Iroshnikov, M., Protsai, L., and Ju. Shelaev. *The Sun set of the Romanov Dynasty.* Moscow, 1992.
69. "Iskusstvo Velikoi Knyagini" [Art of the Grand Duchess]. St. Petersburg, Moscow, 2005.
70. "Istoriya Gosudarstvennogo Soveta Rossiiskoy Imperii. 1801–1917" [History of the State Council of the Russian Empire. 1801–1917]. D. Shilov and A. Chistikov (Eds.). St. Petersburg, 2008.
71. "Khudozhestvennye Sokrovishcha Rossii," [Art Treasures of Russia], magazine, 1901–1907.
72. King, Greg and Penny Wilson. *Gilded Prism – The Konstantinovich Grand Dukes.* Eurohistory, 2006.
73. Kirill Vladimirovich Grand Duke of Russia. "Moyazhizn' na sluzhbe Rossii" [My Life in Russia's Service]. St. Petersburg, 1996.
74. Kiste J. van der and Coryne Hall. *Once a Grand Duchess. Xenia, sister of Nicholas II.* London, 2002.
75. Kleinmikhel M. "Iz potonuvshego mira. Memuary" [Memoires of a Shipwrecked World]. Petrograd, Moscow, 1923.
76. Knodt, Manfred. "Ernst Ludwig, Grossherzog von Hessen und bei Rhein." Darmstadt, 1985.
77. Koefod, A. "Pyat'desyat let v Rossii. 1878–1920" [Fifty Years in Russia. 1878–1920]. St. Petersburg, 2009.
78. Kokovtsov, B. *Out of My Past.* 1935.
79. Konyukhova, E. "Muzyka v zhizni gertsogov MeklehburgStrelitskikh" [Music in life of the Dukes of MecklenburgStrelitz] / /"Russkaya vetv' Meklehburg Strelitskogo Doma". [Russian Branch of Mecklenburg Strelitz Dukes]. Collected Papers of International Scientific Conference 16–18 Oct. 2001. St. Petersburg, 2005. Pp. 183–205.
80. Korneva, G. and T. Cheboksarova. "Byvshiy rossiskiy diplomat Ludwig von Knorring i ego otsenka bolshe vistskoy opasnosti dlya Evropy." (1919). [Former Russian diplomat Ludwig von Knorring and his estimation of Bolshevic danger for Europe (1919)]. Zaru bezhnaya Rossiya. 1917–1939. St. Petersburg, 2004.
81. Korneva, G. and T. Cheboksarova. "Dvor velikogo knyazya Vladimira Alexandrovicha – vtoroi po zna chimosti v rossiiskoy stolitze [Court of Grand Duke Vladimir, the second in rank court in the capital of Russia] / / Staryi Peterburg. Poiski, nakhodki, otkrytiya. [Old Petersburg. Findings and research results, discoveries]. / Krasnova E. (ed.). St. Petersburg, 2009. Pp. 209–228.
82. Korneva, G. and T. Cheboksarova. "Imperator Alexander III i ego syn Mikhail – pokroviteli rossiiskoi elektro tekhniki" [Emperor Alexander III and his son Mikhail – patrons of electrical technique in Russia] / / Poslednie Romanovy i imperatorskie residentsii v kontse XIX – nachale XX veka. St. Petersburg, 2009. Pp. 104–110.
83. Korneva, G. and T. Cheboksarova. "Imperiya Maple". Zakazy rossiiskoi imperatorskoi sem'i. ["Maple's Empire" – Orders of Russian Imperial Family] / / Nevsky arkhiv. Istorikokraevedchesky sbornik. Issue 8. St. Petersburg, 2008. Pp. 289–306.
84. Korneva, G. and T. Cheboksarova. "Korolevskie podar-ki" [King's Gifts] / / "Zerkalo zagadok." Berlin, 2000.
85. Korneva, G. and T. Cheboksarova. "O kollektsii Tatia ny Mainers – urozhdennoy knyazhny Lodyzhenskoy" [About the collection of Tatiana Meiners, born princess Ladyzhenskaya] / / Istoricheskie kollektzii muzeev. Proshloe i nastoyashchee. St. Petersburg, 2007. Pp. 48–53.
86. Korneva, G. and T. Cheboksarova. "Petergofu 300 let" [300 years of Peterhof]. St. Petersburg, 2005.
87. Korneva, G. and T. Cheboksarova. "Protoierej Aleksiy Petrovich Maltsev – sozdatel i rukovoditel Svjato

Bibliography

Vladimirskogo Pravoslavnogo Bratstva" [Archipriest Aleksey Petrovich Maltsev – founder and leader of the Orthodox Brotherhood named after St. Vladimir] // *Nevsky arkhiv*, vol. 6. St. Petersburg, 2003.

88. Korneva, G. and T. Cheboksarova. *"Raboty architec torov nemetskogo proiskhozhdeniya pri Dvore Velikogo knyazya Vladimira Alexandrovicha"* [Work of Architects of German origin for the Court of Grand Duke Vladimir] // *Nemtsi v Rossii*. St. Petersburg, 2004. Pp. 355–370.

89. Korneva, G. and T. Cheboksarova. *"Raboty firmy 'Maple' po zakazam rossiiskoi imperatorskoi sem'i."* // *"Staryi Peterburg. Poiski, nakhodki, otkrytiya"* [Old Petersburg. Findings and research results, discoveries]. / Krasnova, E. (ed.). St. Petersburg,2009. Pp. 191–208.

90. Korneva, G. and T. Cheboksarova. *"Russkaya derev nya Alexandrovka v Potsdame"* ["Russian village" Alexandrovka in Potsdam] // *Arkhitecturnoe nasledie russkogo zarubezh'ya* [Architectural heritage of Russians abroad]. St. Petersburg, 2008. Pp. 305–314.

91. Korneva, G. and T. Cheboksarova. *"Saint Petersburg. By the World Created – By its Beauty Preserved."* St. Petersburg, 2003.

92. Korneva, G. and T. Cheboksarova. *"Sankt Peterburg. Mirom sozdan – krasotoy khranim"* [SaintPetersburg. By the World Created – By its Beauty Preserved]. St. Petersburg, 2011.

93. Korneva, G. and T. Cheboksarova. *"Velikaya knyaginya Mariya Pavlovna. Stranitsy zhizni"* [Grand Duchess Vladimir. Episodes of life] // *Kul'tura Rossii kontsa XIX – nachala XX veka i deyatel'nost' velikogo knyazya Vladimira Aleksandrovicha*. St. Petersburg, 2009. Pp. 65–78.

94. Korneva, G. and T. Cheboksarova. *"Veliky knyaz' Mikhail Aleksandrovich – avgusteishy pokrovitel' Electrotekhnicheskogo institute"* [Grand Duke Mikhail, August patron of Electrotechnical Institute] // *Ural'skaya Golgopha*. Issue 5. Perm, 2010. Pp. 29–37.

95. Korneva, G., T. Cheboksarova and M. Schott. *"Print sessa MecklenburgShverinskaya (Velikaya knyaginya Mariya Pavlovna) v SanktPeterburge"* [Princess of Mecklenburg-Schwerin (Grand Duchess Vladimir) in Saint Petersburg] // *Nemtsi v Rossii*. St. Petersburg, 2001. Pp. 470–481.

96. Krasko, A. *"Peterburgskoe kupechestvo. Stranitsy semeinykh istoriy"* [SaintPetersburg Merchant Class. Pages from Family Stories]. Moscow, 2010.

97. Krog, Ole Villumsen (ed.). *"Kejserinde Dagmar Maria Fjodorovna: en udstillingom den danske prinsesse somblev kejserinde af Rusland"* [Empress Dagmar Maria Feodorovna: an exhibition about the Danish princess, who became empress of Russia]. Copenhagen: Christiansborg Slot. Catalog of an exhibition held in Christiansborg slot. Copenhagen, 1997.

98. *Kunstkatte fra zarernes hof.* 1860–1917 [Treasures of Russia and Gifts to Emperors]. Catalogue of Exhibition. Copenhagen, 2002.

99. Kuzmin, Yu. *"Rossiyskaya imperatorskaya fami liya"* [Russain Imperial Family]. Moscow, 2011.

100. Kyucharianz, D.A. and A.G. Raskin. *"Gatchina. Khudozhestvennye Pamyatniki"* [Gatchina. Places of In terest]. Lenizdat, 1990.

101. Lamzdorf V. *"Dnevnik. 1894–1896"* [Diaries. 1894–1896]. Moscow, 1991.

102. Mager, Hugo. *Elizabeth. Grand Duchess of Russia.* NewYork.

103. Massie, Robert K. *Nicholas and Alexandra.* New York. 1985.

104. Massie, Susanne. *Pavlovsk. The Life of a Russian Palace.* 1990.

105. *Mecklenburgs Grossherzogen. 1815–1918.* Demmler Verlag, 1992.

106. Mosolov, A. *"Pri Dvore poslednego imperatora"* [At the Court of the Last Emperor]. Moscow, 1992.

107. Narishkin-Kurakin, E. *Under Three Tsars: The Memoires of the Ladyi-n-Waiting Elizabeth Narishkin Kurakin.* NY, 1931.

108. Nesin V. *"Zimniy dvorets v tsarstvovanie poslednego imperatora Nikolaya II"* [Winter Palace in the Reign of the Last Emperor Nicholas II]. St. Petersburg, 1999.

109. Neugebauer W. *"Die Wilhelma. Ein Paradies in der Stadt."*

110. *Nicholas and Alexandra. At Home with the last Tsar and His Family.* Marilyn Swezey (Ed.). Washington, D.C.

111. Nicholas, Prince of Greece. *My 50 Years.* Arturo Beéche, Editor. Eurohistory, 2006.

112. *"Niva,"* magazine, 1890–1917.

113. *"Ogonyok"* [Little Flame], magazine, 1899– 1917.

114. Olga Nikolaevna, Queen of Würtemberg. *"Son Yunosti"* [Dream of the Youth]. Paris, 1963.

115. Osborn M. *"Berlin. Ein Rundgang in Bildern."* 1911

116. Papi, Stefano. *The Jewels of the Romanovs. Family and Court.* London: Thames & Hudson, Ltd., 2010.

117. Pashchinskaya, I. *"Prazdniki v Lugovoi i Kolo nistskom parkakh Petergofa v tsarstvovanie Nikolaya I"* [Festivities in Lugovoi and Kolonist Parks in Petergof during epoche of Nicholas I] // *"Istoriya Peterburga"* [History of Petersburg]. 2003, No 3. Pp. 56–64.

118. Petrova, T. *"Komnaty Imperatritsy Marii Alek sandrovny v Zimnem dvortse"* [Private Rooms of Empress Maria Alexandrovna in the Winter Palace]. St. Petersburg, 2007.

119. *"Pod Vysochaishim pokrovitel'stvom"* [With Im perial Support]. Sbornik trudov Mezhdunarodnoi nauchnoi konferentsii v GMZ "Gatchina" [Collected Papers of International Scientific Conference in Gatchina Palacemuseum]. St. Petersburg, 2010.

120. Polovtsov, A. *"Dnevnik gosudarstvennogo sekre tarya"* [Diaries of the State secretary]. Moscow, 1966. 2 vol.

121. *"The Queen: The Lady's Newspaper and Court Chronicle,"* 1890–1906 .

122. Reibnitz-Maltzan, Louise. *"Gestalten vom letzten Zarenhof und andere personliche Begegnungen."* 1928.

123. *Romanov Heirlooms. The Lost Inheritance of Grand Duchess Maria Pavlovna.* London. 30 Nov. 2009. Sotheby's Auction House.

124. *"Romanovy i Krym"* [Romanovs and Crimea]. Collected Papers of Scientific Conference in Livadiya Palace, 2006–2012.

125. *"Die Russische Kapelle in Darmstadt."* München, Berlin. 2007.

126. *"Russkaya vetv' MeklehburgStrelitzkogo Doma"* [Russian Branch of MecklenburgStrelitz Dukes]. Collected Papers of International Scientific Conference 16–18 Oct. 2001. St. Petersburg, 2005.

127. Ryzhenko, I. *Alexander III v Gatchine* [Alexander III in Gatchina]. St. Petersburg, 2011.

128. Saveliev Yu. *"Hikolai Vladimirovich Sultanov."* St. Petersburg, 2009.

129. Saveliev, Yu. *"Vlast' i monument. Pamyatniki derzhavnym pravitelyam Evropy"* 1881 – 1914 [Power and Monument. Monuments to Rulers of Russia and of European Countries 1881–1914]. St. Petersburg, 2011.

130. Sauer, P. *"Wenn Liebe meinem Herzenfehltfehlt mir die ganze Welt"* / Herzogin Wera von Württenberg, Grossfürstin von Russland. 2007.

131. Shelaeva, E. *"Pravoslavnyi mir Rossii v photo graphiyakh kontsa 19 – nachala 20 veka"* [The Ortodox World of Russia in Photographs from the end of the 19. to the beginning of the 20. century]. St. Petersburg, 2002.

132. Shepelev, L. *"Chinovnyi mir Rossii"* [Russian official-dom]. St. Petersburg, 2001.

133. ShilovD.*"Gosudarstvennyi Sovet Rossii. 1801-2001"* [State Council of Russia. 1801–2001].

134. Sokol, K. *"Monumental'nyepamyatnikiRossiis koi imperii"* [Monuments in the Russian Empire]. Catalogue. Moscow, 2006.

135. «*Stolitsa i Usad'ba*» [Capital and Estate], magazine. 1914–1916.

136. *The Strand Magazine.* 1891–1910.

137. Taneeva (Vyrubova), A.A. *"Stranitsy moei zhizni"* [Pages from story of my life]. Moscow, 2000.

138. Tillander-Godenhielm, U. *The Russian Imperial Award System. 1894–1917.* Helsinki, 2005.

139. *Trudy Mezhdunarodnykh nauchnykh konfe rentsiy* in GMZ "Tsarskoe Selo" [Collected Papers of In ternational Scientific Conferences in Tsarskoe Selo Palace muse um]. St. Petersburg, 2000–2011.

140. Tuksen, L. – *pridvornyi khudozhnik* [Tuksen L. – the court painter]. Catalogue of Exhibition. The State Hermitage. 2006.

141. Tuksen, L. *Memoires.* Denmark, 1927.

142. Tyutcheva, A. *Vospominaniya* [Memoires]. Moscow, 2000.

143. Shelaev Ju., Shelaeva E., et al. *"Nikolai II. Stranitzy zhizni"* [Nicholas II. Episodes in his life] SPb., 1998

144. Shelaev Ju., Shelaeva E. *"SanktPeterburg nakanune krusheniya imperii"* [Saint Petersburg on the Eve of the Russian Empire's Collapse]. 2010.

145. Sheremetev, S. *"Memuary grafa Sheremeteva"* [Memoires of Count S. D. Sheremetev]. Moscow, 2001.

146. Ulstrup, P. *"Imperatritza Maria Feodorovna. Zhizn' i sud'ba"* [Empress Maria Feodorovna. Life and Destiny]. Translation of letters from GARF.

147. *"Unter den Linden. Historische Photographien. Herausgeben vom Stadtmuseum Berlin."* Nicolai. Berlin, 1997.

148. *"Upravlencheskaya elita Rossiiskoi Imperii. 1802–1917"* [History of Ministries in Russia. 1802– 1917]. St. Petersburg, 2008.

149. *"Velikaya knyaginya Elena Pavlovna"* [Grand Duchess Elena Pavlovna]. St. Petersburg, 2011.

150. *"Velikiy knyaz' Alexander Alexandrovich. Sbornik docu mentov"* [Grand Duke Alexander Ale xandrovich. Collected Papers]. 2002.

151. Velichenko, M. and G. Mirolyubova. *"Dvorets Velikogo knyazya Vladimira Alexandrovicha"* [Palace of Grand Duke Vladimir Alexandrovich]. St. Petersburg, 1997.

152. Vickers, Hugo. *Alice. Princess Andrew of Greece.* New York, 2000.

153. Vorres, Ian. *The Last Grand Duchess.* London: Hutchinson & Co. Memoirs of Grand Duchess Olga Alexandrovna. 2000.

154. *"Vsemirnaya Illyustratsiya"* [International Il lustrations], magazine. 1869–1897.

155. Wais, G. *"Stuttgart im 19 Jahrhundert."*

156. Witte, Count Sergei. *"Vospominaniya"* [Reminis cence]. Moscow.

157. Yashchik, T. *"Ryadom s Imperatritsei. Vospo minaniya leibkazaka"* [At the service for Empress. Memoirs of Cossack]. St. Petersburg, 2004.

158. Yussoupov, Prince Félix. *Avant l'exil, 1887– 1919.* [Before the exile, 1887–1919]. Paris: Plon. 1952 159. Yusupov F. Prince *"Memuary"* [Memoirs]. Moscow, 1998

160. Zeepvat, Charlotte. *The Camera and the Tsars.* 2004.

161. Zeepvat, Charlotte. *Queen Victoria's Family.* 2001.

162. Zeger, V. *"Imperator Alexander III v Fredensborge"* [Emperor Alexander III in Fredensborg]. St. Petersburg, 1913.

163. Zimin, I. *"Tsarskie den'gi"* [The tsar's money]. St. Petersburg, 2011.

164. *"Zodchie SanktPeterburga XIX – nachala XX veka."* [Architects of Saint Petersburg. XIX – beginning of XX century] Isachenko V. (compiler), St. Petersburg, 1998.

165. *"Zodchiy"* [Architect], magazine. 1872–1914.

Index

Aage (1887–1940) — Prince of Denmark 223-224

Adamson, Amandus (1855–1929) — sculptor 231, (232)

Adlerberg, Nikolai Nikolaevich— count, diplomat 73

Adolph (1818–1905) — Duke of Nassau 307, 309

Adolph (1859–1916) — Prince of Shaumburg-Lippe (146)

Adolph Friedrich VI (1882-1918) — Grand Duke of Mecklenburg-Strelitz 55

Albert (1819–1861) —Prince Consort, husband of Queen Victoria 81, 83, 111

Albert (1843–1902) — Prince of Saxe-Altenburg 55, 307, 309

Albert (1869–1931) — Prince of Schleswig-Holstein-Sonderburg-Augustenburg 214

Albert Victor (1864–1892) — Duke of Clarence (203), 218, (221)

Albrecht (1865–1939) — Duke of Württemberg (45)

Albrecht (1869–1942) — Prince of Schaumburg-Lippe (59)

Albrecht Jr. (1900–1984) — Prince of Schaumburg-Lippe (59)

Alexander (1823–1888) — Prince of Hesse and by Rhine 13, 122, 287

Alexander (b. 1924) — Prince of Yugoslavia 255

Alexander (b. 1945) — Crown Prince of Yugoslavia 255

Alexander I (1777–1825) — Emperor 27, 41, 77, 306, 308

Alexander I (1893–1920) — King of Greece (272), 273, 300, 301

Alexander II (1818–1881) — Emperor 2, 8, (9), (10), (11), (12), 13, 16, 17, 18, 19, 20, 21, 22, 25, 26, 29, 30, 31, 34, 36, (37), 43,46, 51, 55, 65, (75), 77, 80, 81,89, 98, 117, (128), 150, 153, 155, 156, (180), 182, 186, 187, 195, 201, 258, 269, 277, 278, 286, 300, 306, 308

Alexander III (1845–1894) — Emperor 8, 32, 34, 55, 57, 58, 65, 68, 70, 71, 72, 74, 83, 88, 98, 106, 119, 122, 123, 124, 155, 150, 156, 157, 174, 184, 191, (194), 195, (196), 197, (198), 200, 201, 202, 203, 205, 209, 210, (211), 212, 213, (215), 223, 225, 227, 233, 235, 236, (237), 242, 247, 248, 251, 276, 288, 293, 294, 306, 308

Alexander Mikhailovich (1866–1933) — Grand Duke 53, (155), 157, 158, 159, (160), 243, 295, (298), 306, 308

Alexandra (1844–1925) — Queen of Great Britain [also Princess of Wales, née Denmark] 179, (203), (209), (210), 214, 216, 217, 218, 219, (220), 221, 235, 239, 240, (241), 246, 255, (271), 272, 295

Alexandra (1878–1942) — Princess of Edinburgh and Saxe-Coburg & Gotha, married Ernst of Hohenlohe-Langenburg (85), 88, (89), (93), (95), (113), (116)

Alexandra (1882–1963) — Grand Duchess of Mecklenburg-Schwerin [née Cumberland] 165, (171), (196), 222

Alexandra Alexandrovna (1842–1849) — Grand Duchess 16

Alexandra Feodorovna (1798–1860) — Empress [née Prussia] 8, 13, 26, 27, 40, 41, 53, 137, (153), 235

Alexandra Feodorovna (1872–1918) — Empress [née Hesse and by Rhine] 2, 8, (11), 12, 63, 76, 83, 88, (95), 111, (112), (115), 116, 117, (118), (119), (120), 122, 123, 124, (126). 127, (128), 134, 136, 137, (138), 139, (141), 144, (145), 146, 151, 224, 225, 227, (228), (230), 232, 233, 234, (235), (269), 272, 302, 306, 308

Alexandra Georgievna (1870–1891) — Grand Duchess [née Greece] (236), 255, (267), 286, 287, 288, 289, 290, 306, 308

Alexandra Iosifovna (1830–1911) — Grand Duchess [née Princess of Saxe-Altenburg] 55, (58), (129), 151, 221, 226, (256), 257, 260, 267, 268, (269), 270, 280, (289), 307, 309

Alexandra Nikolaevna (1825–1844) — Grand Duchess 306, 309

Alexandrina (1820–1904) — Duchess of Saxe-Coburg & Gotha [née Baden] 81

Alexandrine (1803–1892) — Grand Duchess of Mecklenburg-Schwerin [née Prussia] (153), 162, 308

Alexandrine (1879–1952) — Queen of Denmark [née Mecklenburg-Schwerin] 165, 166, 246, 282, 296, 308

Alexandrina Irene (1915–1980) — Princess of Prussia 170

Alexei I (1629–1678) — Emperor 146

Alexei II (1929–2008) — Patriarch of Moscow and All of Russia (133), 251

Alexei Alexandrovich (1850–1908) — Grand Duke 19, (20), 34, 100, 167, 170, 185, 189, 195, (224), 306

Alexei Mikhailovich (1875–1895) — Grand Duke 156, (157), 307

Alexei Nikolaevich (1904–1918) — Tsarevich 168, (169), 233, (235), (238), 242, 306, 308

Alexei Petrovich (1690–1718) — Tsarevich 2

Alfred (1844–1900) — Duke of Edinburgh and Saxe-Coburg & Gotha 81, (83), (84), (85), 86, 87, (89), (90), 92, 112, (114), (116), (129), 151, 219, 307, 308

Alfred (1874–1899) — Hereditary Prince of Saxe-Coburg & Gotha 88, (89), (114), (116), (129)

Alice (1843—1878) — Grand Duchess of Hesse and by Rhine [née Great Britain] 89, 117, 119, 121, 122

Alice (1885–1969) — Princess of Greece [née Battenberg] (95), (137), (138), 139, (2198), (309)

Alfonso (1886–1975) — Infante of Spain [né Bourbon-Orleans] 88, 114

Amadeo (b. 1943) — Duke of Savoy 255

Amalia (1818–1875) — wife of Otto I [née Oldenburg] 262, 264

Anastasia (1878–1922) — wife of Christopher of Greece [Mrs. Nancy Leeds] 304, 309

Anastasia Mikhailovna (1860–1922) — Grand Duchess of Mecklenburg-Schwerin [née Russia] 2, 73, (129), (138), 151, (152), 153, 154, (155), 161, 162, 163, 164, (165), 166, 167, 168, (170), (171), 184, 222, 296, 307, 308, 309

Anastasia Nikolaevna (1968–1935) — Grand Duchess [née Montenegro] 307

Anastasia Nikolaevna (1901–1918) — Grand Duchess (138), 168, (233)

Andersen, Hans Niels (1852–1937) — Director of the East-Asian Company 247

Andreas (1882–1944) — Prince of Greece (137), (138), 139, (209), (215), (267), (269), (293), 298, (300), 303, 309

Andrei Alexandrovich (1897–1981) — Prince of the Imperial Blood (160)

Andrei Vladimirovich (1879–1956) — Grand Duke (99), 101, (105), (108), 137, (280), 307

Anne (1843–1865) — Grand Duchess of Mecklenburg-Schwerin [née Hesse and by Rhine] 308

Anne (b. 1923) — Queen of Romania (née Bourbon-Parma) 223

Anthony (V. Vadkovsky) (1846–1912) — Metropolitan of St. Petersburg and Ladoga 76

Arthur (1850–1942) — Duke of Connaught, Queen Victoria's third son (85), (86), (116)

Asikritov, D. — photographer 122

Aucock, Louis (1850–1932) — jeweler 282

Augusta (1811–1890) — wife of Kaiser Wilhelm I [née Princess of Saxe-Weimar-Eisenach] 29, (36)

Augusta (1822–1862) — Grand Duchess of Mecklenburg-Schwerin [née Princess of Reuss] 100, 153, (162), (163), 308

Augusta (1826–1898) — wife of Prince Hermann of Saxe-Weimar-Eisenach [née Württemberg] (45)

Augusta (1843-1919) — wife of Prince Moritz of Saxe-Altenburg [née Saxe-Meiningen] 307

Augusta Victoria (1858–1921) — wife of Kaiser Wilhelm II [née Schleswig-Holstein-Sonderburg-Augustenburg] 65, 145, (146), 308

Auguste (1843–1919) — Princess of Saxe-Altenburg [née Saxe-Meiningen] 308

Averov, G. — Greek philanthropist 277

Axel (1888–1964) — Prince of Denmark 224

Babkin, P.I. — photographer (270)

Bach, Johann Sebastian (1685–1750) — German com poser 55

Bachofen, K. – photographer (95)

Baier, R.F. — photographer (260)

Bainbridge, Henrich Charles — an associate of Fabergé 101

Barbara, Sister — Nun 132, 133

Baryatinskaya, Maria — Princess 292

Baryatinskiy, Vladimir Anatolievich (1843–1914) — Prince, Adjutant to Tsarevich Nicholas Alexandrovich 187

Bathildis (1903–1983) — Princess of Schaumburg-Lippe (59)

Bazarov, Ioann (1819–1895) — Protopriest 43

Bazhanov, Vasiliy Borisovich (1800–1883) — Protobresbyter, private priest to the Imperial family 103

Beatrice (1857–1944) — Princess of Battenberg [née Great Britain] (85), (88), (116)

Beatrice (1884–1966) — Princess of Edinburgh and Saxe-Coburg & Gotha (85), 88, (113), (114), (116)

Beckstrøm, Ragnar — Director of the "Langinkoski" Museum 251

Bega, R. — sculptor (35)

Bekker, Jacob — owner of a piano company 54

Beloselski-Belosersky, Konstantin Esperovich (1843–1920) — Prince 123

Benardaki, Dimitry Egorovich (1799–1870) — philan thropist 299, 300, (301)

Benois, Albert Nikolaevich — artist 294

Benois, Alexander Nikolaevich(1870–1960) — art histo rian 24, 55, 135

Benois, Leon Nikolaevich (1856–1928) — architect 76, 118, 136, 137, 147, 227

Bensen, J.W. — jeweler — 88

Benz, Karl (1844–1929) — German inventor 60, 61, 62

Behrens, Peter (1868–1940) — German architect 118, 139, (140), 142, 143

Bergamasco, Karl Ivanovich (1830–1896) — photogra pher 3, (19), (66), (82), (263), (290)

Berlioz, Hector (1803–1869) — French composer 52

Bernstorff, Johann Ernst (1712–1772) — Danish Minister of Foreign Affairs 184

Berthold (1906–1963) — Margrave of Baden 309

Bezobrazov, Vladimir Mikhailovich (1857–1932)— Adjutant-General 62

Bismarck, Otto von (1815–1898) — Prince, Chancellor of the German Empire 29, 38, 39, (66), 67

Blokh, Karl Henrich (1834–1890) — Danish artist 194

Bogdanov, Alexander Nikolaevich — owner of a St. Petersburg tobacco company 76

Bogdanov-Belsky, Nikolai Petrovich (1868–1945) — artist 74

Bogolubov, Alexei Petrovich (1824–1896) — artist (195), 295

Bohm, Albert — German architect 75

Bohringer — photographer (283)

Bolin, Gustav — jeweler 282

Bonfis — photographer (133)

Boris Vladimirovich (1877–1943) — Grand Duke (97), 98, (99), 101, (105), (108), 110, 137, 307

Borwin (b. 1956) — Duke of Mecklenburg 55

Bosse, Harold Haraldovich(1841–1882) — architect 12, 167

Buhre, Paul Karlovich — watchmaker 103

Brandram, Richard 273

Brenna, Vincenzo (1745–1820) — architect (202), 257

Briullov, P.A. 294

Brow, John — Chamberlain of Queen Victoria (88)

Brullov, Alexander Pavlovich (1798–1877) — architect 12

Bruni, Feodor Antonovich (1799–1875) — artist 43

Bruni, Nikolai Alexandrovich (1856—1935) — artist (279)

Brunov, Ludwig (1843–1913) — German sculptor 161

Brusnitsyn, Nikolai Nikolaevich — merchant 76

Budberg, Andrei Feodorovich (1817–1881) — Baron, diplomat 62

Bulla, Karl Karlovich (1855–1929) — photographer (15), (23), (31), (51), (62), (64), (71), (102), (123), (147), (148), (154), (168), (225), (226), (229), (230), (234), (235), (242), (259), (278)

Bulla, Victor Karlovich (1883–1933) — photographer (118)

Butera de Radali, Varvara Petrovna (1796–1870) (née Shakhovskaia) — Princess 41

Cameron, Charles (1745–1811) — architect 257

Carl (1861–1951) — Prince of Sweden 214

Carl Alexander (1818-1901) — Grand Duke of Saxe-Weimar-Eisenach 308

Carl Friedrich (1783-1853) — Grand Duke of Saxe-Weimar-Eisenach 306, 308

Carlow, Ekaterina Georgievna (1891–1940) — Countess von, Princess Galitzine in marriage 54

Carlow, Maria Georgievna (1893–1979) — Countess von, Princess Galitzine in marriage 54

Carlow, Natalia Feodorovna (1858–1921) — Countess von 54, 55, 307, 309

Carlow, Natalia Georgievna (1894–1913) — Countess von 54

Catherine (1821–1898) — Princess of Württemberg (45)

Catherine (1913–1947) — Princess of Greece 273

Catherine II (1729–1796) — Empress 17, 22, 200, 209, 257, 259

Catherine Ioannovna (1692–1733) — Tsarevna 151

Catherine Mikhailovna (1827–1894) — Grand Duchess 51, 52, 53, 55, 73, 307, 309

Catherine Pavlovna (1788–1819) — Grand Duchess, Queen of Württemberg 40, 41, 56, 147, 306, 308

Cavos, Albert Katarinovich (1800–1869) — architect 24

Cavos, Katarino — composer 24

Cecile (1911–1937) — Hereditary Princess of Hesse and by Rhine [née Greece] 309

Cecilie (1886–1954) — Crown Princess of Prussia [née Mecklenburg-Schwerin] (36), 166, 168, 170, (171), 308

Cecilie (1917–1975) — Princess of Prussia 171

Charlemagne, Joseph Josephovich (1782–1861) (27), 167

Charles (b. 1948) — Prince of Wales 255

Charlotte (1860–1919) — Duchess of Saxe-Meiningen [née Prussia] (85), (116)

Charlotte (1864–1946) — Queen of Württemberg [née Shaumburg-Lippe] (45)

Charlotte Amalie — sister of King of Denmark Christian VI 216

Cheremetevsky, Natalia (1880–1952) — Countess Brassova, wife of Grand Duke Michael Alexandrovich 306

Chizhov, Matvei Afanasievich (1838–1916) — sculptor 104

Christian (1885–1901) — Prince of Hannover 222

Christian VI (1699–1744) — King of Denmark 216

Christian VIII (1786–1848) — King of Denmark 184

Christian IX (1818–1906) — King of Denmark 2, 65, 174, (176), 177, 178, 179, 183, 184, (189), 195, (196), 203, 205, 206, (208), (209), (210), 213, 214, 215, 216, 222, (224), 226, 239, 242, 248, 255, 273, (274)

Christian X (1870–1947) — King of Denmark 165, 184, 195, (196), 211, 216, (217), 244, (246), 247, 308

Christiansen, Hans — artist 139, (140)

Christoph (1901–1943) — Prince of Hesse-Kassel 309

Christopher (1888–1940) — Prince of Greece (58), (138), (196), 265, 267, (269), 297, (300), 302, (303), (304), 309

Clare, E. — photographer 299

Constantine, Emperor of Byzantium (190)

Constantine I (Tino) (1868–1923) — King of the Hellenes (138), (146), (236), 266, 272, 273, (274), (276), (286), (289), (293), 300, 301, 302, (303), (304), 309

Constantine II (b. 1940) — King of the Hellenes 255

Daimler, Gotlieb (1834–1900) — German inventor 60, 61, 62

Dal', Vladimir Ivanovich (1801–1872) — writer 260

Danielsen, F. —Danish photographer (178), (184), 211, (213)

Danielsen, I. — Danish photographer (208)

Dannecker, Johann Henrich von (1758–1841) — German sculptor 46

Davydov, Karl Julievich (1838–1889) — cellist 54

Demertsov, Feodor Ivanovich (1762–1823) — architect (123)

Demmler, Adolph (1804–1886) — German architect 161

Diesel, Rudolph (1858–1913) — German inventor 62

Dimitry Alexandrovich (1900–1980) — Prince of the Imperial Blood 160

Dimitry Konstantinovich (1860–1919) — Grand Duke (58), (256), (260), 268, 297, (299), 306, 309

Dimitry Pavlovich (1891–1942) — Grand Duke 93, 130, (131), (138), (250), 290, (291), 296, 307

Dostoevsky, Feodor Mikhailovich (1821–1881) — writer 80

Dragsted — Danish jeweler 197

Dreyer, Nadezhda Friedrich II (1861–1929) — wife of Grand Duke Nicholas Konstantinovich 306

Dunant, Henri Jean (1828–1910) — Swiss public official 47, (50), 51

Dvas, Grigory Viktorovich — Vice-Governor of Leningrad Region (183)

Edward (b. 1935) — Duke of Kent 255

Edward VII (Albert Edward – Bertie) (1841–1910) — King of Great Britain [Prince of Wales] (85), (116), 179, 217, 218, 219, 221, 237

Effern, Renate — German writer 80

Eigtved, Nils (1701–1754) — Danish architect 178, 179, 188

Eleonore (1871–1937) — Grand Duchess of Hesse and by Rhine [née Solms-Hohensolms-Lich] 118-119

Eliseev, Alexander Grigorievich (1839–1918) — banker 75, 76

Eliseev, Pyotr Stepanovich (1834–1901) — banker 73

Eliseeva, Lubov Dmitrievna — wife of Pyotr Stepanovich 73

Elisabeth (1880–1912) — Prince of Hannover 222

Elisabeth (1894–1956) — Princess Romania 304

Elisabeth (1904–1955) — Princess of Greece, married to Count Karl Theodor zu Toerring-Jettenbach (105), 283, 284

Elisabeth Alexeievna (1779–1826) — Empress [née Baden] 13, 77

Elisabeth Feodorovna (Ella) (1864–1918) — Grand Duchess [née Hesse and by Rhine] (27), 73, 76, 81, 83, (85), 93, (95), 111, (116), 117, (119), 120, (121), 122, 123, 124, 130, (131), 132, 133, 135, 137, (138), 139, (142), 228, 286, 287, 290, 302, 307, 308

Elisabeth Mavrikievna (1865–1927) — Grand Duchess [née Saxe-Altenburg] (58), (129), 151, (269), (303), 306, 309

Elisabeth Mikhailovna (1826–1845) — Grand Duchess 51, 307, 309

Elisabeth Petrovna (1709–1861) — Empress 22, 193

Elizabeth (b. 1936) — Princess of Yugoslavia 255

Elizabeth II (b. 1926) — Queen of Great Britain 309

Elsa (1877–1956) — Duchess of Württemberg (45), 57, (59), (129)

Emma (1858–1934) — Queen Regent of the Netherlands [née Waldeck-Pyrmont] 309

Engalychev, Paul Nikolaevich (1864–1944) — Prince, Adjutant-General 62

Engel, Karl Ludwig (1778–1840) — architect 36

Epanchin, Nikolai Alexeevich (1857–1941) — General (98), 149

Erik (1890–1950) — Prince of Denmark 224

Ernst August (1845–1923) — Duke of Cumberland 214, 221

Ernst August (1887–1953) — Prince of Cumberland, son of Thyra (196), 222, 238, (250)

Ernst I (1784–1844) — Duke of Saxe-Coburg & Gotha 84, 86, (87)

Ernst II (1818–1893) — Duke of Saxe-Coburg & Gotha 81, 111

Ernst Ludwig (Ernie) (1868–1937) — Grand Duke of Hesse and by Rhine 63, 81, 83, 87, 88, 89, (90), , (91), 92, (95), 96, 111, (114), 116, 117, 118, 122, (129), 134, (135), 136, (137), (138), 139, 140, 141, 224

Etter, Alexander Sebastianovich (1867– after 1931) — member of the court of Grand Duchess Maria Pavlovna 109

Eugen (1899–1929) — Prince of Schaumburg-Lippe (59)

Eugenie (1910–1989) — Princess of Greece 276

Evlogii (Vasiliy Semeonovich Georgievsky) (1868–1946) — Metropolitan of the Russian Orthodox Church 278

Fabergé, Carl Gustavovich (1846 — 1920) — jeweler 101, 104, 194, 205, 213, 214, 283

Felipe (b. 1968) — Prince of Asturias 255

Feodor Alexandrovich (1898–1968) — Prince of the Imperial Blood 160

Feodora (1807–1872) — Princess of Hohenlohe-Langenburg [née Leiningen], Queen Victoria's Half-sister 145

Feodora (1879–1945) — Princess of Saxe--Meiningen (85), (116)

Ferdinand (1865–1927) — King of Romania (85), (113), (116), (129), 308

Franz Ferdinand (1863–1914) — Austrian Archduke, Heir to the Throne 214

Filimonov, Igor — collector 58

Fisher, Karl Andreevich (1859 — after 1923) – photog rapher 126

Françoise (1844–1925) — Princess d'Orléans, Duchess of Chartres 222

Françoise (1902–1953) —Princess of Greece [née France] 309

Franz Joseph I (1830–1916) — Emperor of Austria and King of Hungary (87)

Franz Wilhelm (b. 1943) — Prince of Prussia 307

Frederik (b. 1968) — Crown Prince of Denmark 251

Frederik II (1534–1588) — King of Denmark 208

Frederik IV (1671–1730) — King of Denmark 188

Frederik V (1723–1766) — King of Denmark 177, 178, 179, 184

Frederik VI (1768–1839) — King of Denmark 177, 178

Frederik VII (1808–1863) — King of Denmark 263

Frederik VIII (1843–1912) — King of Denmark 165, 174, 185, (189), (203), 204, 215, 216, (217), 236, 239, (240)

Frederik VIII (1899–1972) — King of Denmark (250)

Fredericks Vladimir Borisovich (1838–1927) — Baron, Minister of the Imperial Court 63

Anastasia Nikolaevna (1901–1918) — Grand Duchess (138), 168, (233)

Friedrich Franz III (1851–1897) — Grand Duke of Mecklenburg-Schwerin 105, 151, (152), 153, 161, 162, 163, 164, 307, 308

Friedrich Franz IV (1882–1945) — Grand Duke of Mecklenburg-Schwerin 164, 165, (171), 222, (250), 282, 308

Friedrich Georg (1911–1966) — Prince of Prussia 170

Friedrich I (1826–1907) — Grand Duke of Baden 77, 80

Friedrich II (1856–1918) — Duke of Anhalt 306

Friedrich III (1831–1888) — German Kaiser (9), 29, (36), 134, 144, 145, 308

Friedrich Karl (1868–1940) — Prince of Hesse-Kassel (138), (146)

Friedrich Ludwig (1778–1819) — Grand Duke of Mecklenburg-Schwerin 151, 306, 308

Friedrich Wilhelm (1870–1873) — Prince of Hesse and by Rhine 122

Friedrich Wilhelm III (1770–1840) — King of Prussia 26, (36), (153)

Friedrich Wilhelm IV (1795–1861) — King of Prussia 26, 27, (36)

Frolov, Vladimir Alexandrovich (1874–1942) — master of mosaics 136, 279

Gabriel Konstantinovich (1887–1955) — Prince of the Imperial Blood (58), (299)

Gagarin, Grigoriy Grigorievich (1810–1893) — Prince 80

Gagarina (née Valevskaya), Isabella Adamovna (1800–1886) — Princess 80

Gambs, Henrich Daniel (1764–1831) — furniture maker 46

Gekkel, Climentii — gardener 20

Georg Donatus (1906–1937) — Hereditary Prince of Hesse and by Rhine 309

Georg Wilhelm (1880–1912) — Prince of Hannover 222

Georg Wilhelm (1915–2006) — Prince of Hannover 309

George (1779-1860) — Grand Duke of Oldenburg 53

George (1784–1812) — Duke of Oldenburg 40

George (1823–1876) — Duke of Mecklenburg-Strelitz (52), 53, 307, 309

George (1892–1938) — Prince of Battenberg (138)

George (1869–1957) — Prince of Greece (138), (196), (215), 222, (223), (250), (267), 272, 274, 276, (286), (289), 309

George (1902-1942) — Prince of Great Britain, Duke of Kent 285

George I (1845–1913) — King of the Hellenes, also William, Prince of Denmark 2, (138), (203), 205, 206, (215), 235, (236), (240), 255, 256, 261, 262, 263, 264, 265, 266, (267), 269, 270, (271), 272, 273, 286, 288, (289), 292, (293), 297, 298, 300, 302, 306, 309

George II (1890–1947) — King of the Hellenes (146), (272), 273, 292, (293), 300, 301, (303), (304), 309

Georg V the Blind (1819–1878)— King of Hannover 221

George V (1865–1936) — King of Great Britain 218, 219, 221, 246, 272

George VI (1895–1952) — King of Great Britain (250)

George Alexander (1899–1963) — Duke of Mecklenburg, Count von Carlow 54, 55

George Alexandrovich (1871–1899) — Tsarevich (193), (201), (239), 306

George Georgievich(1859–1909) — Duke of Mecklenburg-Strelitz 53, 54, 55, 307. 309

George Maximillianovich (1852-1912) — Duke of Leuchtenberg 44, 306, 308

George Mikhailovich (1863–1919) — Grand Duke (138), 156, (157), 186, (271), 292, 293, 294, 295, 296, 297, (298), (303), 307, 309

George Mikhailovich (b. 1981) — son of Maria Vladimirovna 307

Gertner, F. — German architect 255, 261

Gladstone, Thomas (1804–1889) — Prime Minister of Great Britain 88

Glinka, Mikhail Ivanovich (1804–1857) — composer 3, (23), (24), 25

Glückert, Julius — furniture maker 139

Gogol, Nikolai Vasilievich (1809–1852) — writer 52, 80

Goncharov, Ivan Alexandrovich (1812–1891) — writer 260

Gonzago, Pietro Gottardo di (1751–1831) — architect 257

Gorodetsky, L. — photographer (124), (280), (282)

Gottfried (1897–1960) — Prince of Hohenlohe-Langenburg 309

Grachev, Mikhail Gavrilovich (1863–) — jeweler 213

Grancy, Baron Auguste Senarclens de 13

Grimm, David Ivanovich (1823–1898) — architect 80, 130, 137, (166), 167, (186), 202, 276

Gritsenko, Nikolai Nikolaevich (1856 – 1900) — artist (274)

Grott, Jacob Karlovich (1812–1893) — tutor of 181

Guillome (Wilhelm) (1816–1893) — Duke of Schleswig-Holstein-Sonderburg-Glucksburg 65

Guinuepe, Philippe de la — architect 41

Gun, Andrei Leontievich (1841–1924) — architect (98)

Gustav (1887–1944) — Prince of Denmark (215), 216

Gustav V (1858–1950) — King of Sweden (215)

Gustav VI Adolph (1882-1973) — King of Sweden (250)

Haakon VII (1872–1957) — King of Norway [né Prince Carl of Denmark] 216, (218), (250)

Habikh, Ludwig — German sculptor 118, 135, 139

Halle, Emile (1846–1904) — French designer 216

Halmguber, G. F. (35)

Halske, Johann — one of the founders of the firm "Siemens and Halske" 68, (69)

Hans (1825–1911) — Prince of Schleswig-Holstein-Sonderburg-Glücksburg (215)

Hans-Veit (b. 1935) — Count zu Toerring-Jettenbach 255

Hansen, Georg Emile (1833–1891) — Danish photographer 189, (217)

Hansen, Theophile von — Danish architect 262, 273

Harald (1876–1949) — Prince of Denmark (215), 216, (217), (250)

Heinrich (1858–1896) — Prince of Battenberg (85), (116)

Heinrich Albrecht Wilhelm (1862–1929) — Prince of Prussia (116), 134, (138), 272

Helen (1896–1982) — Princess of Greece, daughter of Constantine I 146, (272), 273, (300), (303), (304), 308

Helen (b. 1937) — Archduchess of Austria [née Toerring-Jettenbach] 255

Helen Georgievna (1857–1936) — Princess of Saxe-Altenburg [née Mecklenburg-Strelitz] 53, 55, (129), 307, 309

Helen Pavlovna (1784–1803) — Grand Duchess, married Friedrich Ludwig of Mecklenburg-Schwerin 51, 151, 306, 308

Helen Pavlovna (1806–1873) — Grand Duchess [née of Württemberg] 50, 51, 52, 53

Helen Vladimirovna (1882–1957) — Grand Duchess [née Greece] 75, 80, (99), 101, 103, (105), (108), 109, (129), (138), 168, (269), (271), 280, 281, 282, 283, 284, 285, (293), 298, (303), 307, 309

Henrik (b. 1934) — Prince Consort, husband of Queen of Denmark Margrete II (251)

Herkomer, Hubert von (1849–1914) — English artist 163

Hermann (1825–1901) — Prince of Saxe-Weimar-Eisenach (45)

Heusler, Jochen — German explorer (34), (69)

Hirsch, Gustav Ivanovich (1828–1907) — life surgeon (195)

Hoffman, Ludwig — architect 118

Hubertus (1909–1950) — Prince of Prussia 170, (171)

Ianyshev, Ioann (1826–1910) — Protopriest, private priest to the Imperial family 137, 190

Igor Konstantinovich (1894–1918) — Prince of the Imperial Blood (58)

Ingeborg (1878–1958) — Princess of Denmark (203), (215), 216, 223

Ioann Konstantinovich(1886–1918) — Prince of the Imperial Blood (58)

Irene (1866–1953) — Princess of Prussia [née Hesse and by Rhine] 83, (85), (116), (119), (120), 122, (134), (138), (141)

Irene (1904–1974) — Princess of Greece, daughter of Constantine I (272), 273, (304)

Isidor (Jacob Sergeevich Nikolsky) (1799–1892) — Metropolitan of St. Petersburg 100

Izmailovich, Vladislav Matveevich (1872–1959) — artist 103

Izvolsky, Alexander Petrovich (1856–1919) — diplomat 109

Jacobsen, Karl (1842–1914) — Danish philanthropist, owner of breweries 203

Jardin, Nicolas Henri — French architect 178, 184

Jellinec, Adriana (Mercedes) (61)

Jellinec, Emile (1853–1918) — Czech diplomat 61

Jensen, David Ivanovich (1816–1902) — sculptor (123)

Johann Albrecht (1857–1920) — Duke of Mecklenburg-Schwerin 164

Kaas, Ove de — Danish diplomat (243)

Kachalov, Nikolai Nikolaevich (1852–1909)– Director of ETI 71

Kann-Rasmussen, Lars — Danish philanthropist 195

Karl (1898–1946) — Prince of Leiningen, husband of Grad Duchess Maria Kirillovna 306

Karl Eugen (1744–1793) — Duke of Württemberg 43

Karl I (1823–1891) — King of Württemberg 40, 41, 43, (45), 49, 306, 308

Karl Leopold (1678–1747) — Duke of Mecklenburg 151

Karl Michael (1863–1934) — Duke of Mecklenburg-Strelitz 53

Karl Theodor (1900–1967) — Count zu Toerring-Jettenbach, husband of Princess Elisabeth of Greece 284

Karnovitch, Olga (1866–1929) — Princess Paley 307

Kazakov, Matvei Feodorovich (1738–1812) — architect (127)

Kegresse, Adolphe (1879–1943) — chauffer to Emperor Nicholas II 63, [64]

Kendler, Johann (1744–1817) — artist on porcelain Kharlamov, M. — sculptor 33, 294

Kira Kirillovna (1909–1967) — Grand Duchess, married Prince Louis Ferdinand of Prussia 98, 105, 306, 308

Kirill Vladimirovich (1876–1938) — Grand Duke 96, 97, 98, (99), 101, (105), 107, (108), 109, 137, (153), (250), 277, (280), 281, 283, 306, 308

Kitner, Jeronim Sebastianovich (1839–1929) — architect 46, (98)

Kleinmikhel, (Peter) Pyotr Andreevich (1793–1869) — Count (30)

Klenze, Leo von (1784–1864) — German architect 30, 255, 261

Klodt, Pyotr Karlovich (1805–1867) — sculptor (26), 27

Klykov, Viacheslav Mikhailovich (1939–2006) — sculptor (133)

Knoblauch, Eduard (1801–1865) — German architect 67

Knorring, Ludwig Karlovich (1859–1930) — Baron, diplomat (66), 73, 145

Kochubei, Victor Sergeevich (1860–1923) — Prince 274

Koefoed (née Obiedova), Elizaveta Petrovna — wife of Andrei Andreevich (244)

Koefoed, Karl Andreas (Andrei Andreevich) (1855–1948) — Danish specialist in agriculture 244, 245, 246

Koefoed, Nina Andreevna — daughter of A.A. Koefoed (244)

Kolchev, Leonid (1871–1944) — Protopriest, private priest to Empress Maria Feodorovna 248

Komarovsky, Alexei Evgrafovich (?–1895) — Count (126)

Konalski — photographer (202)

Konasevich, L.L. — photographer (127)

Koni, Anatolij Feodorovich (1844–1927) — jurist 52

Konstantin Konstantinovich (1858–1915) — Grand Duke (56), 57, (58), 75, (121), 133, 151, 260, 268, (269), 279, 303, 306, 309

Konstantin Konstantinovich (1890–1918) — Prince of the Imperial Blood

Konstantin Nikolaevich (1827–1892) — Grand Duke 55, 166, 256, 257, 258, 259, 260, 267, 307, 309

Konstantin Pavlovich (1779–1831) — Grand Duke 306, 308

Kozlov, Paul Alexandrovich (1841–1891) — Adjutant to Tsarevich Alexander Alexandrovich (195)

Krakau, Alexander Ivanovich (1817–1888) — architect 287

Krasnov, Nikolai Petrovich (1864–1939) — architect 159, 295, 296

Krasovsky, Alexander Feodorovich (1848–1923) — architect 228

Kraus, Conrad — German architect 52

Krebs, Karl Emmanuel (1889–1971) — representative of the Danish Red Cross in Russia 244

Kretzmeyer, F. — photographer (183)

Krieger, Johan Cornelius — Danish architect 188

Krivoshein, Alexander Vasilievich (1857–1921) — Minister 74

Kruger, Franz (1797–1857) — German artist — 36

Kryzhitsky, Konstantin Jacovlevich (1858–1911) — artist (205)

Kschessinska, Matilde (1872–1971) — wife of Grand Duke Andrei Vladimirovich 307

Kulikovsky, Guri Nikolaevich (1919–1984) — son of Grand Duchess Olga Alexandrovna (246), 247

Kulikovsky, Nikolai Alexandrovich (1881–1959) — Colonel 243, (246), 247, 306

Kulikovsky, Tikhon Nikolaevich (1917–1993) — son of Grand Duche7ss Olga Alexandrovna (246), 247

Kurakina, (née Galitsine) Julia Feodorovna (1814–1881) — Hof-Mistress to Tsarevna Maria Feodorovna 195

Kurakina, Alexandra Alexeevna (1840–1919) — Princess, Lady in Waiting to Tsarevna Maria Feodorovna 195

Kuzmin, Roman Ivanovich (1811–1867) — architect 299, (303)

Ladyzhenskaya, (née Kozhukhova) Maria Evgenievna (1864–1941) — Princess (248)

Ladyzhenskaya-Meiners, Tatiana Sergeevna (1919–2006) — Princess (240), (246), (247), (248), (250)

Langberg, M.V. — Danish diplomat 243

Langhans, Karl Ferdinand — architect 29

Lansere, Evgenij Alexandrovich (1848–1886) — sculptor 270

Lapres, V. — photographer 131

Leinz, Cristian Friedrich (1814–1892) — architect 45

Lemer, Bedford — English photographer 249

Leonida Georgievna (1914–2010) Grand Duchess [née Bagration-Moukhtransky] 307, 308

Lermontov, Mikhail Yurievich (1814–1841) — poet 265

Lessner, Gustav Arnoldovich 62

Levitsky, S.L. (1819–1898) — photographer 3, (10), (16), (24), (175), (198), (207), (261)

Liebknecht, Karl (1871–1919) — German socialist politician 26

Likhutin, N.A. — artist 103

Lindner, J. — engraver (40)

Liphart, Ernest Karlovich (1847–1932) — artist 226

Litke, Feodor Petrovich (1797–1882) –Count, Admiral 256

Liubimov, Sergei — private priest to Empress Maria Feodorovna 186

Lobanov-Rostovsky, Alexei Borisovich (1824–1896) — Prince, diplomat 109

Loftus, August — Lord, English Ambassador to Russia 219

Louis (1854–1921) — Prince of Battenberg (85), (116), 134

Louis Ferdinand (1907–1994) — Prince of Prussia 170, (171), 306, 308

Louis Philippe (1838–1894) — Prince d'Orléans, Count of Paris 222

Louise (1776–1810) — Queen of Prussia [née Mecklenburg-Strelitz] 36, 54, 153

Louise (1817–1898) — Queen of Denmark [née Hesse-Kassel] 174, (176), 177, 179, (180), 184, 185, (189), (196), 203, 206, (208), (209), (210), 213, 214, (215), 216, 221, (222), 255, (271), 273, 274

Louise (1838–1923) — Duchess of Baden [née Prussia] (77), 80

Louise (1851–1926) — Queen of Denmark [née Sweden] 203, 214, 215, 216, (217), (218)

Louise (1858–1924) — Princess of Saxe-Coburg & Gotha [née Belgium] (85), (116)

Louise (1867–1931) — Duchess of Fife [née Great Britain] 218, (222)

Louise (1875–1906) — Princess of Schaumburg-Lippe [née Denmark] (209), 216

Louise (1889–1965) — Queen of Sweden [née Battenberg] (138)

Louise (1860–1917) — Duchess of Connaught [née Prussia] (85), (116)

Ludwig I (1786–1868) — King of Bavaria 261

Ludwig I (1753–1830) — Grand Duke of Hesse and by Rhine (138)

Ludwig II (1777–1848) — Grand Duke of Hesse and by Rhine 13

Ludwig III (1806–1877) — Grand Duke of Hesse and by Rhine 117

Ludwig IV (1837–1892) — Grand Duke of Hesse and by Rhine 8, 117, 199, (120), 122

Ludwig Wilhelm (1829–1897) — Prince of Baden 282

Lutzky, Boris Grigorievich (1865–1926) — inventor 61, 62

Maiewsky, Karl Yakovlevich (1824–1897) — architect 22

Maikov, Apollon Nikolaevich (1821–1897) — poet 260

Maltsev, Alexei Petrovich (1854–1915) — protopriest 72, 73, 74, 75, 76

Malyshev, Ignatiy — archimandrite 32, 67

Margaretha (1899–1977) — Princess of Denmark [née Sweden] 223

Margarita (1905–1981) — Princess of Hohenlohe-Langenburg [née Greece] 223

Margrethe (1895–1982) — Princess of Bourbon-Parma [née Denmark] 223

Margarete (1872–1954) — Princess of Hesse-Kassel [née Prussia] (138), (146)

Margrethe (b. 1940) — Queen of Denmark 204, 251

Margrethe II (b. 1940) — Queen of Denmark 204, 251

Maria Alexandrovna (1824–1880) — Empress [née Hesse and by Rhine] 2, 3, 8, (10), (12), 13, (16), 17, 20, (21), 22, 24, 117, 119, 130, 133, 135, 182, 185, 191, 286, 306, 308

Maria Alexandrovna (1853–1920) — Duchess of Saxe-Coburg & Gotha (19), (20), 81, (82), 83, (84), (85), 86, 87, (89), (90), (92), (95), 112, 114, (116), (129), 137, 151, 219, 223, (224), 226, 230, 235, 288, 307, 308

Maria Feodorovna (1759–1828) — Empress [née Württemberg] (13), 50, 148, 257

Maria Feodorovna (1847–1928) — Empress [née Denmark] 2, 3, (20), 24, 55, 123, 124, (128), 159, 165, 174, (175), 186, 190, (191), 192, 193, 194, 195, 196, (199), 200, (201), (202), 203, 205, (207), (209), (210), 214, (215), 218, 219, (220), (221), 222, (224), 225, 226, 227, 235, (236), (237), 239, 240, 241, 242, 243, 244, 245, 246, 247, 248, (249), 250, 251, 261, 282, 283, 288, 304, 306, 308

Maria Georgievna (1876–1940) — Grand Duchess [née Greece] (138), (160), (209), (215), 235, (236), (237), 255, (267), (271), (286), 288, (289), 292, 293, 295, 296, 300, 307, 309

Maria Kirillovna (1907–1951) — Grand Duchess 97, (105), 306, 308

Maria Maximilianovna (1841–1914) — Princess of Baden [née Leuchtenberg] 77, 80, 282

Maria Mikhailovna (1825–1846) — Grand Duchess 51

Maria Nikolaevna (1819–1876) — Grand Duchess 149, 306, 308

Maria Nikolaevna (1899–1918) — Grand Duchess (233), 306

Maria Pavlovna (1786–1859) — Grand Duchess, Grand Duchess of Saxe-Weimar-Eisenach 29

Maria Pavlovna the Elder (1854–1920) — Grand Duchess [née Mecklenburg-Schwerin] (62), (72), 74, 83, (85), (92), (99), 100, 101, (102), 103, 104, (105), (106), 107, (108), 109, 110, 111, (116), (129), 151, 153, 162, (165), 168-170, (226), 227, 228, 229, 280, 283, 284, (285), 288, (302), 306, 308

Maria Pavlovna the Younger (1890–1958) — Grand Duchess 93, (95), (130), (131), (138), 289

Maria Vladimirovna (b. 1953) — Grand Duchess 307

Marie (1818–1907) — Queen of Hannover [née Saxe-Altenburg] 221

Marie (1850–1922) — Grand Duchess of Mecklenburg-Schwerin [née Schwarzburg-Rudolstadt] 308

Marie (1852–1923) — Countess Erbach-Shönberg [née Battenberg] (138), (203), 214, 222, 223

Marie (1855–1888) — Princess of Saxe-Altenburg [née Prussia] 55

Marie (1865–1909) — Princess of Denmark [née Orléans] (188)

Marie (1874–1878) — Princess of Hesse and by Rhine (119), 122

Marie (1875–1938) — Queen of Romania [née Edinburgh] (85), 88, (89), (93), (95), (113), (116), (129), 308

Marie (1882–1962) — Princess of Greece [née Bonaparte] (188), (203), 276, 288, 309

Marie (1888–1947) — Princess of Saxe-Altenburg 55

Marie Louise (1803–1862) — Princess of Saxe-Altenburg [née Mecklenburg-Schwerin] 308

Marie Louise (1879–1948) — Princess of Baden [née Cumberland (Hannover)] 80, 306, 308

Marina (1906–1968) — Princess of Greece, daughter of Grand Duchess Helen Vladimirovna (105), 283, 285

Marsher, Vilhelm Frimann (–1872) — Danish officer 221

Mary (b. 1972) — Crown Princess of Denmark [née Donaldson] 251

Matvienko, Valentina Ivanovna — Governor of St. Petersburg 251

Maud (1869–1938) — Princess of Great Britain, Queen of Norway (196), 197, (209), (215), 218

Maximilian (1817–1852) — Duke of Leuchtenberg 149, 306, 308

Maximilian (Max) (1867–1929) — Margrave of Baden (80), (146), (280), 282, 306, 308

Maximilian (Max) (b. 1933) — Margrave of Baden 255

Maximilian (1894–1914) — Prince of Hesse (146)

Maximilian (1898–1974) — Prince of Schaumburg-Lippe (59)

Meldahl, Ferdinand (1827–1908) — Danish architect 178, 216

Meltser, Roman Feodorovich (1860–1943) — architect furniture maker 213

Mendelsohn, H. — photographer 121

Menelas, Adam Adamovich (1753–1831) – architect 234

Mengden, Zinaida Georgievna (1878–1950) — Lady in Waiting to Empress Maria Feodorovna (246)

Mensdorff-Pouilly, Albert — Count (85)

Menshikov, Vladimir Alexandrovich (1815–1893) — Prince 80

Mestchersky, Maria Elimovna (1844–1868) — Lady in Waiting 187

Mestchersky, Vladimir Petrovich (1839–1914) — Prince, publicist 200

Messmacher, Maximillian Egorovich (1842–1906) — architect (98), 103, 104, 106, 193, 287

Michael (b. 1939) — Prince of Greece 255

Michael I (1596–1645) — Tsar 146, 230

Michael I (b. 1921) — King of Romania 223, 255

Michael Alexandrovich (1878–1918) — Grand Duke 70, (71), (128), 168, 186, (196), 200, (201), 203, (204), (206), (215), (224), (236), (237), (239), (285), 303

Michael Mikhailovich (1861–1929) — Grand Duke 155, 156, 157, 163

Michael Nikolaevich (1832–1909) — Grand Duke 2, 81, (154), 155, 156, (157), 163, (164), 166, (167), 168, (246), (285), 293, 307, 309

Michael Pavlovich (1798–1849) — Grand Duke 50, 53, (227), 257, 258, 307, 309

Michelson, K. — Danish jeweler (190)

Miklukho-Maklay, Nikolai Nikolaevich (1846–1888) — explorer 51

Militza Nikolaevna (1866–1951) — Grand Duchess [née Montenegro] 307

Mirotvortsev, Sergei Romanovich (1878–1949) — surgeon 150

Møller, Maersk MacKinney — Danish philanthropist 195

Monberg, Ludwig — Danish architect 195

Montferrand, Henry Auguste de (1786–1858) — architect 12

Monighetti, Ippolit Antonovich (1819–1878) — architect 18, 20, (22), 157, (159), 193, 194

Mordvinov, Nikolai Semenovich (1754–1845) — Count, Admiral 74

Moritz (1829-1907) — Prince of Saxe-Altenburg 307

Mosolov, Alexander Alexandrovich (1854–1939) — Head of the Chancellery of the Imperial Court (99), 101, (145), (299)

Nabokov, N. — furniture designer 228

Nabokov, Vladimir Dmitrievich (1869–1922) — jurist 74

Napoleon I 27, 86

Napoleon III (1808–1873) — Emperor of the French 46

Natalia Alexeievna (1755–1776) — first wife of Paul I [née Wilhelmine of Hesse and by Rhine] 306, 308

Naumenko, N. — photographer (147)

Nechaev-Maltsev, Yurij Stepanovich (1834–1913) — owner of glass works 76

Neff, Karl Timoleon (Timofei Andreevich) (1805–1876) — artist – (75), 137, 186

Neiman, Johann Kar I (1833–1891) — Danish artist 194

Nesterov, Mikhail Vasilievich (1862–1942) — artist 33, 130

Nikita Alexandrovich (1900–1974) — Prince of the

Imperial Blood (160), 285

Nicholas (1872–1938) — Prince of Greece (105), (106), 109, (138), 168, (196), (211), 255, (265), 266, (267), (271), (276), 280, (281), 282, 283, 284, (285), (286), (289), 292, (293), 298, 300, 302, 307, 309

Nicholas Alexandrovich (Nixa) (1843–1865) — Tsarevich (18), (21), (181), 182, 183, 184, 185, 186, 187, (190), 191, 258, 259, 306

Nicholas I (1796–1855) — Emperor 2, 8, (13), 26, 27, 29, 30, 31, 35, 36, 40, 41, 42, 67, 68, 77, 137, 146, 148, (153), 166, 234, 256, 302, 309

Nicholas II (1868–1918) — Emperor 8, (11), (12), (20), 33, 36, (37), 55, 58, 63, (64), 70, (76), 77, 80, 81, 83, (85), (92), (95), 96, 97, 111, (112), (114), (115), (116), 117, 124, (125), (126), 127, (128), (129), 136, (137), (138), 144, 145, 146, 150, 158, 159, 165, 168, (169), 186, (193), 194, (196), (201), (211), 213, (215), 219, 224, 225, 226, 227, 228, 229, 230, 231, 232, 233, 236, 237, 238, (239), 243, 272, 274, 279, 282, 283, (285), 303, 306, 308

Nicholas Konstantinovich (1850–1918) — Grand Duke (256), 257, (260), 306, 309

Nicholas Mikhailovich (1859–1919) — Grand Duke 155, 156, (157), 163, 168, 296, 297, (299), 307

Nicholas Nikolaevich the Elder (1831–1891) — Grand Duke 151, 166, 307, 309

Nicholas Nikolaevich the Younger (1856–1929) — Grand Duke (296), 307, 309

Nina Georgievna (1901–1974) — Princess of the Imperial Blood 295, 296

Nyblin, Daniel — Finnish photographer 37

Olav V (1903–1991) — King of Norway [né Prince Alexander of Denmark] (218)

Ohm, Feodor Adolphovich (1826–1898) — secretary to Tsarevna Maria Feodorovna (195)

Olbrich, Joseph Maria (1867–1908) — architect 92, 118, 134, 135, 139, (140)

Oldenburg, Alexander Petrovich of (1844–1932) — Prince [Duke] 149, 150, 306, 308

Oldenburg, Eugenia Maximillianovna (1845–1925) — Princess [née Leuchtenberg]

Oldenburg, Georg of (1784–1812) — Prince 40, 306, 308

Oldenburg, Peter Georgievich (1812–1881) — Prince [Duke] 147, 148, 308

Oldenburg, Peter Alexandrovich (1868–1924) — Prince (150), 168, 243, 306

Oldenburg, Theresa (1852–1883) — Duchess 44, 306, 308

Oleg Konstantinovich (1892–1914) — Prince of the Imperial Blood (58)

Olga (1877–1912) — Duchess of Württemberg (45), 57, (59)

Olga (1884–1958) — Princess of Cumberland (196), 222

Olga (1886–1955) — Princess of Saxe-Altenburg 55

Olga (1903–1997) — Princess of Greece, daughter of Grand Duchess Helen Vladimirovna (105), 283, 284

Olga Alexandrovna (1882–1960) — Grand Duchess 168, 186, (196), 200, 203, (204), 205, 206, 210, (224), 226, (236), (237), (239), (241), 242, 243, (246), 247, 306, 308

Olga Feodorovna (1839–1891) — Grand Duchess [née Baden] 77, 81, (154), 155, 156, (157), 166, 167, 295, 307, 309

Olga Konstantinovna (1851–1926) — Queen of Greece [née Russia] 2, (58), (138), 139, 196, (203), (209), 223, 226, 235, (236), (246), (255), 256, 257, 258, (259), 260, 261, 262, 263, 264, 265, 266, 267, 268, 269, 270, 271, 272, 273, 276, 277, 278, 279, 280, 282, 283, 284, 286, 288, (289), 292, (293), (300), 301, (302), 303, (304), (305), 306, 309

Olga Nikolaevna (1822–1892) — Queen of Württemberg [née Russia] 2, 40, 41, 42, 43, 44, 45, 46, 47, (48), 49, 50, 56, 57, 58, 73, (75), 80, 306, 308

Olga Nikolaevna (1895–1918) — Grand Duchess (63), (95), (138), 168, 228, (233), 306

Onou, Mikhail Konstantinovich (1835–1901) — diplomat 174

Opekushin, A.M. — sculptor 34

Orlov, Grigory Grigorievich (1734–1783) — Count 200, 260

Orlov, Vladimir Nikolaevich (1868–1927) — Prince 63, 76

Osten-Sacken, Nikolai Dmitrievich von (1831–1912) — Count, diplomat 65

Ostrovsky, Alexander Nikolaevich (1823–1896) — playwright 260

Ott, Dmitrij Oskarovich (1855–1929) — Life-Obstetrician 146, 147

Ovchinnikov, Pauel Akimovich (1830–1888) — jeweler 103, 213

Panov, V. — photographer 251

Pape, Wilhelm — German artist 170

Parland, Alfred Alexandrovich (1842–1920) — architect 32, 33

Parland, Alfred John 32

Pashkov, Vasilij Leontievich (1849–?) — master of electricity 68

Paul (1893–1976) — Regent of Yugoslavia 284

Paul I (1754–1801) — Emperor (13), 32, 40, 53, 147, 148, (151), 200, 257, 306, 308

Paul I (1901–1964) — King of the Hellenes (272), 273

Paul Alexandrovich (1860–1919) — Grand Duke (19), (20), 72, 83, (85), 92, 93, 95, (116), 130, (131), (138), (285), 286, 287, 288, 289, 290, 297, (298), 303, 307, 308

Paul Friedrich (1852–1923) — Duke of Mecklenburg-Schwerin 100

Pauline Olga (1877–1965) — Princess of Württemberg 41, (45)

Pazetti, Anaklet Alfredovich — photographer 199, 299

Perkhin, Mikhail Evlampievich (1860–1903) — jeweler in the firm of Fabergé (221)

Perovsky, Boris Alexeevich (1815–1881) — Count, Adjutant-General, tutor of Alexander II's children 187

Peter (1908–1980) — Prince of Greece 276

Peter I (1672–1725) — Emperor [The Great] 8, 296

Petersen, I. — photographer 180

Petipa, Marius Ivanovich (1818–1910) — master of the ballet 42

Philip (b. 1921) — Prince of Great Britain, Duke of Edinburgh [né Greece] 309

Philipp (1844–1921) — Prince of Saxe-Coburg & Gotha (85), (116)

Philipp (b. 1970) — Prince of Hohenlohe-Langenburg 255

Phillips — English jeweler 87

Pobedonostsev, Konstantin Petrovich (1827–1907) — Ober-Procuror of the Holy Synod 195

Polovtsov, Alexander Alexandrovich (1832–1909) — state secretary 65, 119, 154

Polovtsova, Nadezhda 287

Pourtàles, Friedrich von (1853–1928) — Count, German diplomat 170

Premazzi, Luigi (1814–1891) — artist 287

Preobrazhensky, Michael Timofeievich (1854–1930) — architect 187

Prosalenti, Sophia — Greek artist 278

Provorov, Alexander Ivanovich — Chairman of the Board of the first Russian Insurance Company 76

Pugni, Cesare (1802–1879) — composer 42

Putiatin, Efim Vasilievich (1803–1883) — Admiral, diplomat 56

Putiatin, Sergei (1893–1966) — Prince 307

Quarenghi, Giacomo (1744–1817) — architect 12

Rachevsky, Zinaida (1898–1963) — wife of Grand Duke Boris Vladimirovich 306

Rappoport, Julius Alexandrovich (1864–1916) — master in the firm of Fabergé 214

Rastrelli, Francesco Bartolomeo (1700–1771) — architect 12, 18, 22, 193

Ratibor — Prince von, Hof-Marshall at court of Saxe-Coburg & Gotha 92

Rat'kov-Rozhnov, Vladimir Alexandrovich (1834–1912) — Mayor of St. Petersburg 73, 76, (212), 213

Rauch, Christian (1777–1857) — German sculptor 27

Razumovsky, Alexei Grigorievich (1709–1771) — Count 193

Reibnitz, Louisa von — Baroness, Hof-Mistress to

Grand Duchess Anastasia Mikhailovna 163, (167)

René (1894–1962) — Prince of Bourbon-Parma 223, (250)

Renie-Gretry, Andre Marie — French architect 84

Repin, Ilia Efimovich (1844–1930) — artist 225, (226)

Retti, Leopold — architect 41

Rezanov, Alexander Ivanovich (1817–1887) — architect (98)

Riabushkin Andrei Petrovich (1861–1904) — artist 33

Rinaldi, Antonio (1709–1794) — Italian architect 200, 257

Robert (1840–1910) — Prince d'Orléans, Duke of Chartres 222

Rossi, Karl Ivanovich (1775–1849) — architect (27), (51), (71), 193, (194)

Rostislav Alexandrovich (1902–1978) — Prince of the Imperial Blood (160)

Rozhdestvensky, Ioann (Ivan Vasilievich) (1815–1882) — priest 189

Rödiger, Alexander Feodorovich (1854–1918) — Minister of the Armed Forces 156

Rubenstein, Anton Grigorievich (1829–1894) — composer and pianist 51, 52, 54, 73, 257

Runeberg, Valter (1838–1920) — Finnish sculptor 38

Russeli, James the Younger — English photographer 84, (115), (116), (145), 224

Saburov, Pyotr Alexandrovich (1835–1918) — diplomat 65

Salvini, Gilbert — French historian (107), (110)

Saveliev, Yurij Rostislavovich — art historian (35)

Savrasov, Alexei Kondratievich (1830—1897) 202

Schinkel, Karl Friedrich (1781–1841) — German architect 25, 26, 36, 67, 84, 111, 161

Schlüter, Andreas (1660–1714) — architect 25, 26

Schmidt, Paul Alexandrovich (1849–1902) — furniture maker (126)

Schott, Mathias — German historian (162)

Schröder, Ivan Nikolaevich (1835–1908) — sculptor 148

Schröder, German Johanovich (Ermolai Ivanovich) (1825–1898) — wood carver, photographer (75)

Schröter, Victor Alexandrovich (1839–1901) — architect (73), 76, (98)

Stackenschneider, Andrei Ivanovich (1802–1866) — architect 156, 167, 193

Schadow, Albert Dietrich (1797–1869) — German architect 25

Schlüter, Friedrich — architect 25

Schultze-Naumburg, Paul (1869–1946) — German architect 170, (171)

Schwechten, Franz — German architect 34

Scott, Bailey (1865–1945) — English architect 118

Selle, H. — photographer (9)

Sergei Alexandrovich (1857–1905) — Grand Duke (19), (20), (27), 72, 83, 92, 93, (95), 100, (106), 111, (116), 122, 123, 124, (127), 130, 131, 133, (224), 286, 287, 289, 290, 307, 308

Sergei Mikhailovich (1869–1918) — Grand Duke 156, (157), 296, 307

Serov, Valentin Alexandrovich (1865–1911) — artist 135, 294

Shatin, Vasilij Vasilievich — coachman of Grand Duchess Vera Konstantinovna 25

Shchusev, Alexei Victorovich (1873–1949) — architect 130

Sheremetiev, Sergei Dmitrievich (1844–1918) — Count 17

Shuvalov, Paul Andreevich (1830–1908) — Count, diplomat 65, (66), 72, 73, 75

Shuvalov, Peter Andreevich (1827–1889) — Count, diplomat — (66)

Shuvalova, Maria Alexandrovna — Countess, Hof-Mistress of Grand Duchess Maria Pavlovna (66)

Siemens, Karl (1829–1906) — German entrepreneur (69), 70, 71

Siemens, Werner (1816–1892) — German entrepreneur 68, (69)

Sinelnikov, Alexei Nikolaevich (1850–1923) — General 109

Singru, Andreas — Greek philanthropist 298

Skavenius, Anna Sophie (1889–1962) — wife of the

Index

Danish Ambassador to Russia [née Stinsen] (243)

Skavenius, Christian (1875–1945) — Director of the Main Northern Telegraph Company 247

Skavenius, Harold (1873–1939) — Danish Ambassador to Russia 244, (243), 296

Slabi, Adolf (1849–1913) — German professor 714

Sofía (b. 1938) — Queen of Spain [née Greece] 255

Sologub, Vladimir Alexandrovich (1813–1882) 80

Sophie (1818–1877) — Queen of the Netherlands [née Württemberg] 307

Sophie (1824–1897) — Grand Duchess of Saxe-Weimar-Eisenach [née Netherlands] 307

Sophie (1865–1939) — Princess of Anhalt [née Baden] 306

Sophie (1870–1932) — Queen of Greece [née Prussia] (138), (146), 272, 273, (293), (300), 303, (304)

Sophie (1914–2001) — Princess of Hesse, Princess of Hannover [née Greece] 309

Sorensen, Karl Frederick (1818–1879) — Danish artist 194

Steen, Mary — English photographer (240)

Stiglitz, Alexander Ludwigovich (1814–1884) — Baron, banker 32

Stiglitz, Ludwig Ivanovich (1777–1842) — Baron, banker 76

Stolypin, Pyotr Arkadievich (1862–1911) — Prime Minister 245

Stroganov, Sergei (1824–1879) — Count (138) 306

Sukhomlinov, Vladimir Alexandrovich (1848–1926) — Adjutant-General, Minister of the Armed Forces (1909–1915) 74

Sultanov, Nikolai Vladimirovich (1850–1908) — architect 34, 158, (159)

Sverbeev, Sergei Nikolaevich (1857–1922) — diplomat 74, 241

Sverchkov, Nikolai Egorovich (1817–1898) — artist 202

Svinjin, Vasilij Feodorovich (1865–1939) — architect (294)

Takanen, I. — sculptor 38

Tatiana Konstantinovna (1890–1970) — Princess of the Imperial Blood (58)

Tatiana Nikolaevna (1897–1918) — Grand Duchess (63), (138), 168, (233), 306

Tchaikovsky, Pyotr Iljich (1840–1893) — composer 52, 54, 260

Theodora (1906–1969) — Margravine of Baden [née Greece] 309

Tietgen, Johan Frederik — furniture maker, father of Karl Frederik Tietgen 194

Tietgen, Karl Frederik (1829–1901) — Danish banker and philanthropist 178, 194, 195, 197

Tietgen, Laura (née Jorgensen) — wife of Karl Frederik Tietgen (197)

Thyra (1853–1933) — Duchess of Cumberland, née Princess of Denmark 174, 179, (188), (189), (210), (203), 214, 221, 222, 238, (262), 282

Thyra (1880–1945) — Princess of Denmark, daughter of Crown Princess Frederik (215), 216

Tjutcheva, Anna Feodorovna (1829–1889) — Lady-in-Waiting 13, (16)

Tolstoy, Alexandra Andreevna (née Chertkova) (1818–1904) — Countess, Lady in Waiting 185

Tolstoy, Dmitry Ivanovich (1860–1941) — Count, Director of the State Hermitage Museum 292

Tolstoy, Leo Nikolaevich (1828–1910) — Count, writer 80

Tomishko, Anton Osipovich (1851–1900) — architect 233

Ton, Konstantin Andreevich (1794–1881) — architect 43

Torby, Sophia Nikolaevna de (1868–1927) — Countess (née Merenberg), granddaughter of A.S. Pushkin 163, 307

Tourett, Nicholaus F. von — architect 41

Tretiakov, Sergei Mikhailovich (1834–1892) — philanthropist, collector (75)

Trubetskoy, Paolo (1866–1938) — sculptor 135

Tsant, Karl Ludwig von (1796–1857) — architect 44, (46)

Turgenev, Ivan Sergeevich (1818–1883) — writer (77), 80

Tuxen, Laurits (1853–1927) — Danish artist 203, (210), 224, 225, 227

Ubri, Paul Petrovich (1818–1896) — Count, diplomat 65

Uhlenhuth, E. — photographer (11), 84, (87), (88), (89), (92), (94), (111), (113), (225)

Ukhtomsky, Esper Esperovich (1861–1921) — Prince (274)

Valdemar (1858–1939) — Prince of Denmark 174, (179), 184, (188), (189), (196), (203), (210), (211), 214, (215), 221, 222, 223, 244, 247, (250), 272, 276

Vallin de la Mothe, J. B. — architect 13

Valuev, Pyotr Alexandrovich (1815–1890) — Count minister 261

Vasilchikov, Alexander Alexeevich (1832–1890) — Prince (122)

Vasilchikov, Boris Alexandrovich (1863–1931) — Prince (245)

Vasilchikov, Maria Alexandrovna (1859–1934) — Princess (122)

Vasiliev, V.V. — artist 103

Vasili Alexandrovich (1907–1989) — Prince of the Imperial Blood (160)

Vasnetsov, Victor Mikhailovich (1848–1926) — artist 33, 118, 136, 229

Vaulin, Pyotr Kuzmich (1870–1943) — mosaics master 229

Vera Konstantinovna (1854–1912) — Grand Duchess, Duchess of Württemberg 40, 41, (43), 44, (45), 47, 56, 57, 58, (59), (129), (138), (260), (263), 303, 306, 309

Vereshchagin, Vasilij Petrovich (1835–1909) — artist (75), 102, 103

Vyacheslav Konstantinovich (1862–1879) — Grand Duke (58), (256), 307, 309

Victoria (1819–1901) — Queen of Great Britain, Empress of India 81, 83, 84, (85), 86, 87, 88, 89, (92), (111), 117, 119, 121, 122, 144, 145, 179, 217, 224, 255

Victoria (1840–1901) — German Empress [née Great Britain], wife of Kaiser Friedrich III 65, (85), 144, 145, (146), 308

Victoria (1862–1930) — Princess of Sweden [née Baden] (215)

Victoria (1863–1950) — Princess of Battenberg [née Hesse and by Rhine] 83, (85), (95), (116), (119), (120), 122, 134, (138), (141)

Victoria (1866–1929) — Princess of Schaumburg-Lippe [née Prussia] (146)

Victoria (1868–1935) — Princess of Wales (138), (196), 197, 209, (215), 218

Victoria Feodorovna (Victoria Melita, "Ducky") (1876–1936) — Grand Duchess of Russia, Grand Duchess of Hesse and by Rhine [née Great Britain] (62), 81, 83, 87, 88, 89, (90), (91), (92), (93), (94), (95), 96, 97, 98, (105), (106), 107, (109), 111, 117, 118, (129), 136, 139, 224, 306, 308

Victoria Louise (1892–1980) — Duchess of Brünswick-Lüneburg [née Prussia] 222

Viggo (1893–1970) — Prince of Denmark 224

Vladimir Alexandrovich (1847–1909) — Grand Duke 8, (19), (20), 46, 65, 68, 72, 73, 74, 75, 76, 83, (85), 92, 97, 98, 99, 100, 101, 102, 103, 106, 107, (108), 109, (110), (116), (128), 153, 170, 185, 186, 187, 188, 189, (224), 280, 281, 282, (285), 288, 306, 308

Vladimir Kirillovich (1917–1992) — Grand Duke 307, 308

Vladimir Pavlovich (1897–1918) — Prince Paley, son of Grand Duke Paul Alexandrovich 303

Volkonsky, Michael — Prince 289

Volkonsky, P. — Prince 12

Volkonsky, Sergei Mikhailovich(1860–1937) — Prince 82, 222

Volkov, Alexei — servant to Grand Duke Paul Alexandrovich 287

Voronikhin, Andrei Nikiforovich (1759 – 1814) — architect 257

Vorontsova, Maria Vasilievna (1819–1895) — Princess 157

Vrubel, Mikhail Alexandrovich (1865–1910) — artist 135

Wagner, Richard (1813–1883) — German composer 52

Weinbrenner, Friedrich — architect 80

Wilhelm (1785–1831) — Duke of Schleswig-Holstein-Sonderburg-Glücksburg 177

Wilhelm (1787–1867) — Landgraf of Hesse-Kassel, father-in-law of King Christian IX (189)

Wilhelm I (1781–1864) — King of Württemberg 40, 41, 44, 56, 57, 148, 307, 309

Wilhelm I (1797–1888) — German Kaiser (9), (24), 25, 26, 27, (28), 29, 34, (35), (36), 38, 46, (66), (75), (153), 161

Wilhelm II (1848–1921) — King of Württemberg (41), (45)

Wilhelm II (1859–1941) —German Kaiser (9), 26, (36), 46, 67, 81, 83, 84, (85), (92), (116), 144, 145, 146, 170, 171, 174, 222, 237, 238, 272, 273, 300, 308

Wilhelm (1882–1951) — Crown Prince of Prussia (9), 168, 170, 308

Wilhelm (1906–1940) — Prince of Prussia 170, (171)

Wilhelm Eugen (1846–1877) — Duke of Württemberg, husband of Vera Konstantinovna 41, 44, (56), 57, 306, 309

Wilhelm Ludwig (1829–1897) — Prince of Baden 77, 80, 282

Wilhelmina (1880–1962) — Queen of the Netherlands 308, 309

Wilhelmine — Grand Duchess of Hesse and by Rhine [née Baden] 13

Willem II (1792–1849) — King of the Netherlands] 309

Willem III (1817–1890) — King of the Netherlands] 309

Winkler, Karl (1845–1900) 33, 34

Witte, Sergei Julievich (1849–1915) — Head of the Council of Ministers 155

Worth, Charles (1825–1895) — French fashion designer 282

Xenia Alexandrovna (1875–1960) — Grand Duchess 157, 158, 159, (160), (193), 197, (201), 203, (204), (209), (224), 235, (236), (237), (239), 244, 247, 285, 292, 295, 306, 307, 308, 309

Xenia Georgievna (1903–1965) — Princess of the Imperial Blood 295

Yashchik, Timofei (Timothy) Xenofontovich (1878–1946) — Life-Cossack to Empress Maria Feodorovna 247

Yousoupov, Felix Felixovich (1887–1967) — Prince 109, 157, 168

Yousoupov, Nikolai Borisovich (1927–1891) — Prince 73

Yousoupova, Irina Alexandrovna (1895–1970) — Princess [née Russia] 157, 168

Zdobnov, Dmitry Spiridonovich (1850–?) — photograph 58

Zeger, Valdemar — Danish journalist 209

Zemtsov, Mikhail Grigorievich (1686–1743) — architect 193

Zhukov, P. — photographer (298)

Zhukovsky, Paul Vasilievich (1845–1912) — artist 34, 36

Zhukovsky, Vasiliy Andreevich (1783–1852) — poet 47, 80

Zichy, Mihaly (Mikhail Alexeevich) (1827–1906) — artist 202, 225

Ziller, Ernst (1837–1923) — German architect 273

Zinoviev, Vasilij Vasilievich (1814–1892) — Hof-Marshal (195)

Zita (1892–1989) — Empress of Austria, Queen of Hungary 174, 223

Zubov, Platon Alexandrovich (1767–1822) — Count 17

Last words...

We are sincerely grateful to the many researchers and professionals who actively supported our work.

In Russia – *Galina Popova, Valentin Privalov, Elena Konjukhova, Valentin Skurlov, Anastasia Tjutjunnik and Irina Feodorova.*

In Germany – *Jochen Haeusler (Nürnberg), Gertraude Bachmann (Coburg), Renate Effern (Baden-Baden), Fritz Falk (Pforzheim) and Christine Grob and Martin Friedel (Pforzheim).*

In Finland – *Ulla Tillander-Godenhielm and Ragnar Backström.*

In Canada – *Joanne Wrangler and Svend Berg.*

In France – *Gilbert Salvini (Contrexéville) and Françoise Ferey (Strassbourg).*

In Great Britain – *Katrina Warne.*

In the USA – *Mark Andersen, Arturo E. Beéche, David Higdon and Henry Wong.*

In Denmark – *Rikke Helms, Lange Olle, Karen Lindberg, Tatiana Ladyzhenskaya, Preben Ulstrup, Hanne Kjer, Bo Ahlberg.*

WE ARE ALSO VERY GRATEFUL TO: *Elena Barkhatova, Natalia Gorbatjuk, Galina Dluzhnevskaya, Vadim Znamenov, Elena Koloskova, Irina Linden, Elena Ljubomirova, Galina Miroljubova, Irina Pashchinskaya, Irina Ryzhenko, Jurij Saveliev, Jurij and Elizaveta Sheliaev from Russia; Berna Bartel (Schwerin), Harald Bachmann (Coburg), Burhardt Goeres and Vasilisa Pakhomova-Goeres (Potsdam), Renate Ulmer (Darmstadt), Mathias Schott (Schwerin), Rose Ebding (Stuttgart), Silvia and Detleth Jahn (Pforzheim) from Germany; Anne-Marie Bruun, Brigit Catter, Morten Jeppesen, Anders Christian Hougard, Lis and Uffe Kornerup, Lars Poulsen-Hansen from Denmark; Stephen de Angelis, Teresa Hudson from the USA; Popi Athanasiou from Greece.*

THE AUTHORS AND PUBLISHERS ALSO EXPRESS THEIR GRATITUDE TO THE FOLLOWING INSTITUTIONS, FOR ALLOWING THE USE OF ILLUSTRATIONS FOR THIS PUBLICATION:
Archives: GARF – State Archive of Russian Federation, Moscow: Fond 618 (Countess N. Karlova), Fond 641 (Maria Alexandrovna), fond 642 (Grand Duchess Elena Vladimirovna), fond 648 (Grand Duke Sergey Alexandrovich), fond 650 (Grand Duke Andrey Vladimirovich), fond 652 (Grand Duke Vladimir Alexandrovich), fond 654 (Grand Duke Boris Vladimirovich), fond 655 (Grand Duchess Maria Pavlovna eld.), fond 681 (Grand Duke Alexey Alexandrovich), fond 637 (L. Knorring)
RGAVMF – Russian State Archive of the Navy: fond 935 (Lifeguard Naval Regiment)
RGIA – Russian State Historical Archive, Saint Petersburg: Fond 468
(Archives of the Cabinet of His Imperial Majesty), fond 472 (Archives of the Chancery of the Imperial Court), fond 487 (Tsarskoe Selo Palaces Administration), fond 491 (Gatchina Palace Administration), fond 496 (Archives of the Office of the Court of His Imperial Majesty Emperor Nicholas II), fond 515 (State Department of Principality), 525 (Archives of the Chancery of Empress Alexandra Feodorovna), fond 528 (Archives of the Office of the Court of Grand Duke Vladimir), fond 544 (Archives of the Chancery of Empress Maria Feodorovna), fond 677 (Archives of the Office of the Court of His Imperial Majesty Emperor Alexander III)
TsGIA SPb. – Central State Historical Archive Saint Petersburg: fond 448 (The Society of Russian Artists support), fond 528 (The Imperial Society of architects of Saint Petersburg), fond 990 (Electrotechnical Institute), fond 1265 (Factory of R.F. Mel'tser)
TsGALI SPb – Central State Archive of Literature and Art of Saint Petersburg
TsGAKFFD SPb – Russian State Archive of Documentary Films and Photographs Saint Petersburg
RGAKFD – Russian State Archive of Documentary Films and Photographs
RNB – Russian National Library, SPb. Library of the State Hermitage, SPb. Theatrical Library, SPb. BAN – Library of Academy of Science, SPb. Memorial Prince Golytsin Library, SPb.
IIMK RAN – Institute of History of Culture of Russian Academy of Science
Foreign Archives and Libraries: *Canada* – Royal Ontario Museum, Public Library, Toronto Reference Library (Toronto); *Denmark* – The Danish National Archive, The Royal Library, The Amalienborg Museum (Copenhagen), Ballerup Museum, The Museum of National History and Archive in Frederiksborg, Museum of Lyngbu; *England* – Library and Archive in Victoria and Albert Museum (London):
Finland – Helsinki University Library; *Germany* – Staatsbibliothek zu Berlin, Staatsarchiv (Coburg), Institut Mathildenhöhe (Darmstadt), Nuenberg, Stadtarrchiv, Weraheim, Mercedes-Benz Museum (Stuttgart), Landeshauptarchiv, Museum of Schwerin Schloss (Schwerin), Schmuckmuseum (Pforzheim); *USA* – Public Library, Newberry Library (Chicago), Ney York Public Library (Ney York), Library of Congress (Washington), The Eurohistory Royal Photo Archive & EUROHISTORY (The European Royal History Journal).